WOMEN'S WORLDS IN SEVENTEENTH-CENTURY ENGLAND

'This rich and exciting collection brings seventeenth-century women to life. Full of unexpected information, the documents are culled from a wide range of sources, much of it archival material which has never been published before. This is a superb volume.'

Lyndal Roper, Royal Holloway, University of London

'Teachers and students have needed a book like this for a long time. Now, at last, we will be able to read the collected words of Englishwomen – *ordinary* English-women – as they spoke in courts, scribbled down accounts, shared advice with one another, and otherwise left records of their experiences, fears, and hopes. Many original documents are printed here for the first time, and all will delight and inform readers. Created by the careful research and attentive teaching of two respected historians, this is a wonderful book.'

Judith M. Bennett, University of North Carolina at Chapel Hill

Women's Worlds in Seventeenth-century England presents a unique collection of source materials on women's lives in sixteenth- and seventeenth-century England. The book introduces a wonderfully diverse group of women and a series of voices that have rarely been heard in history, from a poor Devon servant-girl to Queen Anne herself.

Drawing on unpublished, archival materials, *Women's Worlds* explores the everyday lives of ordinary early modern women, including their experiences of work, sex, marriage and motherhood, their beliefs and spirituality, their political activities, relationships and mental worlds. This book deepens and challenges our understanding of women's lives in the past.

Patricia Crawford is Professor of History at the University of Western Australia, and her books include *Women in Early Modern England* (Oxford University Press, 1998), with Sara Mendelson. **Laura Gowing** is Senior Lecturer in History at the University of Hertfordshire, and is author of *Domestic Dangers: Women, Words, and Sex in Early Modern London* (Oxford University Press, 1996).

WOMEN'S WORLDS IN SEVENTEENTH-CENTURY ENGLAND

Edited by Patricia Crawford
and Laura Gowing

London and New York

First published 2000
by Routledge
11 New Fetter Lane, London EC4P 4EE

Simultaneously published in the USA and Canada
by Routledge
29 West 35th Street, New York, NY 10001

Routledge is an imprint of the Taylor & Francis Group

© 2000 Editorial matter and selection, Patricia Crawford and
Laura Gowing

Typeset in Garamond by Florence Production Ltd, Stoodleigh, Devon.
Printed and bound in Great Britain by
TJ International Ltd, Padstow, Cornwall

British Library Cataloguing in Publication Data
A catalogue record for this book is available from the British Library

Library of Congress Cataloging in Publication Data
Women's worlds in seventeenth-century England / edited by
Patricia Crawford and Laura Gowing.
p.   cm.
Includes bibliographical references (p.   ) and index.
1. Women–England – History Sources.   I. Crawford, Patricia M.
II. Gowing, Laura.
HQ1599.E5W73   1999
305.4′0942–dc21   99–24671
CIP

ISBN 0–415–15637–8 (hbk)
ISBN 0–415–15638–6 (pbk)

CONTENTS

DOCUMENTS

1 BODIES

Conception and pregnancy

Parturition

Breasts and breastfeeding

Menstruation and reproductive health

Health and beauty

2 RELIGION, BELIEFS, SPIRITUALITY

Spirituality: the journey of the Christian soul

The practice of faith

God and the nation

Popular beliefs

3 WORK

Service

Getting a living

Professions

Running a household: domestic tasks

4 POVERTY AND PROPERTY

5 SEXUAL EXPERIENCES

Being a mother

Childcare, health and advice

The maternal relationship

8 RELATIONSHIPS

Neighbours

Families

Friends and lovers

Animals and spirits

9 POLITICS AND PROTESTS

10   MENTAL WORLDS

ILLUSTRATIONS

ACKNOWLEDGEMENTS

From the start this project has been supported by the interest and advice of many friends and colleagues: we would like to thank in particular Amy Erickson, Frances Harris, Anne Laurence, Sara Mendelson, Mary Prior, Lyndal Roper, and Helen Weinstein. We would also like to thank Sarah Barry, Vic Burrows, Shonaidh Marsh and Sarah Toulalan for research assistance. Graeme Hankey, Richard Read, Judy Straton, and Richard Wall kindly gave specialist advice on various questions. Amy Erickson acted as reader for the whole book, Jane Long and Maureen Perkins read sections of the text, Garthine Walker read Chapter 5 and Katharine Hodgkin read Chapter 10; their comments and help were very gratefully received. Helen Weinstein gave valuable help on finding and thinking about illustrations. Amy Erickson, Amy Froide, Frances Harris, Katharine Hodgkin, Sara Mendelson and Claire Walker each contributed documents in their own specialist fields, which are acknowledged in the text.

Staff in record offices and libraries across England, in the United States and in Australia were unfailingly helpful: we would like to thank particularly the Bodleian Library, the British Library Manuscripts Section, Friends House Library, the Folger Shakespeare Library, the Royal College of Physicians and the Wellcome Institute for the History of Medicine.

Laura Gowing thanks the University of Hertfordshire for support of the project with teaching relief; Patricia Crawford thanks the University of Western Australia for general support. Heather McCallum, our editor at Routledge, was always ready with good advice and enthusiasm. Finally, we'd like to thank our students, on whom much of this material was first tested and for whom this book is intended; we hope that the book's readers will find in the documents presented here some of the pleasures we have had researching the histories of early modern women over the years.

PERMISSIONS

Permission from the following authorities to publish the following documents in their copyright or keeping is gratefully acknowledged: the Trustees of Dr Williams' Library, London (for document 2.3); the Catholic Record Society (for document 2.6); the prioress and community of the Priory of Our Lady of Good Counsel, Sayers Common, West Sussex (for document 2.7); the Bristol Record Society and the Rev. Roger Hayden (for document 2.10); the Wiltshire Record Society (for document 5.7); the Bodleian Library; the Borthwick Institute of Historical Research, York; the British Library; the Corporation of London, Guildhall Library and the London Metropolitan Archives; East Sussex Record Office; Essex Record Office; the Folger Shakespeare Library, Washington, DC; the Library Committee, Yearly Meeting of the Religious Society of Friends in Britain; Lichfield Record Office and the Diocesan Registrar; North Yorkshire Record Office; the Public Record Office, Kew; the Royal College of Physicians, London; Somerset Archives and Record Service; the Wellcome Institute for the History of Medicine, London. All efforts have been made to trace other copyright holders.

ABBREVIATIONS

BCE	Before Christian Era
BL	British Library, London
Bodl.	Bodleian Library, Oxford
CE	Christian Era
CKS	Centre for Kentish Studies, Maidstone
fo.	folio of manuscript
Folger	Folger Shakespeare Library, Washington, DC
Guildhall	Guildhall Library, London
LMA	London Metropolitan Archives (previously, Greater London Record Office)
n.d.	No date on document
PRO	Public Record Office, Kew, London
RO	Record Office
sig.	signature, or gathering of pages in an early printed book
Somerset Archives	Somerset Archives and Record Service, Taunton
v	reverse side of manuscript folio [verso]
Wellcome	Wellcome Institute for the History of Medicine, London

INTRODUCTION

This book aims to introduce readers to the wide and rich range of sources on the experiences of early modern women. The last twenty years have seen a transformation in the histories of women in this period. New sources have become available; just as importantly, the innovative work of feminist historians has established new ways of reading familiar kinds of records to uncover women's lives and to make gender a primary category of historical analysis. The experiences of early modern women often strike familiar chords for us, yet the documents here also remind us how differently they perceived their world and themselves. In 1586 the Catholic martyr Margaret Clitheroe was sentenced to be pressed to death for secret Catholic worship; but she expressed herself most concerned with the shame of the public nakedness ordered by the sheriff.[1]

Our focus is specifically on the experiences of women, rather than on cultural representations of them. Prescriptions for and descriptions of female behaviour were manifold in this period, and served as a focus for all kinds of anxieties about public, social, and spiritual order.[2] Literary scholars have focused on the words of elite women, but their lives were very different from those of the mass of Englishwomen at this date. Yet it is not easy to gain access to the words and experiences of ordinary women. Many of women's words survive in records made by others, such as justices of the peace, clerks of courts, physicians, and other male civic authorities. Our book seeks to suggest ways of reading the records created by men in order to understand the lives of women. Even if we were to use the words of women only, we know that ways of thinking and feeling are influenced by the structures of a society; women existed in a social context, and played their own part in shaping cultural representations. Margaret Clitheroe's words are recorded only by her confessor: there is no authentic access to her experience or to her voice.

Early modern England was a patriarchal society, in which women were expected to be subject to their husbands and fathers, and in which male authority was justified by divine and natural law. The preservation of patriarchal power – of the subjection of wives to husbands, children to parents, servants to masters and mistresses – was understood to be central to social, political, and spiritual order. In this society, marriage increased men's authority, enabling them to

1

become masters of households and heads of families; for women, it meant that their persons and their property were merged 'into one mystical person of which the husband is the head'.[3] In the household and in the wider world, men's words tended to carry more weight than women's, which were frequently identified with gossip, scolding, cursing, and immodest talk: 'many women, many words: many geese, many turds', ran one contemporary proverb.[4] Recovering sources for women's history means giving to women's words a weight that contemporaries often did not; but it also necessitates an understanding of the specific context in which such sources were created, one in which the words of both women and men were shaped by law, custom, and the gender order.

Our main chronological focus is on the seventeenth century, extending into a slightly longer period, from 1580 to 1720. Between these two dates, major shifts took place in religion, politics, demography, and economy, but many areas of women's lives remained substantially unchanged. This book is organised around a number of overlapping themes: body and soul, private and public lives, material and mental worlds, individuals and families or communities. However, many of the distinctions through which we understand the world do not make sense in the early modern context. Bodies and minds were interconnected; religion and politics were inseparable; the individual was embedded in the community; business and social lives were often the same.

We begin with bodies, the essential markers of sexual difference for early modern society. On those observed differences, value systems were constructed. Women lived their lives both within a world of discourse and within a material world of embodiedness. The connections between these two worlds continue in the area of belief. It is not easy for late-twentieth-century secular society to grasp the reality of religious belief in early modern times. Life was governed by a sense of the omnipotence of God, and the need for the individual to save her soul. Women's economic and material worlds can be explored through chapters on work and on property and poverty. Chapters on sex, marriage, and maternity follow the female lifecycle, and a chapter on relationships reconstructs some of the social worlds of women. The model of separate 'public' (male) and 'private' (female) spheres does not adequately describe the roles of men and women in early modern society; women's engagement in matters of religious policy and national politics are suggested in a chapter on politics and protests. The final chapter turns to mental lives. Dreams, visions, and mental disturbances suggest some of the less tangible histories of early modern women's worlds. Throughout, the documents are ordered thematically, except in Chapter 9, where women's political activities can be traced through a chronological structure. The illustrations recreate something of the visual world of our subjects; we have focused on woodcuts, many of which would have been repeatedly reprinted with ballads and cheap print of the period and circulated amongst those who could not read as well as those who could.[5]

THE CONDITIONS OF LIFE

The material conditions of early modern women's lives changed relatively little through our period. Infant mortality was high for both girls and boys: in the seventeenth century around one in four children died before the age of 10, and between 1600 and 1750 the rates were rising.[6] On average, women lived longer than men, but their mortality was higher at certain periods of life: in the first ten years of marriage (when women were four times more likely than men to die) and in the early years of childbearing. Maternal mortality increased during the seventeenth century and decreased again in the eighteenth century.[7] From their late forties on, though, women were more likely to survive than men. High infant mortality also meant that the population was an old one, particularly in rural areas, where many young people would have migrated to towns and cities. About 22 per cent of the population in the late sixteenth century were aged 50 or over, and during the seventeenth century, while birth rates were low, the population became proportionately older.[8] The greatest population increase in this period was between 1580 and 1640, to a size of around 5–6 million in 1640. During the second half of the seventeenth century, plague and a lower birth rate kept the population static, and it began to increase again in the early part of the eighteenth century.

For the bulk of the population marriage was comparatively late: in keeping with the western European pattern, both women and men tended to marry in their mid to late twenties, though people in towns, with easier access to a living, tended to marry slightly younger. The age difference between husbands and wives tended to be small. Partly as a result of the late age of marriage, and also because of high rates of miscarriage and stillbirth, fertility rates were lower than we might expect. Women gave birth, on average, to six or seven children, of whom fewer than half might survive; average intervals between births have been calculated as thirty months, if a child survived to one year, but lower if a child died before that.[9]

Elite couples, whose marriages depended on familial and political alliances more than on economic decisions, married younger, from their mid-teens to their mid-twenties. Since many marriages were remarriages for men, the age discrepancy between a wife and her husband was often considerable.

Family structures were characterised by a good deal of flexibility and contingency. High mortality rates meant marriages lasted, on average, as long as those today, when divorce rather than death ends most marriages. As many as one in three early modern marriages – more in areas of high mortality – were remarriages for at least one partner. Widowhood, orphanhood and remarriage created households of complicated relationships between remarried parents, stepchildren, and other relatives, so that although families were not generally 'extended' in the sense of more than two generations sharing a house, they were often extended laterally to include, for example, stepchildren and orphaned nieces or nephews, who might be taken in as children or as servants.[10]

A comparatively high proportion of women did not marry. Of those born around 1600, about 24 per cent remained unmarried – about the same proportion as in modern Britain.[11] Single women tended to live with their parents, as servants, or with other single women. With the high frequency of widowhood, over half the female population were without a spouse at any one time, and 10 per cent of households were headed by women, predominantly widows.[12]

Widowhood transformed a woman's position. Those left with a competency, or a business they could continue, might find in their state a new autonomy; their inheritance might allow them to play a key role in the local microeconomy, loaning out money; and by the late seventeenth century, the numbers of widows remarrying were falling. Those without such fortune were left at the bottom of society, the recipients – if they were lucky – of alms and poor relief.

Throughout our period, women's working practices continued to be centred on the house, garden, and shop, although these were by no means the only female workplaces. The marginalisation of women from trades, such as brewing, continued, but a good proportion of married women still worked separately from their husbands, in retail, the service trades, nursing or midwifery.[13] Despite the introduction of male midwives, most births were still attended by women. For most households, the family economy of farm or workshop remained one in which labour roles were complementary: a household could not survive without a woman's work. At the same time, women's work in and out of the household was consistently underestimated and devalued. Women's wage rates remained between a third and a half of those of men, and single women continued to be the poorest group of people. In the early modern economic world, the line between subsistence and indigence was for many, and particularly for women, a very slender one. Marriage was an economic partnership of shared tasks; but many women were surviving and supporting children on rates that assumed dependence on higher-waged husbands. Poor wives, single women, and widows all resorted to a range of expedients to keep going from week to week and season to season: selling clothes, laundering, charring, gleaning, and petty theft were just some of the options. When these failed, women might have no choice but to turn to prostitution or vagrancy.

The division between rich and poor was widening. In a society and economy without 'classes' in the modern definition of the word, contemporaries distinguished specific social groups: the aristocracy, the gentry, professional men and their wives, 'the middling sort', yeomen, merchants, craftsmen and tradesmen, labourers. Literacy and culture, dress and habits distinguished both social ranks and economic status. The term 'elite' is a useful shorthand to refer to those whose social status and wealth set them apart from the middling sort and the labouring poor.

At all levels, female economic opportunities were defined by a combination of law and custom, which interacted in sometimes unpredictable ways. Inheritance law was changing, so that by the end of our period widows were entitled to a significantly lower legal minimum of their dead husbands' goods; men continued to name their wives as executors, trusting them to administer what remained of their estates, and widows continued – through their inheritances – to play a significant role in local economies.

Property values cannot simply be correlated to those of today. A poor labouring woman might earn 3d. or 5d. a day; servants earned between £1 and £2 per annum with room and board; a gentlewoman's marriage portion might be between £1,000 and £5,000.[14] Movable goods were of high value: beds, with mattress and blankets, could cost over £2, while cottages could be purchased for around £10. Clothes might last over several owners, and could be remade into smaller or more fashionable garments. Thus, for the bulk of the population a lost pair of shoes was a major calamity, and a petticoat worth 6d. might be worth going to court over.

Behind the order of daily life lay the structures of religion and popular belief. Early modern people understood the world in terms of a cosmology that combined popular belief and orthodox Christianity, in which magic, astrology, prophecy, and visions or dreams could make sense of the past and the future, the weather and disease, love and marriage. Particularly in the first half of our period, magical practices remained central to much spirituality and popular custom: magic worked alongside religion to provide a framework for understanding the world. Women's particular relationship to the magical world was reflected in the dynamics of witchcraft accusations and prosecutions for love magic or healing.

The conditions of life were also shaped by political and religious ideas and changes. The mid-seventeenth century saw a breakdown in government: civil wars broke out in 1641, King Charles I was executed in 1649, and a republic and later a protectorate was set up. During this period of crisis, many women were actively involved on both sides. In 1660, King Charles II came to the throne, the Anglican church was restored, and the 'natural order' was reinstated.[15] Between 1580 and 1720 both personal and national religion underwent a series of transformations. After the Reformation women, often in different ways from men, had been active in introducing the new faith and in preserving the old one: by the 1580s, new forms of religious practice were being consolidated.[16] The Elizabethan church settlement, the reforming practices of the 'Puritans', and the persecutions of Catholics established new spiritual practices for both sexes. The comparative religious freedom of the 1640s and 1650s allowed the formation of new churches and religious movements, referred to by contemporaries as sects; whilst they offered new roles for women, restrictions on the part women could play in public spiritual life remained. The years after the Restoration saw the consolidation of a more secular state and a corresponding stress on the spiritual realm as private and hence female.[17]

SOURCES

The sources fall into several categories: records made by women themselves and those, more numerous, created by others. Over the period 1580–1720, the nature of the sources changed. Female capacity both to read and to write increased. Print offered a new way of expressing ideas in public. In the late sixteenth century, few women were able to write. Probably under 10 per cent of women could sign their names, compared to half of the adult male population.[18] Writing was a gentlewoman's accomplishment, although the skills of reading were probably more widely dispersed. (Girls were taught to read before they learnt to write.)[19]

The political, social and economic changes between 1580 and 1720 left women at the end of our period with many more opportunities of recording their voices. By the later sixteenth century the Protestant reformist movement (frequently labelled Puritanism) had acted as a particular spur for women and men to examine their consciences and record their daily spiritual life in personal writings. Religious beliefs and the practice of piety could also lead to public actions. The political events of the 1640s and 1650s prompted women to both individual and collective action. They testified individually, as Quakers and as prophets, and collectively petitioned parliament. After the Restoration, the church courts, whose jurisdiction had been suspended during the Commonwealth, resumed, but their focus became narrower; varying clerical and legal practices saw some courts keeping fewer records, others keeping more. By the 1680s women's literacy was catching up with men's, first in urban areas, later in rural ones: by the end of the period, something like three-quarters of women could sign their names. Although the female literacy rate increased more rapidly than the male during the seventeenth century, still fewer women than men could read and write. The bulk of the population, both female and male, left little trace in written records. Some of the fullest sources for ordinary women are legal records, which began to be kept more fully and methodically from the 1580s. Through the period, the conventions of the sources change. Legal records become fuller, but often less individual in style; spiritual writings use new styles and follow different narratives; new, more secular forms give shape to women's first-person writings.

Comparatively little of what women wrote has been preserved. Some letters and personal writings survive for elite women, but families were more likely to keep those which reflected well upon the religiosity of their female members.[20] Critical writings might be destroyed; Samuel Pepys tore up his wife Elizabeth's account of her unhappy life.[21]

Some manuscripts survive by accident. Sarah Fell's account book remained at Swarthmoor Hall until the mid-eighteenth century, when a Quaker woman rescued it from a grocer who was using it as waste paper. It was handed on by a series of Quaker women, and eventually given to the Library of the Society of Friends in 1915.[22] The letters of Queen Mary II to her 'dearest husband' survived because they were mistakenly thought to be to William, not to her friend, Lady Frances Bathurst.[23] Other manuscripts were deliberately kept and treasured by women; the commonplace books compiled by many literate women were passed on from one generation to the next, sometimes with additions.

Women who could both read and write usually enjoyed more leisure than those who could do neither. They had time to reflect, and many enjoyed the material advantages offered by a private closet, a place originally for prayer, but one that might be a retreat from the household. Yet the purpose of introspection was not so that they might order their lives for greater happiness, but rather that they might understand their sins and direct themselves to God. It is perhaps when we feel closest to early modern women, as they apparently bare their souls, that we are most distant. Ultimately, time spent in reading and writing, as Mary Evelyn explained, was time wasted: 'all time borrowed from family duties is misspent'. What she sought was 'future perfection, without which it were vain to live'.[24] Religious meditations, spiritual diaries, and accounts of the soul's journey towards the divine thus make up a large proportion of both manuscript and printed work by women. Ann Bathurst, a London widow interested in mysticism, wrote voluminously of her nightly visions of God. In 1680, at the end of her fourth book, she wrote of her desire to use her books for spiritual growth by honestly examining her life.[25] Commencing her fifth, she dedicated herself to further spiritual endeavour:

> The particular grace I will endeavour to attain during the writing of this book is spiritual recollection or the constant consideration of God. The Lord give me his grace that at the end I may perceive some increase in this virtue.

For Bathurst, to write was in itself a work of devotion, and furthermore, a work commanded to her by God: 'I seem to receive a direction to set down some, I say some, of the operations of the spirit for there be divers'.[26] We should remember, when reading women's words, the multiple and complex motives of their authors.

Women's motives for diary writing and record keeping varied. Spiritual purposes were stated as the foremost purpose by many. Puritan beliefs in particular encouraged self-examination through the keeping of diaries and records of religious experiences. Sarah Savage, for example, began what proved to be a life-long habit of diary keeping in August 1686 with these words: 'I have had it long upon my thoughts to do something in the nature of a diary – being encouraged by the great advantage others have got thereby and by the hopes that I may thereby be furthered [in] a godly life.' Her diary was a private space in which she reflected upon her spiritual condition and daily struggles. Further, she collected and treasured many of the records of her godly family of origin, thereby sending their piety forward as 'an arrow through time'.[27] Reworked in the nineteenth century, the records of the Henry family, suitably edited, were instrumental both in shaping a view of early Nonconformist piety and in serving as a model of middle-class Christianity to the Victorians.[28]

Many women wrote for their children, sometimes specifically for their daughters, offering both religious and practical advice. In addition to letters, they compiled commonplace books which might include religious, household, cookery, laundry, and even veterinary advice. These volumes were both useful to their authors and also directed to the next generation. Thus Elizabeth Ashburnham explained that she had collected precepts from Scripture 'for the direction of my children; that as God hath made me a means for the life of their bodies, so I may discharge the care that is committed to me . . . for the good of their souls'.[29]

Women's letters, while only a small proportion of surviving correspondence, are nevertheless numerous. Most county archive collections contain fascinating bundles of family papers. To write a letter was not necessarily to engage in a private one-to-one communication. There was always the danger of correspondence falling into the wrong hands. Thus, during the Civil Wars, for example, women who had information to convey used cipher, as the example of Henrietta Maria shows. In the 1690s, two women with significant political interests, Princess Anne and her friend Sarah Churchill, disguised their identities under the names of Mrs Morley and Mrs Freeman and used ciphers to refer to individuals. Most women attempted to control the distribution of their letters. Katherine Whitstone, Oliver Cromwell's widowed sister, wrote that her cousin might show the letter to her father and husband, but to noone else. Sometimes women were ashamed of their orthography and calligraphy. Yet more complex issues were involved, as one young woman explained in a letter to her affianced cousin. Lydia Du Gard was surprised that he had shown one of her previous letters to the President of Trinity College Dublin; she had viewed her letter as speaking to Samuel, a form of thinking aloud, and hence had 'both spoken and writ more freely and unconcernedly than otherwise I would have done'. She comments on how she viewed her writing:

> the truth is I am grown so well acquainted with you, that I have used my self to write as familiarly and freely as I talk, and of late (though the best of my writing is very mean) have taken so little pains with my letters, that they are unfit to be seen by any but by him alone, whose love will teach him rather to excuse than to laugh at, the false spellings, bad English, impertinencies, and perhaps nonsense that some of them may be filled with.[30]

Private letters tell of the material constraints under which women wrote. Frequently messengers or carriers were waiting; paper was finished; eyes were tired. Women more than men worried lest their lengthy letters might be troublesome.

Most of the women's sources we have used remain in manuscript. A few were printed. In seventeenth-century England, works could be published, in the sense of being made known to others, by circulating in manuscript copies.[31]

Print, however, was a more public matter. Some work was printed without the author's knowledge or consent; several of women's writings were published posthumously; others were printed not so much deliberately as by chance. The boundary between manuscript and print might be likened to that today between printed books and web or xerox copies of papers: there is an element of arbitrariness. Some printed women's commonplace books, such as those of the Countess of Kent, and Hannah Wolley, resemble manuscript collections. Jane Sharp's *Midwives Book* is similar to the manuscript which Elizabeth Poeton's husband prepared for her use; both were practical manuals.[32] Wolley's stated motives for her work in physic may have applied more generally.

> So I, when I was to write of physic and chirurgery, have consulted all books I could meet with in that kind, to compleat my own experiences.
>
> If any shall wonder why I have been so large upon it, I must tell them, I look upon the end of life to be usefulness; nor know I wherein our sex can be more useful in their generation than having a competent skill in physic and chirurgery, a competent estate to distribute it, and a heart willing thereunto.[33]

All of the writing which women undertook raises questions about how women found a voice within a society whose language was male, and where the author and reader were 'he'. In the privacy of their own manuscript books, which many writers sought to keep secret during their lifetimes, women struggled to express their aspirations, which were, in many cases, to transcend the world in which they found themselves, for a world beyond.

Ordinary women in early modern England were unlikely to keep any written record of their lives. For most, the only formal trace of their lives was left when they came into contact with institutional record keeping: at birth, at marriage, and at death; in property transfers; over poor relief; and in their contacts with the legal system. For most women, their encounters with the written word were exceptional and recorded unusual, disturbing, dangerous, or illegal events. These records, such as the histories of marital violence presented to the church courts, can nevertheless be as illuminating about normal expectations and everyday events as about extraordinary disruptions and conflict.

Early modern England was a society profoundly concerned with the need for order. Lacking any police force as we know it, the administration of local justice depended on the readiness of ordinary women and men to use the law, and the implicit threat of sanctions that helped ensure co-operation and local harmony. Women found themselves involved with the law as witnesses for their neighbours and family, as victims and as accusers, as plaintiffs and defendants. Many of the proceedings of early modern courts were summary and their records are brief; but some kinds of case demanded more detailed records, full of circumstantial detail and complex stories. As well, the 1580s saw the beginnings of more complete record keeping, and from then, many counties and dioceses have extensive series of records for quarter sessions and church courts, held in local record offices, and often calendared or published by local record societies. The legal records used here are principally from these jurisdictions.

The quarter sessions met quarterly in each county town. Headed by local gentlemen appointed as justices of the peace, they were charged with much local administration (such as licensing alehouses) and with jurisdiction over theft (below a certain level), trespasses, assaults, and bastardy. Crimes such as murder, infanticide, rape, arson, and witchcraft were dealt with at the higher criminal court, the assizes, which met half-yearly in four circuits. Both courts kept a variety of records: of persons admitted to gaol, of processes in court (such as orders made for the keeping of bastards), of persons indicted for crimes, of the examinations of the accused and the informations of witnesses or accusers, of petitions for financial help or judicial clemency, and (in the case of quarter sessions) of recognizances, by which people were bound over to keep the peace.[34] Indictments and recognizances, kept in Latin, contain only the most summary information of a crime: its nature, those involved, and the result. Examinations and informations, which rarely survive for the assizes but often do for quarter sessions, are more detailed. They record, in English, the responses of witnesses, accusers or accused to questions by JPs. They are mostly, but not always, written in the third person, thus: 'She saith that. . . .' Their fidelity to the spoken word cannot be assumed; there is always some mediation by the JP, questioning, and the clerk, writing down a form of the answer. Nevertheless, they represent a version of how women and men told the stories of theft, injury, or bastardy.[35]

The diocesan church courts dealt with spiritual discipline: church attendance, breaking the sabbath, proving wills, tithe disputes, pew disputes, but also illicit sex; marital conflicts; and disputes over reputation ('defamation') where sexual sins were involved. Their jurisdiction overlapped to some extent with that of the quarter sessions, particularly in the regulation of illicit sex and bastardy.[36] Headed in most cases by a bishop, they dealt with two main categories of judicial business: disciplinary or 'office' prosecutions, resulting from a visitation or a complaint by churchwardens or other concerned parties; and 'instance' suits, which involved disputes between two (or more) parties. These longer cases, which included defamation and matrimonial disputes, might cost between £2 and £10 to sue. Church court records often include long and detailed witness depositions, mostly in English, which record not only their knowledge of disputed events, but such details as their age, birthplace, relationship with the litigants, and manner of earning a living: they have been used to study marriage and defamation disputes, and also to examine social life, literacy, migration patterns, and work.

There were many other courts operating in early modern England, with overlapping jurisdictions. Many of them have barely been examined for evidence of female participation. Central courts such as Star Chamber and King's Bench tended to deal with richer litigants and cases on appeal; the Court of Requests dealt with a wider range of litigants; minor property transactions or disputes around land, trespass, business, and debts might be dealt with at local manorial courts, courts of pie-powder, or sheriff's courts.[37]

Despite their notorious inaccuracy about names, places and marital status, even the briefest of legal records can be rich sources for women's history, offering potential profiles of female involvement in the law at all levels. More detailed records present the historian with a series of narratives, all of them mediated by clerks, JPs, or lawyers, but all constructed to be plausible, to make sense to contemporary ears. Seeking to justify, explain, complain, confess, or deny, women in court played on familiar themes, established knowledge, and common fears or assumptions, and gave texture to their picture with a wealth of local, circumstantial detail. Such stories must have been told and retold outside the court as well as inside it. Read as women's narratives, they offer us a new way into reconstructing mental and material worlds.

The sources sampled here are none of them simple, transparent documents. Whether women were writing letters, dictating a petition, or deposing in court, their words were mediated by a set of conventions: established literary forms, the familiar language of pleading or the lawyers' courtroom idiom. The women's words recorded here are often telling a quite different story from that in which the historian is interested; in some cases we have more than one version, leaving us with, for example, a competing dialogue between wife and husband for the history of marriage. In written words or in speech, women told stories that made sense of their own worlds.

NOTE ON TRANSCRIPTIONS

Many of these documents were written by clerks or men unrelated to the women whose experiences we are seeking to represent, and so we have not tried to preserve their original forms completely. We have, however, tried to maintain as much of the original documents as possible for the modern reader. For ease of access by non-specialists, we have chosen to modernise spellings of documents, but we have maintained original spellings of names and particular early modern words (such as 'dexterousness'). We have inserted apostrophes, modern capitals (as in God and Hell), and transposed specific early modern forms to modern ones: *v* to *u*, *j* to *i*, 'yt' to 'that', 'then' to 'than', 'li.' to '£'. Dates are modernised, using the New Style with years starting on 1 January rather than 25 March. Numbers in the Latin form are here printed as Roman figures. Latin text is translated in square brackets. Most abbreviations have been expanded: '&' to 'and', 'wilbe' to 'will be'. Punctuation, with the exception of apostrophes, has been generally left unaltered. This presents some difficulties for the modern reader. Many early modern documents use very little punctuation at all, and writers from clerks to noblewomen write lengthy, run-on texts with no paragraphing and few sentence breaks. Where necessary for comprehension, we have occasionally inserted commas and full stops. Although some of these texts require careful and concentrated reading, their idiosyncrasies preserve a sense of the differences in original documents. Legal records are full of formulas and repetition. Women's letters and personal writings often use only one, if any, form of punctuation; but to make them grammatical in the modern sense involves a wholesale alteration of language and style. Our aim has been to give some sense of the original texts and to encourage readers to examine them for themselves.

1

BODIES

We begin with the body, a subject neglected by historians until comparatively recently. On the whole, historians have found the body of less interest than the mind, and have concentrated on the public sphere of human activity, relegating the body to the 'private' sphere. The history of women's bodies has seemed fundamentally ahistorical, an account of childbearing and rearing. Reproduction, what women 'naturally' do, lacked historical interest. Furthermore, a postmodern focus on the discursive construction of experience has moved attention further away from women's bodies. Yet being a woman was a biological as well as a cultural experience, as this section demonstrates.[1]

The relationship between discursive constructions of the female body and women's lives is problematic. Two discourses were significant, one religious, the other medical. Protestant ministers and biblical scholars explained that as woman was created second, her body was inferior. Medical theorists were largely influenced by ancient texts, especially those of Hippocrates (born c. 460 BCE) and Galen (c. CE 129–199) but sought to reconcile traditional wisdom with a growing body of knowledge based on observation. Hence many medical theories about woman were confused and contradictory. Even so, most medical writers explained the human female as a deviation from the male norm. Since nature sought to make all creation male, a female body was deemed the product of nature's failure.[2] Physiological changes in her body because of her reproductive cycles made her unstable and potentially dangerous to man. Furthermore, the distinctive female functions of menstruation, parturition, and lactation were constructed as potentially damaging to her own health. Popular understandings of the female body likewise reflected negative views of women. While many historians have discussed these theories and beliefs about women's bodies, they have paid less attention to the body as lived experience and to the evidence about how individuals understood their bodies.[3] Although 'experience' is as we know a problematic category, nevertheless it is worth asking questions about how women experienced physiological changes associated with their reproductive functions.

Parturition, lactation, and menstruation are three distinctive female functions, although individual women had different bodily experiences and different remedies for disorders. There are hints in the sources that women's common biology transcended class differences; a wealthier woman might find assistance from a poorer woman, and the midwife who attended a queen perforce had her practice among women of lower social status. Source material, as always, is biased towards the wealthier. While we have diaries, autobiographies, and letters from elite women about their health and bodily experiences, evidence about ordinary women is more difficult to find. Sometimes we can extrapolate from literate women's accounts; their commonplace books reflect their own individual interests, but most included medical remedies for various female health problems. Not all of that material was based on their own direct knowledge; literate women recorded cures offered by others, or copied from a printed book. Yet even here the compilers sometimes added their own annotations, which suggests that women consulted a wide range of people about their health, from the university-trained doctors to the almswoman at the door. Women's commonplace books and letters indicate that they suffered from some of the 'disorders' which were a corollary of the medical theories, such as greensickness, suffocation of the womb, and mother-fits.

For many of the experiences of ordinary women, we depend upon accounts of women in male sources. Yet while the records of courts which prosecuted women for 'bastardy' and infanticide reveal details about conception, pregnancy, and parturition, we must remember that these records were created in extreme situations; the penalty for concealing the birth of a bastard child which was stillborn or died at birth was death. Thus the words of the women themselves before the courts require careful interpretation.[4]

Physicians and medical practitioners offered assistance for women's bodily health and disorders, but their case notes too must be viewed with caution. Female modesty seems on many occasions to have made women unwilling to discuss their bodily ills with men. Ann Barton, testifying in a 1624 defamation case at the London consistory court, reveals two ways in which women's knowledge of the body was asserted – and safeguarded – against young men. When Nathan Webb, an apprentice, asked the widow 'why maids were let blood in the foot', she reproved him 'and told him it was not fitting for boys to know it'.[5] Unlicensed female medical practitioners who advertised their services promised discretion which would not endanger women's concepts of modesty.

We begin with pregnancy, and a woman's puzzlement about whether conception had occurred. Reliable indications were few; the main sign for medical practitioners as well as women themselves was the cessation of menstruation after sexual intercourse.[6] One of the main contemporary theories about conception was that simultaneous orgasm was necessary for conception. Although there were female doubting voices, in general people thought that sexual pleasure could lead to conception at any stage during her menstrual cycle. The link between ovulation and menstruation was not understood until the 1920s, so it is not surprising that women were uncertain about pregnancy.[7]

Women generally viewed childbirth with fear, although Schofield has calculated that the danger of death in childbirth was statistically low, only 10 per

1,000.[8] Nevertheless, evidence from women themselves indicates that they were fearful, and stories were spread of the dangers.[9] From the humblest to the highest woman in the land, ideas and practices about childbirth were similar, until the late seventeenth century, when aristocratic and wealthy women began using the services of the physicians. Likewise, there was a common store of female experience about breast-feeding. Mothers of middling status may have been the experts, since it was they who both fed their babies and were likely to be employed to wet-nurse the babies of others.

Menstruation was referred to variously as 'the flowers' – referring to the flowering or fermenting of beer, when a scum formed on the surface – and 'the courses' or 'the terms', referring to the periodicity of the bleeding. Women linked regular menstruation with general health. Since the absence of menstruation could precipitate a disorder known as greensickness, if women did not menstruate according to their own understandings of their bodily patterns they sought assistance. Menstrual blood was usually thought of as providing foetal nourishment,[10] hence women were anxious about blood-letting in pregnancy. Those who feared that they might be pregnant when they did not menstruate may have sought a blood-letting as a means of abortion. Excessive menstrual bleeding, however, was thought detrimental to health, and women used various remedies to stop the flow.

Women's general health was affected by their reproductive capacities. In addition, they were subject to many illnesses similar to those of men, and to accidents, such as burns and scalds. Daily health care was largely in female hands; women both nursed the sick and prepared many of the herbal remedies.[11]

Bodily appearance and the care of clothing also occupied a proportion of women's time: the higher the social level, the more effort was expended. More rapid changes in fashion later in the seventeenth century meant that wealthier women updated their wardrobes more frequently and passed their clothes to others, including their female servants. However, the bulk of the female population probably spent most of their time in one or two outfits, one for summer and one for winter. The silks and laces of wealthy women were carefully looked after. Some items have survived and can also be seen in the portraiture of the time. Nevertheless, most clothing was passed on until it was worn out.

CONCEPTION AND PREGNANCY

1.1   Pregnancy and primogeniture:
Anne, Princess of Denmark, 1692

For a few women, the birth of a child, preferably a son and heir, was of political as well as personal significance. The menstruation of such women was of interest to a range of people, as well as to the women themselves, for its presence or absence was related to their ability to bear children. Ambassadors to Queen

Elizabeth's court, for example, enquired of her chamber women whether she menstruated.

From the letters of Anne, Princess of Denmark, to her intimate friend Sarah Churchill, later Duchess of Marlborough, we can gain some information about how Anne herself reacted to the absence of menstruation in 1692 and 1693. At that date, Anne's sister Queen Mary had borne no children, so Anne herself and her children were the next in line for the throne, since in 1688 both Mary and Anne had displaced their step-brother, James, born to their step-mother, another Mary (see 1.5 below). Most people believed that the security of the Protestant succession rested on Anne's fecundity. In 1692 Anne had already three children. Ultimately, she bore eighteen children, and experienced even more pregnancies, but at her death in 1714 she had not one living child.

Only Anne's side of the famous correspondence between her and Sarah, under their chosen names of Mrs Morley and Mrs Freeman, survives. (Sarah wanted all her own letters destroyed.) On occasions, Anne wrote almost daily to her friend. Her letters lack any address or signature, and sometimes can be dated only on internal evidence. Anne adopted certain disguises, such as using a numerical cipher to refer to a person, in case the correspondence should be intercepted. Menstruation was termed 'Lady Charlotte', which was possibly a joke between the two women, as the name belonged to a courtier whom neither Anne nor Sarah liked. Sarah at this stage was Groom of the Stole, an appointment which involved certain duties of attending at Anne's court.

Here, one of Anne's letters is given in full, to indicate the range of concerns which the two women shared and the flavour of the correspondence. Brief extracts from subsequent letters continue the story of Anne's absence of menstruation.

Anne, Princess of Denmark, to Sarah, née Jenyns, wife of John Churchill, BL, Add. MS 61415, Blenheim papers, fos 7, 10, 11v, 29, 34.

[25 July 1692?] I have had the satisfaction this morning of receiving a very kind letter from dear Mrs Freeman which I can never thank you enough for, but must assure you as I have often done that one kind word from you is more welcome than anything you can say besides; if you hold your resolution of coming hither next week I hope Thursday will be the latest because I would willingly spend as much of the two days my dear Mrs Freeman is here with her as tis possible, and Saturday being a busy day with me, if she should not come till Friday I should be able to enjoy very little more of her company than I did at St Albans; I have not yet seen Lady Charlotte which I wonder very much at for I used to be very regular and I cannot fancy she has taken her leave for nine months, because since my three first children I have never bred so soon; having writ to my dear, dear Mrs Freeman yesterday and knowing no manner of news I hope she will excuse me for saying no more but that I am more hers than I can ever express.

[ps] Mr Morley sends Mr Freeman these Gazettes believing he may not have heard any thing that is come by the last post, the letters being come but yesterday, and if he cares for them, he will not fail letting him have them every post.

Figure 1 **Anne of Denmark**

By permission of the Ashmolean Museum, Oxford.

Pregnancy was always significant, but especially so when a woman was the heir presumptive to the throne, as Anne, Princess of Denmark, was when she failed to menstruate in mid-1692. Anne bore eighteen children, but had not one living child when she died in 1714.

[?1 August 1692] I am at this time in very splenetic way for lady Charlotte is not yet come to me and I doubt if I should prove with child, tis too soon after my illness to hope to go on with it, and if I am not, tis a very ugly thing to be so irregular, but these and all melancholy thoughts will vanish at the sight of dear Mrs Freeman which I hope she will bless me with some time this week . . .

[?2 August 1692] I have sent to day to the doctors to ask their advice what they would have me to do in case Lady Charlotte should not come to me before the sixteenth of this month, I am mightily inclined to the spa waters myself and I hope they will not disapprove of them . . .

[?1692] [PS] I have taken physic today and Lady Charlotte is come to me just at the time I expected her and therefore I hope you will excuse me for saying no more but that I am faithfully yours.

[c. 9 Jan. 1693] Monday night . . . Lady Charlotte made some little appearance after I writ last, but since yesterday morning I have been quite rid of her company, the medicine I now take was not proposed to me by anybody, but it coming into my head, I got 78 to get it for me (who is the only one besides you and Mr Morely that knows of it,) being so desirous of children I would do anything to go on and having never tried this I had a great mind to take it, but when you mentioned the taking of something I did not think of this, being I am no farther gone, I fancy it can do me no harm for if the child be only weak I hope it may comfort and strengthen it, and if it be loosened I flatter myself it will not stop it for many days. . . . [crossed out]

1.2   A pregnant servant: Deborah Brackley, 1651

Deborah Brackley, a servant, became pregnant in 1651. Her examination before the justices for bastardy reveals conflict between her and her lover, George Jewell, over her knowledge that she was pregnant, and what to do about it. There are intriguing hints about contraception and abortion. Why was George Jewell convinced that Deborah could not be pregnant? Was he reflecting the widespread view that since she had experienced no pleasure in intercourse, she could not have 'spent her seed' and conceived? This deposition is unusual because it is fuller than many others, and Deborah herself signed her statement.

Devon Quarter Sessions Bundles, Devon RO, QSB Box 60, Epiphany 1655/6.

The examination of Deborah Brackley of Lamerton, single woman taken before Francis Glanvill Esquire one of the justices of the peace for the said county the 3d day of September 1651

She saith she is gotten with child by George Jewell late her fellow servant and that he had the carnal knowledge of her body two several times within one month about July 1649 at which time there was a contract of marriage privately passed between them. And she saith the said Jewell oftentimes since hath solicited her to lie with him, and to invite her thereunto he would threaten her to discover what filthiness had formerly passed between them, wherewith she being too much terrified consented to him, and about the latter end of January last he lay with her and had the carnal knowledge of her body two several times in the kitchen one time the first of that month and at another time the same night he returned from Exeter the people being then also gone to bed, and at another time he had the carnal knowledge of her about the midst of February in the said Jewell's own chamber on the bed, he pretending he was sick sent for this examinate, and when she came into the chamber he laid hold of her, and being naked save his shirt lay with her as aforesaid, and she saith that no other person ever had the carnal knowledge of her except the said Jewell. And she also saith that divers times she acquainted him that she feared she was with child and at one time he said he was now revenged of her. At another time he told her that she could not be with child and though the doctors told her so yet they were fools. And if she were with child she knew what to take to bring it going, and advised her to take physic. At another time he pressed her if she were with child to name some other body to be the father and it [would be] better for her and when she told him she would not justly take any other but him he said she might name Thomas Peryn, Cornet Charlton, Peter Tull, or any one of them, and then he would marry her, and now she should see what her great friends would do for her.

[signed]   Deborah Brackley

PARTURITION

(See also Chapter 7, Maternity.)

1.3   Miscarriage: Elizabeth Catterall, 1655

This information from the prosecution of William Hodgson, who was accused of causing the death of Elizabeth's child, offers some details about a woman's activities when she was pregnant. It is also revealing about the access claimed to women's bodies by men.

Northern Assize Depositions, PRO, ASSI 45 5/3/38.

Information of Elizabeth Catterall the wife of Edward of Skipton, taken the 2 April 1655, West Riding.

Who upon her oath saith, that upon the 23th day of December last as she was walking down Skipton town street there came to her one William Hodgson of the same town, a shoemaker, who presently laid his hand upon her belly and griping it fast in his hand told her this informant that he thought she would be as big as Benson's wife and from thence she went to the burial of a child and found herself not well but said nothing to anybody thinking she should be better again in a short space and for that she was persuaded the said Hodgson intended her no harm. But she saith that though she did often go abroad and rid ten miles to a market town yet she had not her health, and that about a fortnight before Candlemas last she was delivered of a dead child being but about sixteen weeks gone with child, but she saith that she did never perceive her self to be with quick child, yet saith that the aforesaid grip given her by the said William Hodgson was the cause of her sudden miscarrying.

1.4   Prayer in time of labour:
Elizabeth, Countess of Bridgewater (d. 1666)

Various papers of Elizabeth Egerton, Countess of Bridgewater (1623–66), were bound up by her husband after her death in a volume entitled 'Meditations'. Many women kept such collections, often in bound volumes, which they might bequeath to a daughter. The countess's collection included a prayer for labour that started and stopped again. Here she refers to the foetus as her 'dear child'.

From copies of loose papers transcribed after her death, BL, MS Egerton 607, pp. 49–53.

A prayer in time of labour

Lord Jesus since thou art pleased my time is come, to bring forth this my babe, thou hast made in me, give me a heart full of all truth and obedience to thee and that I may take this height of pain patiently, without grudging at thy holy will and pleasure; I beg, oh hear, three persons ease me, and that soon: Lord be not angry, that I should limit thee at a time, but sweet Christ bring me out of this my extremity, and fill my mouth with honour and praise to thee, that I may see this my dear child without any deformity, which sight is of the wonderful mercy of my God, far beyond my sins: thus thy name is to be praised with a song, and magnified with thanksgiving; O Lord hear, O Lord forgive, and suffer me not to accompany my sins in the deep, but part us, and make me become a new creature, and if it be by thy will, O God, that I should be no more in this world, Christ raise me to life everlasting in the true belief of thee, who art my only saviour: Amen.

1.5 'The same condition that all other women use to be': the birth of a prince, 1688

When James II became King in 1685, he supported pro-Catholic policies. So long as his heirs were his two Protestant daughters, Mary and Anne, his subjects retained a measure of security for the future since his second wife, Mary of Modena, had borne no child which survived. In 1687–88 Mary was again pregnant. James hoped for a son, who would displace the two Protestant princesses as heirs. Protestants immediately suggested that Mary's pregnancy was a fake, and that a supposititious child would be imposed upon the kingdom. When a son, James Edward, was born, Protestant propaganda alleged that he was spurious, and had been substituted in a warming-pan. In attempt to counter these rumours, James had summoned many respected female courtiers to witness the birth, and most unusually, male members of his Privy Council. Subsequently, he sought depositions as to the authenticity of his son, and ordered that these be printed. Mary's pregnancy and parturition was thus one of the best documented births of seventeenth-century England. Princess Anne kept out of the way. Ultimately, many people found it more convenient to believe that James Edward was not the son of James II, and to support the claims of Mary and Anne to the throne.

At the Council Chamber in Whitehall, Monday the 22 of October 1688 [London, 1688], pp. 8, 10–11, 20, 21.

And the following depositions were all taken upon oath.

Elizabeth Lady Marchioness of Powis deposeth.

That about the 19th of December last, the Queen was likely to miscarry; whereupon she immediately went unto her, and offered her some effectual remedies, which are made use of on the like occasion; which the Queen ordered this deponent to acquaint the doctors with. The day following the Queen Dowager[1] sent this deponent to see how the Queen did; who replied, She had a pretty good night, and did think she had quickened, but would not be positive till she felt it again. That after this the deponent did frequently wait on the Queen in the morning, and did see her shift her[2] several days, and generally saw the milk, and sometimes wet upon her smock. That some time after, this deponent went into the country, and came not up till a few days before the Queen was brought to bed; and from the time of this deponent's return, she saw the Queen every day till she was brought to bed, and was in the room a quarter of an hour before, and at the time of her delivery of the Prince by Mrs Wilks, her Majesty's midwife, which this deponent saw, and immediately went with the Prince, carried by Mrs Delabadie into the Queen's little bedchamber, where she saw Sir Thomas Witherley sent for by the midwife, who gave the child three drops of something which came into the world with him, which this deponent saw done; And this deponent doth aver, this Prince be the same child which was then born, and that she has never been from him one day since.

1. Catherine of Braganza, widow of Charles II.
2. That is, change her linen.

21

Anne Countess of Sunderland deposeth,

That June the 10th 1688, being Trinity Sunday, the deponent went to St James's chapel at eight of the clock in the morning, intending to receive the sacrament; [she was summoned to the Queen] . . . As soon as the deponent came in [to the Queen's bedchamber], her Majesty told her, this deponent, She believed she was in labour. By this time the bed was warmed, and the Queen went into the bed, and the King came in. The Queen asked the King if he had sent for the Queen Dowager; he said he had sent for every body. The said deponent stood at the Queen's bolster, the Lady Roscomon, Mrs Delabadie, and the midwife, on that side of the bed where the Queen was delivered. After some lingering pains, the Queen said, she feared she should not be brought to bed a good while; but inquiring of the midwife, she assured her Majesty, that she wanted only one thorough pain to bring the child into the world; upon which the Queen said, It is impossible, the child lies so high, and commanded this deponent to lay her hand on her Majesty's belly, to feel how high the child lay, which the deponent did; but soon after a great pain came on at past nine of the clock, and the Queen was delivered; which the midwife by pulling the deponent by the coat, assured her was a son, it being the sign she told the deponent she would give her, the Queen having charged her not to let her Majesty know presently, whether it was son or daughter. . . .

Lady Sophia Bulkeley deposeth,

. . . So this deponent ran on to the Queen's bedside, and heard the Queen say to the midwife, Pray, Mrs Wilks, don't part the child (which signifies, don't cut the navel string, until the after-birth is come away.) And while the Queen was with child, this deponent hath heard her Majesty command her midwife not to do otherwise, it being counted much the safest way; But to what the Queen said just then (to the best of the deponent's remembrance) Mrs Wilks replied, Pray madam give me leave, for I will do nothing but what will be safe for your self and child; the Queen answered, Do then, and then cried, where is the King gone; His Majesty came immediately from the other side of the bed (from just having a sight of the child) and answered the Queen, Here I am; the Queen said, Why do you leave me now? The King kneeled on the bed, on that side where the deponent stood, and a little after the midwife said, All is now come safe away; upon that the King rose from the bed, and said, Pray, my Lords, come and see the child . . .

Mrs Judith Wilks deposeth,

That being the Queen's midwife, she came often to her, especially when her Majesty was in any danger of miscarrying, and many times she felt the child stir in her belly, and saw the milk run out of her Majesty's breasts; That on Trinity Sunday last in the morning about eight of the clock, the Queen sent Mr White, page of the Back-stairs, to call her this deponent, believing herself in labour. When the deponent came, she found the Queen in great pain and trembling; the Queen told her she feared it was her labour, it being near the time of her first reckoning, she the deponent desired her Majesty not to be afraid, saying, she did not doubt that it was her full time, and hoped her Majesty would have as good labour as she always had; and whilst her Majesty was sitting trembling, her water broke, and immediately she sent for the King, he being gone to his own side, and let him know in what condition she was, and desired him to send for whom he pleased to be present. . . . about ten a clock that morning the Queen was delivered of the Prince of Wales by her this deponent's assistance, and afterwards she the deponent showed the after-burthen to the physicians, and before them the deponent cut the navel string, and gave the Prince three drops of his blood, to prevent convulsion fits, according to their order. And this deponent further saith, That when the child was born, it not crying, the Queen said she thought it was dead, this deponent assured her Majesty it was not, and she desired leave to part the child from the after-burthen: which the Queen was unwilling to have done, thinking it might be dangerous to her self; but the Deponent assuring her Majesty it would not, her Majesty gave consent; whereupon the child present cried, and then the deponent gave it to Mrs Labadie.

Mrs Elizabeth Pearse, Laundress to the Queen, deposeth,

That about nine of the clock on the 10th of June last in the morning, she came into the bed-chamber, and heard the Queen cry out, being in great pain, in which she continued until her delivery; after which she the deponent saw the Prince of Wales given by the midwife to Mistress Labadie; That immediately after the deponent saw the midwife hold up the after-burthen, showing it to the company, and then the deponent fetched her maids, and with them took away all the foul linen, hot as they came from the Queen. That for a month after her Majesty's lying-in, the deponent well knows by the washing of her linen, that the Queen was in the same condition that all other women use to be on the like occasion; and that some time after her quickening it appeared by her smocks, that her majesty had milk in her breasts, which continued until she was brought to bed, and afterwards during the usual time.

1.6   Midwives and 'man-midwives': Lady Isabella Wentworth, 1713

The letter describes the birth of a daughter and first child to Lady Strafford, the wife of the Tory ambassador at The Hague during the last years of Queen Anne. The baby was delivered by Dr Hugh Chamberlen (1664–1728), of the Huguenot family of 'man-midwives', whose prominence in the field of obstetrics was based chiefly on the secret of forceps delivery. The rivalry between midwives and the new breed of male practitioners specialising in childbirth, in which the latter gradually gained the ascendency, is sometimes represented as a purely professional and social one. Many of Chamberlen's clients, as the letter indicates, were elite Tory women with court connections: the Duchess of Buckingham, Lady Lonsdale, Lady Bathurst, and the Queen's favourite, Abigail, Lady Masham. He appears to have shared their political views, and there may well have been elements of fashion and politics in their choice of him over traditional female practitioners. But the letter provides powerful evidence that their preference, in an intimate matter fraught with personal risk and fear, was based chiefly on direct comparison and experience.

Lady Isabella Wentworth to her son Lord Strafford, 27 Feb [1713], BL, Add. MS 22225, fos 375–6.

This document and its note supplied by Frances Harris.

Lady Anne begs your blessing; she came yesterday in the forenoon . . . my Lady Strafford is as well as is possible and your daughter is very pretty. It looks broad open with her black eyes as pert as if it was a month old. . . . My Lady desired me to thank you for letting her have Dr Chamberlen. She says she is sure he saved her life and she believes the child too. Her labour was not so bad but her fears was great. The woman midwife was with her at ten at night, he came at four in the morning. The woman would fain have brought my lady to bed and gave great encouragement. But my Lady for all she was in great pain was very cold with fear. We warmed the clothes and flannel to wrap her feet in, but as soon as the Doctor came to her, she says she found a great alteration for the better, for although it was the strongest part of her labour, she did not endure so much as with the woman, who is the best we have, but my Lady Royston had possessed herself and my Lady with fear that certainly would have killed her. And Lady Lonsdale and the Duchess of Buckingham has him and Lady Masham says she owes her life to him, next to God, and several more ladies has him and those say they would not for never so much have a woman, it's so much more terrible with a woman. He gives his service to you and says had it been a son he would have wished you joy, but now he fears it will not be welcome, as if a son he was sure it would. I did not say one word of yours to my Lady. I was sure it would have been so much trouble to her, having so much fear upon her because of her mother who died of her. . . . I heard his price [100 guineas] before and writ you word of it, but to be sure of it I not only sent to him but asked him myself, and heard him declare at cousin Hanbury's that he would not take under, for he said people had a notion that he was only fit for that business therefore would never use him as a physician, therefore he would make it up this way and those that employed him as their doctor he would be more moderate with. When you come to England and treat him with a bottle of wine and at dinner as Lord Masham and Lord Bathurst does you may bring him down against the lord [a son] comes, which I hope will be the next. For the other man, your sister Wentworth has him and the first child he brought of hers, it was so bruised that for ten days it was daily expected to die. He is extreme old, he goes almost double. She has

24

had two of the most famous women in England both dead, so she was persuaded to have this old man and she says she would not for never so much have a woman again, there is so much difference . . . and certainly there is no comparison between this and the other.

1.7   Managing childbirth: Anne Glyd, 1656

Anne Glyd, the wife of Richard Glyd (d. 1658), a gentleman in West Kent, compiled a commonplace book with a wide range of medical cures. She sometimes records the source of her information, as in the entry below.

Recipe book of Anne Glyd, Brockman Papers, 'Anne Glyd Her Book 1656', BL, Add. MS 45196, fos 57, 72v.

To cause pains when a woman cannot be delivered
Let her drink a good porringer of her husband's water.
Pro[ved] myself. . . .
Another: Take a cloth that another woman wears when her courses are upon her and it coming wet with her courses from her, lay it upon the belly of the woman in travail. It will cause pain.
Mrs Day

A drink good for the after-pains in women.
Take half a spoonful of coriander seeds as much of carroway seeds as much of sweet fennel seeds 2 or 3 branches of filipendula,[1] which if not to be had you make shift without, bruise all these seeds and boil them in a pint of beer until it be very strong then strain it and sweeten it with sugar according as the party loves it and let it be taken between whiles as their after-pains follow, also make a toast of the bottom of a brown loaf and stick it with cloves and when it is toasted very hot put in a cloth and lay it to the party's belly. You may also before hand, if you know the party use to be troubled much with after pains, take the after-birth when it comes hot from the women, broil it on a gridiron over embers till it be pretty dry, then wrap it in a coarse cloth and lay it to the woman's belly. probatum [proved] Mrs Walker[2]

1.8   Suspected infanticide: Mary Smith, 1672

Abortion before the quickening of the child was not a crime until 1803. However, by the statute of 1624, any unmarried woman whose child was found to be dead was convicted of murder if she had concealed the birth. Mary Smith's pregnancy and parturition was typical of those of single women and servants who kept pregnancy secret and, if the child died, risked accusations of infanticide. The result of

1. *Spirea filipendula*, commonly called dropwort.
2. On fo. 73v Mrs Walker is described as 'an ancient midwife'.

her case is not known: but, despite the severity of the 1624 statute, the courts through the seventeenth century treated infanticide cases with increasing leniency.

Northern Assizes Depositions, PRO, ASSI 45 10/1/120 (22 Feb. 1672).

The examination of Mary Smith of Hipperholme [Yorks], spinster

Who saith that this day sevennight at night about two hours within even, she bore and brought forth this female child now viewed, being then in the bed where she used to lie and no person was then with her, she being at a good distance from the room where the rest of her father's family was, and when all the said family was gone to bed, except her sister who was gone out of doors, she arose and carried the child to the fire to see whether it was living or no, and saith that it never stirred nor cried after it was born and that she had got a fall about a week before in going to Brighouse to pay forth money for her father, which fall as she perceives so hurt the child that she never felt it stir after, and saith that after she had been at the fire with it she lay it by her in the bed till the next morning and then she laid it in her father's garden, and it lay there till yesterday, and saith that neither her mother nor any other to her knowledge did know of it till yesterday, and she fetched it out herself when Susan Wilson told her she had found it there and saith that John Scott of Hipperholme aforesaid, sadler, begot the said child and that she wanted eight weeks of her time when she bore it.

BREASTS AND BREASTFEEDING

1.9   For a sore breast: Constance Hall, 1672

On a mother's success in breastfeeding, the health and sometimes even the survival of the child depended. Women shared information and advice about their breast problems, such as how to produce milk, how to dry up milk and how to ease the pain of sore breasts.

Constance Hall Her Booke of Receipts, 1672, Folger, MS V. a. 20.

For a sore breast
Take hemlock and oatmeal a handful of a lily root. Chop those together and make a plaster. Anoint the place with warm milk twice a day.
To make a sear cloth
Take four pennyworth of salad oil, one pennyworth of stone pitch, one pennyworth of red lead. Boil it together over coals softly till it look black. Then dip the cloths in it. Have a care it do not boil over.

1.10   To manage lactation: Hannah Wolley, 1675

Hannah Wolley (born *c.* 1623) was educated by her female relatives and other women. She was twice married and employed in a range of occupations. She wrote several advice books for women so that they might acquire useful knowledge about female health and housewifery. For her own autobiographical comments, see document 3.19.

Hannah Wolley, *The Gentlewomans Companion: or, a guide to the female sex*, London, 1675, p. 169.

An excellent way to dry up a woman's breast
Of linseed oil and English honey, take of each a penny-worth, and half a quarter of a pound of sweet butter, boil all these together, spread a plaster thereof, and lay it on the breast.
Probatum est.
An infallible receipt to increase milk in a woman's breasts
Take chickens and make a broth of them, then add thereunto fennel and parsnip roots, then take the best made butter you can procure, and butter the roots therewith; having done so let her eat heartily, and her expectations therein will be speedily satisfied.

1.11   To dry breasts: Mrs Corylon, 1606

Women copied remedies for the management of breast problems into their common-place books. One of many cures was that in the book of Mrs Corylon, about whom nothing more is known.

Mrs Corylon, 1606, Wellcome, MS 213, no. 65.

A medicine to dry up a woman's milk troubling her in childbed or to take a wen from any place
Make thin bowls of lead fit to cover the breast or wen and when you do lay it to the breast warm it a little and so whelm it upon the breast and make it fast that it remove not and let it lie as you feel occasion.

1.12   Breast cancer: Mary Astell (d. 1731)

Mary Astell (1668–1731) was born in Newcastle of a merchant family. Well-educated and single, she moved in a circle of pious and intellectual women in London. She led an abstemious life, according to the celebratory memorial published by George Ballard, who termed her 'This great ornament of her sex and country'. She diagnosed her own breast cancer several years before her mastectomy.

George Ballard, *Memoirs of Several Ladies of Great Britain* (1752), ed. Ruth Perry, Detroit, Wayne University Press, 1985, pp. 391–2.

She seemed to enjoy an uninterrupted state of health till a few years before her death, when, having one of her breasts cut off, it so much impaired her

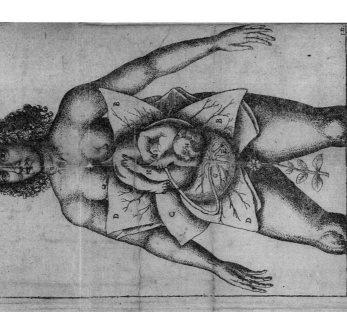

The Figure Explained:

Being a Diſſection of the Womb, with the uſual manner how the Child lies therein near the time of its Birth.

B B. The inner parts of the *Chorion* extended and branched out.

C. The *Amnios* extended.

D D. The Membrane of the Womb extended and branched.

E. The Fleſhy ſubſtance call'd the *Cake* or *Placenta*, which nouriſhes the Infant; it is full of Veſſels.

F. The Veſſels appointed for the Navel ſtring.

G. The Navel ſtring carrying nouriſhment from the *Placenta* to the Navel.

H H H. The manner how the Infant lieth in the Womb near the time of its Birth.

I. The Navel ſtring how it enters into the Navel.

Figure 2 A woman and her womb, from Jane Sharp, *The Midwives Book*

By permission of the British Library

This picture, which opened out from *The Midwives Book*, presents woman as an unfolding plant or flower.

constitution that she did not long survive it. This was occasioned by a cancer which she had concealed from the world in such a manner that few of even her most intimate acquaintances knew anything at all of the matter. She dressed and managed it herself till she plainly perceived there was an absolute necessity for its being cut off. And then, with the most intrepid resolution and courage, she went (with only one person to attend her) to the Reverend Mr Johnson, a gentleman very eminent for his skill in surgery, entreating him to take it off in the most private manner imaginable. She would hardly allow him to have persons whom necessity required to be at the operation. She seemed so regardless of the sufferings or pain she was to undergo that she refused to have her hands held and did not discover the least timidity or impatience, but went through the operation without the least struggling or resistance or even so much as giving a groan or a sigh, and showed the like patience and resignation throughout the whole cure, which that gentleman, to his lasting credit and honour, soon performed.

MENSTRUATION AND REPRODUCTIVE HEALTH

1.13   Greensickness: Alice Corfield, 1649

Greensickness was widely believed to be a disorder to which women were prone from the suppression of menstruation or from excessive seed. Seed, a distillation of the blood, would drive a woman to sexual activity. Contemporaries believed that the best remedy for greensickness in maids was marriage; in wives, vigorous sex. Alternatively, physic might assist.

A book of physicall receits for Mrs Alice Corfield, 1649, Royal College of Physicians, London, MS 232, no 7.

A sovereign medicine for the green sickness
Take a handful of herb grace, and a handful of red sage leaves, stamp them and strain out the juice, then take a pint of honey, hot and well clarified, and put it into the juice aforesaid, with a great spoonful of pepper bruised, but not too small then stir it well and give the patient a spoonful and a half morning and evening. If she take early in the morning, then to sleep upon it, is better, it must be taken last at night; also she must eat every day raisins of the sun; 5 or 6 at a time, this will cure it although it will appear not at first, but if you see not the party mend at the end of ten weeks, give her the like receipt again, and she shall be perfect whole by God's grace.

1.14   Greensickness: Johanna St John, 1680

Johanna St John was the daughter of the famous lawyer and Parliamentarian, Oliver St John. Her commonplace book is an interesting one. Small notes scribbled inside the covers, such as 'cow piss will cure a dog of the mange washing therewith', and the division into alphabetical sections for ease of use suggest that it was a working manual. Most of the ingredients mentioned below were herbs.

Johanna St John 1680, Wellcome, MS 4338 (unfoliated).

G. A bitter drink Dr Lower prescribed Betty when she had the greensickness and a cough and was swelled.

Species Hira picra one dram, tops of centaury one handful, white horehound a quarter of a handful, tops of St John's wort 2 pugels,[1] filings of steel cleansed one ounce, roots of gentian one dram, infuse these in 3 pints of good white wine. Let them steep in it while the [illegible] liquor is drawn. Drink 8 spoonfuls every morning less and more. This was to be taken 3 or 4 days, and then she took a spoonful of syrup of steel and as much cream of tartar as will lie on a groat and after both a little water wherein centaury has been infused like tea, taking the powder in a little of it, and about 4 or 5 spoonfuls after it and every third or fourth morning, the bitter drink so much as may work 3 times or a pill of pill russi.[2] Do this three months together.

1.15   Excessive menstruation: a poor woman's remedy, late seventeenth century

The following remedy has been taken from a late seventeenth-century commonplace book. The author obtained it from one woman, who had it from a woman begging at her door. The recipe itself was also in the book of Sarah Wigges (1616), almost word for word the same, but lacking the provenance (Sarah Wigges, Medical Receipts, 1616: Royal College of Physicians, London, MS 654, p. 160). These two records from the beginning and end of the century thus suggest that the magical cure was known both to literate and to beggar women.

Collection of medical receipts, late seventeenth century, Royal College of Physicians, London, MS 504, p. 28.

28. To stop women's courses

If a woman that is too much weakened with her courses doth cast the same, or let the same run into a hole made in the ground, with a three-squared stake, the same stake immediately after being put or drove into the same hole, and so remain there in unremoved, her said flux will cease, being thought before incurable. An honest woman revealed this who had proved it to be true; and she learned it of a poor woman that required alms at her door.

1. Pinches.
2. This obscure term possibly refers to some purchased pill.

1.16   Excessive menstruation: Anne Glyd, 1656

Despite the range of negative attitudes towards menstrual blood, some women took a positive view of its magical and healing properties. For Anne Glyd, see 1.7 above.

Recipe book of Anne Glyd, Brockman Papers, 'Anne Glyd Her Book 1656', BL, Add. MS 45196, fo. 57.

For flooding of the courses. Take a cloth that comes from the woman that floods and wring it into a glass of beer and let her drink thereof. Let her take this three or four times and it will stop them in four and twenty hours. This may be given in a posset drink when they have the small pox.
Mrs Day.

1.17   Mother-fits: Elizabeth Butler, 1679

Fits of the mother were thought to be a choking sensation caused by the womb rising. The following remedy was to be taken according to the phases of the moon, which were believed to affect the time of menstruation. The fits could be precipitated by a shock. According to the original MS catalogue the name of the compiler was Hester Gullyford.

Book of Elizabeth Butler 1679, BL, Sloane MS 3842, fo. 32v.

This book humbly begs Madam Elizabeth Butler her acceptance from her faithful servant: Poor Colly
March the last 1679
An excellent receipt for fits of the mother:
Take the liver and heart of a hare, and bake it in a pot, in an oven after brown bread is drawn, and make it into a powder; then take in motherwort[1] and make it into a powder and mix it with the other, only let there be twice as much powder of hare as of motherwort, then let the party take as much as will lie on a shilling in a wine glass of black cherry water, first in morning and last at night take it a fortnight together, then rest a week, take it again, a week before the full of the moon and a week before new moon. This with God's blessing has cured many.

1.18   Mother-fits in a 17-year-old: Mary Henry, 1658

Philip Henry, a minister, recorded the mother-fits of his 17-year-old sister in his diary. The original manuscript for this period cannot now be traced, and the chronology around Mary's fits is a little uncertain. Mary's fits appear to have lasted a whole year.

Diaries and Letters of Philip Henry of Broad Oak, Flintshire, A.D. 1631–1696, ed. M. H. Lee, London, Kegan Paul, 1882, from pp. 41–3, 65–6.

1. Motherwort was commended in contemporary herbals for settling the womb.

30 January 1658 I was ill, I thought unto death, but the Lord had mercy: it was the occasion through inordinate fear and grief of sister Mary's fits of the mother, in the first whereof she continued near 8 hours, without sign of life. . . .

1 February. Another violent fit . . .

2. I began to mend, . . . but sister Mary continued ill.

17. Sister Mary let blood.

20. Sister Mary very weak and in much danger, the Lord be her support. I do verily believe she is in Christ and therefore best for her to be with Christ.

– her distemper turned about this time from the fits of the mother to a violent ague . . .

17 December. Sister Mary returned from Shrewsbury, not rid of her mother-fits which she had before; the time of her being there was chargeable, it cost between thirty and forty pounds; I bless God I had it for her use.

1.19   Infertility: Jane Sharp, 1671

Barrenness in wives, according to the Bible and to contemporary wisdom, was deeply unfortunate. Jane Sharp, one of the first women to publish health-care advice for women, here reflects upon a range of causes for infertility. Her comments were in many cases similar to those contained in manuscript commonplace books. In a society in which many marriages were arranged, Mrs Sharp's allusion to medical theories about conception were a timely reminder that aversion between a couple would lead to infertility. Unlike many, she did not identify infertility as exclusively the woman's 'fault'. Her observation that blood-letting to provoke menstruation could be dangerous seems widespread among women.

Jane Sharp, *The Midwives Book*, London, 1671, pp. 97–101.

Notwithstanding that God gave the blessing generally to our first parent, and so by consequent to all her succeeding generations, yet we find that some women are exceeding fruitful to conceive; and others barren that they conceive not at all; God reserving to himself a prerogative of furthering and hindering conception where he pleaseth, that men and women may more earnestly pray unto God for his blessing of procreation. . . . Some women are by nature barren, though both they themselves and their husbands are no way deficient to perform the acts of generation, and are in all parts, as perfect as the most fruitful persons can be: Some think the cause is too much likeness and similitude in their complexions . . .

Some say again the cause of barrenness is want of love in man and wife, whose seed never mixeth as it should to procreation of children, their hatred is so great. . . . The cause of this hatred in married people, is commonly when they are contracted and married by unkind parents for some sinister ends against their wills, which makes some children complain of their parents' cruelly herein all the days of their lives; but as parents do ill to compel their children in such cases, so children should not be drawn away by their own foolish fancies, but take their parents' counsel along with them when they go about such a great work as marriage is, wherein consists their greatest woe or welfare so long as they live upon the earth.

Another cause that women prove barren is, when they are let blood in the arm before their courses come down, whereas to provoke the terms when they flow not as they should, women and maids ought rather to be let blood in the foot, for that draws them down to the place nature hath provided, but to let blood from the arm keeps them from falling down, and is as great a mischief as can be to hinder them; wherefore let the terms first come naturally before you venture to draw blood in the arm, unless the cause be so great that there is no help for it otherwise. The time of the courses to appear for maids is fourteen or thirteen, or the soonest at twelve years old; yet I remember that in France I saw a child but of nine years old that was very sickly until such time as she was let blood in the arm, and then she recovered immediately; but this is no precedent for others, especially in our climate, blood-letting being the ordinary remedy in those parts when the Patient is charged with fullness of blood, of what age almost soever they be.

There is besides this natural barrenness of women, another barrenness by accident, by the ill disposition of the body and generative parts, when the courses are either more or fewer that stands with the state of the woman's body, when humours fall down to the womb, and have found a passage that way and will hardly be brought to keep their natural order; or when the womb is disaffected, either by any preternatural quality that exceeds the bounds of nature, as heat or cold, or dryness, or moisture, or windy vapours.

Lastly, there is barrenness by enchantment, when a man cannot lie with his wife by reason of some charm that hath disabled him; the French in such a case advise a man to thread the needle *Noer C'eguilliette*, as much as to say, to piss through his wife's wedding ring and not to spill a drop and then he will be perfectly cured. Let him try it that pleaseth.

1.20 Gynaecological disorders: unlicensed practice, late seventeenth century

From the later seventeenth century, unlicensed medical practitioners used small printed bills to advertise their services. These followed a conventional form, similar advertisements often appearing for different practitioners. Female practitioners specialised in disorders of women and children, cosmetics and beauty treatments;

several claimed to be gentlewomen, thereby suggesting respectability. Hints of 'most rare secrets' with promises of confidentiality would have encouraged women seeking abortions to consult as well as those troubled with sexually transmitted diseases.

Compilation of medical advertisements, 1675–1715, BL, 551 a. 32, no. 31.

In Holborn over against Southampton-Square, at the Coffin and Child, against the Watch-house, next door to the Sugar-Loaf and Roll, where you will see the Golden-Ball hanging over the passage door, liveth Anne Laverenst a German gentlewoman.

Being but very lately arrived in this kingdom, and so consequently a stranger, I could not propose a better method to make myself known, than by this printed paper, without which I might for some years have remained unknown to you; and so consequently incapable of implying that talent which heaven hath bestowed on me, for all your benefits and good. My parents before me were so far skilled in the art and knowledge of physic that they have removed the most dangerous distempers, and have seldom or never failed wholesomely to assist nature in the discharge of her duty. From them I received the great knowledge and experience that I now profess, and question not but (by the blessing of God) I shall be able to cure any distemper incident to woman-kind: a few of which I shall here give you an account.

First, I cure all women or maids of the suffocation or rising of the mother, which may be occasioned through any rotten substance, or through a corruption in nature, or by an imposthumation[1] in the womb, which may be easily discerned, for there oftentimes proceeds a great dizziness in the head, anguish of heart, an inclination to vomit, much rising and tumbling in the belly, from whence oftentimes proceeds very fatal accidents; as barrenness, imposthumes, inflammations of the lungs, an unusual paleness, and shivering in the limbs, colic, strangulation; obstructions, wringings, and tertians of the guts, &c.

Secondly, I cure outsinking, downfalling, out-hanging of the matrix, that is when the ligaments or strings that bind the mother fast to the body, removes from its place, occasioned either by bearing of children, violent coughing or heavy work. In 14 or 20 days, I artificially return to its proper place, which I challenge any person to do but myself.

I also cure women or maids that are subject to vomiting, and take from them, the quivering and shaking, occasioned by the same infirmity. I also cure hard bellies, swelled as with child, or as if troubled with the dropsy. There is yet another sort of sickness, when the melancholy is not cleansed and taken away, it occasions grief and heavy thoughts, nay sometimes ragings, and an ill mind towards themselves and others. I cure the piles or haemorrhoids in the fundament, all warts, excrescences, or superfluous flesh in the mouth of the bladder or womb.

1. A purulent swelling or abcess.

I also cure ruptures or bursten-bellies either in women or children, nay though they have had it many years. I take the stone[2] from women and maids, nay without cutting, which no woman (except my mother) did before me. I have also an approved remedy for a pain in the loins, or small of the back, whether proceeding from gravel[3] or child-bearing, as also a pain in making water, or those that cannot hold their water, but are troubled with a constant leaking or dropping as they go, let it proceed from what cause it will. I drive away all gouty pains in the joints; nay though your arms and legs were grown crooked through a contraction, or sinking of the sinews; nay though you have kept your bed for many years, by the blessing of God, I don't doubt but to relieve you. I cure many sad accidents in the eyes, as spots, specks, pearls, water-sinkings, hot and violent rheums, and many more too tedious here to relate. I also cure the morbus gallicus or French pox, with all its symptoms, and dangerous effects, with ease, speed, and secrecy; nay, though tampered with and almost ruined by others. I dare presume few has arrived to the perfection in this cure as myself. There are many other cures in women, I shall conclude with this, that I correct all vices, of the matrix, and refresh all the weak faculties of the body, by this means rendering a woman capable of conception, that before was barren, this is the best time of the year for all cures.

Those that are not able to come to me, let them but send their urine, and on sight thereof, I will resolve them what their distemper is, and if curable will perform it at a reasonable rate, but if not curable, will plainly and honestly tell them, that they may not be defrauded by others.

If any persons troubled with distempers, whether through weakness, or that the nature of the distemper requires a close confinement to their chambers, if desired they may be lodged at my house, and accommodated with all things necessary at a reasonable rate.

My hours are from eight in the morning till twelve at noon, and from two till nine at night.

HEALTH AND BEAUTY

1.21   The virtues of a temperate life: Katherine Austen, 1664

Katherine Austen (*c.* 1628–83) was a young London widow, who married with a dowry of over £2,000. Her husband died in 1658, and around the same time so did his father and younger brother, leaving her in charge of the family properties and of her three children.

Katherine Austen Collectanea, BL, Add. MS 4454, fo. 51.

---

2. Disease characterised by the formation of a calculus.
3. Urinary crystals causing pain.

I observe what a long and healthy age my grandmother Rudd lived, above 80, and Mr Smith of Aldermanbury 90, and parson Wilson about 80. All lived in the city and did not love the country. Their diet was temperate, their exercise little. A softly pace ever went, not put nature scarce ever in any violence by over stirring or heating which makes a faintness often times and a decay. Yet I attribute the chief part of their long life to the quiet of their minds. Never engaged in any thing disquieted or disordered that peace within them. How was my own mother's strong nature worn out by too much stirring and walking. And the many cares and businesses which a great family gave occasions to her. That nature was spent which in likelihood by indulging to retirement would have prolonged. The distractions of the times wherein she lived gave her many discomposures and crosses by abuses. Dear mother, thou hadst a great estate and a great burden too.

1.22 'My crazy health': Anne Dormer, 1686

Anne Dormer, daughter of Sir Charles Cottrell and his wife Elizabeth, was unhappily married to Robert Dormer of Rousham. She confided her difficulties to her sister, Lady Elizabeth Trumbull, who was in Constantinople with her husband, Sir William, the ambassador there from 1687 to 1691.

BL, Add. MS 72516, fos 163–164v. (24 Aug [1687].)

My dearest heart

Two letters I have received from thee since that from Sir James Ox: and at this distance from thee nothing can equal the joy it gives me to hear thy self my dear brother and all with you are so well . . .

The world is so full of miseries and I am so sensible of my own in particular that I esteem fortitude the most necessary virtue now; when I remember how you begged of me to do what I could to live that you might find me if you did come home again I apply myself to tend my crazy health, and keep up my weak shattered carcase broken with restless nights and unquiet days. I take the king's drops and drink chocolate and when my soul is sad to death I run and play with the children. After I have prayed and almost read my eyes out the thought of my friends and the concern they take in my life and health makes me ashamed to suffer all their and [sic] pains to be lost, and therefore I strive to cheer up my self but it is so unnatural to me to be guttling and tending my self, that I have sometimes much ado to do it, and then comes a new supply of some good thing as the other day a vessel of rare wine from thee the kindness of which gave me a greater joy than if I had it full of pearl some other way. I must say as poor people do I can but love you and thank you, and I am sure never sister loved more passionately, nor gave thanks more gratefully, than I do. . . .

I promise that I will take it for your sake, and when my heart low I'll go for two or three spoonfuls of thy wine, for Solomon says give wine to the afflicted, and now I have had four years' trial of my self that I am sure there is no danger I should ever love wine, to sit and sip by my self, I allow myself all I can drink of any sort, which never exceeds six spoonfuls, and unless my spirits be very low indeed I cannot prevail with my self to take any for many days, and twice in a day when I need it most is all I drink of any wine, which is great content to my mind, for did I love it I would never touch a drop . . .

My most affectionate service to my dear brother, my respects to Mr Haley, and to thyself. I am more than words can express thy faithful friend and loving sister.

1.23   Skin-care: Elizabeth Butler, 1679

In the late seventeenth century, ideals of beauty were for a white skin, high fore-head, golden hair, and youth, ideals more attainable by wealthy, leisured women than those who laboured. Elite women could more easily protect their complexions from the elements, and had maids to help to curl and arrange their hair. Commonplace books contain many instructions for improving the appearance.

Book of Elizabeth Butler 1679, BL, Sloane MS 5842, fos 39, 40v.

To do away freckles.
Take the gall of a goat and meal, of a cockle of either a like portion, mingle them together and anoint the place therewith.

To cleanse and smooth the skin:
Take oil of almonds new-drawn, and put to it as much oil of tartar only to turn it make it look white: so beat them well together and at night wash the face with it and do it again.

1.24   Hairdresser, early eighteenth century

From a compilation of medical advertisements, 1675–1715.

BL, 551 a. 32, no. 4 [post 1702].

Removed from the next door to the Still, near the Fleet-Gate, to the next door to the Golden Bell in St Bride's Lane, Fleet Street; where liveth a gentle-woman, who cutteth and curleth gentlemen's, gentlewomen's, and children's hair; and selleth a fine pomatum,[1] which is mixed with ingredients of her own making, that if the hair be never so thin, it makes it grow thick; and if short, it makes it grow long: if any gentlemen's or children's hair be never so lank, she makes it curl in a little time like a periwig. She waits on ladies, if desired, on Tuesdays and Fridays; the other days of the week, she is to be spoken with at home.

1. Pomade, a scented ointment used especially for the skin of the head and hair.

1.25   The old made young: the services of the
beautician, *c.* 1700

As well as offering services in attaining ideals of female beauty, the 'gentlewoman'
advertises her experience in other bodily ills.

BL, 551 a. 32, no. 24.

The gentlewoman who lived in Red-Lion-Court, is now removed to Racket-
Court near Fleet-bridge, the third door on the right-hand, who hath a most
excellent wash to beautify the face, as many of the greatest quality can testify:
its virtue is to take out all manner of wrinkles, freckles, pimples, redness,
morphew, sun-burn, yellowness, or any other accident, caused too often by
mercurial poisonous washes: it also plumps and softens the skin, making it
smooth and tender as a sucking child. In a word, the young it keeps always
so, and the old it makes appear fair and young even to a miracle, there is
nothing of paint relating to it, neither hath any person the secret but myself,
having (with much difficulty) obtained it of a great lady at Paris, which is
now dead, who sold it there to the Queen and court for above twenty thousand pistols in one year. You may have it from half a crown to five pounds
the bottle. She can furnish you with all sorts of delicate pomatums, whit
pots[1] that cannot be compared with, and also an admirable powder for the
teeth, which makes then as white as snow, and a water to wash the gums,
which preserves from all scorbutical humours, and cures where it is already
come. She has also an admirable spirit for the scurvy, which being taken one
spoonful in a morning, and another at night, certainly cures it, tho' the
patient were broke out all in blotches, and never so far gone. Another excellent remedy against that cruel distemper called the stone, and ulceration of
the kidneys, and a most pleasant diet drink which cures the worst of consumptions, tho' the patient have been left off by others in a month or six weeks
time at farthest. She has also great skill in all manner of sore eyes, or any
cold or hot rheum, caused by the small-pox curing the black or white cataracts,
tho' the patient have been stark blind, and also a most delicate ointment to
anoint the face so soon as the small-pox, begins to dry which certainly
prevents all scars or pits, as also a most excellent secret to prevent hair from
falling, causing it to grow where it is wanting in any part of the head, and
can alter any red or grey hair to a most delicate light or dark brown which
will continue for ever without any soil or smoothing. She also shapes the
eyebrows, taking off the uneven hair, and making them perfectly beautiful,
without any pain, and makes low foreheads as high as you please, taking off
the hair so that it shall never come again. You may have in the same house
all manner of cordial waters, and a most delicate paste to smooth and whiten
the hands, with a curious red pomatum to plump and colour the lips, which
keeps them all the winter from chopping, and a plaster to take off hair from

1. Small pomatums?

38

Figure 3 **A fashionable woman**

From the Pepys Ballads, vol. III, no. 80. By permission of the Pepys Library, Magdalene College, Cambridge

Late-seventeenth-century ballads often featured images of fashionable women with beauty spots and revealed breasts, and commentators such as Pepys remarked on the display and exposure of Restoration London fashion. Many of these pictures and ballads referred specifically to urban style: to a rural audience, this might have been a figure of fun. And for women whose experience of breast-feeding had damaged their nipples or breasts, the idea of fashionable exposure of the breast might have seemed extraordinary.

any part of the body. She cures also any sorts of agues, removing the cause, so that the patient shall never need to fear a relapse, but will be more healthful all their life after; with several other rare secrets in physic, not fit here to mention; which if any person desire to be satisfied in they may speak with her every day in the week, from 10 in the morning till 8 at night. She has also an excellent remedy for barrenness in women.

2

RELIGION, BELIEFS, SPIRITUALITY

One of the major differences between seventeenth-century English society and that of many western countries today is the centrality of religious belief. Everyone, with only a few minor exceptions, believed in God. Most people's lives were dominated by their search for salvation and by their desire to lead a Christian life. Protestant Christians turned to the Scriptures and their ministers for guidance; an indispensable reference work for the reader of these documents is the King James version of the Bible.

During the sixteenth century, in a series of momentous changes, England ceased to be part of the Catholic church and become Protestant.[1] Monasteries and nunneries were abolished and Catholicism was persecuted. While many people embraced the new faith, others defended the old. Women as well as men had views about religious changes, and their beliefs, which were central to their lives, could engage them in public religious controversy and activism.[2] Many women remained faithful to Catholicism, and struggled to preserve their beliefs. Some provided the networks of support which allowed priests to move around the country offering the mass to the faithful. Those, always a minority, who wanted to become nuns, were forced to travel abroad.[3] During the seventeenth century, anti-Catholicism was strong among English Protestants, and was an established feature of Protestant nationalist history. Subsequently, Catholic spirituality, especially that of nuns, has been neglected by many historians who have concentrated on Protestant believers.

Reformation was an ongoing process. Many Protestants believed that the monarchs of the sixteenth century had failed to reform the church thoroughly; Elizabeth was a sluttish housewife who had swept the dirt under the carpet, and not cleaned down the building thoroughly. However, during her reign many of her subjects came to accept and to love the established church, although Reformers continued their efforts to Protestantise the church. Broadly, Reformers, who were often termed Puritans, emphasised a faith based more on the Bible than church traditions, on preaching rather than sacraments, and on less distinction between the clergy and laity. More extreme Puritans believed that the Anglican church was so unreformed that they should separate from it, and form a true church. Such separatist churches, which contemporaries usually referred to as

41

'sects' or even heresies, were open only to true believers. Women were prominent in what was termed the 'gathering' of churches, and many found that their spiritual aspirations were better satisfied than in the established churches.

After the Civil Wars broke out in 1642 and during the Interregnum of the 1650s, separatist churches multiplied. Prominent were the Independents and the Baptists, churches whose organisation was derived from Scriptural models. More experiential churches, in which believers emphasised the work of the Holy Spirit as a direct source of inspiration, were the Fifth Monarchists and Quakers. The Quakers, who were named for their trembling, or quaking, in the power of the Lord, believed that God was present in all. By looking to the inner light, to the divine within, the individual gained direct access to God. Women as well as men were fearless in bearing witness to their faith. The public testimonies of Quaker women placed them in regular conflict with magistrates, church authorities, and most of their contemporaries, who feared the social upheaval their beliefs seemed to entail (see Chapter 9).

Some religious movements also challenged the gender order. Amongst the Quakers, Phyllis Mack has argued, gender was more fluid: women could transcend the limitations of their female bodies, and take on the roles of prophet and visionary. The boundaries of gender were reconfigured by the use of language, with men talking of themselves as breastfeeding mothers, and women adopting the language of heroic warriors.[4]

After 1660, when the Anglican church was restored, all of those who refused to attend its worship were punished as Nonconformists. By the early eighteenth century, Nonconformists may have been only around 5 per cent of the total population. However, Nonconformist women, particularly Quakers, attracted a disproportionate share of public attention.

One of the effects of the Reformation was to 'internalise' spirituality, validating the practice of inward contemplation and private prayer. It was in this context that literate women began to write diaries and memoirs, recording their sins and God's grace towards them. But religious practice in this period also led women into a more public sphere. In the years of the Civil Wars, women's prophesying, membership of sects, and publication of pamphlets and tracts claimed for sectarian women a public ground.

Expressions of religiosity were gendered. Women's opportunities to express their spirituality were different from men's. No women had a role or office in the established church in the seventeenth century; nor were women admitted to study theology in the universities. On the other hand, women had opportunities for piety and charity which men lacked. While their contemporaries believed that women were more liable to sin, they acknowledged that women might possess a particular, often a special, kind of access to God. Women were more prominent among those who prophesied, especially while in trance.

The first section illustrates a range of female spirituality across the century. Historians have often adopted a functionalist analysis to understand women's beliefs; they have argued that faith comforted women through the dangers of pregnancy and childbirth. Certainly women did turn to God for help, but to see their beliefs solely in instrumental terms is too narrow. What many of the documents tell us of is women's desire to be at one with God; they longed, like Ann Bathurst, whose extraordinary account of some of her religious experiences begins this chapter, to lose their sense of self in the divine.

Embodiment was central to female religious experience, and women had differing views about how their bodies, souls, and gender were related. Social levels as well as gender influenced expressions of spirituality. Literate first-hand accounts survive from wealthier women whose houses were spacious enough to offer a closet for prayer and meditation. Nevertheless, we should not make the mistake of thinking that illiterate, poorer women lacked spirituality because we lack sources. The unnamed bearer of Katherine Gell's letter was troubled by religious matters as was her mistress, but she was too shy even to speak with the minister directly without some introduction from Mrs Gell.

The documents in the second section raise questions about the connections between gender, private beliefs, and public action. Belief could provide women with opportunities for meditation and reflection; their sense of self was intimately related to their spiritual beliefs as well as to their bodily experiences. Given that women engaged less in theological disputes than men did, adherence to particular tenets of belief – what later became denominational differences – may have mattered less. Wealthy Catholic as well as wealthy Protestant women shared similar patterns of piety: prayer, meditation, and charity. Yet many women did take a keen interest in religious doctrine, read their Bibles, and developed their own theological views. During the Civil Wars, when some women embarked on more public religious activity, the inner conscience became, briefly, a guide for public action.[5]

The second section also illustrates how religious belief was no private matter: women were vitally concerned with large social issues and political events. Public and private boundaries were fluid; personal religious beliefs could become a public matter of supreme importance. Women justified their public actions in religious terms.[6]

Not all women's beliefs were Christian. Some of women's healing practices (as we saw in Chapter 1, 'Bodies') involved non-Christian beliefs. Although women healers claimed that their practice was orthodox because it involved prayers, they could be accused of witchcraft. Witchcraft beliefs were shared by women as well as men, and threatened the lives of those accused. This third group of documents about popular beliefs reminds us that people did not draw firm lines between their beliefs in spirits and fairies and orthodox Christianity.

SPIRITUALITY: THE JOURNEY OF THE CHRISTIAN SOUL

2.1 'The word divine multiplies in me': Ann Bathurst, c. 1690–93

Ann Bathurst left several volumes of spiritual meditations, each of around 600 closely written pages. She was influenced by the ideas of the sixteenth-century Silesian mystic Jacob Boehme, and was part of a London group which included Jane Lead, another mystical visionary. Bathurst's writings stand out from others. She wrote in an ecstatic vein more extensively than anyone else we know of in the seventeenth century. Although her concern is with spiritual things, she conveys a stronger sense of a physical body than any male writer and than many other women. The following passages have been selected to illustrate her intention in writing, and some of her ideas about the relationship between body, spirit, and the divine.

Bodl., MS Rawl. D1263, 1693 (unfoliated), pp. 1, 2; Bodl., MS Rawl. D 1262, fos 7, 9, 10, 11, 13, 15, 45–6, 47.

Having had many considerations of the love of God, some are set down for my better understanding and memory: and being often led in the depths of endless love, the Soul breaks forth, O thou bottomless love! Thou spring of praise! And being as one besides myself, I cry out, O Jubilee of praise, when shalt thou be sung in our streets, and we as a well-tuned instrument of praise sing thee forth! for thou art our beloved, thou feedest among the nuts. O thou offspring of David and of the house of Jesse, how the virgins love thee! And thy spirit gives thee praise. All hallowed sweetness be given unto thee thou Song of Love and Divine Jubilee.

The word <u>Divine</u> has such an emphasis in it. I am as one with solace, with divine sweetness. But the word divine multiplies in me and fills me, taking away my heart's life into it. . . . O sea of redeeming love, what wilt thou not do! and fountains of blood what canst thou do! O, a fountain sealed, breasts full of consolation.

I am as pent milk in the breast, ready to be poured forth and dilated into Thee, from whom my fullness flows with such fullness and plenitude, and pleased when eased. O flow and overflow! O thou milk of the world! to the well of life that springeth up in me as a fountain, to reach all the branches. . . . But the word Divine is still too big for me to speak. It fills me with that which is unutterable, sweet and pleasant, yea satisfactory to an excess! O Lord thy fullness is fullness I fill as from a sea, and well I may, when the sea has broke in upon me, upon my understanding . . .

Beloved I say, in the bridal chambering is sung the song of love by our beloved. There we have our fill of love. And it is often that we are brought into the bed-chamber of our King. While we are in this body. And hence it is that we know not how to demean ourselves to the world, nor will know

Figure 4 **Ann Bathurst, London mystic, 1707**

By permission of the Bodleian Library, Oxford

Ann Bathurst was a mystic who experienced oneness with the divine in her visions, which she recorded in her notebooks.

how to carry it as before our King. For we are such novices in the high kingly court, and our ecstasies, yea our often ecstasies make us forget his greatness by reason he has manifested himself in such familiar sweetness, like as God and we were one: even as a father to a child; as a brother a Joseph to his brethren; a spouse, a Lord, a bridegroom to the soul with such rejoicing essence, as if all of God were mine, when I to him am joined.

For Divine is like word before it became flesh. O when this Divine thing in us has clothed itself with us then we shall name the divine word with power. O word, word of the Lord, power and spirit put on flesh, and come and serve amongst us! put on thy wisdom in thy manhood in us. Is not thy manhood in us as well as thy Godhead? We wait for the perfect manhood thy Godhead to act as thy manhood . . .

O the showering of thy spirit, will it not bring forth and cause an increase? O multiply thy own seed of life in us. Wilt thou bring to the birth in us and not bring forth for us? Shall not the holy Jesus's childlike life be born of us in spirit and truth in perfect births?

[An account of her spiritual journey follows. After various struggles, and ten years in a state of desolation which she termed 'the wilderness', aged about 40 years, Bathurst found the spirit.]

After this for my support, on June 23rd 1678 a year of Jubilee was proclaimed, and prophesied to me by an angel or spirit in a dream or vision; and after confirmed by another angel in such a like dream; . . . at the end of six months, being December 23rd 1678 . . . I was taken out of his bewildered place, and put into such a calm as is not to be expressed.

That as the very day, hour and minute of my being set in the wilderness were so plainly felt and perceived, being so different an air. So the taking out of it was as sensible, leaving all storms behind me, I was as set into a sweet still haven, and new senses given me as one not in a body. So that I felt myself quite taken out of all disturbances of outward senses and set in a new air or another climate, and another spirit given me that was accompanied with new understanding. Being as one who had put off an old garment, nay like one unclothed of this mortal body, and a new body brought forth to manifestation, which caused great joy and admiration much more felt than can be expressed.

There opened a view of the heavenly Canaan as follows:
A transportation or manifestation made to me, whither in the body or out of the body (as St Paul saith) I cannot tell; but I was often made sensible, where my body lay, and that my eyes did abide open, by my spirit's return to it <u>which was on Monday night, March 17th 1679.</u>

[She sees Paradise]

Yet did not this fully satisfy me except I might also see the kingdom of Christ. Then was I caught up higher, where I saw Jesus in the appearance of a man, all surrounded with a most glorious light, which greatly transported me; for now I knew I was come to the place which I had so long desired to behold. Whilst I was here I appeared to my self (I mean my angel appeared to me, but I understood it not) at which being surprised, and the flesh shrinking at the greatness of the glory, I perfectly felt a touch on the top of my head, which drew my spirit out of me, as you draw a knife or sword out of a sheath, and it cut as it was drawn forth. I felt it cut like a two-edged sword. Thereafter I appeared as a spark of light, and according to my desire I sometimes mounted up to see Jesus, and then descended again into Paradise; all which motions were very swift.

After this I desired to see the Father, and after a little stay in the Kingdom of Christ, I was had up to God the Father. But Oh! Oh! Oh! the glory! the splendour! the brightness! the exceeding inexpressible glory that was there! at the sight of which I threw myself down before Him, crying continually for above a quarter of an hour, My God! My God! I'm now come to the place to which thou hast called me; and which I so long desired to see . . .

[She desired to see Hell.]

Then I desired to behold Christ again, and to see his heart, as some had seen, which I beheld flaming with love to the Saints. Then I desired to enter into the heart of Christ, and so I did, entering in and coming forth again very swiftly for several times. After I was desirous to enter into the whole Christ. And presently I was in the person of Christ, where I felt and saw my self. I saw my eye in and through Christ's eye, and I saw my head, neck and breast in Christ's, as through a glass. So I was satisfied. Yet I desired also to see and feel, whether my hand was in Christ's hand, and I found it was.

Then I desired that one of my children might come up, and she came a little after. And then another of them, and so till all were come in. . . . And as they came up, I remembered two little children[1] which died one at fourteen weeks, the other at fourteen days' end. And immediately as soon as I began to desire it, they came like two bright sparks, one after another, and entered into the great light and became one with it, as a spark is swallowed up of the flame.

There was, towards the end of this vision, as I came nearer the Earth a request put up by me (finding I had nothing denied me) Lord, what wilt thou do with this nation? And straight way there appeared an hand and arm stretched out towards them, with a slight moving of the hand twice, looking like the warning or putting by of my request, with these words: <u>Concern not yourself with that</u>, implying that I was to attend to my inward teachings, and not to look out after national concerns, or the public affairs of the world . . .

7 Sept. 1679 The blessed glory of God came to me, filling me with great influences and quickening, raising my soul to an unexpressible delight (often I saw Christ in his glorified person behind me) as I lay, as in a circle of divine love, with great freedom and intimate familiarity with the Father, who stood as a breath or spirit of air by me. And being very desirous, I was taken

---

1. Presumably, two of her own babies.

into the glory of the Father. And I was, that is, my spirit was in his hand, as clay in the hand of the potter. [Margin: Divine embraces in a manifestation of the Father's glory]

Sept. 8 [She records that she found her spirit dead] and hoped at night that I might lie in his arms as I had done the night before. . . . I lay in a bed of his Love-presence and security and loving embraces. There I held him and would not let Him go, but that he would lie all night as a bundle of myrrh between my breasts, and He was willingly held . . .

9 Sept. And I looked and said, let him kiss me with the kisses of his mouth. Then I said, This is more than Isaiah desired, which was that God would touch his lips with a coal from his altar; but God has touched me with fire from his lips, a pledge of his love. And then the nuptial, for so it was that I turned to see him again being very desirous of his enjoyment [Margin: drawing of a pointing hand] . . . O the love of God! O Jesus, I am thine, thou hast ravished me, Thou has taken away my heart. I am full wanting words to vent! O the sweetness and full satisfaction!

[In Christ's embraces and with the Trinity:] sometimes we were all one, sometimes as three, sometimes I taken into them, sometimes they filling me, even the whole man with such transports, that though all the senses were delighted, yet not as in this body; but a body fitted for such an union far surmounting all earthly delights, which are not in the least to be compared to it.

For these several years I have desired to enjoy as much here as the soul is capable of. So that hereafter I might enjoy as much glory as the souls glorified are capable of enjoying, but I little thought that so much we had been capable of here, as I have received.

2.2 Maternal religious instruction: Lady Anne Halkett (b. 1623)

Anne Murray (1623–99) was brought up in orthodox Anglican belief. Her mother was responsible for her religious education. Anne was active in the Royalist cause in the 1640s and subsequently married Sir James Halkett. Her autobiography has been printed in *The Memoirs of Anne, Lady Halkett and Ann, Lady Fanshawe*, edited by John Loftis, Oxford, 1991.

BL, Add. MS 32376, fos 1v.–2.

But my mother's greatest care, and for which I shall ever own to her memory the highest gratitude, was the great care she took that even from our infancy we were instructed never to neglect to begin and end the day with prayer, and orderly every morning to read the Bible, and ever to keep the church as often as there was occasion to meet there either for prayers or preaching. So that for many years together I was seldom or never absent from divine service at five a clock in the morning in the summer and six a clock in the winter till the usurped power put a restraint to that public worship[1] so long owned and continued in the church of England; where I bless God I had my education and the example of a good mother, who kept constant to her own parish church, and had always a great respect for the ministers under whose charge she was.[2]

2.3   Some account of my state: Katherine Gell, 1655

Katherine Gell (born *c.* 1623) was the wife of a military commander, John Gell (1613–89). The spiritual melancholy from which she suffered, a lack of assurance of salvation, was common among the godly. Richard Baxter, of Kidderminster, a famous Nonconformist minister, answered her letter, and a correspondence ensued. In a subsequent letter, Baxter advised her to keep cheerful and to 'be much busy in your necessary employments in the world'. Such epistolary relationships with ministers were not unusual. Many women looked to their ministers or priests for spiritual direction.

Katherine Gell to Richard Baxter, July 1655, Dr Williams' Library, London, Baxter MS V, fos 216–216v. (The correspondence is calendared in N. H. Keeble and G. F. Nuttall (eds), *Calendar of the Correspondence of Richard Baxter*, Oxford, Oxford University Press, 1991, 2 vols.)

at Westminster, Sabbath morning lecture, July 1655

Honoured Sir,

Though I never yet saw you, I hope having seen so much of you it may be an encouragement to me to write for some satisfaction from you in something in your own writing in The Saints Rest.[3] Before I come to it I suppose being altogether a stranger, it will be fit to give you some account of my state which in brief I shall relate thus; I was brought up under such parents as took great care to educate me well. My father being a man of eminent holiness whereby I was as formal as any and constant in duties till near 20 years of age that a sermon of Mr Marshall's[4] did work so far as to make me seek out for a better way than I was in. Indeed before that I was very much convicted and saw clearly that I was out of the right way but yet did not desire to come in till that sermon, which I as near as I can (by recollecting all things) conceive to be the time when my will was changed, for I cannot remember that ever I stood out after, but this produced many sad troubles

---

1. The Parliamentarians reformed the Anglican church in 1646, replacing the services with a Presbyterian form of worship.
2. Halkett here is reflecting adversely on the practices of those who travelled to hear other preachers if they were dissatisfied in their own parishes. Such 'promiscuous' gadding to sermons was widely criticised by the orthodox.
3. First published in 1649, Baxter's work, *The Saints Everlasting Rest,* was reprinted many times during the seventeenth century.
4. Presumably Stephen Marshall (*c.* 1594–1655), the most famous of the Parliamentary preachers during the Civil Wars.

in my soul, and raised many thoughts within which I concealed [for] two years. And in that time through God's mercy many words supported me in my hearing of sermons. At the 2 years' end I revealed it to my husband from whom I had much comfort but would not suffer any other to know till 2 years after. I writ to Mr Marshall and received much comfort from him but since that reading your book wherein you earnestly press the helping others to that rest and in particular by admonishing I was so clearly convinced of my neglect and unfitness to it and my uselessness in my family that way that I have drawn the conclusion from it that I am not in a state of grace and that upon that account that whoever lives in the constant omission of a known duty or commission of a known sin is not in a state of grace but I have done etc: this has cost me much sorrow for indeed sir, I have endeavoured it very much since and could speak but for a natural foolish bashfulness that attends me in all other matters hindering me much from doing or receiving good, alas this is much aggravated by the checks of conscience for I seldom see an object for me to speak to but I have a motion to do it and refuse it and then I am sure to hear of it this much greatens the sin, it's true. I can hardly instance in any that perform this duty as you profess it but it's no excuse to me if I am convinced of it; though I believe were it set home so on their consciences that are gifted for it and neglect it, it would put them on the speedy practice. Many other doubts I might trouble you with but that I have imparted them of late to our own minister and another in this county from whom I have received much satisfaction but though he hath writ to me about this yet I desire to have your opinion and you can best tell how far you extend that exhortation and therefore having a friend [torn] resolved to write this that I might be more fully satisfied in that particular. Many times condemned my self. Pray sir deal clearly in giving me your advice both what to judge of myself, and do, though it may be my portion to be in sa[d] troubles while I live, yet I would not by any means so far indulge them so as to wrong God in robbing myself of my comfort, but since that change, which I think was wrought 12 years since, I never have been free from inward troubles nor could ever see myself to have clear interest in Christ. My great support hath been in casting myself wholly on him, adhering to him resolving to venture my self on him only and not to part with him what ever he do with me, neither would I live in any sin or omit any duty, no my earnest desires are after universal obedience to have respect to all God's commands and I long after more holiness as much does desire grace here as glory hereafter, but the naughty base heart hinders performance and is a clog in every duty; our ministers tell me I must submissively strive against temptation which I think a very hard lesson. I shall say no more of myself, but if you desire any further information this bearer may inform you of any thing she knows who lives in our family, and being one that hath many outward afflictions and inward troubles of conscience, I desire you would please to examine her of her own condition who would be very glad

of some words from you but it may be can hardly speak to you if you take not some notice to her of it. I told her I would write a word for her. Sir I hope your leisure will permit some lines back to me, I heartily wish we could see you one week in this county that we might also hear you of which I have an earnest desire and had I not too great a family to leave, I should endeavour the fulfilling of my desires in coming to you; the great care you have showed to poor souls made me the willinger to write this fit opportunity. I having had it often in my thoughts and if I could conveniently have sent letters you had heard of me sooner. I entreat you to excuse both style English and all other defects herein by considering it's a woman's and so shall leave you to the keeping of your God and with my service rest,
Being one that honours you for your work's sake – Katherine Gell

July 55
none hath seen this neither doth any know of my writing but my husband and this bearer therefore I desire your concealment. [crossed over: 'for yourself'.]

2.4   Catholic mystic: Gertrude More (d. 1633)

Helen More (1606–33) was a descendant of Sir Thomas More. In 1625, aged 19, she became a nun in the Benedictine cloister at Cambrai, taking the name Dame Gertrude in religion. After a period of spiritual desolation she encountered Father Augustine Baker, who encouraged her to trust her own spiritual inclinations. Gertrude More proceeded to achieve great spiritual satisfaction, and she was widely recognised as a mystic who had attained close union with the divine. More's influence survived her early death from smallpox, and in 1658 her spiritual writings were published as *The Spiritual Exercises* (more commonly known as *Confessiones Amantis*). Here we see her approach to the divine, who is invoked as both lover and father. In the second piece, from the book's preface, More defends her own spiritual independence in a Counter-Reformation church which insisted upon close clerical supervision of nuns; and she foreshadows her own deathbed refusal to seek comfort from clerics, declaring she could confidently leave this world without the assistance of any man.

Gertrude More, *The Spiritual Exercises*, Paris, 1658, pp. 55–7, 98–100.

This document and its note supplied by Claire Walker.

The XVI confession

I have had myself a confessor who though he had the largest conscience that ever I knew good man have in my life, in what he pleased, yet out of the difficulty he had with me in his nature, and out of his aptness thereby to take all I did and said in another sense than I meant it: he could, and did turn twenty things, which my other confessors made no great matter of, into horrible mortal sins, and would have frighted me from the sacraments till I had settled my conscience according to his will, and mind. What was I to do in this case? I had been warranted by three former confessors, two of which were my chief superiors and doctors of divinity; and now this present wholly doubted my case. He had (as he pretended) a greater reach into my case then all the rest, and they were simple to him in discovering truly the state of my soul. But should I in this case put my soul into his hands, who desired to know all that had passed in my life to inform him in some things he desired to know out of policy, thereby also to tie me to him self more absolutely? Verily if I had thus put myself on him, I had done great wrong to God and I might have bid farewell to all true peace hereafter. But standing to my former warrant, and giving him the respect was due to him, and being reserved towards him, I have hitherto God be praised kept myself out of his fingers. And also by the grace of God [I] hope to hold on my way in tendance towards God, thereby raising myself (according to his divine Majesty shall vouchsafe to enable me) out of my natural fear to the love of God, who is only able to satisfy, and satiate our soul. And not as this my confessor would have had me to plunge my-self by reason of his words, and threats of my miserable state: which notwithstanding his apprehensions is so much, and no more, as it is in the sight of God, who changeth not his opinion of us, as the humour of the confessor may be: but imagineth us according to what we really are in very truth. But these spiritual men of this kind would be so absolute that there is no power left in the soul thus under such to have relation, or confidence in God, whereby those for the most part under them, if they be poor simple women, of how good spirits soever, live miserable dejected lives: for it is their only way to bring their politic, and absolute government about. And ordinarily under this pretence they do it; saying that there is no way to make this, or that soul humble, but to bring them into such fear, that they neither dare speak, think, or do any thing without their approbation. At least so far they must have relation to them, as it may serve this turn to inform them of what is for their purpose: and then that soul is happy in their eyes, and they will declare that they are so to others: that they may follow their example. Then the perplexity the soul suffereth they term a profitable pill to cure their disease with all. And the confusion they suffer to see themselves disloyal to God and man, to serve their confessors turn; he termeth a suffering for justice, and warranteth them. What harm, disquiet, or confusion soever cometh by this their doings to others, or themselves out of obedience to him, he will answer for it, and therein they have done God, and their congregation great, and faithful service. . . .

Oh Lord my God; Father of the poor, and true comforter of all afflicted souls; be merciful to my desolate heart, and stir it up to perfect love of thee, that I may simply seek thee, and sigh after thee my beloved absent, and not for the sorrow I feel at the present. Let me long to embrace thee with the arms of my soul, and think it little to endure any misery in body, or soul, to be at last admitted into the bosom of my love, fairest and choicest of thousands. Let all fall down, and adore my God, the glory of my heart. Let the sound of his praise be heard to sound, and resound over all the earth.

Oh when shall my soul, having transcended itself, and all created things, be firmly united to thee, the beloved of my heart, resting in thee, not in thy gifts or graces, and neither desiring, nor taking any satisfaction in any work, or exercise whatsoever, but in all pains, temptations, contempts, desolations, poverties, and miseries either of body, or mind, conforming my self to thy sweet will for time and eternity, who as justly as ever thou didst any thing, mayst (yet God forbid!) condemn my soul eternally to hell, from which nothing but thy mere mercy were able to save and deliver me; and daily I should incur this sentence if thou didst not, out of thy goodness ever help and protect me, thy sinful servant.

This only I desire, this only I ask, that I may in all things praise thee, and that I may desire no comfort, but to be able, without all comfort, human or divine, to be true to thee, and not offend thy Majesty . . .

THE PRACTICE OF FAITH

2.5 'It is with soul as with the body': Elizabeth Joceline, 1622

Elizabeth Joceline, née Brooke (*c.* 1595–1622?) was orphaned at an early age. She was taught by her grandfather, a famous Cambridge theologian, Laurence Chaderton. Married at 20 years of age, she feared death in childbirth, and wrote instructions to her husband about how to rear her child if she should die. She died giving birth, and her husband subsequently arranged for the printing of her thoughts. The work was well known, and reprinted many times.

The Mothers Legacie to her unborne childe, London, 1624, sig. B1v.–B2, pp. 78, 86–91.

To my truly loving, and most dearly loved husband, Tourell Joceline.

Mine own dear love, I no sooner conceived an hope, that I should be made a mother by thee, but with it entered the consideration of a mother's duty, and shortly after followed the apprehension of danger that might prevent me from executing that care I so exceedingly desired, I mean in religious training our child. And in truth death appearing in this shape, was doubly terrible unto me. First, in respect of the painfulness of that kind of death, and next of the loss my little one should have in wanting me. But I thank God, these fears were cured with the remembrance that all things work together for the best to those that love God, and a certain assurance that he will give me patience according to my pain.

The Mother's Legacy

... Remember that thou keep holy the Sabbath day ...

So approach and enter with reverent and fervent zeal, the house of God and throwing away all thoughts, but such as may further the good work thou art about, bend thy knees and heart to God, desiring of him his holy Spirit, that thou mayst join with the congregation in zealous prayer, and earnest attention to his word preached. And though perhaps thou hearest a minister preach, as thou thinkest weakly, yet give him thine attention, and thou shalt find that he will deliver something profitable to thy soul, either that thou hast not heard before, or not marked, or forgotten, or not well put into practise. And it is fit thou shouldest be often put in mind of those things concerning thy salvation.

Thus, if thou spend thy time at church, thou wilt be ready to give thyself to meditate of the holy Word thou hast heard, without which truly hearing profiteth little. For it is with soul as with the body, though meat be never so wholesome, and the appetite never so great, if any ill disposition in the stomach hinder digestion, it turn not to nourishment, but rather proves more dangerous. So the Word if after hearing it be not digested by meditation, it is not nourishing to the soul. Therefore let the time thou hast to be absent from church be spent in praising God, praying to go, and applying to thyself what thou hast heard. If thou hast heard a sin reproved that thou art guilty of, take it for a warning, do it no more. If thou hearest of a good action which thou hast overslipt, strive to recover time, and resolve to put it in act. Thus by practising what thou hearest, thou shalt bind it to thy memory, and by making it thine own, make thyself most happy.

Learn of the true observation of the Sabbath. If thou turn away thy foot from the Sabbath, from doing thy will on any holy day, and call the Sabbath a delight to consecrate it as glorious to the Lord, and shall honour him, not doing thy own ways, nor seeking thine own will, nor speaking a vain word: then shall thou delight in the Lord, and I will cause thee to mount upon the high places of the earth, and fee thee with the heritage of *Jacob* thy father, for the mouth of the Lord hath spoken it, *Isaiah 58.13*.

2.6 'Exactness in all regular observances': Catherine Wigmore (d. 1656)

Elizabeth (Abbess Catherine) Wigmore (d. 1656) became a nun at the Ghent Benedictine Abbey in 1626. Renowned for her intense spiritual relationship with God, and for her capable exercise of household offices, in 1652 she was chosen to head the filiation, the daughter-house, to Boulogne. This extract from her lengthy obituary, which was probably written by one of the senior nuns, reveals the variety of personal devotions undertaken by nuns, as well as the qualities nuns deemed worthy in their abbess.

'Obituary Notices of the English Benedictine Nuns of Ghent in Flanders, and at Preston, Lancashire (now at Oulton Staffordshire), 1627–1811', in *Miscellanea 11*, Catholic Record Society, vol. 19, London, printed privately for the Catholic Record Society by J. Whitehead and Son, 1917, pp. 58, 61–2.

This document and its note supplied by Claire Walker.

In the year 1656 on the 28 of October, most happily departed this life the Right Reverend Lady Catherine Wigmore, Abbess of the English religious of the holy order of St Bennet [that is, Benedict] then at Boulogne, but now translated from thence to Pontoise. She was clothed[1] on Low Sunday 1625 and made her holy vows[2] 2nd of July 1626. Her most remarkable virtues was a most singular great charity and exactness in all regular observances, humility, obedience, patience, compassion and self contempt, with a continual zeal of the divine glory, love of spiritual exercises and union with God. She died in the years of her profession thirty, and four months of her age sixty, and four months of her prelature. . . .

When my Lady Mary Roper of happy memory died, she [Wigmore] prayed in a manner incessantly and got all the prayers she could of others that the chief superiority might not be laid upon her, and God in his chief providence provided otherwise most comfortably for us and reserved her for what in his eternal decree he had determined concerning her supreme government elsewhere. For in the year 1652, the beginning of January, our Right Reverend and dear Lady Abbess, my Lady Mary Knatchbull, sent a little colony of virgins to Boulogne, and Dame Catherine Wigmore being then our prioress, her Ladyship and my Lord Bishop had ordered her for their chief commander. . . . Her life there and prudent government, accompanied with a great zeal mixed with a mother's compassion, together with her exactness, not only to teach, but also to do on all times and occasions the perfect will of God in the most punctual observance of our holy rule and statutes,[3] is most constantly affirmed by all her children[4] in that new plantation; and for the greater authority, by those also, into whose hands she put the charge of her soul,[5] unto whom she perseverently remained most candid and clear in the account of herself. Retaining in that chief dignity[6] her wonted spirit of holy poverty, humility, patience and charity, not only mending the poor and few accommodations for her own use, but also patching her children's clothes and mending their stockings, excusing herself from better works [by saying she was] blind and unable to do anything of neatness. And she was so careful

1. Clothing refers to the ceremony in which the woman was first dressed in her religious habit, after which she became a 'novice'.
2. Ceremony of religious profession in which the novice made her final vows.
3. Rule: guidelines for the structure of monastic life written by the founder of a religious order. Statutes: adaptation of the rule for use in a particular cloister.
4. Nuns.
5. Her spiritual directors.
6. Position of authority.

of expense of time that even [in] the hours allowed in our statutes for recreation she would always be mending or making somewhat for common good. Nor did she grow slack in her ordinary penance and austerity, which were rods, discipline, bracelets, chains, and haircloth, still punishing herself for anything amiss in her actions. And the summer before she died being vehemently hot, yet would she not be dispensed from wearing woollen[7] which indeed is feared did hasten her death for she got a fever and other great indispositions by it. 'Tis credibly believed she had a certain knowledge of her death, running on in her first fervour to a midday height. She had the virtue of modesty in a most eminent manner, and always blushed at her own praise. She loved God entirely and would all her life in religion seem transported speaking of him. She wore an hour glass at Ghent in her pocket, secretly turning it each hour, renewing acts of virtue and memory of our Saviour's passion, with an invocation to the nine choirs of angels and orders of saints. Her prayer was always pure and intense, [and] her death was like her life: remarkable for piety. Some clergy of the bishop's and some seculars too were present at her most saintly and happy departure, who received such edification that in their whole life the[y] had not experienced the like. 'Tis believed by them that [knew] her exercises of spirit that she had chiefly bent her whole endeavours to emulate our Saviour to the utmost of her power in her life and actions. She received all the rites of [the] holy church in perfect sense, breathing out the ardent affections of her heart to our blessed Saviour, her only Lord and love, and sweetly expired in [the] midst of her truly afflicted children, pouring forth tears and prayers. Her virgin body in his manner of burial had some resemblance with our blessed Saviour's, for it was interred in a garden where yet never any had been laid.

2.7 'Our Most Reverend Mother, Margrit Clement' (d. 1612)

In 1557 Margaret Clement (c. 1539–1612), daughter of Dr John Clement and Margaret Giggs, became a nun in a Flemish Augustinian cloister in Louvain. Noted for her piety and virtue, in 1569 she was elected prioress at the youthful age of 30, thereby attracting several of her countrywomen to the monastery. In 1609 the English nuns left their Flemish sisters to establish their own monastery. When Margaret Clement died in 1612, her biography was written by Sister Elizabeth Shirley, who described the former prioress' life and acts as 'a firebrand to enkindle in me the love of God'. In this extract Elizabeth Shirley explains how Margaret Clement cared for the spiritual welfare of not only her own nuns, but also for spiritually troubled women sent to her for counselling by the clergy and other religious superiors.

7. Woollen: woollen underclothes which were part of the religious habit. They were worn even in hot weather as a form of penance, but sick nuns were permitted to take them off.

Elizabeth Shirley, 'The Life of Our Most Reverend Mother, Margrit Clement', 1626, Priory of Our Lady of Good Counsel, Sayers Common, West Sussex, St Monica's MS Q29, fos 48–50, 51–2. (This is a copy of the original manuscript held by the Priory of Our Blessed Lady of Nazareth in Bruges.)

This document and its note supplied by Claire Walker.

Her fame was such over all the country that whosoever had any such troublesome persons as they could no way with, they brought them aright unto her, and her charity was such, and zeal of souls so great, that she had not the power to deny them how desperate soever their cause were. The archbishop himself was fain to use her help in such difficult matters and hath wonderfully admired at her prudency therein. Oh would to God I were anyways able either by words or pen to declare her great labour and travail to gain souls to God; her devout prayers, her watchings, her tears, her continual exhortations, her long suffering with such unspeakable patience without any show of wearisomeness therein, when they were such crooked persons as was tedious and irksome to the whole company. . . . Now if I should tell what she had to suffer for this her labour of the better sort of the religious, it were unspeakable. Some would tell her in plain terms that she was partial, and that she esteemed more of those troublesome persons than of their[1] good. Some said that she hung so much time on them that it hindered her other duties. These and other such like speeches which were too long to rehearse was her daily bread: all which she bore with invincible patience, only she would sometimes sweetly with a mild word reply and say, sisters if we knew how dear and precious those souls are in the sight of almighty God we would afford them willingly what help we could. And well might we see that her pains came to good effect, for such persons as one would have thought was unlikely ever to have been brought to any thing, came after by God his grace and her good endeavour to be good religious, as themselves did well confess that next unto God they did ascribe unto her the whole cause of their salvation. . . . She would many times comfort us in telling us that temptations were necessary for young religious, for by that they came to know themselves and to make their recourse the more to God. . . . Therefore she would say that if she should see any novice or young religious that passed through with out any difficulty she should be greatly afraid for them; by this and such like, I must confess she did greatly comfort me and gave me strength to bear the better my impediments which I found in myself.

1. I.e., her own nuns' good.

GOD AND THE NATION

2.8 Catholic martyrdom: Margaret Clitheroe, 1586

During Elizabeth's reign, in 1586, Margaret Clitheroe, a butcher's wife, was indicted for treason for secret Catholic worship. Fearing that if she entered a plea, her children and servants would all be examined, and more details of the Catholic networks would be revealed, she declined to answer whether or not she was guilty. The Protestant judges gave her every opportunity to enter a plea, since the punishment in such cases was the particularly savage one of being crushed to death with a stone. When she refused, the judges sentenced her to be stripped naked and pressed to death. Her confessor, John Mush, depicts her as preoccupied with modesty when she comes to die. Clitheroe used a claim based on conscience to counter the implicit charge that she was a bad wife for not obeying her husband in religious matters.

John Mush, *A True Report of the Life and Martyrdom of Mrs Margaret Clitheroe*, printed in John Morris (ed.), *The Troubles of Our Catholic Forefathers*, vol. 3, 1877, pp. 412–14, 431–2.

The 14th day of March, being Monday, after dinner, the martyr was brought from the Castle to Common Hall in York, before the two judges, Mr Clinch and Mr Rhodes, and divers of the Council sitting with them on the bench.

Her indictment was read, that she had harboured and maintained Jesuit and Seminary priests, traitors to the Queen's Majesty and her laws, and that she had [heard] Mass, and such like. Then Judge Clinch stood up, and said: 'Margaret Clitheroe, how say you? [Are you] guilty of this indictment, or no?' Then she [being] about to answer, they commanded her to put off her hat, and then she said mildly with a bold and smiling countenance: 'I know no offence whereof I should confess myself guilty.' The judge said: 'Yes, you have harboured and maintained Jesuits and priests, enemies to her Majesty.' The martyr answered: 'I never knew nor have harboured any such persons, or maintained those which are not the Queen's friends. God defend I should.' The judge said: 'How will you be tried?' The martyr answered, 'Having made no offence, I need no trial.' They said: 'you have offended the statutes, and therefore you must be tried;' and often asked her how she would be tried. The martyr answered: 'If you say I have offended, and that I must be tried, I will be tried by none but by God and your own consciences.' The judge said, 'No, you cannot so do, for we sit here,' quoth he, 'to see justice and law, and therefore you must be tried [by the country].' . . . After a while the judges said to her again: 'Margaret Clitheroe, how say you yet? Are you content to be tried by God and the country?' The martyr said, 'No.' The judge said, 'Good woman, consider well what you do; if you refuse to be tried by the country, you make yourself guilty and accessory to your own death, for we cannot try you,' said he, 'but by order of law. You need not fear this kind of trial, for I think the country cannot find you guilty upon this slender evidence of a child.' The martyr still refused. They asked if her husband were not privy to her doings in keeping priests. The martyr said: 'God knoweth I could never yet get my husband in that good case that he were worthy to know or come in place where they were to serve God.' The judge said: 'We must proceed by law against you, which will condemn you to a sharp death for want of trial.' The martyr said cheerfully: 'God's will be done: I think I may suffer any death for this good cause.'

[The following day she was examined again, refused to plead, and was sentenced to death, and brought to execution a few days later.]

Then [Sheriff] Fawcet commanded her to put off her apparel; 'For you must die', said he, 'naked as judgment was given and pronounced against you.'

The martyr with the other women requested him on their knees that she might die in her smock, and that for the honour of womanhood they would not see her naked; but that would not be granted. Then she requested that women might unapparel her, and that they would turn their faces from her for that time.

The women took off her clothes, and put upon her the long habit of linen. Then very quietly she laid her down upon the ground, her face covered with a handkerchief, the linen habit being placed over her as far as it would reach, all the rest of her body being naked. The door was laid upon her, her hands she joined towards her face. Then the sheriff said, 'Nay, you must have your hands bound.' The martyr put forth her hands over the door still joined. Then two sergeants parted them, and with the ankle strings, which she had prepared for that purpose bound them to two posts, so that her body and arms made a perfect cross. They willed her again to ask the Queen's Majesty's forgiveness, and to pray for her. The martyr said she had prayed for her. They also willed her to ask her husband's forgiveness. The martyr said, 'If ever I have offended him, but for my conscience, I ask him forgiveness.'

After this they laid weight upon her, which when she first felt, she said, 'Jesu! Jesu! Jesu! have mercy upon me!' which were the last words she was heard to speak.

She was in dying one quarter of an hour. A sharp stone, as much as a man's fist, put under her back; upon her was laid to the quantity of seven or eight hundred weight, at the least, which, breaking her ribs, caused them to burst forth of the skin.

Thus most victoriously this gracious martyr overcame all her enemies, passing [from] this mortal life with marvellous triumph into the peaceable city of God, there to receive a worth crown of endless immortality and joy.

This was at nine of the clock, and she continued in the press until three at afternoon. Her hat before she died she sent to her husband, in sign of her loving duty to him as to her head. Her hose and shoes to her eldest daughter, Anne, about twelve years old, signifying that she should serve God and follow her steps of virtue.

2.9 'A city upon a hill': the gathering of a true church, 1640

Historians frequently refer to women 'joining the sects', yet frequently it was women who were instrumental in the gathering of a congregation into 'a true church'. The following extract from the Church Book of a congregation at Broadmead, Bristol, describes some of the early stages of separation in the late 1630s in which the widowed Dorothy Kelly, an independent woman who kept a grocer's shop, played a significant role. Mrs Kelly was troubled at what she considered to be the church's superstitious attitudes to festivals, such as Christmas. Since she did not believe that the church building was in itself holy, but rather that the holiness resided in the worshippers, a private house could be a church, 'a church with a chimney'. Later, Quakers outraged their contemporaries by referring to parish churches under the derogatory epithet of 'steeple houses' and by meeting for worship in taverns and fields.

The Records of a Church of Christ in Bristol, 1640–1687, ed. Roger Hayden, Bristol, Bristol Record Soc., 1974, p. 85.

Now at this, Mr Kelly being some years deceased, his widow persevered in godliness; and it might be said of her as of Ruth, iii. 11 (*all the City did know her to be a virtuous woman*). She was like a he-goat before the flock; for in those days Mrs Kelly was very famous for piety and reformation, well known to all, bearing a living testimony against the superstitions and traditions of those days, and she would not observe their invented times and feasts, called Holy days. At which time she kept a grocer's shop in High-street, between the Guilders Inn and the High Cross, where she would keep open her shop on the time they called Christmas day, and sit sewing in her shop, as a witness for God in the midst of the city, in the face of the sun, and in the sight of all men; even in those very days of darkness, when, as it were, all sorts of people had a reverence of that particular day above all others. And as the Apostle saith, I Cor. viii. 7, *There was not in every man that knowledge; for some, with conscience of the idol unto this hour eat it as things offered unto an idol, and their conscience being weak is defiled.* But this gracious woman (afterwards called Mrs Hazzard), like a *Deborah* she arose, with strength of holy resolution in her soul from God, even a mother in Israel. And so she proved, because she was the first woman in this city of Bristol that practised that truth of the Lord (which was then hated and odious), namely, *separation.*

Now the way that the Lord took to bring her, with some others the professors[1] in this city, to separate from the world, was this. After they had (as before rehearsed), been awakened, and met first together to repeat sermon notes, then they kept many days of prayer together, as a company of good people, sensible of the sins and snares of their day. In doing of which duties they began to be more humble and spiritual, and grow more resolved for

1. Believers, those who professed the truth.

God, heaven, and eternal happiness, and for the worship of God according to Holy Scriptures . . .

Now these meetings of prayer etc, as aforesaid, being so frequent, and many resorting unto it, they became such a light, as a city upon a hill[2] that could not be hid, especially from the bishops, who instead of being promoters and encouragers in such acts of piety, they were the obstructors, and could not bear it, for they endeavoured to suppress them. And God made his people not to bear them, nor their ways of worship; for the professors meeting one day in a house in High-street, the house was assaulted by the rude multitude and seamen, so that they broke all the windows, because they heard there was a conventicle of puritans; which to them was a very strange and unheard of thing for people to meet in a church with a chimney in it, as they termed it.

2.10 'Let not the sun go down upon this monarchy': Lady Dorothy Pakington, 1649

In 1679, these private prayers were found after the death of Lady Dorothy Pakington, and were copied, possibly by her daughter. Lady Pakington's sense of sinfulness, magnifying the smallest faults, was common among seventeenth-century Christians, who trusted in their faith in Christ for salvation, rather than their own merits. Lady Pakington viewed the threatened execution of King Charles I as a horrifying sin against God's commands to obey the King. Fearing lest the Lord would turn against the nation if the King's blood were shed, punishing the whole nation for the sin of blood guilt, she sought by prayer to avert this horrible deed and the Lord's wrath. Included in her collection are prayers for a child, for a woman in childbirth, and another for the nation.

Bodl., MS Add B 58, fos 133v., 131, 4v., 5v., 26, 33, 33v., 43.

A Confession

See Oh Lord and consider for I am become very vile, my heart is deceitful above all things and desperately wicked. The imaginations of the thoughts of my heart are only evil and that continually. I weave the spider's web in vain impertinent childish thoughts such as are below the dignity of a reasonable creature, such as would render me (if seen) ridiculous to man, how base and contemptible must they make me in thy all-judging eye to whom even the wisdom of the wise is foolishness. And how much oh Lord of my time how much of my thinking faculty do I thus squander away.

Behold, Oh Lord, a perishing sinner, and as I want, so let me find the [rescues?] of a Saviour, and that not only in expiating the guilt, but in subduing the power of sin; his blood cannot only reconcile but purify, O let me find it in both these effects.

2. Matthew 5.14.

Thou God of peace compose the distempers, allay the flames, bind up all breaches that are among us, Thou God of Israel interpose thine immediate hand of power for the quelling those enormous designs of men against the life of our Sovereign Lord, whom thou hast set over us, Lord suffer not the effusion of his blood to be added to the many provocations of a rebellious people, lest it fill up the measure of the land, and leave us no place of mercy with thee, but if thou hast pleasure in thy people, suffer not our glory thus to be put out in obscurity, suffer not this amazing judgment to fall upon us, show thyself a Lord of power, and grace in averting this horrible fact, in upholding and vindicating distressed innocence, in owning thine own cause, thine own ordinance, thine own inscription, that image of thine own power, thus violently invaded and defaced in thine Anointed. Father if it be possible let this cup pass from us, O let the life of the Lord the King be precious in thy sight, let not the sun go down upon this monarchy, be not wroth very sore, O Lord, behold see, we beseech thee, we are all thy people . . .

And Oh let the soul of our Lord the King be bound up in the bundle of life.

[Prayer for an infant]

We call upon thee for this infant, whom thou hast received into the number of thy children, that thou wilt deal with us in him, according to the measure of a father, that thou wilt support him with thine hand, supply him with thy strength, remove all indisposition or disease, or weakness from him, assist him with that aid from thee, which may fit him for a long and happy course of many prosperous days to be spent before thee to the joy of his parents whom thou hast so signally blest with this late mercy, to the benefit of many, and to the glory of thy name, and abundance of fruit to his own account, Sweet Jesu that tookest infants in thine arms, and blessedest them, and invited them to thee, and designest thy kingdom to be made up of such, be thou now pleased to lay thy healing hands of grace and mercy upon this child . . . that he may live to praise thee, or if otherwise thou hast disposed of him, to receive him calmly to thyself, to give him an easy pass to the sacred rest of thine everlasting joy, into the glorious estate of thy chosen saints in heaven.

[Prayer for woman in labour]

. . . We thy poor creatures desire to adore and make our humblest approaches toward thee. And O let not the Lord be angry, that being most unworthy to petition or demand any good thing from thee, we yet dare importune thee with our united intercessions for this thy servant, which lies here before thee; Lord that thou wouldst at this time refresh, and support with thy strength, enable her to bear and carry and to bring forth that fruit conceived in her, if not that yet in all thy sharp prescriptions and methods thou wilt please to intermix the sweet and comfortable allays of thine own most gracious hand . . .

[Another prayer]

Lord we are a sinful nation, a people laden with iniquity, that have added drunkenness unto thirst, one extremity and contrariety of sin unto another, and at last advanced to that highest pitch that any Christian nation hath at any time been known to be guilty of. And Lord thou hast in some degree proportioned thy vengeance to our sins, thou hast abased our glory, thou hast spit in our very face, cast reproach upon all that is most precious among us, judged us as women that break wedlock and shed blood are judged, and given us blood in fury and jealousy. The whole head is sick, the whole heart faint, from the sole of the foot to the crown of the head there is no whole part in us . . .

2.11   Warning to sinners: Martha Simmonds, 1655

Martha Calvert (whose brother Giles was her printer) was born in Somerset in 1624. She married a printer, Thomas Simmonds, and embarked on a spiritual quest in the late 1640s which she describes here. Eventually she found the Lord within herself, and this inner light guided her subsequent spiritual development as a Quaker. Around 1656 she found the power of the Lord so strong within her that she took on a leadership role, challenging both George Fox and James Nayler.

A lamentation for the Lost Sheep of the House of Israel written by one of the children of Light, who is known to the world by the name of Martha Simmons, London, 1655, pp. 2, 3, 5–6.

Oh England, England whence art thou; groping in the dark and stumbling at noon day; art thou grown so high in thy fallen wisdom, and in the pride of thy heart that thou canst not stoop to a measure of God in thee? . . .

And now to you high priests of the nation; and teachers of all sorts of opinions, who have been groping and hunting in your wisdom to find out that precious pearl to defile in your filthy nature; but you have not yet found it, nor cannot find the door to enter into the kingdom . . .

And now all people that hath sobriety, and love to your souls, come out from among these idle dumb shepherds that feed themselves, but not you, and if you put not into their mouths they will soon show violence to you: come out from among them, and be no longer partaker of their uncleanness, for they are broken cisterns that can no longer hold water; and come into the fountain that runs forth freely, the streams whereof would refresh your hungry fainting souls: in my father's house there is bread enough: Oh why will you perish for hunger? mind the light the measure of Christ in you, that with it you may see where you are, that you may see his eternal love, how he calls and invites you into the kingdom, that he may take off your filthy garments, that he may clothe you with the garment of right-eousness, and marry you unto himself; and now day of his mighty power is appeared, and the fountain of life set open to wash and cleanse you from your sins, and baptize you into his death and sufferings: Oh be not stub-born and stiff-necked against him, for we that do follow him do find his paths pleasant pure and sweet, and the further we follow him in the straight gate and narrow way, we see his love is past finding out: And now in the tenderness of my heart longing for your souls' good am I made open to you, having had a habitation in this City of *London* sometime; for seven years together I wandered up and down the streets inquiring of those that had the image of honesty in their countenance, where I might find an honest minister, for I saw my soul in death, and that I was in the first nature,[1] and wandering from one idol's temple to another, and from one private meeting to another, I heard a sound of words amongst them but no substance could I find, and the more I sought after them the more trouble came on me, and finding none sensible of my condition, I kept it in, and kept all close within me; and about the end of seven years hunting, and finding no rest, the Lord opened a little glimmerings of light to me, and quieted my spirit and then for about seven years more he kept me still from running after men, and all this time durst not meddle with any thing of God, nor scarce take his name in my mouth, because I knew him not, it [I?] living wild and wanton not knowing a cross to my will I spent this time; yet something I found breathing in me groaning for deliverance, crying out, oh when shall I see the day of thy appearance; about the end of the last seven years the Lord opened my eyes to see a measure of himself in me, which when I saw I waited diligently in it, and being faithful to it I found this Light more and more increase, which brought me into a day of trouble, and through it, and through a warfare and to the end of it, and now hath given me a resting place with him; *and this is my beloved, and this is my friend O ye daughters of* Jerusalem: And now all that have a desire to come this way must lay down your crowns at the feet of Jesus, for now a profession of words will no longer cover, for the Lord is come to look for fruit, all types and shadows is flying away; and he that will come in may inherit substance, and he that will not shall be left naked.

FINIS

---

1. The first nature was the unredeemed, fallen human being whom Christ came to redeem.

POPULAR BELIEFS

2.12 'Their shoes by the fire': popular customs before the Wars

John Aubrey (1626–97) recorded many traditional customs in his manuscripts, viewing these as relics of paganism. These examples tell of women's faith in divination, their desire to know who would marry whom, and who would die. Bargains were struck with God: a woman might promise her unborn child to the Lord, clearly hoping for a son. In some circumstances to attempt to foretell the future was an offence. For an example of a prosecution for a woman's attempt at love magic, see 6.1.

John Aubrey, *Remaines of Gentilisme and Judaisme*, ed. James Britten, London, Folk-Lore Society, 1881, pp. 24, 96–7, 125.

Of casting or drawing lots

... When I was a boy in North Wilts (before the Civil Wars) the maid servants were wont at night (after supper) to make smooth the ashes on the hearth, and then to make streaks on it with a stick; such a streak signified privately to her that made it such an unmarried man, such a one such a maid: the like for men. Then the men and the maids were to choose by this kind of way, their husbands and wives: or by this divination to know whom they should marry. The maids I remember were very fond of this kind of magic, which is clearly a branch of Geomantie.[1] Now the rule of Geomantie is, that you are not to go about your divination, but with a great deal of seriousness, and also prayers; and to be performed in a very private place; or on the sea shore.

Memorandum: the sitting up on Midsummer-eve in the church porch to see the apparitions of those that should die or be buried there, that year: most used by women: I have heard them tell strange stories of it.

Vowing of children by barren women

Mr George Dickson, now rector of Brampton, near Northampton, was by his breeding mother devoted to the office of the ministry, to which he was bred and ordained, though heir to a plentiful estate.

Fairies

When I was a boy, our country people would talk much of them: they swept up the hearth clean at night; and did set their shoes by the fire, and many times they should find a threepence in one of them. Mrs Markey (a daughter

1. Divination.

of Sergeant Hoskyns, the poet) told me, that her Mother did use that custom, and had as much money as made her (or bought her) a little silver-cup, of thirty shillings value.

2.13   Witchcraft: Wilman Worsiter, Dorothy Rawlins and Katherine Wilson, 1651

The 1650s saw a local witch panic in Kent. Accusations emerged as people reviewed everyday and more extraordinary incidents in the light of witchcraft beliefs. None of those accused of witchcraft were marginal figures, but were clearly integrated into the local community networks. Nicholas Widgier's death, which may have been caused by a series of epileptic fits, is linked by one of the witnesses to Rawlins' presence as a suspected witch. None of the witnesses was apparently literate except Deborah Swayne.

Kent Quarter Sessions Papers, Centre for Kentish Studies, Q/SB 2/12–14.

The examination of Anthony Harlott mariner of the Isle of Guernsey, mariner, sworn and examined concerning the accusation of witchcraft against Wilman Worsiter the wife of George Worsiter of Ashford sawyer as followeth. August 16 1651.

That being brought unto the house of John Harris of Ashford shoemaker upon the sixth day of August last to look upon Sarah the daughter of the same John Harris being there sick in bed and suspected to be bewitched, this examinate was asked if she were bewitched yea or no he answered that if she were the party that had done it should come in a sad condition, and accordingly the said Wilman Worsiter did speedily come, being not well, and upon her first coming in he this examinant asked her the said Wilman Worsiter how she did, to which she answered, Lord am I brought hither to be a wondering stock to all the company, and then kneeling down on her knees she said to this examinate, Good Sir shew mercy on me and do not accuse me or to that effect, and acknowledged that she had deserved death indeed. Whereunto he this examinate replied, speak not to me but to the child and see in what a sad condition it lie, whereupon she laid her hands on the child and said I pray God bless thee God send thee well to do, whereupon the child presently arose and dressed herself and went away in all appearance well.

The examination of Deborah Swayne the wife of Albertus Swayne of Ashford aforesaid, innholder, sworn and examined the day abovesaid. Who saith that on Sunday last in the afternoon she this examinate hearing that Sarah the daughter of John Harris of Ashford shoemaker was very ill, she went to see her, she found her in very strange fits much striving and catching at every one that came near, much raving and crying out against Wilmer Worsiter, saying she would use that jade as bad as she had used her for that God had now given her victory over her, and being in her naked bed she suddenly start up, put on her clothes and ran into the street, saying she would go to a bakehouse over against her father's house to seek out the said Wilmer Worsiter, saying that if she could find her she would pay her as she had tormented her, and joins with Anthony Harlott in the matter of his examination.

The examination of witnesses upon oath against Dorothy Rawlins wife of William Rawlins of St Dunstans in the said county brewer taken the 16 of August 1651 ...

Elizabeth Widgier widow late wife of Nicholas Widgier of St Dunstan's, wheelwright, upon her oath saith that about seven weeks ago the said Dorothy Rawlins came to this examinate's house for fire and this examinate's late husband said unto this examinate, have nothing to do with her for she is naught, and said that she had the eyes of the witches were hanged at Faversham[1] and that upon Thursday last was sevenight her said husband was taken sick in the morning with an extraordinary pain in his side, and in his sickness he said unto this examinate, Pray God goodwife Rawlins that witch over the way have no power over me for she knoweth that I say she is a witch and she cannot abide me, and when I met her at any time she leereth on me and will not speak unto me, and upon the Monday next after in the evening this examinate's husband died in a strange manner being taken with extraordinary and unusual fits.

Margaret Ken of St Dunstan's, spinster, upon oath saith that this examinate upon Sunday night last in the time of the sickness of the said Nicholas Widgier, watching with him, heard him say that he thought he should be ridd[en] to death by Goodwife Rawling, for he thought she had bewitched him for she never went by him but she gave him an leering look, but if he lived he would scratch out her eyes, and the next day in the evening he was taken with four extraordinary fits which drew his mouth on one side and was speechless divers hours, and died speechless, and the bed and rooms shook before he died, and died in the last fits: And this examinate saith that the said Rawlins told her before that the said Nicholas Widgier married the said Elizabeth, that she durst lay her life of it that they should not live 8 weeks together. And about a month ago the said Dorothy Rawlins gave the examinate a piece of cheese which she ate and the same night this examinate was pinched upon the arms and stomach and the next morning was black and blue with it.

Mary Hollandine wife of Andrew Hollandine of St Dunstan's, brasier, upon oath saith that the said Dorothy Rawlins for some years last past hath been suspected to be a witch and that she was several times with the said Nicholas

1. Joan Cariden and others, in 1645.

Widgier in the time of his sickness and that the night that the said Widgier died he had some extraordinary and unusual fits and was speechless all that time, and in his fits his eyes were ready to fly out of his head, his mouth was drawn on one side, and he foamed in the mouth and his arms and legs beat violently, and departed near the end of the last fit and that the bed whereon he lay shook very much and strangely.

Mary Blyth wife of Thomas Blyth of St Dunstan's, brewer, upon oath saith, That this deponent went about a fortnight since to the house of the said Dorothy Rawlins to buy some seething[2] and the said Dorothy at that time gave some seething unto her and lent her a pot to carry it home in, and when this deponent was come home and going to use the same, of a sudden the pot gave a great blow and flew and broke, and the seething flew about her ears and up unto the ceiling and only the handles of the pot and a small part of the pot remained in this deponent's hand, and for many years past the said Dorothy Rawlins hath been reputed and suspected to be a witch, and this deponent hath heard the said Dorothy's husband say she was a witch if there were any in England for she knew what was done seven miles off.

Joane Claringbold wife of Richard Claringbold of St Dunstan's, labourer, upon oath saith that about a quarter of a year since Richard Claringbold her son, a boy about fifteen years old, told this deponent (he being then sick) that he had never been well since that the said Dorothy Rawlins gave him a piece of cheese which he ate (as he told her) and that he was sick about a month together after that time and that the said Dorothy Rawlins hath been many years reputed and suspected to be a witch.

The examination of Katherine Wilson of Boughton Alaph in the county of Kent widow being accused for bewitching of George Cheeseman the son of George Cheeseman, of Boughton Alaph aforesaid, husbandman, taken at Ashford . . . the 4th day of September 1651.

She saith that there have some times of late been some small fallings out between her this examinate and Mary the wife of the said George Cheeseman, but doth not remember that she had threatened the said Mary, but she saith that it may be that she this examinate hath formerly threatened the said Mary but she saith she doth not well remember it, nor did she think to do her any evil, and she doth deny the doing or procuring any evil or hurt to the said George Cheeseman the son whereof she is accused.

The examination of George Cheeseman the elder then taken before the said justices Who saith that about five weeks ago there was a falling out between the wife of him the said George Cheeseman and Katherine Wilson of

2. Seething: something hot or boiling.

Boughton Alaph widow, and thereupon she, the said Katherine, being withdrawn to her chamber he this examinate heard her say to her daughter being then with her, that she would be avenged of that woman, meaning the wife of him this examinate as he verily believeth. And about a month after the only son of him this examinate and Mary his said wife was very suddenly taken with a very great pain in both his legs so that he was presently unable to go, being before a very healthy busy child, and so continued and rather worse than better until this afternoon, at which time by some means she the said Katherine was brought to see the said child, and prayed to God to bless the said child and make it well or to that effect, and the said child presently looked up very cheerfully and better than it had done a long time before and did in all appearance amend and leave groaning and take some sustenance with a spoon which it had not done but with a feather for the space of four and twenty hours before.

Anthony Harlott sworn and examined touching the said matter saith that he verily believes that George, the son of George Cheeseman of Boughton Alaph, is bewitched for that some of the hair of the head of the said child being cut off and set on the fire in water, the water in which the same boiling would rise up above the lip of the skillet but would not run into the fire, though there were a great fire kept under it and red hot irons put into it to enforce it to run over if it might be, but he further saith that he doth not know who hath bewitched the said child. The said George Cheeseman the elder concurred with the said Anthony concerning the boiling of the child's water.

2.14   Healing by faith: Elinor Burt, 1660

All Christians were exhorted to pray to God, so that prayers for good health were in theory orthodox. But some claims to heal by prayer were suspect, largely because of the status of those who offered them. Elinor Burt was summoned for questioning before two Justices of the Peace because she had no authority to lay on hands and pray for the sick, and was thus suspected of witchcraft.

Worcester Quarter Sessions, Worcester RO, QS 97/60.

The examination of Elinor Burt, taken the 26th day of May 1660 . . .
Being examined whether she hath not taken upon her to cure several persons afflicted with several diseases and distempers in their bodies, Answereth and saith that she did not take upon her so to do, but confesseth that when diverse have come to her that had aches in their heads and other infirmities she had and hath a gift from God by good prayers and laying her hands upon their heads or faces often times to recover and heal them of their diseases. And being examined what other means she useth to recover such persons saith no other means but good prayers. And further doth not materially confess.

3

WORK

Women in early modern England were workers, as Alice Clark demonstrated in her classic study many years ago.[1] Their working lives varied according to their life stages and their social status. The basic business of getting a living was arduous for most women, and at different stages of their lives, they might engage in multiple occupations or even in illegal work. The concept of 'family wage economy' disguises the reality of women's working lives; 'the family' never provided for the majority of women who laboured both inside as well as outside marriage. Wives needed the larger wages men could command as well as their own to support their children; and should their husbands fall ill, die, or desert, female wages were usually insufficient to maintain a family. Widows and orphans were classic recipients of poor relief.

Working lives were affected by marital status. The majority of women married late, around 26 years of age. Young single women had to provide for themselves as young adults. Most were employed in domestic service and husbandry.[2] Not all women married; of those born in 1600, around 20 per cent of the population remained single, and the proportion never married fluctuated over the century.[3] Married women usually continued to work at a range of occupations, as well as housekeeping and childcare. Deserted wives and widows could be responsible for maintaining their children as well as themselves.

The bulk of the female population worked in agriculture or as domestic servants. In the towns, retail shopkeeping developed, and by the end of the century London was attracting many young women to supply the city's demands for services. All women received lower pay than men in similar occupations and for like work. Labouring women's training was limited, and their pay poor. In this period before the Industrial Revolution, many of the crafts and trades were still controlled by guilds; young women were unlikely to gain apprenticeships. Their labour as family members or as servants might gain them skill in a particular craft but without a formal apprenticeship they were unable to set up in their own business. We do not know how many women in English towns and cities married into the same craft or trade as their families of origin; in France, Natalie Davis found that daughters of silk-weavers and printers in Lyon frequently married craftsmen in other trades.[4]

Getting a living involved a range of varied activities at different social levels. Women's work is not easily separated into paid and unpaid work, nor were their occupational identities always distinct. Certain work could be for pay or not, depending on a woman's status. Cleaning, for example, might be part of the duties of a servant, an occupation for older women in cities, or the expected task of wives. Much of the paid work of married women was combined with childcare and housewifery.[5] Over their lifetimes, labouring women might be independent wage earners during their teens and early twenties. After marriage, they were responsible for housewifery and childcare, and in old age still required to labour at poorly rewarded tasks such as spinning. Those who depended upon poor rates could be forced into unpleasant work, such as searching bodies, as the price of their continued relief.

Women's self-identification as workers was stronger than many contemporary labels suggest. The courts might describe women by their marital status, as 'wife' or 'spinster', but women themselves spoke of their art or profession; a cheese-maker's wife described herself as 'a butterwoman by profession'.[6] Those most likely to be able to establish an occupational or professional identity were usually in the middling levels of society. Their occupations included midwifery, medical practice, teaching, and nursing. Many of these were pursued also by poorer women, but they have been separated because wealthier women were more likely to have a professional identity than their poorer counterparts. Cultural areas, such as painting, singing, the stage, and even writing, were opening up for women after the Restoration in 1660, but around the same time middling women were being challenged in traditional areas, such as midwifery, by professionalising men. In trades such as brewing, ale-wives were being marginalised by larger-scale brewers.[7] The multiple occupations of poorer women militated against contemporary recognition of female work identities.

Social class influenced women's housekeeping and housewifery. While women of the elite did not themselves labour, they supervised their servants who performed the tasks of maintaining their households. Possessions were more numerous higher up the social scale. Gentlewomen might therefore need skilled and specialised servants to look after their possessions. Ladies employed other women for time-consuming and delicate tasks such as the washing of silks and lace.

As Chapter 4 shows, the majority of women experienced relative and absolute poverty at some stages of their lives. Furthermore, sexuality and reproduction impacted on women's working lives. Heterosexual activity in young women servants could lead to pregnancy, dismissal, and punishment for bastardy; wives bore a baby roughly every three years.[8] Poverty meant malnourished babies too, making the work of rearing children even more difficult.

Since so much of women's work was invisible, taken for granted by their contemporaries, it is not easy to find records which document female labour. We have selected a variety of documents to illustrate the possibilities of reading apparently unprepossessing material to reveal details about women's working lives. The documents have been grouped thematically. Many of these documents require a different kind of reading from those in other chapters: more deduction is needed, and information about work is often in the incidental detail. Further relevant sources may be found in Chapter 4, 'Poverty and Property'.

SERVICE

3.1 Advice for servants in larger households: Hannah Wolley, 1675

Most young women worked as domestic servants from their early teens until their mid-twenties, living in the households of their employers, and subject to their masters' commands. The majority of households employed at least one general servant, but in larger households there were several, many of whom had specialised tasks. Young women might begin in a lowly capacity, rising through the ranks as they learnt more and grew older. Hannah Wolley (see 1.10) advised about a range of different kinds of employment and cautioned young women against sexual temptation.

Hannah Wolley, *The Compleat Servant Maid*, London, 1677, pp. 110, 157–8; *The Gentlewoman's Companion*, London, 1675, p. 214.

Directions for such who desire to be Nursery-Maids to persons of honour or quality, or else to gentlewomen either in city or country.
If you intend to fit your self for this employment, you must naturally incline to love young children . . .

Directions for such as desire to be dairy maids.
Those who would endeavour to gain the esteem and reputation of good dairy maids must be very careful that all their vessels be scalded well, and kept very clean, that they milk their cattle in due time, for the kine by custom will expect it though you neglect, which will tend much to their detriment.
. . . I look upon it to be altogether needless, for to give you any directions for the making of butter or cheese, since there are very few (especially in the country) that can be ignorant thereof.

Instructions for under-cook maids
It behoves you to be very diligent and willing to do what you are bid to do; and though your employment be greasy and smutty, yet if you please you may keep your self from being nasty, therefore let it be your care to keep yourself clean. Observe everything in cookery that is done by your superior, treasure it up in your memory, and when you meet with a convenient opportunity, put that in practice which you have observed; this course will advance you from a drudge to be a cook another day.
Every one must have a beginning, and if you will be ingenious and willing to learn, there is none will be so churlish or unkind as to be unwilling to

teach you; but if you are stubborn and careless, who do you think will trouble themselves with you? Beware of gossips, for they will misadvise you; beware of the solicitations of the flesh, for they will undo you; and though you may have mean thoughts of your self, and think none will meddle with such as you; it is a mistake, *hungry dogs will eat dirty puddings;* and I myself have known a brave gallant to fall foul with the wench of the scullery, when some others would have hazarded their life for one sole enjoyment of that incomparable lady his wife, he so ungratefully slighted.

3.2   Wages dispute: Elizabeth Lytten, 1691

Most contracts for service were informal, so if women had difficulty in receiving their wages, legal recourse could be hard.

Norwich City Records, Informations and Examinations, Norfolk RO, Case 12b(1), 1690–99.

The information of Elizabeth Lytten of Drayton in the county of Norfolk single woman taken upon oath the 28th of January 1691 before Jeremy Vynne Esq, Mayor of the City of Norwich

Who saith that the last Michaelmas was twelve months she went to Eaton petty sessions to see for a service and did then and there before the chief constable let herself to one Daniel Cooper of Drayton aforesaid for thirty shillings for one year ending at Michaelmas last, and the said informant received for her half year's service of her master Cooper aforesaid fifteen shillings for the first half year, but when her year was near expiring she desired the other half year's wages, but he refused and told her that he would not pay it to her, and she asked him why, or whether she had not done her work, or had hindered him of anything, he answered no. And the very last week of her year's service, she asked him again to pay her the wages due to her, and the said Cooper fell upon the said informant and beat her with a great staff, knocked her down the first stroke, and continued beating her and likewise rent all her linings[1] of her head and burnt them, and endeavoured to burn this informant, dragging of her to the fire and had not one John Bun ran in to her relief, he the said Cooper had burnt her. And further she saith that the said Daniel Cooper is now come to dwell in Heigham in the liberty of the said city where she have made her applications to him for the remainder of her wages and he refused to pay it, saying she shall get it by order of the law. And further saith not.

Sworn the day and year above
Signed before me, Jeremy Vynne, Mayor
The mark of Eliz. Lytten

---

1. Linens, meaning head-cloths.

3.3   Service and prostitution: Margaret Atkinson, 1617

Service involved frequent changes of employers. In the course of her examination at London's Bridewell Hospital in September 1617, accused of prostitution and of misnaming the father of her illegitimate child, Margaret Atkinson gave a brief history of her working life after her arrival in London five years earlier.

Bridewell Hospital Records, Guildhall Library, BCB 6 (microfilm), 23 Sept. 1617.

Margaret Atkinson called and examined saith she came to London about 5 years since next spring, whereof the first year she served as a servant with one Mr Smyth in Basinghall an upholsterer, from thence she went to the Lady Wiseman a prisoner in the Fleet,[1] and dwelt with her one year, from thence she went to the Lady Skynner by Vinisten House in Southwark and dwelt with her three quarters of a year, and from thence she went to Lambeth to one Mrs Wotton and there she remained a quarter of a year, and from thence she went to one William Stanley in Hosier Lane, and continued there about four months.

Being demanded who had first the use of her body, saith one Thomas Strackey, a gentleman, had several times at his chamber at one Wilcock's a shoemaker in Fleet Lane the use of her body, and afterwards a stranger at Lambeth Marsh at one Goodwife Clarton's house who gave her 12s. in silver.

And she further saith, That about February last past one Garrett a clock-maker had the use of her body at the Seven Stars a victualling house at London Wall, and he gave her 52s., and about a fortnight after he had the use of her body there again, and lay all night with her and had there several times that night afterward the use of her body. She further saith that Garrett sent for her to come to him to one Goodwife Lee's in Dairy Lane, he staying at one Mrs Lifte's, and both the son and daughter of Mrs Lifte came severally to Goodwife Lee's house to see if she wert come in, and she followed the child[2] to Mrs Lifte's, and when she came thither Mr Garrett was above-stairs and demanded of her whether she knew him or no, and she then before two others that were there present charged him that she was with child by him. But he answered that he was a broken man of his body and not able to get a child.

She further saith that at the beginning of Lent she met with Mr Elkyn in the walk at Moorfields, and he asked her if she would drink a pint of wine, which she refused, and told him she dwelt hard by at the postern by Moorgate, and there he followed her in, and went up a pair of stairs, and then had the use of her body once. Afterwards she saith at the Grange by Lincoln's Inn Mr Elkin came by chance as a stranger, and she being at work at the door of Mrs Lifte, he made a stand there, and looked this examinate in the face, as Mrs Lifte told her, asking if she knew him, and she answered

1. The Fleet was a prison.
2. The messenger.

she did. And this examine further saith that he turned [the] lock and came in, and asked if he might not have a bottle of ale, which was sent for, and Mrs Lifte leaving the room went into her garden, and then she saith he had the use of her body, and at this time he gave her 2s. 6d.

And she further saith that one James Ward a cook or victualler near Holborn Conduit and William Stanley were with her at the devising of a father for her child, and advised her that if Mr Garrett could not beget her with child, if anybody else had had to do with her, they willed her to name him to them, and they would labour in her behalf for a warrant for them, and they procured a warrant from Mr Recorder, for Mr Elkin . . .

3.4 A freed slave in service: Katherine Auker, 1690

English traders sold African people as slaves to planters in Barbados. Because it was unclear whether Christians could be enslaved, planters resisted Christianising their slaves, and colonial assemblies passed Acts denying that baptism made free. However, slavery in England theoretically was another matter. Englishmen boasted that as the very air of England was inimical to slavery, so any slaves who set foot there were free. Katherine Auker had some grounds for believing herself to be free: she was living in England, and had been baptised as 'Katharine Anker a black' at St Katharine's on 29 January 1688. However, her status and future seem very unclear.

Middlesex Sessions Bundles, LMA, MJ/SBB 472, p. 41 (Sessions Feb. 1690).

[margin] Order for Kath' Auker a Black to be at liberty to go to service until her master shall return from Barbados and provide for her.
Upon reading the humble petition of Katherine Auker, a Black, exhibited unto this court setting forth that she was servant to one Robert Rich a planter in Barbados, and about six years since came over with her master and mistress into England and about two years since was baptized in the parish church of St Katharine's near the Tower of London as appeared by certificate under the hand of the minister there produced in court. And that after her being baptized her said master and mistress tortured her and turned her out of doors. And her said master refusing to give her a discharge she could not be entertained in service whereby she was likely to perish. And that her said master procured kidnappers to take her up and carry her by force on shipboard several times threatening to cut off her nose and ears, and had caused her to be arrested and kept prisoner in the Poultry Counter[1] London. And thereby praying to be discharged from her said master, he being in Barbados, and her friends refusing to entertain her in service till lawfully discharged, her said master threatening to sue such persons as should entertain her. Now upon examination of the matter upon the oaths of several

1. The Poultry Counter was a prison.

credible witnesses, it appearing that the said Robert Rich had neglected to provide a service for the said Katherine Auker or to allow her necessary relief and maintenance, This court thought fit and doth accordingly order that the said Katherine Auker be at liberty to serve any person or persons that shall entertain her in service until such time as the said Robert Rich shall return from Barbados and provide for her the said Katherine necessary apparel and maintenance of which the person that doth entertain her is to have reasonable notice.

GETTING A LIVING

3.5   Whereby she maintains herself: witnesses' statements from the court records, 1610–24

Those who came to witness in cases at the church courts were often asked about the financial compensation they expected from the litigant. They might also be asked about their own financial circumstances – how they maintained themselves, what was the manner of their lives – to establish their honesty, reputation, and social and economic status (generally, such questions were posed by the defence in an attempt to proved that the prosecution witnesses were expecting financial rewards from the litigant, or were poor and of low standing). Some were also, apparently, asked who their fathers had been. The answers to these varied questions supply a range of otherwise inaccessible information about the working lives of women. Whereas many married women stated simply, 'she is a married wife and knoweth not her husband's estate', and many servants answered, 'she hath nothing but her service', other women gave more detailed responses about the work they did, with or apart from their husbands, and the earnings they lived on. These extracts are from the London church courts early in the seventeenth century, and are preceded by the biographical details which witnesses gave at the start of their testimony. The parishes mentioned are in London unless otherwise noted. Ages are generally approximate, with 'or thereabouts' noted by the clerk.

Consistory Court of London Deposition Books, LMA, DL/C 219, fos 152, 154v; 176–v.; DL/C 224, fos 82–v; DL/C 225, fos 37, 39v–40, 42v, 43, 73–v, 74–v, 76–v, 77–v, 78v, 79v, 326v; DL/C 226/4 fo. 37v–38; DL/C 226/5 fos 12–13v; Guildhall, MS 9189/1 fos 76–v, 130v–131.

[Ann Hawes wife of Edmund Hawes, of the parish of Holy Trinity in Trinity Lane, where she has lived for 9 or 10 years, and with whom she has lived for about 14 years, and previously she lived in Botolph Lane for a year and previously she lived in the parish of St Michael Cornhill for a year, born in Charlwood, Surrey, aged 50.] She keepeth a sempster's shop and her husband is a musician and by that means they get their living. [1610]

[Emma Kene, wife of John Kene, of the parish of St Nicholas Colchester, bricklayer, with whom she has lived for four years, and in which parish she has lived all her life, and was born, aged 30.] She useth[1] to spin, do her household business and to wash and starch sometime at home and sometime abroad if she be hired. [1610]

[Elizabeth Ellell, widow, of St Mary Whitechapel, where she has lived for a year, and previously in the parish of St Botolph without Algate, for about 2 years or thereabouts, and previously in Froginford in Southampton for about 15 years, born on the Isle of Wight, age 50.] She is a sempster and teaches young children to read and work with their needles, and thereby getteth her living. [1615]

[Elizabeth Devell, wife of Robert Devell, hatdresser, of the town of St Albans in Hertfordshire where she has lived all her life and was born, aged 26.] Her father was a haberdasher of small wares and this respondent hath and doth towards her maintenance wash and scour at men's houses where she liveth. [1617]

[Katherine Carter, domestic servant of John Shelford of the parish of St Mary Aldermary, for the last 3 years, and previously in the parish of St Michael Cornhill, previously in the parish of St Nicholas Cole Abbey for 4 years, born at Thissetton in the parish of Kirkham in Lancashire, aged 35.] She hath none other means to live by but by her service and is worth in her goods her debts paid 40s. [1617]

[Ann Soome, wife of John Soome of St Mary Aldermary, threadmaker, where she has lived for the last 11 years, born in St Stephen Coleman Street, aged 42.] Her father was while he lived a basketmaker of London and this respondent for her part useth to make thread ... she liveth of her self by her husband's means and by her own means in the trade she useth, and is little worth of herself. [1617]

[Ann Burges, of St Mary Aldermary, widow, where she has lived for 14 years, born in Winchester, aged 35.] Her father was a weaver, and she useth to wash and starch for her maintenance having no other means to live. [1617]

[Elizabeth Gaskyn, of St Bride's, widow, where she has lived for 20 years, born in Kendal, Westmorland, aged 60.] She useth to keep women in childbed and doth use to wash at several men's houses, and thereby getteth her living. [1617]

[Ann Pace of St Bride's, widow, where she has lived for 16 years, born in North Mimms in Hertfordshire, aged 50.] She useth to mend stockings and thereby liveth. [1617]

---

1. I.e., she still does.

[Marie Cable, wife of Barnabe Cable, of Wapping in the parish of Stepney in Middlesex, butcher, where she has lived for the last 9 months and previously in the precinct of St Katharine by the Tower and St Botolph without Aldgate for 20 years, born in Warwick, aged 50.] She keepeth shop for her husband's trade. [1617]

[Ann Lee, wife of Thome Lee of Wapping, Stepney, painter, where she has lived for 8 years, born in Great Malvern in Worcestershire, aged 55.] She windeth raw silk from the throwsters[2] and thereby getteth her living and hath some maintenance from her husband. [1617]

[Margaret Peirce, wife of Henry Peirce of Wapping, Stepney, farmer, where she has lived for 14 years, born in Carmarthen in Carmarthenshire, aged 50.] For the manner of her life she spendeth her time as other women use to do in spinning and carding. [1617]

[Ann Brand, wife of John Brand, of the parish of St Katherine Cree, cheesemaker, whose wife she has been for 23 years, born in Southall, Suffolk, aged 54.] . . . being a butterwoman by profession and tending on the market at Leadenhall . . . [1618]

[Frances Andrewes, wife of Thomas Andrewes, of St Andrew Holborn, yeoman, whose wife she has been for the last 10 years, but has lived in this parish for 1 year, and previously in St Martin in the Fields in Middlesex for 3 years, born in Amptill, Bedfordshire, aged 30.] She is a starcher, and starches to shops, and by that means getteth her living, and what her husband's estate is she knoweth not, in regard he liveth from her and so hath done these 4 years. [1619]

[Ellen Jefferey, widow, of St Martins in the Fields where she has lived for 36 years, born at Ludlow, Shropshire, aged 50.] She liveth by keeping of an alehouse or victualling house. [1619]

[Magdalen Holmes, wife of John Holmes, of St Martin in the Fields, born in Cardiff, Glamorgan, aged 34.] She hath dwelt in the parish of St Martin in the Fields these 12 years or thereabouts and this respondent's husband is pot-scourer in the King's privy kitchen and always at court for the most part, and this respondent for the most part useth her needle and knitting and sometimes washing and starching and by this means she helps to get her own living. [1619]

2. Those who twist raw silk into thread.

[Joan Blackborn, wife of John Blackborn of the parish of Whitechapel in Middlesex carter whose wife she has been for the last 3 years but she has lived in the same parish for the last 12 years, born in Deptford in Kent, aged 21 or thereabouts.] She is a wife and liveth partly of her husband's labour and partly of her own by winding of silk and making of buttons for handkerchers. [1623]

[Ann Booton, widow, of the parish of St Dunstan's in the West, where she has lived for 1 year and previously in the parish of St Bride Fleet street for 12 years born at Haworth in Yorkshire, aged 60 and more.] She is a poor widow and little or nothing worth . . . she doth belong to Seargent's Inn in Fleet Street where she is employed there by the cook of the house in the termtime[3] to turn the spit and wash dishes and such like drudgery. [1624]

3.6   Small-scale retail: Judith Joanes, pedlar, 1631

Many smaller items of consumption were sold by pedlars. Although geographical mobility was more frequent among male workers, women too could be employed on the roads. Seventeenth-century authorities suspected that anyone found wandering was a rogue, thief, or vagabond, and feared that they might settle in the parish as a charge on the rates.

Somerset Quarter Session Rolls, Somerset Archives, Q/SR 64/1 (1631).

The examination of Judith Joanes the wife of William Joanes of Little Torrington in the county of Devon husbandman, taken before William Walcond Esq one of his Majesty's Justices of the peace the twenty third day of August the seventh year of King Charles now of England etc Anno domini 1631

Who saith that her dwelling is in Little Torrington near unto Great Torrington in the said county of Devon; and that her husband William Joanes doth rent a house in Little Torrington aforesaid of one Robert Carter, a glover there, for the yearly rent of twenty shillings. And being demanded what occasion of business her husband and she had in Chard where they were now apprehended, Saith that she had no other business, but to sell such wares of her own as she had in a box which she now showeth (wherein there are divers small commodities of little value, saving two yards of holland which she saith she bought of one Mr John Prows a linen draper in Exeter about three weeks since, and paid for it four shillings a yard, that there was three yards of it when she bought it whereof she hath used one yard since). This examinate also saith that her husband William Joanes doth carry about the country at his back a crate of earthenware, which was partly their occasion of being at Chard yesterday being the market day to sell the same. And being

3. Term time – the law courts met for three legal terms per annum.

demanded whether she hath ever been in a gaol, or burnt in the hand, denieth that ever she was in any gaol as a prisoner or ever burnt in the hand. There being also a pair of new shoes taken upon her and she being questioned where she had them saith that she bought them about fortnight since of a man to her unknown as he was going unto Axminster Market and paid for them 17d. and further confesseth not.

3.7   Working lives of London market women, 1699

Evidence about the working lives of ordinary women is rare in early modern times. A petition from London market people, occasioned by a rise in fees and reorganisation, offers some evidence about women's role in marketing. The information was taken by the rival claimants for the market, who would have been sympathetic to retailers' claims that Thomas Killner's demands were extortionate and contrary to custom.

The petition of the oppressed market people, humbled offer'd to the consideration of the Lord Mayor, Aldermen, and Common Council of the City of London [London, 1699], pp. 3, 4, 5, 10, 12, 13, 16.

An Abstract of an Information for Extortion exhibited against Mr Thomas Killner, . . .

That the defendant . . . unjustly, unlawfully and extortiously took of one Mary Palmer the wife of Samuel Palmer, 4s. 8d. for permitting her to have the use of a board about five foot long, and three foot broad in Newgate Market aforesaid, for selling and exposing to sale of butter, eggs, oat-cakes, hogs-puddings and sausages upon, for the space of two weeks then past (to wit) 2s. 4d. per week, whereas he ought not to have received of the said Mary, for the use of the said board, more than 2s. (to wit) 1s. per week.

Also, . . . took of one Anne Milbourn, wife of Daniel Milbourne, 40s. for permitting her to place two dossars[1] in Newgate Market, for selling and exposing to sale of flesh, butter, and other provisions upon, [he should have taken no more than 13s. 4d.] to wit 2d. per day.

The Case

That the said Joan Laxton, Mary Palmer, Anne Milbourne, Mary Cooke, Anne Geeves, Mary Bignell, Elizabeth Page and Anne Sutton are poor people, who sell small provisions in Newgate Market, viz. lamb, pork, butter, eggs, oat-cakes, hogs-puddings, sausages, &c. in small quantities, none of them ever bringing more than an horse-load on any one market-day, for which by the ancient custom of the City of London, as also by an Act of Common-Council, made the 17th September 1674, they ought not to pay more than 2d. per day . . .

1. Panniers.

Divers affidavits, touching the information exhibited against Thomas Killner, &c.

Joan Laxton of the parish of St Sepulchres, London, widow, maketh oath, That she this deponent selleth small butchers' meat in Newgate Market in London, under the pent-house belonging to the house of Thomas Whitmore, upon a board about three foot and an half in length, and about three foot in breadth; . . . And further this deponent maketh oath, That she hath kept the same standing in the market, with the like conveniencies, for about eighteen years last past; and until of late years, she paid no more than 2d. per day for such days only as she came to the said Market, and she paid nothing for such days as she did not come, but now the present Farmers compel her to pay the rent aforesaid, if she doth not come one day in the week to the said Market.

[Sworn 8 Feb. 1698]

Anne Milbourne, wife of Daniel Milbourne, of London, in county of Middlesex, farmer, maketh oath, That she hath for divers years kept Newgate Market, in London, commonly two days in a week with only two dossars

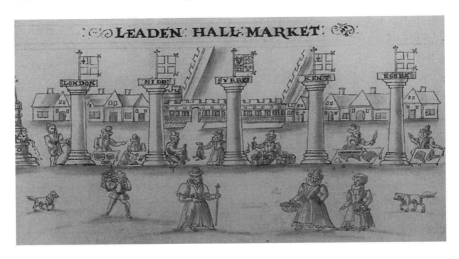

Figure 5 **Leadenhall Market**

From [Hugh Alley], A Caveat for the Citty of London [1598], Folger MS V.a.318. By permission of the Folger Shakespeare Library

Market women brought small provisions for sale, either riding in with their goods in 'dossars' or carrying their wares in baskets. Although this picture of a London market is dated to the end of the sixteenth century, little had changed by the end of the next century. Markets were still regulated, and under the supervision of men.

of small provision each day for which formerly she paid no more than two pence per day, but when she did not come she paid nothing.

Mary Cooke, wife of John Cooke, of the parish of Christ-Church, London, butcher, maketh oath, that she selleth small butchers' meat in Newgate Market, London, under the pent-house of John Whiteing, upon a board about six foot in length, and about eighteen inches in breadth, for which the Farmers of the markets have ... demanded ... 2s. 4d. per week, for several months last past.

[Sworn 6 Feb. 1698]

As the ground for the said Markets was purchased with money raised upon the public by virtue of the aforesaid Act of Parliament, so no doubt the Markets were designed to be free, open and common, and for the public advantage of all the King's subjects, who have occasion to use the same, either to sell or buy food and victuals, upon paying a reasonable toll or duty ...

3.8 Pegg Dodgson and Jenny Colton: employees of Sarah Fell, 1674–75

The selections here from the account book of Sarah Fell, the Quaker daughter of the wealthy gentlewoman, Margaret Fell, allow us to trace details of two women's work over two years. (Sarah's accounting was originally in columns, with 1d. listed as 000 00 01.)

The Account Book of Sarah Fell of Swarthmoor Hall, ed. Norman Penney, Cambridge, Cambridge University Press, 1920, introduction by Alice Clark, from pp. 75–263.

Entries concerning Pegg Dodgson, 1674–76

23 May 1674 by money paid Pegg Dodgson for filling manure, scaling manure, washing, harrowing, and dressing meadows 17 days Mother's account. . .   2s. 6d.

1674 June the 13 by money paid Pegg Dodgson for rubbing 1 day for sister Lower ...   1d.

by money paid her more for spreading peats, washing, rinsing and weeding 12 days Mother's account ...   1s. 5d.

July the 1st By money paid Ann Geldart and Peggy Dodgson for setting and dressing 5 daywork of peats in Conniside Mosse, Mother's account ...   2s. 6d.

1674 Aug the 17 To money received of Pegg Dodgson that she owed me ...   1d.

1674 Aug the 16 by money paid Pegg Dodgson for working at hay, and about pulling hemp and line[1] &c 5 weeks and 4 days Mother's account . . .
2s. 10d.

by money paid her more for rubbing for sister Lower 2 days . . .   2d.

1674 Aug the 27th by money paid Pegg Dodgson for working hay and picking line, and pulling, and for washing clothes 6 days Mother's account . . .   8d.

by money paid her for washing and rubbing for sister Lower 3 days . . .
4d.

October the 10th by money paid Pegg Dodgson for swingling[2] and raking brackens 8 days . . .   2d.

by money paid her for rubbing 1 day for sister Lower . . .   1d.

October the 28th by money paid Pegg Dodgson for swingling, washing and rinsing 5 days her account . . .   8d.

by money paid her for 5 days for sister Lower . . .   5d.

November the 12th by money paid him [Higgins] for bringing a stone of flax from Lancaster from Pegg Dodgson . . .   2d.

1674 December the 4th to money received of Pegg Dodgson for 1 stone of line, that I bought for her of Henry Coward and for carriage . . .
6s. 2d.

Dec the 4th by money paid Pegg Dodgson for filling manure and scaling manure, when the wheat was sown 8 days; her account . . .   1s.

by money paid her for rubbing 2 days for sister Lower. . . .   2d.

by money paid her for 5 yards of tare of hemp, at 10d. per yard and 1d. more at all for Nelly, and Richard Mother's Account . . .   4s. 3d.

by money said Pegg Dodgson owes me . . .   5d.

Dec the 17th by money Jenny Atkinson owes me about a cabbage that Pegg Dodgson bought . . .   2d.

1675 March the 23rd to money received of Pegg Dodgson that she owed me . . .   5d.

1675 March the 23rd by money paid Pegg Dodgson for washing and rubbing for sister Lower . . .   8d

1. The fibre of flax.
2. To beat and scrape flax.

by money paid her for footing a pair of stockings for sister Rachel . . .
3d.

by money paid her more for scalding manure and 3 days Mother's account
. . .
4d.

April the 1st by money lent Pegg Dodgson . . .   1s.

1675 May 28 To money received of Pegg Dodgson that I lent her the 1st of April last . . .   1s.

1675 May the 28th by money paid Pegg Dodgson for weeding in the garden, filing and scalding manure spreading peats and other work 22 days her account . . .   2s. 7d.

by money paid her for a pair of stockings for George Jackson, Brother Lower's account . . .   1s. 4d.

Dec the 16 To money received of Pegg Dodgson for 5 lbs of wool sold her of ours at Marsh . . .   2s. 6d.

To money received of her for 1½ lbs of ewe butter of Mother's sold her . . .
4d.

1675 Dec the 16th by money paid Pegg Dodgson for working here at several sorts of work 8 weeks and odd days Mother's Account . . .   4s. 11d.

By money Pegg Dodgson owes me . . .   11d.

1676 Feb the 26th by money paid Pegg Dodgson for washing rinsing, rubbing, and scalding mole hills 13 days her account . . .   1s. 5d.

1676 March the 25th by money paid Pegg Dodgson for washing, rubbing, and other work 13 days her account . . .   1s. 3d.

1676 April the 15th by money paid Peggy Dodgson for rubbing scouring and other work 12 days her account . . .   1s.

Entries concerning Jenny Colton, a buyer of commodities for sale, 25 March 1674–25 March 1675

1674 Mar 19 by money I lent Jenny Colton upon her manure   1s.

1674 June the 12 by money Jenny Colton owes me 3d   1s. 2d.

1674 June the 18 To money received of Jenny Colton that she owed me
. . .   3d. 2 farthings

To money received of Jenny Colton that she owed me . . .   1d.

1674 July the 9th To money received of Jenny Colton that she owed me about buying butter . . .   3d.

1674 July the 16th To money received of Jenny Colton that she owed me about butter buying ... 4d.

1674 July the 8 By money Jenny Colton owes me . 3d.

12 by money Jenny Colton owes me ... 4d.

1674 July the 16 by money paid for a mande[3] lent to Jenny Colton to buy butter in ... 6d.

by money Jenny Colton owes me about butter buying ... 1d. 2 farthings

1674 July the 25 To money received of Jenny Colton that she owed me about buying butter ... 1d. 2 farthings

1674 July the 29 To money received of Jenny Colton that she had of me to buy chickens with ... 1s. 6d.

1674 July the 29 by money paid for 9 chickens that Jenny Colton brought her account ... 1s. 6d.

July the 30 by money Jenny Colton owes me about butter 1d.

1674 Aug the 13 To money received of Jenny Colton for 1h of our Marshgr: beans ... 1s.

1674 Aug the 6 by money paid Jenny Colton in part of 5s the Women's Meeting[4] ordered her out of their stock ... 6d.

1674 Aug the 13 By money paid Jenny Colton in full of 5s. given her of the Women's Meeting stock per their order ... 4s. 6d.

1674 Aug 13 To money received of Jenny Colton she owed me about butter ... 1d.

1674 Oct the 5 by money lent Jenny Colton for a week ... 6d.

1674 Oct the 18 to money received of Jenny Colton that I lent her the 8th instant ... 6d.

1674 Nov the 12 To money received of Jenny Colton for 1 hoo: of wheat sold her of ours there at Marsh Grange ... 1s. 4d.

1674 Dec the 22 To money received of Jenny Colton for 1 hoo of old wheat of ours at Marsh: ... 1s. 4d.

3. Mande: a carrying vessel.
4. From the 1650s, Quaker women met together separately from men for charitable purposes. The separate meetings became contentious in the 1670s.

1675 Jan the 14 To money received for 2 hoo of rye of Jenny Colton being part of that I bought of Robert Elletson of Stenerley for her ...

1s. 6d.

1675 Jan the 21 To money received of her more for 2 hoo of said rye ...

1s. 8d.

To money received of her more for 1 hoo of old wheat of ours at Marsh: ...

1s. 3d.

1674 Feb the 11 To money received of Jenny Colton in part of 3s. 4d. for 1p[eck?] of rye, that I bought for her of Robt Elletson of Stenerley ...

2s.

3.9   Single Southampton businesswoman: Elizabeth Wheeler, 1698–1702

Single women faced limited employment options in early modern English towns. Urban authorities preferred to have never-married women work as servants or live with their relatives, instead of working independently. This does not mean that single-women were incapable of working for themselves, but those who did so were usually of a mature age (at least 30 or 40) and of at least middling social status. One other factor helped single women establish their own businesses: family assistance, especially from female relatives. The Southampton singlewoman Elizabeth Wheeler received training and material assistance from her two spinster aunts, Jane and Alice Zains. Forgoing her father's trade of a cutler, Wheeler informally learnt her aunts' occupation of linen drapery and assisted them until Jane and then Alice Zains died. Wheeler inherited shop goods from her aunt Alice, as well as her aunt's position as a linen draper (and it seems her shop) in Southampton. Whereas most male and widowed traders paid an annual Stall and Art fee of 2d. to trade in Southampton, the Zains sisters paid twelve times as much, or 12s. a year. When their niece Elizabeth Wheeler took over their business in 1701 she paid the even heftier sum of £5. Despite this, the civic authorities challenged Wheeler's ability to work as a linen draper. Interestingly, Wheeler was the last singlewoman in eighteenth-century Southampton to have her right to trade questioned. After her, more than thirty single-women between 1700 and 1750 paid Stall and Art to work as shopkeepers, teachers, milliners, glovers, and even ironmongers. Wheeler's working history can be pieced together from a range of documents.

This document and its note supplied by Amy Froide.

Elizabeth Wheeler:

1. Southampton Record Office (hereafter SRO), 6/1/73 (1698) Court Leet records: Stall and Art Rolls.

All Saints Infra [parish of Southampton]:
Jane or Alice Zains – 2s.

2. Hampshire Record Office (hereafter HRO), 1701 A107 Will of Alice Zains, spinster (16 July 1701).

Item I give unto my cousin [niece] Elizabeth Wheeler all my household goods except which is hereinafter otherwise disposed of and in shop goods I give her the value of fifty pounds according to a just and reasonable appraisement.

3. SRO, SC 6/1/74 (1701) Court Leet records: Stall and Art Rolls.

All Saints Infra [parish of Southampton]:
Alice Zains – mortuus est
Elizabeth Wheeler £5

4. SRO, SC 9/1/63 July 1702) Southampton Quarter Sessions Rolls.

Recognizance:
Elizabeth Wheeler, Southampton spinster, bound in £10 to appear at next sessions and execute her traverse with effect and not depart the court without leave then this recognizance to be void.

Informations:
n.d.
Information of Rebecca, wife of John Lambert: says in the month of June last she bought of Elizabeth Wheeler in All Saints parish one yard of blue ditty.

3 July 1702:
Information of Ellis Antram, seargeant: says he went to warn Elizabeth Wheeler, spinster, to appear and went to the shop where Elizabeth was and told her to appear immediately and she told him she would do her own business first.

Recognizance: 4 July 1702:
Elizabeth Wheeler, spinster, bound in £40 with Robert Zains Southampton hatter – £20 John Wheeler Southampton cutler – £20 for Elizabeth to appear and answer and in mean time be of good behaviour.

Indictment of Elizabeth Wheeler, spinster 11 January [1702]:
[The spinster Elizabeth Wheeler is indicted for practising the trade of a linen draper in Southampton for the three months between April and July 1701, which is illegal since she never served a formal seven-year apprenticeship in this trade. She is found culpable for practising the trade of a linendraper for the one month after her aunt, Alice Zains, died, and is fined £2.]

88

3.10   Wet nursing for the gentry: Mary Page, 1639

Once married, women's employment opportunities were restricted by their child-care responsibilities and their domestic duties. Wetnursing had the advantage that married women could combine it with their own childcare and housekeeping. On the whole, the pay for such work was better than other female employment. Here a literate wetnurse responds to the request of Sir Simonds D'Ewes, a wealthy gentleman, to undertake the duty of suckling his wife's expected child. Although much contemporary literature abuses wetnurses as being neglectful of their charges, Mary Page's letter suggests a degree of commitment to the infants in her care.

Mary Page to Lady D'Ewes at London, 10 May 1639, BL, MS Harleian 386, fo. 182.

To the right worshipful the Lady D'Ewes give this I pray at London

Right Worshipful,

Good Madam I should be exceeding glad to see your Ladyship and that your Ladyship might see your little ones, which I thank God are both very well and merry. Sir Simonds write unto me to know if I could nurse your Ladyship another. I thank God I have my health and am well and have good store of milk, and if I continue so to be I am willing to nurse your Ladyship another. I would desire to know when your Ladyship does look you, because I would speak to a woman that does use to be with me at the first month to be with me again. If I do not speak to her betimes she will be promised to others. I delivered the letter to Mr Chamberlane privately. I pray God make thankful for the good news that was in it; it hath much comforted and joyed all our hearts that heard it, but if your Ladyship should not come to Stow that would grieve us. My husband and myself desire to remember our service to your Ladyship. My husband is willing I should nurse your Ladyship another. Yesterday my husband went to see Mrs Sissilia;[1] he saith she looks very hearty and well. I pray God your Ladyship may go your full time and give your Ladyship a safe and comfortable deliverance in due time. Desiring your Ladyship's prayers I rest

Your Ladyship's to command in all Christian duty

Mary Page.

3.11   Plague searchers: parish pensioners, 1592

The task of searching dead bodies to discover if the cause of death was the plague was hazardous work. Parishes usually required those poor people who were in receipt of parish relief to perform the job. The wage of 5s. weekly was better than for much other unskilled work, but the pay could be viewed as danger money.

E. Freshfield (ed.), *The Vestry Minute Book of the Parish of St Margaret Lothbury in the City of London, 1571–1677*, privately printed, London, Rixon and Arnold, 1887, p. 26.

---

1. Cecilia, daughter of D'Ewes.

At a vestry lawfully warned and holden the 24th day of September 1592. There was called before the parish, these persons hereafter following that have weekly pension out of the parish for their relief, To say, Axton's widow, Bristowe's widow, Jonne Abowen, Elizabeth Chaulkeley, Elizabeth Foxe, Ralph Brokefield his wife for her husband's pension, Katheren Crye, and Annys Tysse, and these being thus called to choose amongst them 2 persons to be the viewers of the dead corpses of such as should die in this parish, and to give true knowledge unto the clerk of such as should die of the plague. There was chosen Annis Tyse and Katheren Crye and they to take their oath before the deputy concerning that charge according to the order in that behalf provided, etc.

And for provision for the payment of the said 5s. a week to both our viewers, it is ordered that there shall be gathered of every man in the parish so much as they seized at in the collectors' scroll that is gathered for the hospital for one month, and to be gathered by Humphery Lydall and Jeames Hill, and delivered to the churchwardens, and they to pay it and be accountable for the same.

3.12   Lying-in services: Margaret Jackson, 1609

As an extension of their own housekeeping, many women made a living by taking in lodgers, or caring for children, the sick, or the old. Here a midwife provided the service of looking after mothers of illegitimate children when the man-midwife refused.

Bridewell Hospital Records, Guildhall Library, BCB 5 (microfilm), fo. 366, 19 July 1609.

Margaret Jackson brought in by warrant from my lord mayor. She is the midwife which the wife of the said John Barnes undertook last court day, to bring in. Examined, she saith she brought two women to bed at Barnes his house, and the child of the first lived about four days and then died and was not christened at all, but was buried at Stepney. That the last was still-born, and buried there also: She brought in one Helen Redgrave a widow dwelling in Fetter Lane, to testify that the last child was still-born, which Helen Redgrave accordingly testified, and that it was dead in the womb, a whole day before it was born. Further the said Redgrave saith she doth dwell in Fetter Lane, and there hath dwelt four years and that she was sent for to the travail of her that had the last child in the morning but did not come until about six of the clock at night and within two hours after her coming the woman was delivered (the man midwife having before been with her and had refused to undertake the business) and that the child was dead and black long before it was born.

She [Helen Redgrave] further saith she was the means to the said Margaret Jackson the midwife to place the said woman in some house where she might lie and be delivered of her said child, because, by means of the examinate's brother, the mother of the said child had helped the examinate to do business in her kitchen in the Terms[1] and had laid open herself to the examination and confessed to her that she was with child. The said midwife having formerly told the examinant . . . that there was many more people dwelling about her, and many escapes were there helped both of merchants' maids and others who were there delivered, and did well after. The said Margaret Jackson the midwife further examined denieth that she ever said any such matter to the said Redgrave. But saith the said Redgrave had a mischance in her house, one of the maids being gotten with child, whereupon the said Redgrave dealt with Mr John Hayes a neighbour of the examinate's to receive and harbour the said servant, who did so and her said servant being in travail was brought through London to Stepney to his house, when the examinate brought her to bed of a woman child which is yet living and christened at Stepney. And the said Redgrave and her brother gave bonds to discharge the parish of the child.

3.13 Prostitution in London: Frances Baker and Elizabeth Hoer, 1598–99

Elizabethan London saw a series of campaigns against prostitutes, bawds, and clients. The first case documents the hazards of sex-work. Elizabeth Hoer (was this truly her name?) was punished with a whipping and sent to St Thomas's hospital 'to be cured of the foul disease'. The second case suggests the importance of dress: in a society where social status was meant to be clearly marked by dress, the right clothes could be used to represent or impersonate gentility. The case also gives details of how women were moved to different places. Mrs Hibbens admitted her offence, and was ordered to pay £30 (a large sum) towards the relief of the poor, to depart from London before 24 June 1599, and to be of good behaviour. She had previously been ordered to leave the city at least once, nine or ten years earlier.

Bridewell Hospital Records, Guildhall Library, BCB 4 (microfilm), fos 46v., 64.

[11 Nov. 1598] Elizabeth Hoer being this day re-examined saith that about three quarters of a year now past, one Captain Pettfield brought her this examinant to Mistress White's house in Elbow Lane, and there the said Mistress White brought this examinant and the said Pettfield into her chamber and shut the door to them, and there the said Pettfield had the use of her body, and the said Mistress White had 12d. for her pains and she further saith that the said Mistress White told this examinant that she looked through the wall and saw the sayd Pettfield use the body of this examinant, and further saith that she did pay 3s. a week for her lodging besides her diet and that she was spoiled[2] in one Mistress Barlett's house in Duck Lane by a man whose name she knoweth not . . .

1. The law terms?
2. Probably, the loss of her virginity, but could also mean that she contracted the pox.

[Sat. 17 Feb. 1599] This day Frances Baker, late servant unto Mistress Holland dwelling at the Picket Hatch at the upper end of Aldersgate Street, sent into this hospital by the Treasurer of the said house by reason of the complaint of one Mr Bagnall grocer who dwelleth thereabouts. Being examined the day and year abovesaid, saith that during the time she did dwell with her mistress Holland, there did resort usually to her house young men which had the use of this examinant's body, and would give her sometimes two shillings and sometimes more and sometimes less, and would give her mistress for her pains sometimes 18d. and sometimes less. Their names she knoweth not but one whose name is Mr Bradley, a citizen, but where he dwelleth she knoweth not, but saith they were guests which did usually resort to her now house before she this examinant did dwell with her mistress, for that her mistress did usually keep a young wench before she came to dwell there. And she this examinant further saith that Mistress Hibbens dwelling near the Half Moon in Aldersgate Street did usually send for this examinant to the intent that divers should have the use of her body. And that a fortnight before Christmas last and at Christmas, the said Mistress Hibbens sent for this examinant at those two several times, at whose house there were two gentlemen which had the use of the body of this examinant, whereof one gave her five shillings and gave Mistress Hibbens money but how much it was she knoweth not and the other gentleman gave her nothing after he had the use of her body nor Mistress Hibbens, but fell out with her saying that Mrs Hibbens promised him four days before that she would provide him a gentlewoman and therefore he would give this examinant nothing. And she this examinant further saith that when she did usually send for this examinant to her house that gentlemen might use her body, the said Mistress Hibbens did cause this examinant to put off all her own apparel and put on one suit of apparel or other either silk, or silk rashe[2] or stuff gowns which she the said Mistress Hibbens thought good and put on a white holland smock with a durance[3] petticoat of two or three yards of velvet, and the cause why the gentleman aforesaid would give this examinant no money was because he knew the apparel which this examinant had on her back when he used her body to be the apparel of the said Mistress Hibbens. And further this examinant saith that the said Mistress Hibbens hath always lying in her house ready of her own divers suits of apparels for women viz. silk gowns of several colours as also silk rashe gowns and other stuff gowns, petticoats of durance with two or three yards of velvet as also smocks of holland,[4] and do use that when any gentlemen do come to her house and be desirous of gentlewomen, then she will send for such young wenches as she is acquainted withall, and will shift them from top to toe and put on such apparel as she thinketh the frankness of the gentlemen will be unto her, and

2. A kind of silk.
3. Stout durable cloth.
4. A linen fabric.

so doth in like sort when any other sorts of people do come to her house, she will array such wenches for them as she thinketh they will be in liberality towards her.

PROFESSIONS

3.14   Schoolteacher: Dorothy Traske, vegetarian, *c.* 1617

The information we have about Dorothy Traske comes from a hostile heresiographer. Dorothy Coome married John Traske in 1617. The couple were teachers. Both were imprisoned in Maidenlane prison for life in 1618 for Sabbatarian views (namely, that the day which the Lord commanded should be kept holy was Saturday, not Sunday). Although her husband recanted in 1620 and was released, Dorothy remained in prison. She kept herself by sweeping rooms and helping other prisoners, refusing alms even for her lame child. She was transferred to the Gatehouse prison in 1640, where she died in 1645. Ephraim Pagitt, whose *Heresiography* was first published in 1645, mentioned her briefly, but his account was expanded in the 1662 edition with a letter purporting to come from one whose child Dorothy Traske had taught to read, presumably before her imprisonment. The anonymous author provides a rare comment on one woman's methods of conducting her school. There is no evidence to suggest that Mrs Traske was licensed as a teacher (*Biographical Dictionary of British Radicals*, iii. 251–2).

Ephraim Pagitt, *Heresiography*, London, 1662, pp. 209–10.

She was a woman endued with many particular virtues, well worthy of the imitation of all good Christians, had not error in other things, and especially a spirit of strange unparalleled opinionativeness and obstinacy in her private concepts, spoiled her. She lived at Fleet bridge, and there taught children to read. She would teach them only five days in the week, for Saturday she would not teach them, because she esteemed that the Sabbath day; and upon Sunday (which is the Christian Sabbath) I suppose she durst not; and unless parents would cause their children to come precisely by seven of the clock in the morning, and send them their breakfasts at nine, she would not teach them. Her price was four pence a week, and under that she would not teach; yet if any of their parents were poor, she would oftentimes send them somewhat of the price back again; as she would likewise do at times when she thought that for some scholars she deserved not so much. This she professed to do out of conscience, as believing she must one day come to be judged for all things done in the flesh. Therefore she resolved to go *by the safest rule*, rather against than for her private interest. There was hardly any to be found that did equal her for speedy bringing of children to read. She taught a son of mine, who had only learned his letters in another place, at the age of four years or thereabouts, in the space of nine months, so that he was fit for Latin; into which he was then entered. She had a maid-servant of her own opinion, who helped her to teach; and their course was never to receive above their fixed number of children: So that by reason thereof, sometimes in two or three months space, a child could hardly be then admitted to their school.

... Her husband was prisoner with her at the same time in the same prison, yet she would not by any means be persuaded to bed with him, but left him to his chamber, and gat for her self a place, where she was penned up betwixt a few boards. Here she lay, till the Parliament, called November the third 1640, dissolved that prison, after which she was carried to the Gatehouse, where she continued until her death.

All the time of her imprisonment, notwithstanding whatever extremity, she would never either borrow or receive alms, saying it was a dishonour to God, whom she served, if she should do so: for God had promised his people, *thou shalt lend to many nations*, Deut[eronomy] 28.12, *and shalt not borrow*. She would *eat her own bread*, she said, meaning what she earned by sweeping some rooms of the prison, and helping some certain prisoners; which with an annuity of forty shillings at the most was all her maintenance. She eat no flesh, nor drank wine, but water only for many years together.

3.15 Working artist: Mary Beale, 1677

Mary Beale (1632–97) was born in Suffolk. She married Charles Beale and worked as a popular Restoration artist. Her husband's diary chronicles her work. Sir Peter Lely was a famous painter at this period. Mary Beale probably used the cast of her arms in alabaster when she painted her own self-portrait. (For an extract from Mary Beale's treatise on friendship, see 8.13.)

Diary of Charles Beale, husband of artist Mary Beale, on blank pages in William Lilley almanack book, Bodl., MS 8 Rawlinson 572.

6 January 1677   Mr Lely was at our house together with Mr Ulemberg to see us, and upon showing him Mrs Clarke's, Dr Pselk's last, Miss Russell's, 2 Monsieur Counsellor Bat's pictures upon the 3 quarters cloth, the lord Falconbridge's, Mrs Stillingfleet's, Sir William Turner's, and the nameless gentlewoman's pictures, he told me that Mrs Beale was very much improved in her painting. We showed him also some of the hands we had cast in alabaster (especially many of those of my dearest heart's in various postures which are cast up to the elbows), and he was very much pleased with them and would hardly believe we could cast them so curiously ourselves.

30 January 1677   My Dearest Heart painted Sir William Turner's picture from head to foot for our worthy and kind friend Mr Knollys, in consideration of his most obliging kindness to us upon all occasions. He gave it to be set up in the hall at Bridewell, Sir William Turner having been chosen president of that House, in the year he was Lord Mayor of London ...

20 August 1677 My Dearest Heart painted upon square Sir John Lowther's picture a second time. Finished the face and breast of Mrs Fanshaw's picture at the fourth sitting. And dead coloured[1] Mr Jolivet's picture.

3.16 Application for surgeon's licence: Margaret Neale, 1691

Licences for midwifery, surgery, and schoolteaching were granted by the ecclesi-astical authorities. Because the boundary between licensed and unlicensed practice was blurred, women found it difficult to sustain an occupational identity. Although many middling and wealthier women undertook the care of the health of their poorer neighbours, those licensed by the ecclesiastical authorities to practise surgery were few. In these two documents, Margaret Neale, a single woman in Norfolk, presented the supporting testimonials to obtain her licence.

Licensing Papers, Norfolk RO, TES 8.

Sept. 2 1691

These are to certify that Margaret Neale, born and bred in Reepham, an industrious maid and of sober conversation, by the instructions of an artist in surgery and by her own practice (with good success) hath attained to much expertness in blood-letting (having bled many gratis) as also dextrous-ness[2] in pulling out teeth, and is reasonably well versed in dressing and healing all sort of common and ordinary sores, pain, cuts, wounding and ailments belong to the art of surgery; and we do hereby recommend her to the favour of the court, for a license ad practicandum, she likely to do much good among her neighbours and to other that will have recourse unto her.

Charles Rowbotham BD and rector of Reepham,
[& 15 other male signatories]

[To] Mr Welsh, the Register within the close near the Cathedral in Norwich

Sir, the bearer hereof (Margaret Neale) hath attained to a faculty of blood letting, and pulling of teeth, and something of surgical cures, by which she may be very beneficial to her neighbours. And though she hath performed much hitherto gratis yet for her better security for any peevish disturbance, she desires to be put into a legal capacity by a license, and eatemus practi-candum; I desire therefore you would please to afford her your favour. She is and hath been my servant for divers years, her father hath been a man of some fame but now fallen to decay. What favour you shall please to her, will

1. Dead colouring is a stage in the preparation of a painting that involves sketching out of the final composition in monochrome shades.
2. Dexterity.

much oblige her, and shall after be acknowledged by your respectful friend and servant,
Charles Rowbotham,
Reepham, 27 Nov. 1691 [seal]
She hath a testimonial subscribed by some clergy and some lay.

3.17 Application for midwife's licence: Mary Cooper, 1695

Applications to practise legally as a midwife required a licence of the ecclesiastical authorities. Some testimonials referred to the woman's training and skill, but those here supporting the application of Mary Cooper stressed her qualities as a good, pious woman.

Wellcome, MS 3544, no. 4.

To the worshipful Charles Baldwin, Esq, Doctor of Laws, his Majesty's Chancellor for the diocese of Hereford
We whose names are hereunto subscribed do humbly certify that Mary, the wife of Langley Cooper of the parish of Liddom, is a woman of good life and conversation, descended of pious and religious parents, well instructed both in learning and religion, a constant frequenter of the church, and one that bringeth up her children in the fear of God, a peaceable and quiet neighbour, and one (to our knowledge) who hath good skill and fit to be employed in the office of a midwife. In testimony whereof we have hereunto set our hands the first day of May in the sixth year of the reign of our sovereign lord King William the third over England, A.D. 1695.
[signed] Mary Meredith, Grace Speak, Jane Powell, Hanah Manning, Mary Powell, Margaret Sankey

7 April 1695
[Licence granted] C. Baldwin

3.18 A London midwife's receipts, 1702

An anonymous London midwife kept a record for twenty-two years of the babies she delivered and the payments she received. The fees varied according to the social status of the mother, ranging from two shillings and six pence to £6.19s.0d. At the rate of two or three deliveries a month, she was not working full-time as a midwife, and may either have had other work or other means of support. The record for the old style year, 1702 has been transcribed from 25 March onwards, starting at Lady Day. Contrary to historians' beliefs that a number of midwives attended each birth, there is no evidence that other midwives were present at the deliveries.

Diary of a London midwife, December 1694 to 11 May 1716, Bodl., MS Rawlinson D1141, fos 45–49v.

1702 March the 27 laid Mrs Richards in Whitechapel of a son being Friday between 3 and 4 in the morning. 2s.

March the 31 1702 laid Mrs Twine on Fish Street Hill on a Tuesday morning a little before three given £2.3.0.

Laid Mrs Jeland in Old Street of a daughter being the 20 day of April about 7 in the morning being Monday 1702. Given me 10s.

April the 22 1702 laid Mrs Rose in the Minories of a son on a Wednesday at 8 of the clock at night. 7s 6d. Given by the gossips 4s 2d.

April the 24 1702 laid Mrs Broome of a son the 24 being Friday about a quarter before 12 at night. 15s.

May the 10 day laid Mrs Fell in Goodmans Fields of a daughter on a Sunday at night being about 8 of the clock. Given me 10s.

May the 14 1702 laid Mrs Jackson of a daughter in Miles's Lane on a Thursday about 8 of the clock at night. 10s. 9d.

May the 18 day 1702 laid Mrs Stuens of a daughter on a Monday morning about 7 of the clock. 10s.

June the 26th 1702 Laid Mrs Bagg of a son being of a Friday at night at 9 of the clock. Given me 10s.

July the 9 day 1702 laid Mrs Marksbridge of a son being Thursday a little after 5 in the morning in red cross street in ship yard over against Jewin street. 5s.

Laid Mrs Burton in St Katherine's Hospital Tower Hill of a daughter the 21 of July being on a Tuesday morning a little after 2 of the clock 1702. Given me 10s 9d.

July the 29 1702 laid Mrs Starnd by London Wall of a son of a Wednesday about one of the clock in the day. Given me 8s.

August the 8 day laid Mrs Too in Tasy [?] lane of a son being Wednesday a quarter before twelve in the forenoon. Given me £1. 8. 6.

Laid Mrs Gale in Redriffe of a son the 4 day of September being on a Tuesday about 12 of the clock in the forenoon. 10s.

Laid Mrs Coock in Sun Court of a daughter between 11 and 12 of the clock being Wednesday the 16 of September 1702. Given me £2.0.0.

September the 3 day at 11 of the clock at night being Wednesday 1702 laid Madam Legg. Given £1.1.6.

October the 4 1702 laid Mrs Jons of a son being on a Wednesday night half an hour after 8 of the clock in Worely's Court in Holborn. Given me £1.0.0.

Laid Madam Yonge of a son the 10 of September given me £2. 5. 0.

Mrs Burin gave me 5s Oct the 28 1702.

Laid Mrs Littel of a son being Wednesday. Given 10s.

Laid the bakers wife in St Martins of a daughter on the 6 of November being on a Friday morning about 5 of the clock 1702. Given me 7s. 6d.

Laid Mrs Foulde on the 2 day of November 1702 being on a Monday morning about 11 of the clock. Given me £1. 0. 0.

Laid Mrs Litell of a son the 28 of October being on a tuesday morning. Given me 7s. 6d.

January the 5 1702 laid Madam Preson of a daughter being on a Tuesday at night half hour after 12. £2. 0. 0.

January the 12 day laid Mrs Heal in Fox Court in Gray's Inn Lane of a son being on a Tuesday between 7 and 8 of the clock at night. Given me £1. 5. 0.

Laid Mrs Hakins in Scalding Alley in the Poultry of a son being the 13 of January 1702 on a Wednesday night a little after 6 of the clock. Given me 5s.

Laid Mrs French in Smithfield of a son the 19 day of January being on a Tuesday between 11 and 12 of the clock at noon. 5s.

January 25 laid Mrs Shepard in the Minories of a son on a Monday at 2 of the clock in the afternoon.

[In the remainder of the year, she delivered 7 more babies.]

3.19   Inventing her own work identity: Hannah Wolley, 1674

Some women created new work roles. Hannah Wolley (see 1.10) turned her traditional female skills into an occupation for herself. Like many other married women, she was part of a team, acting as a matron in the Free-school of which her husband was the master.

Hannah Wolley, *A Supplement to the Queene-Like Closet*, London 1674 (bound with *The Queene-Like Closet*), London, 1675, pp. 10, 12, 13, 16, 61.

I have spoken enough concerning your clothes, and face and hands; now I will give you direction for to be your own chirurgeons and physicians, unless the case be desperate: but before I begin to teach, be pleased to take notice of what cures I have done, that you may be assured of my ability.

First, take notice that my mother and my elder sisters were very well skilled in physic and chirurgery, from whom I learned a little, and at the age of seventeen I had the fortune to belong to a noble lady in this kingdom, till I married, which was at twenty four years (those seven years I was with her) she finding my genius, and being of a charitable temper to do good amongst her poor neighbours, I had her purse at command to buy what ingredients might be required to make balsams, salves, ointments, waters for wounds, oils, cordials and the like; besides she procured such knowledge for me from her physicians and chirurgeons (who were the best that all England could afford) and also bought many books for me to read, that in short time, with the help of those worthy men before mentioned, I soon became a practitioner, and did begin with cut fingers, bruises, aches, agues, head-ache, bleeding at the nose, felons, whitlows on the fingers, sore eyes, drawing of blisters, burnings, tooth-ache, and any thing which is commonly incident; and in all those cures God was pleased to give me good success.

When I was about the age of two and twenty years, I was sent by this noble lady to a woman in hard labour of child, who being quite wearied out with her pains, she fell into strong convulsion fits, which greatly endangered both herself and her child; but by God's help those remedies which I gave her caused her fits to cease, and a safe delivery followed . . .

When I was married to Mr. Wolley, we lived together at Newport Pond in Essex near Saffron Walden seven years; my husband having been master of that Free-school fourteen years before; we having many boarders my skill was often exercised amongst them, for oftentimes they got mishaps when they were playing, and oftentimes fell into distempers; as agues, fevers, measles, small-pox, consumptions, and many other diseases; in all which, unless they were desperately ill, their parents trusted me without the help of any physician or chirurgeon: likewise the neighbours in eight or ten miles round came to me for cure.

A woman who had had a sore leg one and twenty years I quite cured.

Another being kicked by a churlish husband on her leg, so that a vein was burst, whereby she lost at the least a pottle[1] of blood; I stayed the blood and cured her leg.

A young maid as she was cutting sticks with an axe, by chance cut her leg sorely, she having long time been afflicted with the green-sickness and dropsy; I not only cured her leg, but also her other distempers at the same time . . .

A gentleman having got a bruise on his leg by the lash of a whip, and being in a desperate condition with it, so that he was in danger of his life, I in a competent time did cure.

Many of the convulsion-fits, and rickets among children I did cure.

One being bitten with a mad-dog, I in very short time did cure him.

Several women who had sore breasts and sore nipples, I cured.

Many who had violent fits of the stone, I eased them.

A man being much bruised with the fall of a cart upon him, I cured.

One being much bruised by rogues meeting him on the way, and after they had beaten him down, kicked him on one side of his head, so that his ear was swelled you could see no shape it had, and withal fell into a fever: I, by God's help did cure.

A woman who for divers months had a very great flux upon her, I speedily cured.

A man lying sick of the measles, and being all struck in, so that it was thought he could not possibly have lived, I gave him a cordial which brought them forth again and recovered him . . .

I cured a man-servant to a gentleman, who had a sore leg by a fall from an high place, and it was grown so dangerous, that it was thought incurable.

---

1. A measure equal to half a gallon.

I cured a bricklayer who had a sore leg by the fall of timber, and because he was poor his chirurgeon gave it over.

I cured a shoe-maker of a sore leg, who had spent three pounds on it before he came to me.

I cured a poor woman of a sore leg, who was advised by a chirurgeon to have it cut off . . .

The green-sickness in many, dropsy, jaundices, scurvy, sciatica, griping of the guts, vomiting and looseness.

And for the palsy, whether dead or shaking, I am sure none can give better remedies, nor know it better than I do, having bought my experience at a dear rate; there is none who have been more afflicted with it than my self, and (I humbly bless God for it) there is no person more freer from it than my self, nor from any other disease, and that is very much, I being now in my two and fiftieth year . . .

I have set down every thing as plain as I can; and I know there are many who have done things very well by my books only: but you may imagine that if you did learn a little by sight of my doing, you would do much better; for if my pen can teach you well, how much better would my tongue and hands do? The one to make answer to any objection or question; the other to order or to shape any thing. So that in my opinion you would not lose by having some personal acquaintance with me; neither would I willingly lose my time and labour in informing you: therefore I beseech you let it be thus;

Be pleased to afford me some of your money, and I will repay you with my pains and skill. That I judge to be fair on both sides.

RUNNING A HOUSEHOLD: DOMESTIC TASKS

3.20   To scour sarcenet hoods: Mary Chantrell and others, 1690

Housewifery occupied women's time and labour. At the upper levels of society, where material goods were more extensive, the tasks were more specialised.

Mary Chantrell [and others], Book of Receipts, 1690 (unfoliated), Wellcome, MS 1548.

To scour sarcenet[1] hoods

If they be very foul lap them together and put them in cold water and soap them well and rub them well, then lay them on your board very smooth, and soap them well, with an indifferent hard brush and water, scour the

1. A very fine soft silk material.

Figure 6 Hannah Wolley, *The Queene-Like Closet*, frontispiece
By permission of the British Library

The frontispiece of Hannah Wolley's work of domestic advice, published in 1670, pictured middling-status women and their servants at work in the kitchen. Many household tasks would have increased in volume and complexity in the seventeenth century, as households accumulated more consumer goods.

same way that the selvedge goes, putting water on as your rub, when they are clean, rinse the first time in warm water, with a little blue, and then in cold. Wipe your board dry, and wash your sponge and wring it dry, then lay your hood on the board again very smooth and with the sponge dry up the way and sprinkle in your isinglass,[1] and rub it well on, and make them very stiff, let them hang on the line till half dry, then hold them over the smoke of brimstone, let them not be over dry before you glaze them, your iron must be pretty hot, always take care you hold your left hand stretching the silk the same way that the selvedge goes.

The woman as gave these two receipts I knowed her to get the greatest part of her bread by them in London a great part of her life ...

This last receipt of washing sarcenet hoods I learned to wash them myself: it's a very good way and they look as well as any new hoods when they are done.

3.21   To whiten clothes: Rose Kendall and Ann Cater, 1682

In many families, women kept books of domestic and medical advice, and passed them to their female descendants. This book, inscribed 'Rose Kendall and Ann Cater their book 1682', was in 1725 inscribed with the name of Anna Maria Wentworth.

Folger, MS V. a. 429, fo. 17.

To whiten cloth

Lady Sillyard's
In June which is the best time lay your flaxen cloths in hot water. Let it lie in that water 2 or 3 days then beat it out of that water and rinse it well in cold water. Lay it abroad but do not water it unless it rain then take it out in a nights and put it in fresh water and when it hath lain a week then buck[2] it [and] so do every week. If your cloth be fine you may betwixt your bucks give it a lather of soap or two. Lay it abroad in your suds without rinsing. When it is white enough give it lather of soap and rinse it in blue water. Lay it abroad and as it dries, wet it with your blue water while [till?] it be all spent then order it as you please.

3.22   To wash lace: Constance Hall, 1672

Lace-making employed many women in seventeenth-century England. The care of hand-made lace, or point, was time-consuming and painstaking. Here Constance Hall included in her book of receipts her instructions for the laundering of lace. She may well have instructed a servant in the task.

Constance Hall her Booke of Receipts 1672, Folger, MS V. a. 20, unfoliated.

1. A firm whitish substance, a comparatively pure form of gelatin.
2. Bleach.

To wash point

Take your point and soap it on the right side. Let it lie in water all night. Warm your suds and wash it out of it. Make a lather. Wash it well out of it. If it be yellow, lay it on the grass a night or 2. First boil it and put it to some cold water. If you see it not white then set it to whiten. Give it a lather. Run it with water that has no blue. After that run it in blue water that is made with stone blue. Starch it with Holland. Starch it on the wrong side. Lay it on a cloth. A little dry it in your hand. Pull it as even as you can. Let it not be too dry nor too wet. Iron it not with too hot an iron. Let the cloth be pretty thick that it is iron on. If the point be high raised take the gloss off with a dry cloth rub it pick every pearl in his place.

3.23   'My sister's way to make mead': Rose Kendall and Ann Cater, 1682

Larger households were productive units, and women's labour provided much of the food and drink.

'Rose Kendall and Ann Cater their book 1682', Folger, MS V. a. 429, fo. 33.

My sister's way to make mead.

To every gallon of water put 2 pennyworth of honey. Mix the honey and water well together cold, then boil and skim it as long as any will rise, and in the boiling take a sprig of rosemary and 2 or 3 sprigs of sweet briar. Hold it in your hand and stir it round till it has 3 or 4 boils, then put it into a tub fit for it with the rinds of 2 lemons and the juice. And when your liquor is almost cold, spread a toast or two with good ale yeast and put to it and the next day put it into a vessel that will just hold it. You may tie a few cloves and mace in a rag and put it in the vessel, and the whites of 6 eggs beat. You may put in primrose flowers or cowslip. It will be ready to bottle in 10 days.

3.24   Lemon delicious pudding: Mrs Meade, late seventeenth century

Literate women copied recipes into their books, and exchanged them among their relatives and friends. The following is one of many from the book of Mrs Meade and others, 1688–1727. In the same book, Meade included veterinary remedies.

Wellcome, MS 3500.

To make a lemon pudding

Take eight eggs. Leave out the whites of three of them. Put to them half a pound of beaten sugar. Grate in the peel of three lemons and squeeze in the juice. Beat them well together and just before you set into the oven pour into it a quarter of pound of melted butter, beating the pudding while you pour it into the dish. If in a quick oven, half an hour will bake it.

4

POVERTY AND PROPERTY

Economic documents are some of the fullest sources we have for early modern women, yet they are also amongst the most problematic. Only a small proportion of women had sufficient property for it to be recorded in marriage settlements, wills, or inventories. The economic life of those without property is often revealed only in times of great need, through the medium of officers of the parish and the law. And for women of all social statuses, marriage was legally understood to remove much of their right to hold and use their own property.

A large proportion of the female population were poor. Poverty is hard to measure, but it has been estimated that at any one time, half the female population could be described as poor, and that two-thirds probably experienced poverty at some point.[1] Poverty could be permanent, with many children born into poverty and remaining poor; or it could be a lifecycle condition, with women falling into poverty through misfortunes, illness, or widowhood. Old age made women even more likely to become indigent. The working practices of poor women are described in Chapter 3; women without work turned to forms of relief and to a makeshift, marginal economy of expedients. Women were the majority of those receiving poor relief. The Poor Law of 1601 provided for regular support of the poor from rates collected by the parish, in the form either of occasional aid or weekly payments. The parish might also provide women with a dwelling, with food or with fuel, and it might make arrangements for poor women to work for their relief. Most such arrangements were made locally, by churchwardens, overseers of the poor, or vestry meetings, but appeals were also made to the quarter sessions, who were empowered to order local overseers to help. Parishes, hospitals, and guilds also administered private bequests to the poor, sometimes of money, sometimes of fuel or food. Most informally, alms might be given at the door, in the street or in the fields. However, poor relief was dependent on reputation. Petitions constructed narratives to show worthiness, hard work, and misfortune; women considered not to be honest, respectable, or chaste would be unlikely to receive relief. The only other means of support were on the margins of the law or outside it. Expedients for survival for poor women included such activities as grazing on others' land, milking others' animals, taking eggs, or shearing sheep; in towns, taking employers' clothes or small sums of money.

In some areas women also constituted a third or more of those arrested as vagrants. Some were travelling to find work, others to escape from, or to be reunited with, husbands. Some were forced or expected to abandon their children. Vagrancy was a crime, but it was also a trap from which it was hard to escape: parishes moved vagrants on before they could achieve a legal settlement (which took a year to establish, reduced to forty days in 1662). Poor single mothers or mothers-to-be were likely to be a particular anxiety.

Even the poor had property. In an economy where moveable goods and clothes were very valuable, property such as petticoats, lace, working tools, or cooking utensils were passed on or inherited. In marriage, women passed their ownership of all property to their husbands. Nevertheless, married women often had a very clear sense of the ownership of goods, and made sure that their husbands knew what arrangements they desired. Gentlewomen had estates and incomes to plan for, and property law offered a few ways (such as pin money, or the provision of a separate estate) through which women retained an independent income or estate. Women with much less might mark the household goods they brought into marriage, or keep them in their own chests.

Only a few women, most of them widows and spinsters, made wills, or had their goods inventoried after their deaths; the majority either did not leave enough goods for them to be valued, or their estates were not differentiated from their husbands'. Nevertheless, wills and probate inventories provide an enormous range of economic and social evidence. Women's wills, made for different reasons from their husband's, fulfilled different functions, serving (for example) to register neighbourhood relationships and honour a different series of family ties. They also testify to the place women, particularly spinsters and widows, occupied in families, local societies and economies. Spinsters might leave money to other single women in need, or to sisters and nieces; some widows left records of the numerous small-scale loans that made them central to local economies.

Both single and married women at a wide range of social levels demonstrated significant investment in personal property. Clothes lasted a long time and might be inherited more than once: when stolen, they might be recognised by personal lace patterns or individual touches. Other material goods were bequeathed with care and thought: women's wills recognise a wider range of legatees than men's, with goods of less value. As consumption patterns changed in the late seventeenth century, middling status and gentry women were prominent in the development of new markets for clothes and ornaments.

At the same time, women's relationship to their property was becoming more rigidly regulated by marital property law. The right to 'reasonable parts', which entitled a widow to one-third of her husband's moveable goods, had already been abolished in the Southern Province by 1600; in the Northern Province it was abolished between 1692 and 1725. Those widows whose husbands had not made wills found, from 1670, that the probate courts enforced their restriction to a third of their husband's goods more severely.[2] Widows' rights to their husbands' estates, and the freedom with which some of the courts which dealt with inheritance matters had interpreted them, were eroded. At the same time, the age of first marriage was also falling, and the value of moveable goods which women were likely to inherit rather than land was decreasing. The late seventeenth century saw female economic independence become even harder to attain. Nevertheless, the private arrangements by which wives and husbands, daughters, and parents, and siblings negotiated their own economic positions remain largely invisible to us.

MAKING SHIFT

4.1 Service and petty theft: Elisabeth Brand, 1621

Elisabeth Brand's examination at the Essex Quarter Sessions in 1621, when she was suspected of theft, records some of the employment and financial transactions of one servant. Her services are often temporary and casual; she 'places herself'; and her informal contract involves not just pay, but the theft of portable goods from her mistress, not to sell but to wear herself.

Essex Quarter Sessions Bundles, Essex RO, Q/SBa2/2.

The examination of Elisabeth Brand of Barking . . . the 7th day of October 1621

This examinant she saith that she was born at Barford in Oxfordshire and served one Mr John Collins of the said town for three years last past and about six months since she came to London, where she placed her self with one goodwife Parker a buttonmaker near the spital[1] in Bishopsgate Street, who as she saith did take away all her apparel and turned her out of doors, and then she came to Barking to seek a service and was there received upon liking by the wife of Peter Debett of Barking fisherman upon Wednesday being the third day of this month, and the next morning about seven of the clock her dame sent her forth to one Daniell Overell's house in Barking for 4d. of broom and the said Elisabeth Brand went accordingly, but did take with her one petticoat of cloth of her dame's feloniously being worth 10s. and put it upon her body which when the said Overell perceived he did apprehend her and did bring her back again to her dame who presently committed her to the constable's charge as a felon.

4.2 Stealing clothes: Elizabeth Warde, 1635

Elizabeth Warde was in service with a relative. It was not uncommon for servants to augment their wages with petty theft from the household, and some employers seem to have tacitly recognised such thefts as supplements to meagre wages. However, in the eyes of the law, the violation of trust and obedience involved in

1. Hospital.

opportunistic theft by a household member might make it a particularly serious offence. Elizabeth's examination also indicates the existence of connections and networks by which stolen goods could be sold. Elizabeth confessed her guilt and was ordered to be whipped.

Staffordshire Quarter Sessions Rolls, Staffordshire RO, Q/SR 220/74 (5 Oct. 1635).

The examination of Elizabeth Warde late servant to John Baggely of Staffordshire glasier . . .

Who saith that she served the said Baggely a quarter of a year, and confesseth that upon Sunday night last being the fifth of this present October she took away out of the parlour there one old waistcoat one petticoat two old bands[1] and one apron with other things, which she saith she took for want of clothes, having but eight shillings a year wages, and being further asked where she intended to carry them she saith to Chester, to an aunt that she hath there whose name is Elline Baggely and more she saith not.

4.3 Pawning goods: Elizabeth Stevens, 1695

Elizabeth Stevens' want of money drove her to a neighbour to pawn a brass kettle; her neighbour's advice reveals some of the possibilities for petty theft, and of the unwritten rules that decreed what was acceptable and what was not.

Staffordshire Quarter Sessions Rolls, Staffordshire RO, Q/SR 196/4 (23 July 1695).

Information of Elizabeth Stevens of the parish of East Coker . . .

Who upon oath saith that about three weeks since this informant [came] to one Elener Daniell of the said parish of East Coker and desired her to take a brass kettle in lieu of one shilling and eight pence which this informant desired the said Elener Daniell to spare her. But the said Elener Daniell would spare her but one shilling and four pence upon the said kettle and the said Elener Daniell told this informant that her husband might go to one Mr Mitchell of Aurington and steal away a dozen and half of yarn and bring it her and she and her son would spool it up, and told this deponent that after the yarn was spooled up the devil could not know it again and further told this informant they were fooled if they would want as long as they could have it, and that they should not steal any from any of their own parish and further saith not.

1. Collar-bands.

4.4   Vagrancy: Elizabeth Tucker, 1608

Elizabeth Tucker was examined by the Somerset Quarter Sessions on a charge of vagrancy: like so many, her examination records a detailed history of her movements and how she lived.

Somerset Quarter Sessions Rolls, Somerset Archives, Q/SR 13/1/52 (Aug. 1608).

Elizabeth Tucker, late of North Cheriton within the County of Devon, examined . . .

Saith that about Wednesday last was a month she came from North Cheriton aforesaid and travelled unto Fowey in Cornwall to a kinsman of hers called William Crase where she stayed about seven nights and from there came to Bodmin where she lodged that night. The Wednesday or Thursday following she met with John Crasman at a mill near Mr Arthur Harris his house some three or four miles from Torrington and so kept company together with him the space of three weeks wandering up and down the county begging, until on Wednesday late they both came to Dulverton in which place they lay that night at a tithingman's[1] house whose name she knoweth not. The Thursday morning about ten of the clock the same Crasman leaving her (as she saith) she went unto Dunster where she lodged that night at a poor woman's house there and the Friday about ten of the clock in the forenoon she met with the said Crasman again in Dunster where she sold a pair of shoes unto a man whose name she knoweth not for 7d. and bought a new pair of shoes of the woman at whose house she lodged as before, and about sun setting she departed with the said Crasman towards Brompton Regis near which place they lodged that night (as she saith) in a meadow and the Saturday following she travelling towards Dulverton about two or three of the clock in the afternoon, was apprehended in Brompton Regis aforesaid but denieth that she was in the house of Ambrose Langdon there or that she hid any clothes in a brake of furze near his house [as] confessed by the said Crasman or did steal the shoes which she sold at Dunster.

POVERTY AND RELIEF

4.5   Managing poverty: the Braintree 'Company of Four and Twenty', 1619–24

The majority of poor relief was organised at parish level, through the poor rates, the overseers of the poor, and occasionally, as in Braintree in Essex, through vestry and similar local groups. The Four-and-Twenty was a select vestry meeting of twenty-four substantial male parishioners, which met monthly, usually over a dinner, to discuss parish business of disorder, poverty, and poor relief. These selections are

1. A kind of constable.

from their minute book and include all those referring to women (except tangentially) for the years 1619–24. Through these minutes, we can trace the ways in which women's poverty was dealt with at the most local level. Here, poor relief involved both co-operation and conflict, negotiation with the poor, and confrontation with the troublesome. Women were heavily involved in the operation of the whole system. Over this five-year period we get some sense, too, of the microeconomic changes of households and individuals, as women move in or out of almshouses or claim more relief.

Minutes of the 'Company of the Four-and-Twenty', Braintree Parish Records, Essex RO, D/P 264/8/3, fos 3v–33 (extracts).

August 2 1619   Imprimis[1] at this meeting it was agreed that the widow Browne and her son if she do live and recover shall be removed to the almshouse at Braintree bridge, where we the last day did appoint Eliot should be.

September 6 1619   Imprimis order was taken at this meeting that Anne Gay shall be warned with all speed to provide her a service, or else that she shall be sent to the house of correction. . . .

Item notice is given us by William Stebbing of a wench entertained at John Beckwith's dwelling on Cursing Green, that is supposed to have a great belly; which the constables have warning to look after, and to take order to remove her if they find the report to be true.

February 8 1620   Imprimis it was agreed that Widow Gay be placed in the almshouse with Howell, and the widow Coe shall be put into the house where she is.

September 4 1620   Imprimis it was agreed that Anne Hill's house shall be mended that it may not rain in by the churchwardens. . . .

It is further agreed that the business touching Margery Eagle's money now resting in Gervase Bradshawe's hands shall be finished the next court day which shall be the last Saturday of this present month.

November 6 1620   Item at this meeting the binding of Elizabeth Linwood the daughter of John Linwood with Henry Meade of Fairstead his wife tailor for the term of ten years is approved by the townsmen.

February 5 1621 [On the disposition of five shillings which had been received from the constables for the use of the poor]   It was agreed that Richard Loveday shall have two shillings of this money, in regard of the extraordinary charge he hath been at for the washing of his wife being lame.

It is agreed that the widow Gay shall have 12d. of the said money for pains taken with the widow Eliot and that for the time to come she shall

1. Firstly.

have 6d. a week for attendance given upon the said widow, during the time the overseers shall think fit.

Item it is agreed that Margery Pierson shall be provided of an almshouse at the discretion of the overseers, because she is helpful woman at their request to those that are sick. . . .

Item the other 12d. was given to the widow Boltwood.

March 5 1621   It is agreed that the widow Coe shall be provided of an almshouse in the Hyde at the discretion of the overseers and that the widow Gay shall be displaced out of the almshouse.

October 8 1621   Item it is agreed that the widow Boltwood shall have 2s. 6d. allowed her out of the poor man's box and that she shall have an almshouse offered her which if she refuse she shall have no more allowance.

November 5 1621   Imprimis it was agreed that Widow Ingram's boy that should be taken from her and put into the hospital and that she being incorrigible in her idle and vicious course that she shall be sent to the house of correction.

December 3 1621   Imprimis it was agreed that Richard Loveday shall be allowed out of the poor man's box to pay the widow Gay for the washing of him and his wife and further the widow Gay shall during her continuance in the almshouse wash them freely in consideration of her dwelling. . . .

It is further agreed that the widow Elyot and the widow Randall shall have 18d. a week allowed them during the time of their weakness or what else the overseers for the poor shall see their present necessity require for the winter.

January 7 1622   Item it is agreed that the widow Whitehead shall have 6d. a week allowed by the collectors, and continue released of all other town charges. . . .

Item it is agreed that Scott's wife shall have some allowance for her attendance upon the widow Randall, at the discretion of the overseers.

Item it is agreed that Johnson's wife shall be for the wintertime in the Almshouse in the Hyde that's empty.

February 4 1622   Imprimis it was agreed that forsomuch as the widow Whitehead is grown so aged and feeble, as to do nothing towards the earning of her living, that her son shall have 12d. a week allowed by the town, towards the keeping of her.

March 4 1622   Item Robert Whaples doth inform that the wiredrawer's wife is still at Arthur Harris his house.

Item it is agreed that the widow Wallinger shall be allowed 4d. a week by the overseers.

It is agreed that Jeremy Whaple's wife, during the time of his sickness shall be weekly allowed towards her charge 3s. a week or more if they see cause.

Item it is agreed that Richard Tophand's wife shall have ten shillings given her to supply her want in her present necessity whereof 5s. shall be allowed by the overseers, and the other 5s. shall be taken out of the poor man's box.

April 1 1622 Imprimis it is agreed that the widow Wallinger shall have 6d. a week allowed her by the overseers.

Memorandum that Robert Preston's wife had now warning: to remove one Richard a married man, coming from Chelmsford, that lodges there and may be chargeable to the parish.

May 6 1622   Item it is agreed the widow Coe shall go into the almshouse out of which the widow Eliot died.

July 8 1622   Item it is agreed that the widow Whaples shall be allowed 20s. by the overseers for the poor towards her rent upon that condition that she hereafter shall be not further chargeable; nor keep any alehouse.

Item it is agreed that the widow Randall shall have half a load of wood allowed her by the overseers.

December 2 1622   Item Margery Carter is presently to be sent to the house of correction if she get no service before the holy days.

January 6 1623 Item it is agreed that the youngest child of Howard shall be continued with Ferdinand Brook's wife, and that she shall have allowance of 20d. a week for the nursing thereof.

Item it is agreed that Tophand's wife shall have five shillings lent her by the overseers.

February 3 1623   It is agreed that Carter's daughter that's out of service and now keeps at Adam Ward's and the sister of Bradey that married Casse's daughter shall by the justice's warrant the next Wednesday be sent to the house of correction.

December the first 1623   Item that Palmer is required to send his daughter back again to Colchester to her former service, which Palmer hath promised presently to do.

February 2 1624   Item at this meeting Widow Boltwood had 6d. given her by the churchwardens and she hath once again an almshouse offered her. It is agreed that Mason's wife shall have a quarter's rent given her because her child hath been long sick.

March 1 1624   Item notice is given of one Grace that's out of service that keeps at Little's of Bocking that was seen privately in a chamber locked up with Joseph Pullin.

April 5 1624   It is agreed that the overseers for the poor shall hire Halle's house at the further end of the town and so many Crosier's houses as are to be let for the use of our poor and that the widow Beckwith shall be placed in one of them.

May 3 1624   Imprimis it's agreed that the widow Whaples shall have 20s. towards the payment of her rent.

September 7 1624   Imprimis at this meeting Tibell's wife making complaint that she hath been at extraordinary charge and pains by reason of the infection of the smallpox that hath been in her house and other trouble with Richardson that is very diseased that she shall have another straw bed allowed by the overseers, and a pair of sheets and that she shall be allowed 6d. a week for the washing of him[2] and further that the overseers shall take an inventory of all the goods that are the town's in Tibball's house . . . .

Item Dean's wife complained that her husband hath yet allowed her nothing but wood and therefore it's agreed that the constables shall procure warrant from the justices to bind him over to the quarter sessions if he persist in this course.

December 6 1624   Imprimis it was agreed at this meeting that the constables assisted by those in whose walk it is[3] shall before the next quarter sessions entreat Sir Thomas Wiseman and Sergeant Darcy being the two next justices to our town, to appoint some convenient time to meet here to set down an order for Praxedy Bullen's bastard and for Stephen Gower's servant who is great with child.

4.6   Settlement disputes: Elizabeth Webb and Elizabeth Corfield, 1716, 1720

From the late seventeenth century, examinations in poor law settlement disputes survive. In an effort to establish the liability of a parish for poor relief, they investigated the last places of settlement of poor men and women.

Poor Law Settlement Disputes, Staffordshire RO, D1197/5/6/4 (2 Jan. 1716), D1197/5/6/9 (3 Feb. 1720).

---

2. Presumably washing him, but could also refer to washing his linen.
3. Each member of the Twenty-Four was responsible for walking a certain part of the parish to check for disorders.

The examination of Elizabeth Webb of Kinfare in the said county of Stafford spinster touching her last legal settlement . . .

Who deposeth that she was last hired for a servant for a year with Richard Phillips of Wollaston in the parish of Old Swinford and county of Worcester and served him one whole year and received in money and clothes the sum of five and thirty shillings for the year's wages. And further she saith that during her service her master removed from Wollaston aforesaid to the parish of Halesowen in the county of Shropshire where she served the latter part of her year's service but saith that to the best of her knowledge she did not live forty days in the said parish of Halesowen and further she saith not.

The examination of Elizabeth Corfield taken upon oath touching her settlement . . .

Who deposeth that her last legal place of settlement was within the parish of Kingswinford in the said county where she lived an hired servant by the year with Margaret Willmott of the said parish, widow, and served the said Margaret Willmott one whole year and received one pound and seven shillings for her said year's service; And further saith that she hath not gained a legal settlement in any other parish or place since she left the parish of Kingswinford aforesaid and this examinant further saith not.

4.7   Injury and lameness: Alice Shelley, 1609

In cases where the parish's responsibility was disputed, or where parochial poor relief was refused, women and men might petition the quarter sessions. Alice Shelley petitioned the Kent quarter sessions for financial help in 1609. She does not mention her age, which suggests she was, like most servants, in her twenties. Here, it is illness and injury – allegedly caused by her work – that have pushed Alice over the poverty line; the details she gives reveal the costs of illness and the mobility forced on servants in such situations, as parishes tried to establish a settlement for them. The first document is an order in response to Alice's petition, the second an examination of Alice's circumstances.

Kent Quarter Sessions Papers, CKS, QM/SB 809, 810 (12 April 1609).

Upon the examination of Alice Shelley spinster it appeareth unto us that she the said Alice did some fourteen days before Christmas last enter into covenant for one whole year for the wages of twenty shillings with the wife of Henry Knock of the parish of Pluckley yeoman and did there continue until Thursday last during which service she the said Alice did fall impotent and lame and was upon Sunday last brought unto the parish of Ulcombe where she the said Alice was neither born nor yet had her last abode: these are therefore in his Majesty's name to charge and command you the Barholder of Ulcombe that you remove and safely convey the body of the said Alice and her deliver unto the overseers for the poor of the parish of Pluckley or to one of them likewise we command you . . . to . . . receive the said Alice . . . and her settle and relieve according to her former covenant or otherwise as the case shall require and accordinge to his Majesty's laws. . . .

The examination of Alice Shelley, spinster

First she saith that she dwelled almost three whole years with one Robert Hope of Ulcombe in which time she was lame by the space of a quarter of a year and that she was struck about Michaelmas last past with a bore[1] after which time she continued with the said Mr Hope until about Pluckley fair and then she came unto Pluckley since which time she hath dwelled one quarter of a year with one Henry Knock: and saith at the quarter's end which was on Wednesday before the fair of which she departed from her master Knock by and with his and her own consent: and then returned again to her later master Hope's and there stayed three or four days and then went back unto the foresaid Knock's for that the said Robert Hope said unto her that he would send one Woodland unto her to help her of her lameness which Woodland had had before that time of her said master Hope the best part of five shillings for leeches and drinks which this examinant had received of and from the said Woodland, and further saith that her master Hope told her that if she would go unto the said Knock's if Woodland did not come unto her the said Hope would fetch her again from the said Knock's and have the said Woodland to keep to his own house, whereupon she went unto the said Knock's and when she had stayed two or three days she went unto Egerton and there stayed two or three days and then unto Lenham and there stayed one day and then again to Egerton and there stayed three or four days and back to Knock's and stayed two days and then to Egerton and stayed two days and there then requested one Brally to help her to Ulcombe, who pitying her seeing her so lame lent her a horse and a boy and so she went to her late master Hope's and there she asked why Woodland came not unto her and her dame Hope's son which lying thither with one Robson said that the said Woodland promised him that he would come unto her. Thus being at the said Hope's after two days she was sent by warrant to the overseers of the peace of Pluckly.

4.8   Petitioning for relief: Agnes Harvey, 1663

The poor might also apply to local charities for aid. Petitions such as this one, addressed to the governors of the hospital in Bruton, Somerset, who administered the funds of Sexey's charity, would generally have been written out by a clerk. They show some knowledge of established methods of appealing to charity on the grounds of poor health, inability to work, and inadequate housing.

Sexey's Charity, Somerset Archives, DD'SE/38 (1663)

---

1. An iron tool.

To the right worshipful the feoffees of the hospital in Bruton these –

The humble petition of Agnes Harvey a poor widow of Bruton

Humbly sheweth that your petitioner hath five children and being well towards threescore years of age by mishap of a stripe[1] in one of her eyes very lately was blind about 8 weeks and yet now by God's help hath recovered the sight of one of her eyes again but the other never like to be recovered. It is well known to the town that your petitioner hath been and yet is a great painstaker for purchasing a present livelihood for her poor family. But meeting of late with such miserable hard pinching times and cold winters hath so much impoverished your petitioner that she hath nothing scarcely at all left her for to keep alive doth humbly beseech your good worships to bestow some such of your charitable benevolence on her after such so hard tedious times of penury towards the present relief and comfort of your poor petitioner and her children.

And she shall be ever bound to pray etc.

4.9   The effects of war: Joane Burt, 1654

During the 1640s and 1650s petitioning Parliament was one of the principal ways in which women staked a claim in affairs of state and religion. At a more personal level, they used the same tool – the petition – to secure financial help for the hardships and injury imposed by war and its aftermath. As well as local help from JPs, as Joane Burt was requesting, for the first time some war widows petitioned for and received state pensions. Both types of petition appealed to a rhetoric of the sufferings of women and families in the cause of the Commonwealth, their contributions to the war, and their part in the state. Burt's petition, signed by the mayor and two other men, resulted in an order to the overseers to relieve her poverty. Petitions such as these would not have been written by the women themselves, but by a local scribe or clerk; this one is reproduced here (Figure 7) and original spelling has been retained.

Somerset Quarter Sessions Petitions, Somerset Archives, Q/SR Pet I/42 (1654).

To the worshipfull the Justices of the Peace for the County of Somerset now in Session assembled.
The humble Peticon of Joane Burt of Darleigh widdowe: Sheweth:

That your Petitioner haveing only one Sonne & Daughter, who through many Straites and Difficulties, by the labour of her handes, shee bred up, which said Sonne Jeffry Burt, out of his good affeccon to the Parliament, in the beginning of the late Warres voluntarily betooke himselfe to their Service under the Command of Colonell Blake, and haveing continued in the same Service by the space of two or three yeares, was att length taken in the Actuall Service of the State by the Enemy then in Garison in Bridgwater, where after

---

1. A blow.

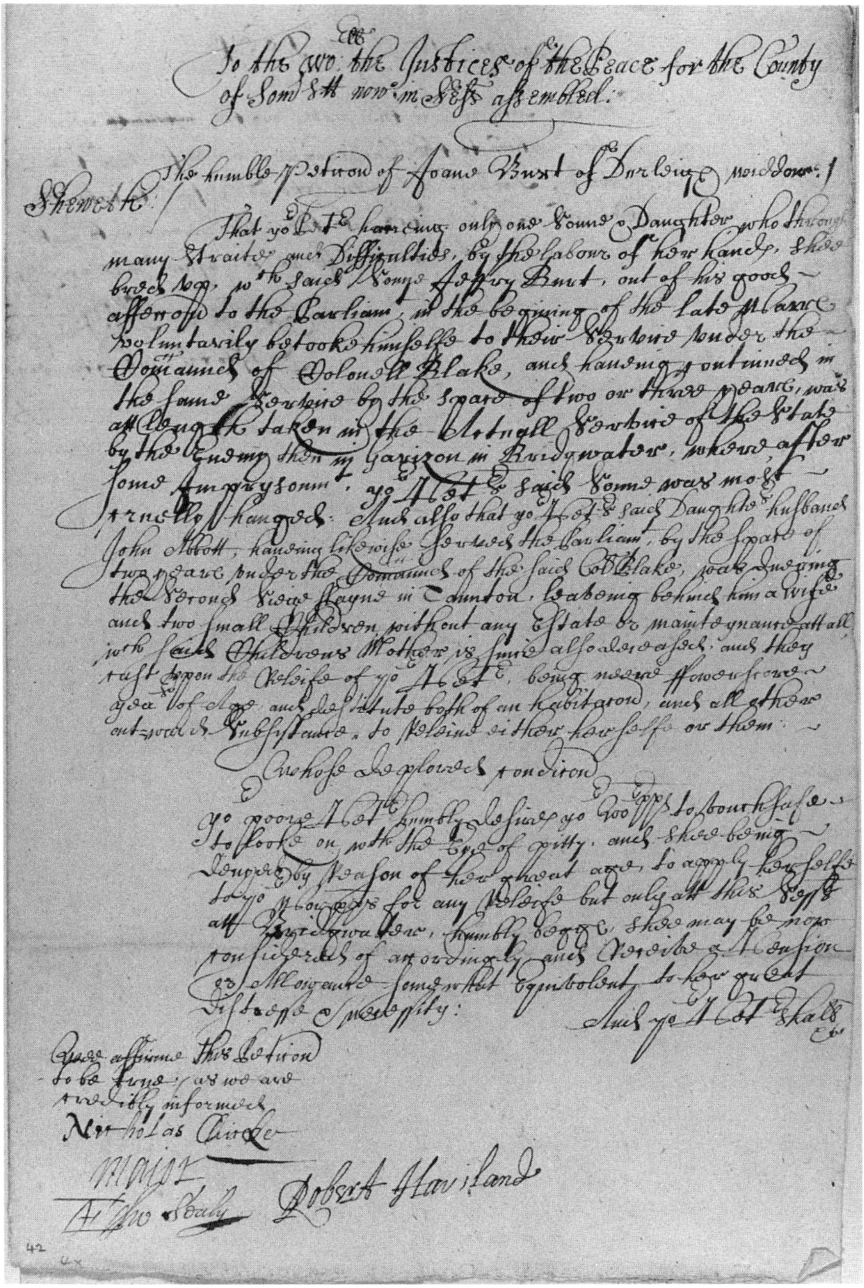

Figure 7 Petition of Joane Burt

By permission of Somerset Archives and Record Service

This petition is transcribed in document 4.9.

117

some Imprysonment, your Petitioners said Sonne was most cruelly hanged: And also that your Petitioners said Daughters husband John Abbott, haveing likewise served the Parliament, by the space of two yeares under the command of the said Colonel Blake, was duering the Second Siege slayne in Taunton, leaveing behind him a Wife and two small Children, without any Estate or mainteynance att all, which said Childrens Mother is since also deceased, and they cast uppon the releife of your Petitioner, being neere fowerscore years of Age and destitute both of an habitacon, and all other outward Subsistance, to releive either herselfe or them:

Whose deplored condicon your poore Petitioner humbly desires your Worships to vouchsafe to looke on with the Eye of pitty, and shee being denyed by reason of her great age, to apply herselfe to the Worshipps for any relief but only at this Sessions at Bridgwater, humbly begges shee may be now considered of accordingly and receive a Pension or Allowance some-what equivalent to her great distresse & necessity: And your Petitioner shall &c[1]

Wee affirme this Peticon to be true: as we are credibly informed

Nicholas Chicke, maior

Edward Sealy

Robert Haviland

4.10 Vagrancy and the death of a child: Katherine Talbott, 1656

The mobility of the very poor was often forced upon them. For Katherine Talbott, the birth of an illegitimate child and the want of poor relief when her child was ill resulted in her being accused of infanticide and tried before the Northern Assizes in 1656. Her responses to examination by the JP tell a story not just of poverty but also of anger and frustration; her final abandonment of her child, after its death, was perhaps her last attempt to make local authorities responsible.

Northern Assizes Depositions, PRO, ASSI 45 5/3/94 (29 May 1656).

Examination of Katherine Talbott of Bashall, West Riding . . .

This examinate Katherine Talbott saith she was delivered of a bastard child begotten by William Swinglehurst of Slaidburn a year and half since, which better for which child this examinant had sought two several times at private sessions and once at the quarter sessions at Wetherby for relief and could get none but was referred to the constable of the Forest of Bowland and overseers of Slaidburn then being to relieve her want and necessity and complained to them daily and could get no help from them till at length she this examinate was advised to leave her child where it was born, which accordingly this examinate did and saith the churchwardens and overseers or

---

1. I.e., shall pray [for the justices].

some of them then caused the town of Slaidburn to maintain the child three quarters of a year and afterward this examinant saith that Ambrose Boulton the overseer and James Banke the constable both of Slaidburn came to this examinant into Bashall, and took her this examinant and carried her back to her child at Slaidburn and desired her to take her child and they would help her to maintain the child so this examinant took her child and said she would gladly live with it. And often requested the officers of the town to get a house or place for her to sit in and she would work for her child and her own maintenance, and craved relief from day to day but was neglected and could get no help from them although often and daily at their houses she craved and told them she and her child was both like to starve and could not move them to pity nor do anything at all for them. So this examinant was constrained to leave and beg with her child from place to place and town to town for relief till about Shrovetide 17th of February last her child was very sick with [unidentifiable] and she lay at Thomas Bidsborrowe's at Great Barugh a pieceman's house there, this examinant saith they can witness that the child was not like to live one hour yet this examinant was forced to go on with it and about the next day to seek relief. And upon the common at the head of the way this examinant sat down with her child and it died in her arms there and she laid it down under a hill side and left it there and acquainted nobody. Since that time this examinant hath wrought for her living by spinning here and there as she could get work.

THE WORLD OF GOODS

4.11   Household goods: Isabel Wharton, 1610

Isabel Wharton and her husband Charles lived in the fenland of south Lincolnshire. Charles's inventory shows a two-room cottage consisting of a 'hall' or main room with two beds for all five children and their parents, and a rather grandly named parlour, which the contents reveal to have been actually the workroom. Charles, who died in January 1610, was a day labourer. Isabel is not identified by her work, but from the evidence of her own and Charles's inventories she must have been active in spinning, dairying, and keeping the pig, cows, sheep, hens, and horse, as well as the house. Isabel died in December of the same year. She appears to have sold or eaten three of the five sheep they had in January, but the fact that both cows and the calf survive the year suggests they were more important for milk than for meat. The cheesevats, butter, and cheese in Charles's inventory (not itemised in Isabel's) indicate that Isabel makes her own. What appears as 'hemp pilled and unpilled' in Charles's inventory becomes yarn and cloth in Isabel's, and by December she has the hempseed for the next year ready for planting. If the Whartons had a garden or an orchard Isabel probably kept this as well, but gardens, orchards, and their produce do not appear in inventories for technical legal reasons. Debts owed by the deceased are not normally included in an inventory either, since they were not part of her assets; they seem to be used in Isabel's inventory as notes towards the account.

Charles had left her with a balance of £12 after his debts and expenses were paid. But in December Isabel's property was valued at over £19. The disparity is partly explained by three factors: first, a different time of year and profits accrued from the family's labour; second, different valuation of the same goods (the linen and woollen spinning wheels are valued at 3s. 4d. in Charles' inventory, and at 4s. in Isabel's); third, goods which she had either acquired since his death or considered her own during marriage and so held back from Charles's inventory (the pair of reckons, pair of tongs, the brandle and hatchet, the hen, and eight ducks).

Isabel's inventory starts out with the normal grouping by room, but this gives way to a more unusual order: items are grouped not by location but by her bequests, allowing the value of these to be quickly deducted in her account. Charles had not made a will, but it was important enough to Isabel to pay someone to write her will, perhaps a week before her death. The careful division of household goods is typical of women's wills. Her bequests are reproduced in the account filed by one of the two 'true and faithful friends . . . in whom my trust is' that she appointed supervisors of her will, 'that they will see my children honestly brought up' (Carnell and Groome). The unusual gift of her gown to her son Thomas was 'to make him clothes'.

Lincolnshire Archives, INV110/213; Ad Ac 11/7.

This document and its note supplied by Amy Louise Erickson.

Isabel Wharton's inventory

A true and perfect inventory of all and singular such goods and chattels as Isabel Wharton late of Gedney widow deceased had valued and praised[1] the 3d day of December 1610 by Thomas Johnson Rycharde Thornton James Craxton John Gaunte John Peeke with others

	£	s	d
Imprimis in the hall:			
Item a trussbed[2] with a mattress and a coverlet a pillow and bolster		10	0
five sheets 2 table napkins		14	6
Item five yards of woollen cloth		12	0
Item 9 yards of harden[3] and 9 pound of linen yarn		6	0
Item a chest and a pewter platter		3	4
Item a bed and a coverlet and bolster		8	0
Item 4 sheets and 2 table napkins		10	6
Item the little table and 6 pound of woollen yarn		4	2
Item 4 sheets 2 table napkins and a table cloth		12	4

1. Appraised.
2. Travelling bed whose frame and hangings can be taken apart (trussed).
3. Coarse parts of flax or hemp.

Item a linen wheel and a woollen wheel		4	0
Item a table a chest 2 pewter platters a brass pot and a red petticoat		10	4
Item a brown cow an ewe and a lamb and a gown	3	6	8
Item a mare a cow and a burlen[4]	6	1	8
Item 2 pillowbears[5] and old wearing linen		4	0
Item coals and trash forgotten[6]		6	8
Item certain cheese		4	6
Item 4 brass pans 2 candlesticks a frying pan 2 pewter platters 2 sallers[7] 2 pails and a little tub		6	8
Item a pair of reckons[8] a pair of tongs a brandlet[9] a hatchet		2	8
Item 2 chairs and a cushion		1	6
Item hemp and hempseed	2	3	4
Item hay and wood	1	6	8
Item a shoat pig[10] a hen 8 ducks		7	2
Item 3 pots with other trash forgotten		1	8
[Total]	19	8	4
Debts from the testator			
Imprimis to Thomas Johnson		12	3
Item to John Groome		13	4
Item to Roberte Darkinge	1	0	0
Item to James Craxton		15	0
Item her funeral charges	1	10	0
[Debts total]	4	10	7
[Balance]	14	17	9

Isabel Wharton's account (2 April 1612)

Thaccompt of John Grome of Gedney in the County of Lincoln administrator of the goods and chattels of Isabel Wharton late of Gedney aforesaid in the County aforesaid widow deceased, as well of and for such and so much of the same goods and chattels as came to his hands as of and for his payments forth of the same – followeth

The said accomptant chargeth himself with all and singular the goods and chattels of the said deceased specified in an inventory thereof made by him exhibited into the registry of the Diocese of Lincoln amounting to the sum of

4. A yearling calf.
5. Pillowcases.
6. The usual catch-all phrase for anything not itemised.
7. Salt cellars.
8. Scales.
9. A brandreth is a gridiron or tripod for the fire.
10. Young weaned pig.

	£	s	d
	19	8	4

Whereof

	£	s	d
Made and expended by the said accomptant in and about the funeral charges of the said deceased		1	10
Item paid for the mortuary of the said deceased		3	4
Item made and expended in fees and other necessary expenses, viz. the fees of the letters of administration with the bonds seal and oath, the writing and engrossing of the testament and inventories double, the charges of praising the goods, expenses of travel and other necessary expenses, to the sum of		15	4
Item owing by the said deceased for debts at her death and since her death paid by this accomptant viz.			
To Thomas Johnson		12	3
To John Grome		13	4
To Robert Darkinge		15	
To James Craxton		15	
[Total of debts]	2	15	7

	£	s	d
Item the legacies bequeathed in and by the said deceased her last will and testament and chargeable upon this accomptant as followeth viz.			
To Agnes Reader daughter of the said deceased a truss bed, a pair of hemptear[11] sheets, and a flaxen sheet, and the new russet[12] for a gown, two table napkins a great chest and 9 pound of hemptear yarn, which this accomptant hath paid, to the value of	2	5	10
To Margarett her daughter a posted bed, a pair of hemptear sheets, a flaxen sheet, the little table, two table napkins, 6 pound of woollen yarn, to the value of		1	7
To Joane her daughter, a woollen wheel a linen wheel a chest in the hall, a table cloth, two table napkins, two hemptear sheets, a pair of harden sheets and a flaxen sheet, the table in the parlour, a brass pot, a red petticoat, and two pewter platters, to the value of		1	3
To Thomas her son an old brown cow, an ewe and lamb and a gown valued to £3 6s. 8d. and in money 10s.	3	16	8
To John Carnell and John Grome bequeathed		2	0
[Total of legacies]	8	14	6

11. A coarse linen cloth.
12. Coarse homespun woollen cloth of reddish-brown, grey or neutral colour.

Item the fees of drawing engrossing this accompt, the			
quietus est seal and oath and citation and dismission	1	1	4
Item the accomptant's charge spent at the making of this			
accompt with his horse charge		4	
Sum total of the said payments debts legacies and			
expenses	15	4	1
And so remaineth the sum of	4	4	3

Which is bequeathed in the said testament of the said deceased unto James Wharton her son and executor by the name of all her goods and chattels unbequeathed, and is to be paid to him accordingly

4.12 Second-hand clothes: Mary Richards, 1688

Many women were engaged in selling, reselling and buying secondhand and stolen goods. This is a typical case of women's theft, involving easily resaleable material goods and transactions of secondhand goods with women and men whose names are now, conveniently, forgotten.

Somerset Quarter Sessions Rolls, Somerset Archives, Q/SR 212/16 (1 June 1688).

The examination of Mary Richards of Staplegrove . . .

Who saith that the bundle of worsted yarn now found under the thatch of her house above a quarter of a year since she found it in the little lane over against the bridewell as she was coming out of Taunton. And as for the linsey-woolsey that she had she bought of a person unknown to her in Taunton since Christmas last and gave 1s. 8d. per yard for it, and the little parcel of linsey-woolsey she bought it of the same man and gave 1s. 5d. for it, and the little camlett of serge she bought of a woman that came into her house to light a pipe of tobacco and gave her two pence for it.

4.13 Fashion and consumption: Elizabeth Jeake, 1701

Elizabeth Jeake, a gentlewoman, left her children at Rye, East Sussex, to visit London. Her letters detail the business of finding fabrics, garments, and accessories for the new fashions. Women were to play a leading role in the new markets of the late seventeenth and early eighteenth centuries.

Frewen Papers, East Sussex RO, FRE 5340–1.

London May the 24th 1701

This serves dear Mother to inform you anew of my health which thanks be to God is still continued. I hope the same blessing attends you and my children. . . . I have bought you petticoats but for head linen am at a loss knowing you will not conform to high heads which young and old wear here no glove tops worn. Tell Betty her hair frused as mine uses to be is the way, low dresses and two double ruffs. . . .

London May the 27th 1701
. . . I shall take care dear Mother to execute your commands in all the particulars . . . let Betty send me the piece of red Indian satin by Mr Chiswel to leave at Mrs Tomkins's if it be not sent per carrier I would know what Mrs Seal would have instead of her carnation tape I have forgot. I am glad you have so much good company. Madam Miller advises Betty to weave bone lace rather than point which is quite out of vogue if she incline to the lady's sentiments will buy a piece of lace. . . .

4.14   Business dealings: Dorothy Bresbeech and Ursula Goodspeed, 1661

Records of litigation over business debts can reveal much about the roles women played in the wider world of business, debts, and accounts. In this case from London in 1661, Dorothy Bresbeech, an account-keeper for Ursula Goodspeed, came to testify in Ursula's behalf at the Mayor's Court in 1661, in an attempt to get her debt to the estate of Hillary Hancock cancelled. Hillary had supplied Ursula (who may have been running an alehouse) with beer and ale. Dorothy Bresbeech's deposition records a good deal about the ways in which some women were involved in business.

London Mayor's Court, Corporation of London RO, MC 6/113, fos 2–3 (20 June 1661).

Dorothy Bresbeech wife of John Bresbeech of the parish of St Bride's London gentleman aged 47 years or thereabouts sworn and examined upon certain interrogatories administered unto her on the part and behalf of Ursula Goodspeed widow, complainant, against Richard Beazar executor of the last will and testament of Hillary Hancock and Judith his wife, defendants, deposeth and saith upon her corporal oath as followeth viz.:

1   To the 1st interrogatory this deponent saith that she . . . hath known the complainant about 13 years and the defendants and either of them about 2 years now last past. Also this dept did know Hillary Hancock before mentioned in his lifetime about 5 years before he died.

2   To the 2nd interrogatory this deponent saith that she knoweth that there was in the lifetime of the said Hillary Hancock great dealings between him and the complainant for beer and ale that the said complainant had of him by which the said Hillary Hancock received many great sums of money of the said complainant for many years together. And this deponent knoweth the same because she this deponent did lodge and dwell in house with the said complainant and was employed by her to keep her books and accounts for many years together aswell while she this deponent dwelt in house with the said complainant as long before in which books and accounts

all the beer and ale received and monies paid for the same were entered and written.

3   To the 3rd interrogatory this deponent saith that about 2 years and a half ago the said Hillary Hancock came to the complainant's home in Three Legged Alley in the parish of St Bride London and did urge and persuade the said complainant to come to an account with him for the remainder of some monies due upon his book for beer and ale. And this deponent saith that the said complainant was willing and did come to an account with him at the same time for the same. And this deponent and her husband were then present all the while of such their accounting together and until the business was fully completed touching the same. And the said Hancock having cast up the monies which he pretended to be resting due amounting to about £80 demanded payment thereof whereupon the said complainant exceedingly wondered that the said Hillary should make so large a demand and told him that she did not owe him any such sum nor indeed according to the best of her memory and as she had reckoned not near half so much and told him that his clerks had omitted to set down in her book what she had paid them at any time in the absence of this deponent (for that this deponent had often occasion to be absent for a month or 6 weeks together). And thereupon the said complainant brought forth £10 and paid the same to him and told him that she did not in her conscience believe that she ought him more then £20 more if so much. . . .

4   To the 4th interrogatory this deponent saith that the said Hillary Hancock at the time of making up the account as aforesaid did desire the said complainant with very much importunity to enter into a bond unto him for payment of the remaining monies (after her payment of the said £10) which he so pretended to be due as aforesaid whereunto the said complainant answered that she did in no sense owe him the same and wondered he should desire any such thing and that it was unreasonable or to that effect howbeit the said Hancock did much importune her thereunto and told her that his wife had taken a view of his accounts and had advised him to settle the same and take bonds for the monies thereby due and that he desired it only to satisfy his wife and did thereupon promise and affirm to the said complainant that if she would seal and deliver to him a bond it should be for payment of the said monies by 2s. 6d. per week for their two joint lives which said he cannot be long we being both very old. And that he the said Hillary before he died would either cancel the said bond himself or take such course that the same should be cancelled and that she should never be troubled for the same after his death. And the said complainant giving credit to the said Hillary's words and promises which he then also bound with a most solemn imprecation upon his soul if he did not perform or cause to be performed that which he so declared and promised as aforesaid she the said complainant did seal and deliver a bond unto him the said Hillary for payment of the said 2s. 6d. weekly accordingly. But more to this

interrogatory this dept saith that she cannot depose. Save that the said Hillary did amongst his other words and fair speeches now and then give the complainant many threats what he would do to her in case she would not assent to the giving him the same bond and what with that and his imprecations and fair promises that it should be only for payment of 2s. 6d. a week so long as they two should live together was the reason of her making the said bond.

4.15 Remarriage, death and property: Margaret Rothwell, 1639–40

Although three of the following four documents nominally relate to a man, they describe family property and family relationships amongst women as much as men. Margaret and Thomas Rothwell were much better off than Isabel and Charles Wharton (document 4.11) although Thomas was only a husbandman, who would not have had to work for wages but who would have had only a small amount of land compared to a yeoman. He might have owned or rented land, but it doesn't appear in any of the documents relating to Thomas. Only in the account of Margaret's estate do we see from rent and taxes due that they rented from several people. In addition to the hall and parlour, the Rothwell house had a milkhouse, allowing dairying on a much larger scale than Isabel Wharton, a chamber over one of the rooms, a barn, and many more animals, suggesting meat production. Margaret died very soon after Thomas, and the inventory filed under his name appears actually to be a joint one for both of them: note for example the last item, 'her apparel and ready money in her purse'.

The inventory contains a quantity of pewter dishes, and does not mention wooden or earthenware, although the household certainly had some (compare Isabel Wharton's inventory, with all three types of vessel). Similarly, while the chamber contains hemp, hempseed and wool, no spinning wheels are mentioned; they may not have been considered worth listing.

In Thomas's will each of his three sons and four daughters was to have the same amount, £1 'with the increase', or interest, when they turned 21. Margaret is expected to invest the pounds and keep track of the interest for the intervening twenty years. It is clear from their accounts that both Thomas and Margaret had been married previously. She brought one son (Humfrey Wyley) and Thomas two to their marriage, and they had four daughters together. Remarriage highlights the problems of keeping property straight, although Thomas's lack of distinction between his stepchild and his own children is typical. The two deductions from Thomas's estate for Humfrey Wyley – one a portion from his own father's estate and one given to him by Margaret before she remarried – were probably secured by legal documents at the time of their marriage, although these are not specified. Humfrey's share of £15 is much larger than Thomas's bequests to each child of £1: was Margaret the wealthier partner at marriage? Or did Thomas expect her to divide up the bulk of the estate after his death?

High mortality (a problem particularly in fenland areas like this) also had dramatic effects on inheritance. When Thomas wrote his will in 1637 he named seven children. By the time his account was filed in July 1640, his son Anthony (age 15) and their youngest daughter, Annis, had died. Three weeks later, when Margaret's account was filed, only two daughters and one son were left. The survivors inherited the portions of their dead siblings.

Lincolnshire Archives, Inv 150B/643; Misc Wills D/80; Ad Ac 27/62; Ad Ac 27/78.

This document and its note supplied by Amy Louise Erickson.

Thomas Rothwell's inventory (18 March 1639)

The inventory of the goods and chattels of Thomas Rothwell of Pinchbeck in the County of Lincoln husbandman late deceased administered of by Margaret his wife, taken and prized the 18th day of March anno domini 1639 by Richard Keyes Samuell Purdie William Mitchemson Thomas Garner as followeth

	£	s	d
In the Hall			
Imprimis one halling[1], 2 tables, 3 forms[2], 4 chairs and five stools		13	4
Item one cupboard a dishbench[3] 4 cushions and the fire irons		1	5
Item 7 brass pots 8 brass pans a mortar a chafingdish 3 brass candlesticks 40 pieces of great and small pewter and a dripping pan with other implements there	5	7	6
In the Parlour			
Item 4 beds with the furniture[4] lying on them	7	0	0
Item 7 pair of hempen sheets 1 pair of fine linen sheets 2 tablecloths 1 towel 4 pillowores[5] and a dozen and a half of napkins	4	0	0
Item 4 chests one stand bed with the furniture 1 box with other implements there	1	0	0
In the Milkhouse			
Item one table 3 shelves 2 churns 2 barrels the milk vessel 2 tubs five pails with other necessaries there	1	0	0
Item 2 bacon flickes[6]	1	0	0

1. Tapestry or painted cloth hanging on the walls of the hall.
2. Benches.
3. Sideboard.
4. Mattresses, linens, etc.
5. Pillowcases.
6. Flitches, or sides of cured bacon.

	£	s	d
In the Chamber			
Item 13 stone of hemp 2 quarters of hempseed a quarter and a half of wheat rye and barley 2 stone of wool a piece of harden[7] cloth and other implements there	5	10	0
In the Barn			
Item rye unthreshed and rette[8] hemp	1	11	0
Item a cart and cartgears plough and ploughgears and a harness	4	10	0
In the Yard			
Item 2 hovells[9] 2 stone troughs [illegible] and compass and old wood about the yard	2	0	0
Item the hay	1	0	0
Item 8 cows	20	0	0
Item 7 calves	3	10	0
Item 4 burlings[10]	6	0	0
Item 3 mares and 3 foals	17	0	0
Item 3 swine	1	3	4
Item one acre and a half of wheat and rye sown	1	10	0
Item her apparel and ready money in her purse	6	0	0
[Total]	91	10	2

Thomas Rothwell's will (12 January 1637, probated 15 February 1639)

... Item I give to Richard Rothwell my son 20s. to be paid by Margaret Rothwell my wife whom I make executrix with the increase when he attaineth the age of 21 years. Item I give to Anthony Rothwell my son 20s. to be paid when he attaineth the age of 21 years with the increase by my executrix. Item I give to Humfrey Wyley my son 20s. to be paid when he attaineth the age of 21 years with the increase by my executor [*sic*]. Item I give to Margaret Rothwell my daughter 20s. to be paid when she attaineth the age of 21 years with the increase by my executrix. Item I give to Alice Rothwell my daughter 20s. to be paid when she attaineth the age 21 years with the increase by my executrix. Item I give to Elizabeth Rothwell 20s. when she attaineth the age of 21 years with the increase by my executrix. Item I give to Annis Rothwell my daughter all the linen her mother brought and one chest to be put into the hands of Richard Preist within one month after my decease. And if it happen that any of the said children die before they have their portions then my will is that it should be equally divided amongst the

7. A coarse fabric made of the hards of flax or hemp.
8. Soaked to separate the fibres.
9. Shelter for cattle.
10. Yearling calf.

rest. Item I give to Raph my kinsman the foal that sucketh now on the gray mare to be kept two years if he tarry with his aunt if not to take the foal with him. And my will is that all the rest of my goods and chattels not given nor bequeathed I give them to Margaret my wife wholly to bring up my children whom I make executrix of this my last will she to take my debts and pay my debts and bring my body in seemly manner to the ground. And I make and appoint Richard Hall supervisor of this my last will and testament in witness whereof I have subscribed my name and set to my seal the day and year abovesaid.

Thomas Rothwell's account (1 July 1640)

The accompt of Richard Richardson administrator of all and singular the goods rights and chattels of Thomas Rothwell late of Pinchbeck in Holland deceased unadministered [by the executrix], according to the term of his last will and testament, made of and upon such and so much of the goods and chattels of the said deceased, as have come to his hands and possession by virtue of his administration as also out of his payments and disbursements out of the same as followeth

The Charge
Imprimis the said accomptant chargeth himself with all
    and singular the goods and chattels of the said
    deceased comprised in an inventory thereof made
    and exhibited into the Registry of the Archdeaconry
    of Lincoln at Lincoln remaining, amounting as
    by the same it may and doth appear to the sum
    of   £91   10s   2d
Whereof the said accomptant craveth allowance of the
    sums hereafter following, viz. Imprimis the said
    accomptant craveth allowance of ten pounds as a
    portion allotted by the Ordinary[11] out of the goods
    for Humfrey Wyley which was remaining in the
    hands of the said Thomas Rothwell and owing to him
    at his death   10   0   0
Item the said accomptant craveth allowance of the
    sum of £5 which was given to the said Humfrey
    Wyley in the widowhood of his late mother
    deceased which the said Thomas Rothwell died
    possessed of   5   0   0
Legacies in the will of the said Thomas Rothwell

---

11. Church court official.

Item this accomptant craveth allowance of certain portions given by Thomas Rothwell deceased unto certain children which he had by a former wife viz. to Richard and Anthony	2	0	0
Item this accomptant craveth allowance of the sum of £3 given by the said Thomas Rothwell to Margaret, Alice and Elizabeth Rothwell children which he had by Margaret his later wife viz.	3	0	0
Item this accomptant craveth allowance of £1 given to Humfrey Wyley by the said deceased's testament viz.	1	0	0
Item the charges of this accomptant in taking the letters of administration the bond fine and engrossing of the inventories, being done at the request of this accomptant		15	0
Item a proctor's fee at the same time		3	4
Item to the judge for his fees of the administration		6	8
Item the fees of this accomptant to the registrar for drawing this accompt 3s. 4d. for engrossing this accompt 3s. 4d. for registering this accompt 3s. 4d. letters testimonial 3s. 4d. in all		13	4
Item the judge's fees of this accompt letters testimonial seal and oath		6	8
Item this accomptant's charges in coming to Lincoln thrice vizt when he took administration and his sureties charges and now passing of this accompt in all and other necessary charges	3	0	0
[Total] [crossed out]	25	16	8

And so remaineth in the hands of this accomptant the sum of ['£76' crossed out] which is bequeathed in the said deceased's testament unto Margaret his late wife and executrix, since his death also deceased, wholly to bring up his children.

Margaret Rothwell's account (22 July 1640)

The accompt of Richard Richardson of Pinchbeck administrator of the goods and chattels of Margaret Rothwell late of the same town deceased, made as followeth viz.

The Charge
Imprimis the said accomptant chargeth himself with all and singular the goods chattels and rights of the said deceased comprised in an inventory thereof made and

	£	s	d
exhibited into the principal Registry at Lincoln amounting to the sum of	£65	10s	2d

The Discharge
Whereof the said accomptant craveth allowance of these sums following Imprimis paid for the deceased's mortuary — 10 0
Item spent for the funeral and charges of the said deceased and of Richard Rothwell her son in law[12] — 3 1 6

Specialties[13]
Item owing by the deceased upon bond and paid by this accomptant to John Tilson — 5 8 0
Item paid to Captain Agle for Lady Day rent last past to him and to other landlords — 6 10 0
Item owing by the deceased at her death for the church assessment 2s. 6d., to the Constable for the King's provision 1s. 9d., to the dike graves[14] 1s. 8d., to the Constables 3s. 4d. and also owing to Richard More 1s. 8d. — 10 11
Item owing for Easter offerings — 7 0
Item paid for clothes for the deceased's children vizt for Humfrey Wyley Margaret Rothwell and Alice Rothwell in woollen and linen — 1 17 4
Item paid more for hoses and shoes and hats — 17 8

Necessary charges
Item for the fees of the administration to the registrar the fine the bond engrossing of the inventories and exhibiting of them — 10 0
Item the judges fees of the said letters of administration seal and oath — 6 8
Item the fees of this accomptant to the registrar for drawing registering and engrossing of this accomptant's letters testimonial and assignation of portions — 16 8
Item the judge's fees of this accomptant's letters testimonial seal and oath and assignation of portions — 13 8
Item for a proctor's fee two several times about taking the said letters of administration and passing of this accompt — 6 8
Item this accomptant's victuals in passing this accompt

12. I.e. stepson.
13. Debts secured by written instruments.
14. Dikereeves, who looked after the dikes in the fens.

and with the charges of his sureties and other necessary charges	1	15	0
Total expenses	23	2	1
Balance	42	8	10

Disposition:

Humfrey Wyley, age 11	11	13	4
Margaret Rothwell, age 8	11	13	4
Alice Rothwell, age 7	11	13	4
Accountant for £5 which he promised to pay a man to bring up Humfrey Wyley, and other expenses bringing up children	7	8	1

An inventory of the goods and chattels of Margaret Rothwell widow late of Pinchbeck deceased vizt

The goods and chattels of the said deceased are the sum of £65 10s. 2d. being the remainder of the goods and chattels of Thomas Rothwell late of Pinchbeck aforesaid deceased . . . in his last will and testament as appeareth by the accompt of the goods of the said Thomas Rothwell deceased; made by Richard Richardson administrator of the said Margaret Rothwells goods which said Margaret Rothwell was executrix of the last will and testament of the said Thomas Rothwell deceased and which sum of £65 10s. 2d. is part of the goods of the said Thomas Rothwell deceased mentioned in the inventory exhibited by Richard Richardson administrator of the goods of the said Thomas according to his will viz.	65	10	2

4.16 A widow's will: An Toynby, 1679

An Toynby died in March 1679 in Waddington, a village 5 miles south of Lincoln. She had been the second wife of a husbandman whose will had left to An 'the homestead wherein I now live' and an oxgang of land for her life. The land was to be tilled by her stepson Thomas at his own expense. The 'homestead' included a hall or house, parlour, buttery, kitchen, milkhouse, and chambers above these rooms. After An's death it went to her eldest stepson Robert. An also had two stepdaughters, both of whom were married with children. All of the household goods, indoors and out, An had received from her husband outright, so she could dispose of them in her own will. She made her will one year after his death, but lived another six years. At this point her goods amounted to just under £35, not including the debts she listed due to her, including £40 from her stepson Thomas. An had no children of her own, and uses the common term 'in law' to refer to her stepchildren. She also names a wide range of 'kin' and 'cousins', godchildren and friends. Her small gift to 'all the widows' in the village suggests a particularly female form of charity.

Lincolnshire Archives Office, LCC Will 1678/61.

This document and its note supplied by Amy Louise Erickson.

In the name of god Amen the 21th day of January 1673 I An Toynby of Waddington within the County of the City of Lincoln widow being sick of body but of perfect memory God be praised, do make and ordain this my last will and testament in manner and form following, that is to say: first I commend my soul into the hands of God my creator and saviour desiring him for Christ Jesus sake to pardon and forgive me all my sins and to make me partaker of everlasting life and my body to be buried in the parish church of Waddington and for all my other goods I do dispose of as followeth:

Item I give unto James Haryson and John Haryson of Canwick my kinsmen seven pounds apiece in silver to either of them and either of them one ewe and lamb within one year after my decease, and in case either of them die before the said time, then my will is the survivor of them to have the said legacies to them and their heirs for ever.

Item I give unto Casander Haryson and Catherine Haryson of Canwick my kinswomen either of them seven pounds apiece in silver and either of them one ewe and lamb within one year after my decease and in case either of them shall die before the said time, then my will is the survivor of them to have the said legacies to them and their heirs for ever.

Item I give unto my foresaid kinswomen Casander and Catherine Haryson my two best coverlids and two pair of the best blankets and two of the best linen sheets and two of the best linen towels and two of the best linen pillow-bears[1] and all my hempen yarn and harden yarn and two of the best pewter dishes to be equally divided betwixt them to them and their heirs for ever.

Item I give unto Thomas Toynby my son-in-law one cow and one coverlid and one pewter dish and one steepfatt[2] and the featherbed I lie on and half of the winter corn.

Item I give unto John Toynby my son-in-law one cow and one coverlid and one pewter dish and twenty shillings in silver and the fan and the skreele[3] and one swine hog and half of the winter corn.

Item I give unto Elizabeth Prockter my daughter-in-law one cow and one pan that stands in a furnish and one swine hog and half of the other household stuff unbequeathed of in the house and parlour.

Item I give unto An Craven my daughter-in-law one yearling calf and that moneys that her husband doth owe to me I freely forgive him and I give unto her the other half of the household stuff unbequeathed of in the house and parlour to be equally divided betwixt her sister Prockter and her.

1. Pillowcases.
2. Vat to steep barley for malting.
3. Screen for dressing corn.

Item I give unto all my godchildren twelve pence apiece and to Mr Edward Colson and his wife either of them a pair of gloves and a mourning ribbon and to John Newcome and his wife the like and to William Hammond and his wife the like and to my cousin Mary Newcome and William Newcome and Roberte Newcome the like and to Martha Smyth and her son the like and to my cousin An Dickinson the like and to my sister Haryson and all her children every one of them gloves and ribbons at my funeral and to Mary Newcome the like.

Item I give unto Isabell Hales two shillings and six pence and one linen apron.

Item I give unto my sister[4] Margaret Toynby one piece of woollen cloth.

Item I give unto Widow Poole six pence and to Widow Dawlin six pence and to Widow Jackson six pence and to Widow Newcome six pence and to all widows in Waddington four pence apiece, to be paid within one month after my decease.

Item I give unto Roberte Toynby my son-in-law all my other goods unbequeathed of whom I do make full and sole executor of this my last will and testament paying all my debts legacies and funeral expenses. In witness whereof I have set hereto my hand and seal the 21th day of January in the year of our Lord 1673.

Debts owing to me

Thomas Toynby my son-in-law doth owe unto me £30 upon a bond and £10 that he doth owe to me besides that he never gave me any account of. William Prockter doth owe unto me for one sack of malt.
Roberte Toynby doth owe the sum of one pound and four shillings.

4.17   My desires and advice: Lady Peregrina Chaytor, 1697

Peregrina Chaytor, wife of a Yorkshire baronet, wrote this letter to her husband when she was about to lie in in 1697. Like many early modern women (see also the Countess of Bridgewater in Chapter 1, and Mary Carey in Chapter 10), she anticipated childbirth with foreboding, but this response is a more practical, material one. Peregrina lived until 1708, but had only four surviving children from thirteen births: this child died eleven days old of the gripes. The Chaytors' financial situation was troubled, and Peregrina's husband was imprisoned for debt from 1701. Peregrina's letter in Chapter 6 is also revealing of the independent financial arrangements envisaged for her daughters as well as her sons.

Chaytor Papers, North Yorkshire County RO, ZQH 9/12/54 (?July/Aug. 1697) (also published in *Sir William Chaytor (1639–1721)*, Northallerton, North Yorkshire County Council 1984).

---

4. In this case meaning sister-in-law.

My dear

I being to pass the great peril of child bearing and not knowing how God may please to dispose of me could not but write you down my desires in this paper which I hope you will so far take notice of as to take care they be observed, and in the first place must recommend our dear children to you which I beg you will take true care of and be a very kind father to and if possible let every one of them have some provision and be put to employments but above all take care that they understand their duty to God and to practice it and pray be not too severe with Tom for my sake and if this child live which I am now with I desire you will be kind and careful of it and if it be a girl add something to what I have left it by will and if it be a boy take care that it have some reasonable provision. I have left you an account of what plate I have at Mr Crest's which I desire you will dispense of amongst my children not forgetting this child I am with and also the old gold in my green purse taking what piece you like best for your self and pray take care that the five guineas in the same purse be kept for Tom and Clarvaux two of them being Tom's and the other three Clarvaux's, there is also twenty-five shillings in money in the same purse belonging to Harry and given him by Sir William Bowes the rest of the money in the said purse belongs to Tom and Clarvaux and I must desire you to let my Nancy have my best diamond ring and my 2 lockets but if this child I am now with prove a daughter then I would have it have my lesser locket and my other diamond ring with one diamond in it and if there come any monies to you out of my father's personal estate pray take care that every one of my children have ten pound a piece and if you can not pay cousin Hutton and cousin Bowes their interest for the 2 hundred pounds out of your estate then I would have it paid out of the farms of Thornly and Greenwell Hill and pray my dear take care to pay Mrs Parks her money and Nanny Peacock and Betty Coetts theirs and if you think fit to get an Act of Parliament I beg it of you never to consent to lay more monies upon Croft than £2500, five hundred pound of which I request may be a portion for Nancy and if I die I think it may be better to charge the whole estate of Croft with the above said £2500 by which means the whole estate may come to your son which I think it cannot do if you lay so great a sum upon that part of it mentioned in the writing Mr Hillton drew up the last year, for you can not raise £2500 upon so small a part of Croft without selling part of it so I think it better if you think fit to charge the whole estate of Croft with the £2500 which your son may redeem if God think fit and if this monies rest upon Croft and what you sell your other lands for should not pay all your debts you must then live so frugally as to pay every year part to those which are left unpaid, for I cannot consent to charge Croft with more than the abovesaid sum and doth beg it of you that no persuasions prevail with you to the contrary. My dear, I have willed you in this paper my desires and advice to which I hope you will observe and not take amiss they coming from a faithful wife who doth and will to her last breath most truly love you which is all the return I can make you for your great kindness to me which I beg you will continue to my dear children after my death and in particular to Nancy and be not troubled at my death for you know my life has not been very easy for some time and if God think fit to take me out of my troubles to himself it will be of great happiness for me neither would I have you make any great funeral for me but with as little charge and company as can be and pray take care my will be observed and that you take advice which way will be the best to charge Croft with the abovesaid sum before you proceed to an Act of Parliament and I beg it of you to be kind and careful of my dear children and I pray God bless you and them and grant us all a happy meeting in the next world and send you and them much happiness in this which is the prayer of

your most truly affectionate wife
Pe. Chaytor

5

SEXUAL EXPERIENCES

Because of the concerns of both secular and ecclesiastical courts with illicit sex, sources on sexual activity are fuller than those for many other areas of women's lives. They are also very selective. They register, as much as anything else, the concerns of local authorities – constables, churchwardens, anxious neighbours, sometimes more organised campaigns for the reformation of manners. In the late sixteenth century the church courts did much disciplinary business, presenting and punishing offenders with penance; such presentments tend to decrease in the years leading up to 1642, when the courts ceased to function, and the responsibility for sexual regulation was assumed, to some extent, by the quarter sessions, to be resumed by the church courts in 1660.

The records of sexual activity are characterised by evasions, elaborations, and inventions. In court, the majority of women who were examined for bastardy claimed to have had sex once and with one man only; only a proportion of them were likely to be telling the truth. Testimonies in adultery and fornication cases involved convenient holes in walls, through which neighbours happened to observe the suspicious events: the resulting narratives are at least partly formulaic, although they also represent familiar and fairly plausible stories.

The courts, of course, were interested only in illicit sex. Sex in marriage, or between betrothed partners, was far less likely to leave any record. Women's own writings rarely if ever mention sex or sexual desire. A few women's and men's letters are explicit; many more use veiled language to convey a meaning clear only to the couple.

Sex between women is even harder to reconstruct. Whereas sex between men was punishable as sodomy in the secular courts, sexual acts between women had no legal meaning, and there are only a few exceptional instances of women punished for sex with other women. Lesbianism was not understood in terms of sexual identity, although the category of 'hermaphrodite' constituted in some senses a forerunner for such an identity. Contemporary culture construed lesbian acts at least partly as a preliminary to heterosexual sex, or occasionally as an unfortunate substitute for it. Romantic friendship provided another matrix for understanding potentially erotic intimacies between women: sometimes such relationships seemed laudable, sometimes scandalous and dangerous.

Occasionally, women dressed as men married other women; some were discovered, sometimes becoming legendary; others may have passed unnoticed.

The context within which female sexuality was understood was shaped by a range of legal, medical, and customary ideas and expectations. Popular and elite medical texts, broadsides, and ballads presented women as relentlessly desiring. Their lust, more than men's, was the hardest to control. This discourse was a source of profound misogyny, used against women both individually and collectively. However, it might also have been a means by which women could claim sexual passion. Descriptions of reproduction, relating male and female physiologies more closely than was to be the case in the later eighteenth century, presented conception as the result of both male and female orgasm. In some cases at least, this made married men keen to learn how to please their wives. It may also have meant that unmarried men connected the pursuit of female sexual pleasure with the dangers of conception.

As the records of rape and sexual assault suggest, it could be hard for women to assert control over their perceived sexual availability. Rape was rarely pursued in court and was difficult to prosecute; as a legal concept it had traditionally been associated with property offences. Discussions of the crime in the later seventeenth century suggest that it was becoming more clearly perceived as a sexual offence, involving lack of consent.[1] More broadly, women questioned about sex in court rarely speak of themselves as consenting partners. This was, of course, their main defence; but it may also bear witness to a culture in which active female desire was problematic and unacceptable.

The lack of effective contraception was a crucial determinant of female sexual experiences. Despite the lack of evidence for any widespread use of contraception, illegitimacy rates in sixteenth- and seventeenth-century England appear to have been surprisingly low: it has been argued that a good deal of heterosexual sexual activity before marriage involved non-penetrative sex.[2] Young men and women, waiting for the chance to marry, engaged in kissing, petting, and 'love play' on their own or in front of friends and family. Once a firm marriage contract had been made, though, many felt sexual intercourse was permissible and accordingly, many women examined for bastardy claimed a promise of marriage.

SEX AND SINGLE WOMEN

5.1 To mark him for her own: Joane Waters, 1611

For most women and men sex and marriage began with love play, fondling, and 'bundling'. Joane Waters, a widow pregnant with her dead husband's child, was sued at the London consistory court in 1586 over a marriage contract she was alleged to have made with John Newton, a London actor. George Ireland, who deposed in Newton's favour, testified that the couple had made a written contract, and that their public love play (in front of William Duke and John's sister as well as George Ireland) demonstrated Joane's readiness to marry John, although she at first refused to marry 'till she was delivered of the child she then went with being her late husbands child deceased for avoiding scandal'. Joane herself denied discussing marriage or reading the contract, but the couple were married in August, 1611.

Consistory Court of London Deposition Book, LMA DL/C 219, fo. 417 (17 Feb. 1611). The case is discussed at greater length and with a longer extract in Loreen L. Giese, 'Theatrical citings and bitings: some references to playhouses and players in London consistory court depositions, 1586–1611', *Early Theatre*, 1 (1998), pp. 113–28.

[George Ireland, of Gray's Inn, gentleman, where he has lived for 3 years, previously of Brasenose College, Oxford for 3 years, aged 22, who has known the plaintiff for two years and the defendant since the feast of St Bartholomew.

[To the second article he deposes and says] that . . . as he now remembreth about a fortnight before Michaelmas last past tharticulate John Newton and Joane Waters by means of the said Duke as this deponent taketh it met together at the sign of the Crown and Goat in West Smithfield London being a tavern, whither this deponent came into their company hearing that they then were there, for that he was well acquainted with the said parties, where he saith he saw the said Joane Waters and John Newton together in very loving and extraordinary kind manner, making love and showing great kindness each to other by drinking one to another and kissing and embracing together very lovingly and he verily believeth that the said Waters was then very much affected to him the said Newton in the way of marriage for that she the said Waters did then with her lips suck his the said Newton's neck in a manner of kindness whereby she made three red spots arise whereupon the said Newton asking her what she meant by it she answering said that she had marked him for her own. And after much kindness and conference then and there passed betwixt them she the said Waters requested him the said Newton to go home with her saying that he should be very welcome, which this deponent thinketh he did. . . .

5.2   Promising her marriage: Mary Marvell, 1656

When illicit sex was detected, many women claimed to have been drawn into it by a promise of marriage. Mary Marvell's examination, in the Commonwealth period when the sessions, rather than the church courts, had jurisdiction over sexual offences, is also revealing about patterns of sociability between men and women.

Essex Quarter Sessions Bundles, Essex RO, Q/SBa 2/97.

The examination of Mary Marvell of Great Braxted in the said county singlewoman taken the tenth day of October 1656 before Jeremy Aylett esquire one of the justices of the peace of the said county

Figure 8 **Courting couple**

From the Pepys Ballads, vol. IV, no. 119. By permission of the Pepys Library, Magdalene College, Cambridge

Idealised, romantic wooers like these feature over and over again in cheap print. In practice, as some of the documents here (and Figure 9) show, courtship was not always so decorous.

Who saith about Thursday was a month one Alexander Hall cordwainer was with this examinant at the White Hart in Maldon, and promising her marriage prevailed with her to lie with him as his wife. Then next morning she came with him to her mistress Joan Rouse's house in Great Braxted to whom the examinant is a servant, and there he the said Alexander took his leave of her. The next Lord's day he met her the said Mary beyond Kelvedon and forthwith they came to Larkin's house an alehouse keeper in Braxted aforesaid. And that night the said Alexander and the examinant lay together again as husband and wife, he promising still to make her his wife.

5.3 Sex by appointment: Mary Bathron, 1656

In contrast to the previous examination, at the same sessions Mary Bathron admitted to sex with a man who had made her no promises.

Essex Quarter Sessions Bundles, Essex RO, Q/SBa 2/97.

Figure 9 **Couple with cupid**

From the Pepys Ballads, vol. III, no. 138. By permission of the Pepys Library, Magdalene College, Cambridge

This image appeared in a series of ballads with different words for the cupid: here, it illustrates 'The Ranting Whores resolution: wherein you find that her only treasure, consisteth in being a lady of pleasure'.

The information and examination of Mary Bathron alias Bathrope taken ... upon the 31th of October 1656

This informant saith that about a fortnight after Michaelmas last was a twelvemonth not long before the wedding of Jeremy Right of Debden, she was in company with Henry Searle of Debden at the house of John Eliott. And that he the said Henry Searle followed her, when she went home from thence and that about six of the clock in the evening of the said day the said Henry Searle had the carnal knowledge of her body, in a ditch, between two closes near Debden Hall and that she was with child by him of a bastard child, of which she hath been since delivered.

This informant further saith that several times after by appointment she met him the said Henry Searle who had the carnal knowledge of her accordingly viz. two several times in the granary of Debden Hall.

And further she saith not.

5.4   A servant and her master's friend: Suzan More, 1608

For many women, their first sexual encounters would happen while they were in service; and while many courted fellow servants, others might be propositioned, harassed, or assaulted by their masters and their master's married friends. Suzan More appeared in the London consistory court in 1608 as witness in a prosecution of Thomas Creede for fornication and bastardy. Although only 25, she had a long and varied employment history, and was then working as a servant to a bookseller whose wife she helped make points. Thomas Creede was a married friend of her master's, a printer in the Old Exchange from 1593 to 1617; he printed some of Shakespeare's plays and in 1608 was printing, amongst others, treatises against temptation. The case was prosecuted by John Scales, a friend of Suzan's, rather than being presented by churchwardens as a disciplinary complaint. Suzan More's testimony is an account of the stated facts of the accusation against Thomas Creede, detailing his courtship of her, their relationship, and his response (and that of his wife) to her pregnancy; she also counters the allegations ('interrogatories') he made in his defence, that her master, Randall Birke, was the real father of her child, and that Suzan had cleared his name publicly. Anna Birke, Suzan's mistress, also testified Thomas had tried to seduce her, telling her 'she had a sweet pair of lips and if she were a good wench she would let him have some part with her husband'; other witnesses deposed that Suzan had named Thomas as the father in her labour. There is no mention of the child, who may have been stillborn, died shortly after birth, or been put out to nurse.

Consistory Court of London Deposition Book, LMA, DL/C 218, pp. 138 ff. (18 June 1608).

[Suzan More, servant of Hugh Jackson, stationer, of the parish of St Bride's Fleet St, where she has lived for six weeks, and previously in the house of Edward Handby for ten weeks or thereabouts and previously with one Randall Birke in the parish of St Giles without Cripplegate for about a year and previously in Holy Trinity Minories with one Mrs Long for three months or thereabouts and previously with one Arthur Goodgame of the parish of St Laurence Pountney for about one year and previously with one Mrs Lambert of the parish of St Margaret New Fish Street for a year or thereabouts and previously with Mrs Lynsey widow in the parish of St Peter Cornhill for about 2 years and previously in the town of Cambridge since her birth, where she was born, aged 25, she has known John Scales for 7 years and Thomas Creede since Easter 1607 and before as she says.]

[To the first, second, third, fourth and fifth articles she says and deposes] that the week before Easter last was twelve months she this deponent dwelling with one Randall Birke a bookseller without Cripplegate whose wife using the trade of pointmaking which she this deponent could do, she saith there came one day the articulate Thomas Creede who used to come often thither, he the same Thomas Creede being a printer and Randall Birke a bookseller, and she saith that he the same Thomas Creede began one day to talk with her this deponent first asking her name and she telling him Suzan he then said he had a sister of that name, and therefore quoth he you

Figure 10 **Couple on bed**

From the Pepys Ballads, vol. IV, no. 95. By permission of the Pepys Library, Magdalene College, Cambridge

Another much-used woodcut representing courtship and sex: this one is from 'The Hasty Bridegroom'. The bed is a typically solid, ornate one: beds were often the most significant and valuable pieces of household furniture, and they were rarely reserved exclusively for a married couple.

being so like my first wife as you are and your name Suzan I must needs love you, then asked her this deponent if she would go drink some time with him which she this deponent denying as she saith he asked her this deponent's mistress Mrs Birke leave for her this deponent and desired Mrs Birke to go with them herself, which she often denied, yet at last through his importunity both Mrs Birke and she this deponent went with him to the King's Head in Red Cross Street where they drunk wine with him, and then Mrs Birke and she this deponent returned home again and he the same Thomas Creede brought them home and she saith that sundry times after that he the said Creede would come thither and procure her this deponent to go with him to drink wine.

And she saith that about Midsummer last she this deponent going with him to the Sun Tavern in Aldersgate Street he gave her this deponent so much wine as she was drunk and sick withall and then he the same Creede had her this deponent to one Widow Grimes' house by Picket Hatch an alehouse and had her up into a chamber where she this deponent as she saith lay down on a bed to sleep and she saith at that time he the same Thomas Creede had the carnal knowledge of her this deponent's body, and she saith that after that time he the same Creede did sundry times entice her to go with him to taverns and she this deponent sometimes denying he would be very angry and then he would set others, sometimes tavern boys and sometimes the boys of the forenamed Widow Grimes to come and stand over the way against her this deponent's mistress's house and shop and ask her this deponent to come to them and she saith that twice after that first time she this deponent met him the same Thomas Creede at Widow Grimes house, both which times he the same Creede had the carnal knowledge of her this deponent's body, in so much as she this deponent being with child she this deponent acquainted him with it and then he said unto her this deponent thus, if you had gone from your master and left his house and would have been at my disposition as I told you I would have had you to have done then I would have provided for you and you should have wanted nothing but seeing you have continued still there at Birke's go fetch you another father for your child if you will for I mean not to father it, I will shift it off well enough and my wife will help to clear me of this matter and to shift it off as she hath shifted me of such matters as this is before now. And she saith that after that he the same Creede procured her this deponent's master and mistress and her this deponent to go to a tavern to supper in or near Old Fish Street, and she saith he the same Creede meeting with her his deponent and her fellow maidservant in Birke's house (named Blanche) by Cripplegate he gave each of them a cake and desired them to meet him at Islington the next day and he would give them a pig. And she saith that night he and his wife supped likewise in that tavern in Old Fish Street and then her this deponent's said master fell sick and that of the plague and so she this deponent did not go to Islington.

And she saith that after that when she this deponent perceived for certainty that she was with child she sent the maidservant being the kitchen maid in Birke's house named Blanche unto him to desire him but to provide a house for her and she would not farther trouble him, whereunto he the same Creede answered that Birke and she should not gull him so. And she this deponent told then her said master and mistress and they understanding thereof being much grieved sent for him the same Thomas Creede to a tavern, whither he the same Creede came and his wife after him, and there at that tavern the same Creede's wife at the first did so terrify her this deponent with words as she this deponent could not tell what to do, she saying that if she this deponent laid her child to her husband she would make her this deponent repent it all the days of her life. But at last she this deponent telling her Mrs Creede all the circumstances afore by her this deponent now deposed, she the same Mrs Creede began to speak her this deponent fair and persuaded her to go into the country to her friends, and so she gave her this deponent 10s. to get her away and she went with her this deponent to the Cambridge carriers and did see her placed in the wagon, but she this deponent being not able to endure the uneasy going of the wagon, it being in the great frost time last, she this deponent returned back again when she came at Ware and coming to London could not get a place to lie in of a great while but lay abroad in the streets.

At last she saith she got to lie in a poor woman's house in Gravel Lane in Houndsditch, where she lay two days without meat or drink, and then she saith there was one More a poor man of her this deponent's name, that had some little acquaintance of her this deponent, understanding of her this deponent's being there came unto her and persuaded her this deponent to procure him the same Creede to be called before some justice and then he would take some order for her this deponents keeping, but she this deponent was (as she saith) unwilling to take such course yet he the same More unknown to her this deponent procured a warrant from Sir Stephen Sones and called Thomas Creede before him and likewise her this deponent. And she saith that there she this deponent being examined privately by Sir Stephen she this deponent told in substance and effect as much to him as now she hath deposed whereupon he the same Thomas Creede was bound over to the sessions. And she the same Creede's wife being then there seemed to make very much of her this deponent, bidding her this deponent to come to her to her house and she should have such as she had to do her good until she were delivered and then when her time should come to be delivered, send for me, quoth she the same mistress Creede.

And she saith by reason of her kind words she this deponent within a week after went to the same Creede's house, where first he, espying her this deponent, began to speak very churlishly asking her in a furious manner wherefore she came thither and she this deponent told him that if his wife had not bid her she said she would not. And then his wife came to her this deponent and spake something roughly to her, but yet called her this deponent Suzan by her name and willed her this deponent to get her a place to lie in and when you are delivered, quoth she, my word will go for a bastard I warrant you.[1] And these premises or at least some of it she this deponent hath confessed and acknowledged to some of her friends and she saith that she thinketh there is a common fame and report in the parishes articulate of this matter by her deposed of by reason of his the same Thomas Creed's own speeches and his wife's together with his continual visiting and familiar behaviour to and with her this deponent at taverns and at her said master's house [And otherwise she knows nothing to depose].

[To the 6th article she says] that he the same Thomas Creede told her this deponent after they had been the first time at the tavern as aforesaid together that if he had given her this deponent's mistress but a pint more

---

1. It's not clear whether Mrs Creede means here that she would testify that her husband was the child's father, or deny it, as had earlier been threatened.

he said he could have done what he had would with her. And Blanche Howell mentioned in this article coming one day home to Randall Birke's house with some extraordinary behaviour and her face red that she this deponent perceived she had been drinking wine, through her this deponent's insistence confessed unto her this deponent that she had been with Mr Creede and he had willed her to bring home her master's child which she then had and then meet him at Goodwife Grimes' house but she this deponent would not suffer her to go at that time [. . .]

[To the interrogatories of Thomas Creede]

[To the 4th . . . she answers] that she is a poor servant little or nothing worth but liveth by her service . . .

[To the 11th she answers as deposed above] and saith it was in the daytime and in an upper chamber in Widow Grimes' house he having a suit of fustian on when he came to her and she this respondent a violet coloured waistcoat and a stuff kirtle and he had the same clothes on every time that they met at Widow Grimes' house aforesaid his fustian suit being cut with a small cut and she saith she knoweth his name to be Thomas Creede by his own confession.

[To the 15th . . .] saith she had no wages but wrought her points by the gross and was paid by the gross for them viz. 5s. 4d. a gross. . . .

[To the 23rd she answers] that Sir Stephen Sone said indeed that it were good there should be a strange midwife to bring her this respondent to bed but he said expressly thus not provided by you Mistress Creede nor yet by Birke and therefore there was such a midwife as that neither she this respondent nor either of the other women Creede's wife or Birke's wife ever knew or saw provided and sent for. . . .

[To the 24th she answers] and saith that so soon as she this respondent fell in labour and travail of childbirth both Mrs Creede and Mrs Birke were sent for but she this respondent was delivered before they came . . .

5.5   The master's son: Elizabeth Hodson, 1633

Elizabeth Hodson appeared at the Staffordshire quarter sessions in 1633 whilst pregnant; after giving birth, she submitted a petition for relief, saying that her master, 'a man of great wealth', refused to help her. It was not unusual for servants to find their daily work interrupted with sexual propositions from their masters, or to have to leave their services pregnant by them, their sons, or their friends; see also the previous document, and the testimony of Susan Lay in Chapter 10.

Staffordshire Quarter Sessions Rolls, Staffordshire RO, Q/SR 213/19.

The information of Elizabeth Hodson taken at Eccleshall Castle . . . on the 2 November 1633. . . .

She saith that she dwelt with John Johnson of the parish of Chebsey, father to the said Thomas Johnson whom she accuseth to be the father of the child that she now goeth withall, and farther saith that the Saturday sevennight after Stafford fair and being the third day of May she coming into her master's stable with a candle for the men to dress their horses by, and the said Thomas Johnson aforesaid put out the candle and worked his pleasure with her, and after that had to do with her in the kitchen in his father's house, and another time in the hall chimney, and saith that he promised to marry her.

5.6   Showing her privities: Joane Cranckland, 1605

Joane Cranckland, single mother of a bastard child in a Somerset village, was sexually troublesome to the local authorities. Showing one's privities in public was something men were generally more likely to be accused of than women; the words and acts attributed to her record a kind of sexual aggressiveness that represented many of the great fears of female sexuality. For both women and men, such visions might have been at once menacing and enticing.

Consistory Court of Bath and Wells Deposition Book, Somerset Archives, D/Dcd 34 [n.p.] (1605).

[Thomas Burridge alias Mills of Raddington, Somerset, husbandman . . .]
. . . [he deposes and says] that this jurate being one of the churchwardens of Raddington . . . did present together with the said Hill, and on the report of John Hill, Edmund Hill, and John Stockham the said Joane Cranckland that she shewed to them her privities twice in one day, And that upon the report of the said Richard Chubberie alias Hill, he did . . . present[1] the said Joane Cranckland that she made a jest that the said John Stockham could not bridle his nature at the sight thereof, And that she having a base child in her house of the age of eight years of thereabouts caused the said child to lie down and shew how a woman did lie when a man had his pleasure of her. And also that upon the report of Mr Toby Davies parson of Chipstable, she should report and say[2] that when she answered the matters at Wells, there was a man that took up her clothes as high as her knees.

SEX AND MARRIAGE

5.7   Kind wanton letters: Maria Thynne, c. 1606

Maria Audley, a gentlewoman, married Thomas Thynne in 1602; he inherited Longleat in Wiltshire in 1604. There was some family displeasure at their marriage. Maria's letters tease Thomas with her failure to submit to the expected role of submissive

1. Complain to officials.
2. I.e., she said.

wife. This is a brief extract from a much longer letter, one of many discussing house-hold arrangements in Thomas's absence, but also revealing the kind of passionate marriage that often left little traces in records.

Maria to Thomas Thynne, *c.* 1606. Reproduced by kind permission of the Wiltshire Record Society from Alison Wall (ed.), *Two Elizabethan Women: Correspondence of Joan and Maria Thynne 1575–1611*, Trowbridge, Wiltshire Record Society, vol. 38, 1982.

My best beloved Thomken, and my best little Sirrah, know that I have not, nor will not forget how you made my modest blood flush up into my bashful cheek at your first letter, thou threatened sound payment, and I sound repay-ment, so as when we meet, there will be pay, and repay, which will pass and repass, allgiges ultes fregnan tolles,[1] thou knowest my mind, though thou dost not understand me. Well now laying on side my high choller,[2] know in sober sadness that I am at Longleat, ready and unready to receive thee, and here will attend thy coming. . . .

. . . I salute thy best beloved self with the return of thine own wish in thy last letter, and so once more fare ever well, my best and sweetest Thomken, and many thousand times more than these 1000 000 000 000 000 000 000 00 for thy kind wanton letters
Thine and only all thine Maria

5.8   Without an unchaste thought: Dame Sarah Cowper, 1700–1

Dame Sarah Cowper's diary records a somewhat different attitude towards married love from that of Maria Thynne. Cowper, a merchant's daughter born Sarah Holland in 1644, married the Whig MP and lawyer Sir William Cowper in 1664. She had four children before the age of 26, but by 1700, at least, the couple were barely on speaking terms, and Sarah Cowper, who described herself as a Protestant of the 'truest blue', spent many hours alone reading. Cowper's diaries, recording a combination of spiritual reflections and daily events and grievances, and her common-place books, cover the years 1700–16. In these extracts, written in 1700 and 1701 when she was 57, she reflects on her sexual virtue and the chastity she prided herself on maintaining within marriage, with a satisfaction that was apparently not echoed by her husband.

Diary of Dame Sarah Cowper, vol 1, Hertfordshire Archives, D/EP/F29, pp. 13, 60–1.

[9 Oct. 1700] In the evening Sir William fell into a wrangling discourse wherein he compared, or rather would level me with a liar and a whore, saying, pride was a worse sin than either, and a chaste woman that over-valued herself was in greater fault. However I shall not be persuaded, but the virtuous have some reason to value themselves, and to expect esteem

1. Distorted Latin probably meaning something like 'you will frequently rise up'.
2. Pun on choler, collar, colour.

from others, and I spared not to tell him, that my manner of living with him, did deserve all the praise, love and respect, that he could give me. But my comfort was if I missed of that, I had a sure promise: Do that which is good and thou shall have praise &c.

[10 Feb. 1701] Came a penny post letter without a name, the contents were to dissuade me from appearing to be a friend to the Lady Te. – for that she kept ill company as would bring her to shame and ruin. Now knowing by experience, that sometimes such as suffer the wrong, bear also the blame, the only friendship I hath shown hath been charity: when occasion hath been offered, to speak favourably of her: Many times when young women are ill used they commit indiscretions that yet may not come within the verge of a crime, and I hope that to be the worst of her case. This subject occasions me to reckon myself a mirror of chastity, even beyond the most entire Virgin. For to conceive four children without knowing what it is to have an unchaste thought or sensual pleasure and being but 26 when the last was born have ever since then remained pure – is a thing scarce to be matched by a married woman, and a reflection that without vanity may justly delight me.

SEX BETWEEN WOMEN

5.9 Whorish ways: Susannah Bell, 1694

Susannah Bell's story appears only briefly and faintly in the written records of early modern London. She was claimed to have been married to an alleged bigamist, Ralph Hollingsworth. Hollingsworth was sued by his later wife, Maria Seely, at the London consistory court in 1694, and in the proceedings a letter from him to Maria Seely was produced, in which he defended his previous marriages as being clandestine or unconsummated. The extract describing Susannah Bell is from this letter to Maria Seely. We know nothing more of her.

Consistory Court of London Allegations, Libels and Sentence Book, LMA, DL/C 146, fo. 531 (11 May 1694).

... now as to Susannah Bell: she knowing her infirmity ought not to have married; her infirmity is such that no man can lie with her, and because it so she has ways with women as well, as with her old companions men, which is not fit to be named but most rank whorish they are ... the said Susan belongs to a company of clippers and coiners, as she herself was telling me and relating the great benefit of it, which was one main thing, which frighted me from her. ...

Figure 11 **Two women in bed together**
From the Roxburghe Ballads, vol II, no. 29

This image is used in at least two seventeenth-century ballads, one of them 'The Bloody Battle at Billingsgate, beginning with a scolding bout between two young fish-women, Doll and Kate'. There is no clue as to what these two women in bed together are doing: the image might represent a mistress and servant, or two friends sharing a bed as many did away from home; but they are apparently embracing. (This is a nineteenth century redrawing of the original.)

5.10 Cross-dressing: 1692

Cases of women passing as men were notorious, although rare, in the seventeenth century. Stories of women discovered in the army or the navy, sacrificing their natural gender for the good of their country, passed into popular myth. Occasionally, the stories also include reference to such women courting or marrying other women; some did so and remained undiscovered for years.

From *The Gentleman's Journal: Or the Monthly Miscellany* [ed. Pierre Antoine Motteux], April 1692, London, 1692, pp. 22–3.

Courage is so natural to the English, that even the tender sex give a frequent mark of theirs: We have had but two years ago a young lady on board the Fleet in man's apparel, who show'd all the signs of the most undaunted valour. Several others are still living, and some of them in this town, who have served whole campaigns, and fought stroke by stroke by the most manly soldiers. The last letters from Genoa give us an account of an English heroine who, they tell us, is of quality. She had served two years in the French Army in Piedmont as a volunteer, and was entertained for her merit by the Governor of Pignerol in the quality of his Gentlemen of the Horse; at last playing with another of her sex, she was discover'd; and the Governor having thought fit to inform the King his master of this, he hath sent him word that he would be glad to see the lady; which hath occasion'd her coming to Genoa, in order to embark for France: Nature has bestow'd no less beauty on her than courage; and her age is not above 26. The French envoy hath orders to cause her to be waited on to Marseille, and to furnish her with all necessaries.

SECRECY AND ADULTERY

5.11 'I mean to have a good turn of you': Clement Underhill, 1598

Clement Underhill was brought to the London Bridewell accused of adultery, on the testimony of her neighbour Margaret Browne, who claimed to have seen her through a hole in the wall, and to have heard the precise words with which she greeted her lover.

Bridewell Hospital Records, Guildhall, BCB 4 (microfilm), fo. 23.

The examination of Margaret Browne ... taken the thirtieth day of May 1598 before the Lord Mayor and Court of Aldermen....

Margaret Browne the wife of Henry Browne, citizen and stationer of London dwelling in Houndsditch in the parish of St Botolph without Bishopsgate in the ward of Bishopsgate London saith that upon the thirteenth day of this present month of May 1598 being Saturday Michael Fludd and Clement Underhill the wife of John Underhill were making merry together in the house of the said John Underhill being the next house unto this deponent's house in the parish and ward aforesaid he the said John being from home. And as they were eating their victualls Underhill's wife said unto Fludd these words eat no more cheese for that it will make your gear[1] short and I mean to have a good turn of you soon, immediately after that went up into her chamber and lay upon her bed and there continued until six of the clock or thereabouts at what time she shut in her shop windows and

---

1. Genitals. Cheese was thought to have magical properties, but there are no further clues to the meaning of this phrase.

went up unto him with a rapier in her hand and asked him whether he had spoken with all his friends or not whereupon the said Fludd took the rapier out of her hand laying it aside took her in his arms and brought her to the bed's foot and took up her clothes and she put her hand into his hose and he kissed her and pulled her upon him upon the bed's feet. And after that they went to the bed's side and he taking her in his arms did cast her upon the bed. He plucked up her clothes to her thighs, she plucked them up higher (whereby this deponent saw not only her hose being a seawater green colour and also her bare thighs) then he went up to her upon the bed and putting down his hose had carnal copulation with her and having so done he wiped his yard on her smock and this deponent had in the meantime called up the said Henry Browne the husband of this deponent to see this deed, who came and saw Fludd come from the bed with his hose down whereupon this deponent's husband went away and would see no more. Then this deponent saw the said Fludd to go to a pail or a tub of water in the same chamber and washed his yard then Underhill's wife departed from him to fetch a pot of beer and out of the cupboard in the table took bread and butter which they did eat together and then she left up the pot and said to him, Here now I drink to thee.

5.12   The maid's story: Agnes Brampton, 1612

This is an excerpt from a long church court case between Agnes Brampton, a London woman with a good portion, and her husband Walter, who was suing for separation on the grounds of Agnes's adultery. As this testimony reveals, he appears to have been at least complicit in any adultery that did take place. Martha Robinson, the couple's servant, testified to her master's attempts to get her to spy on her mistress, her mistress's lover's attempts to seduce her, and her mistress's confidences in her. The words she reports of Agnes Brampton might be a rare instance of a woman's own words about her sexual and emotional desires – or an imagined scene of confidences that supports the case against Agnes. Martha also reported that Agnes visited a cunning woman, thus hinting at attempts to ensure the shortness of her husband's life. Yet the last part of her testimony – her answers to Agnes's defence – concedes that the events were stage-managed by Walter, who paid her £10 to spy on her mistress, encouraged Edmund Holland to visit the house in the hopes of 'alluring' Agnes into adultery, and hoped, now he had security for her portion from her father, to be divorced and to 'allow her no more than the law would give her'. It remains unclear what actual circumstances lay behind the stories.

Consistory Court of London Deposition Book, LMA, DL/C 220, fos 657–60 (Oct. 1612).

[Martha Robinson, maid, of the parish of St Giles Cripplegate, London, who previously lived with the plaintiff for half a year, aged 23; she has known the litigants since the beginning of Quadragesima[1] last]

... [To the 12th article ... she deposes and says] that from Shrovetide

1. First Sunday in Lent.

last past as she says being the time of this deponent's coming to dwell with the articulate Agnes Brampton she the said Agnes dwelt in the lane articulate called Cony House Lane and she saith that for the time of her dwelling with the said Agnes being about half a year, she this deponent hath seen the articulate Theophilus Holland resort to the said house divers times, and hath known him once as she saith to have been there alone in the company of the said Agnes Brampton, and for Edmund Holland she saith he likewise hath been divers times in the said house with her master and mistress and once in private as she saith with her mistress the articulate Agnes, and for Bowker articulate she saith she only saw him once at her said master's house in company with her said mistress and Theophilus Holland being likewise with him as she says. . . .

[To the 14th article . . . she deposes and says] that one day in the time articulate and as she remembreth upon Good Friday last past this deponent's master the party producent being to ride a journey out of town into Suffolk or Norfolk called this deponent unto him and told this deponent in private that he was then to ride forth and to stay long forth and therefore willed her to have a care of his said house or to that effect and likewise said to this deponent talking of his wife that he suspected that the said Theophilus Holland, Edmund Holland and the foresaid Bewker and other of his wife's lovers and acquaintance would in his absence take occasion then to resort to the said Agnes his wife and therefore willed and charged this deponent that if any of the said parties or any other should happen to resort to his wife and that they or her said mistress should command her to go this ways or that ways or did send this deponent of any messages or errands or send any letters or that if the said Agnes her mistress should offer or be desirous to go any whither abroad that she this deponent should not gainsay anything her mistress did or refuse to go whither she should send her, only he willed this deponent to be secret and not to let her said mistress know what he then said unto her, and that this deponent should mark and observe the behaviour of her said mistress and the foresaid parties and that she should be ready to go upon any errands for her said mistress if it were, rather than fail to be her bawd, and that she this deponent should make her said mistress believe that she would do any thing for her. For, said he to this deponent, do but speak her fair and she is of that disposition that thou shalt have anything of her.

. . . she saith that the same Good Friday about ten of the clock this deponent and her said mistress being then alone in her said mistress's house the articulate Theophilus Holland and Edmond Bewker came to the said house and were letten in to the house by this deponent's said mistress, and went up together with her mistress into the hall where this deponent was, and they being there the said Bewker would have sent this deponent for some wine and this deponent refused to go, telling them if they would have any wine they should fetch it themselves and then they would have sent her for beer and she said as she did before and began to find fault with their so late coming into the house, and many other words they then had.

And after they had sat all a while in the hall they went up into the kitchen being above the hall where the said Holland and her mistress sat down by the fire side and Bewker taking a pack of cards in his hand would have had this deponent to have played with him but she would not, and soon after that, this deponent's mistress went into her bedchamber and went to bed and this deponent following her and helping her to bed and the said Holland and Bewker staying above in the kitchen, and after her mistress was in bed the said Holland and Bewker came down into her chamber to her said mistress and Bewker went presently away out of doors and this deponent shut the door after him and returned again to her mistress and sat in her said chamber the space of an hour all which time the said Theophilus Holland sat upon the bedside by her mistress talking with her.

And at last she saith the bellman coming by and this deponent saying that the bellman would find fault with their light the said Holland with his rapier put out the candle which before was burning by them and then her said mistress asked this deponent angrily (as she saith) what she meant that she came not away to bed and thereupon this deponent having put off her clothes went into the bed to her mistress on the further side from Holland, he sitting still upon the side of the bed for at the least half an hour, and soon after the said Holland reaching his hand to this deponent and jogging her asked this deponent if he should come to bed to her and she answered him no for by report he had enough already, and thereupon this deponent being angry said if he could not be quiet that she would get her away from thence, and her mistress bid her do so.

And then this deponent went from them into her own chamber, and left the said Theophilus Holland and her mistress all alone, but what they did there she cannot depose but saith that after they had been together half an hour or more they fell out one with another so that the said Holland calling to this deponent departed from out of her said mistress's house and went away. . . .

[To the 18th article she deposes and says] that in the time of this deponent's dwelling with the said party producent and the foresaid Agnes, she this deponent hath heard the said Agnes say to her husband . . . in a kind of merriment that her first husband lived but nine weeks and if she had thought that he . . . would have lived above eighteen weeks she would never have married him. . . .

[To the 22nd article she deposes and says] that she knows nothing to depose other than she has predeposed, saving that sometimes when as this deponent upon some occasions hath talked with the articulate Agnes concerning her keeping company with the forenamed Holland and Bewker and some others she the said Agnes hath sometimes wept thereat, and sometimes hath said a pox on them for rogues they have been my overthrow and that she would not care if it were not for John at Lane's (meaning as she saith John Wright . . .) but other manner of confession she saith she heard none. . . .

5.13 'Knowing herself to be fruitful': Elizabeth Higgs, 1665

Elizabeth Higgs was a married Somerset woman engaged in a long-term relationship with a neighbour. In 1665, however, she found herself widowed and pregnant by her lover, who then refused to marry her. With little or no means of contraception, women such as Elizabeth Higgs might develop a clear sense of their fertility and its risks; but this did not always protect them against unwanted pregnancy.

Somerset Quarter Sessions Rolls, Somerset Archives, Q/SR 106/6a (11 Mar. 1664).

The examination of Elizabeth Higgs of Donyatt taken before Henry Walcond. . . .

Who saith upon her oath that George Grubham of Donyatt in the county of Somerset having formerly begotten two children on the body of this examinate, and both being dead did as before frequent oftentimes the company of this examinate, and by many promises as by marrying of her if her husband were dead did tempt this examinate to have the carnal knowledge as before of her body. This examinate did say unto the said Grubham that she would not have him do any such thing, for that it would be a great disgrace unto both for that she knew her self to be so fruitful that she should be soon begotten with child in case he had to do with her. This examinate saith that this answer of hers would not make him desist, but did still solicit this examinate to have the enjoyment of his desires. This examinate saith that being wearied out with his often solicitations did between a fortnight and five weeks of St James tide last permit and suffer the said George Grubham in the ring chamber or lower room (which of the two this examinate cannot well remember) to lie with her twice, after which this examinate did happen to be with child by the said Grubham, who acquainting him with it, said that this examinate must hang her self. This examinate another time telling the said Grubham of her being with child [he] made this answer that he could forswear it as well as he could other things. This examinate being demanded whether any other person beside himself have ever had the carnal knowledge of her body saith upon the oath she have taken that he alone and no other man is the only reputed father of the child she now goeth withall. And more this examinate cannot say.

5.14   Spying through the wall: Mary Babb, 1666

Mary Babb and her brother-in-law were prosecuted for adultery and incest (their relationship being within the forbidden degrees) at the consistory court of York in 1666. Like many other such cases in the late seventeenth century, the testimony of her neighbours follows a familiar narrative model with its own conventions, though there are some personalised touches like the words of love. Certainly, early modern buildings made it relatively easy to spy on illicit sex; but stories like these, whilst heavily based on established convention, also allow room for creative flourishes.

Consistory Court of York Cause Papers, Borthwick Institute of Historical Research, CPH 2688.

[Elizabeth Tullett, wife, of Clipsten Forge, aged 26 . . .]

[She deposes that . . .] She this examinant hath lived at Clipsten Forge these four years last past and more where the articulate Ottiwell Babb and Mary Babb also lived. . . . Richard Babb hath by times yearly during the same years lived with the said Ottiwell Babb and tabled with him in his house, and saith that for and during the same time this examinate hath seen and observed the articulate Mary Babb and Richard Babb much company together both on foot and horseback and been together they two alone in secret and apart places to commit incontinency together and to carry themselves too lightly and wantonly not becoming civil persons. . . .

[She deposes that] she this examinate living . . . next house to the said Ottiwell Babb having only a wall betwixt them hath several times seen and observed very uncivil passages betwixt them . . . in the said Ottiwell's house and especially about the month of May last past this examinant looking though the wall at an hole did see her the said Mary Babb pass by the said hole having her clothes and smock pulled up to her breast none being in the house with her but the articulate Richard Babb. And also upon a Tuesday in the beginning of July last past this examinate did see the said Mary and Richard Babb alone together in the said Ottiwell Babb's house she the said Mary being making of ash balls and there they two did frequently kiss each other with as much eagerness and familiarity as man and wife could do and he put his hand under her clothes in an uncivil manner which she allowed without resistance.

And the day after being Wednesday this examinate did see and observe the said Richard Babb go into the said Ottiwell Babb's house several times and pull the door after him and this examinate looking in at the said hole through the wall did see him take her on his knee and there kiss each other very freely and too familiarly and he put his hand under her clothes in very uncivil manner several times and at the last she this examinate did see them the said Mary Babb and Richard Babb in the very act of adultery or incest in a very beastly manner she the said Mary holding up her hinder parts and having her clothes and smock pulled up above her loins and he thrusting at her behind nine times together, where this examinate did see him draw his yard and thrust it into her body in such postures and gestures used in acts of carnal copulation and she the said Mary did answer him accordingly in which posture they continued the space of half a quarter of an hour in the presence and sight of this examinate and her precontest Richard Vintin and his wife who also were with this examinate and looked in at the said hole, who being much troubled at such passages did hastily go into the house where they were so uncivilly acting, thinking to have taken them in the very act. But they hearing a stir, the said Mary clapped her down on her breech on the hearth and he did sit on the bench by her and the said Mary said Lord Bless me but Alice Vintin wife to the said Richard replied, the Lord hath nothing to do with thee, and then the said Richard Vintin said to them Woe worth you what have you been doing, to which the said Richard Babb said what have we been doing? and Vintin said You have been playing nought with your brother's wife thus and thus (speaking in plain terms), whereat the said Richard Babb looked very pale and shamefully but have no answer nor did deny it; and so they went away.

5.15 Doing penance: Ursula Shepherd, 1589

Prosecutions for illicit sex at the church courts generally resulted in penances which were meant to signal both public shame and reconciliation with the community of the church. They were usually performed at Sunday service, and might involve standing in the church porch in a white sheet, or with a paper declaring the offence round the culprit's neck, and the saying of a penance. This extract from a London church court act book records, first, Ursula Shepherd's admission of leaving her husband for another man, and secondly, the penance decreed by the judge. The case was brought by Ursula's husband, who requested (and was granted) a separation which would allow them to live apart (though not to remarry).

Consistory Court of London Instance Act Book, LMA, DL/C 13, p. 16 (1589).

She responds that she this respondent being free from all contracts of matrimony for her own part did about one and twenty years now sithence[1] contract lawful matrimony by words of present time[2] with him the said Henry Shepherd and after that did solemnize marriage with him the said Henry Shepherd ... and hath had by him ten children ... about midsummer last past she left the company of her said husband and played the whore with Richard Mathewe her husband's servant and with him went down to Cambridge and both by the way and also in Cambridge town and other places where she was with him did commit whoredom with him ... and lived with him as his harlot from that time until about a month now since. ...

1. Since.
2. I.e., a promise of marriage in the present tense, such as 'I take you to be my husband', which was the essential requirement for a legally binding union.

[Her penance is to say:]

Good people I do here before God and you all confess that whereas I have been a married wife unto Henry Shepherd for the space of twenty years I (forgetting god and my duty unto my husband) have committed adultery and played the harlot with one Richard Mathewe my servant now of late time. And for the same I am by order of law divorced from my husband and enjoined to do this my penance. And therefore I desire you all to take example by me and I do promise hereafter to lead a chaste life and this her penance is to be done upon Sunday next following in the parish church of St Mary Woolchurch in London in service time.

RAPE, ASSAULTS, AND ATTEMPTS

5.16 'A simple body': Agnes Clement, 1609

Agnes Clement, a husbandman's wife from Midsomer Norton in Somerset, reported her assault by a man she knew to the quarter sessions in April 1609. A note at the foot of the document recorded: 'he hath attempted other women for the like: which shall be proved'.

Somerset Quarter Sessions Rolls, Somerset Archives, Q/SR 3/1/10 (19 April 1609).

The examination of Agnes Clement the wife of John Clement of Midsomer Norton in the county of Somerset husbandman

Who saith that between Midsummer and St James tide last, John Peyrce thelder of Midsomer Norton aforesaid, sent for this examinant by a boy of his to request her to come presently to his house to winnow whilst that the wind did serve which she then refused. Whereupon the said John Peyrce sent for her again, within a quarter of an hour after. At which time, she this examinant went presently to his dwelling house, where the said Peyrce was, she saying unto him I am now come to winnow your corn. But the said John Peyrce, then presently took his privy parts in hand, and informed her to take the same in her hand, striving with her, for the use of her body. And further this examinant saith that the said John Peyrce was too strong for her, and with long striving did with force use her body against her will, throwing her against a board, in such violent manner, that he brake the skin of her hand. And this examinant crying out, that he was the utter undoing and spoil of her, she saying that she was but a simple body for any such matter: Who answered that he did account of her to be as fit for such a purpose, as the best lady in the land and willed her to hold her peace, and said, thou durst not know what is good for thine self, who hath to do with me, and also further saith that the said John Peyrce sent for her again within some fortnight or three weeks after, by the same boy, that she this examinant should come again unto his uncle Peyrce, who would be very angry, he said, if she came not. But this examinant refused to go, her husband demanded of her, why she went not, who answered she would not go any more unto him, but the cause wherefore, she was loath to discover. And being troubled in mind and conscience, did afterwards confess it, first to a friend of hers, named goodwife Miller, desiring to know of her, what was left to be done in it, who advised her to speak the truth and no more. But afterwards this examinant saith, she could not choose but make it known to her husband how wickedly the said Peyrce had used her and taken her against her will.

5.17   Resistance with all her strength: Joan Brown, c. 1601

Joan Brown testified in the prosecution of Thomas Hellyer for illicit sex with a number of unmarried women in Lottisham, near Datchett, Somerset. Her testimony is a particularly long and detailed one, recording her anger at her assailant and her attempts at self-defence, as well as her experience of powerlessness as a woman and a servant. Her description of Hellyer's 'careless' assumption of her complicity, in line with the other servant he has abused, is particularly striking. It suggests that this was at least one working woman who expected the court to hear her complaint of attempted rape with an outrage to match her own. Unusually, as well, Brown signed her own deposition.

Consistory Court of Bath and Wells Deposition Book, Somerset Archives, D/D/cd34 (1601/2).

[Joan Brown of Lottisham, spinster, who has lived there for a year and a half and previously lived in West Bradley for half a year, born in Baltonsbrough in the same diocese, aged 40, she has known Thomas Hellyer well for the last half year.]

[To the third, fourth and fifth articles she knows nothing to depose:] saving that on a certain Sunday, or holy day in the afternoon happening about some fortnight or three weeks next after the feast of Whitsuntide last past before this her examination, and within fortnight next after that the articulate Marie Loxton was delivered of child or near thereabouts, this examinate did see the articulate Thomas Hellyer to lift up the latch of a barn's door of the articulate Thomas Quarman's, in which barn the said Marie was delivered of child, and finding the door to be locked so that he could not get in, he departed away again. . . .

[She deposes and says] that on a certain Sunday or holy day happening about St James tide now last past, and in the afternoon of the same day, the articulate Thomas Hellyer came unto this deponent as she was in the backside of her master the articulate Thomas Quarman's house in Lottisham within the parish of Datchett articulate, going to fetch in a tankard of water, and took away the tankard from her, and thrust her by violence into the entry of the said house, and closing the door thereof with his heels, he by main force threw her down upon the ground, lay down upon her, and told her that he would occupy her, and earnestly entreated her so to do, and finding her in no wise consenting to his lascivious and filthy lust, he took up her clothes near as high as her girdle not withstanding any resistance she could make, which she did with all the strength she had. And then the said Hellyer took forth of his breeches his privy member or yard, and strived and struggled with her in the said entry for the space of an hour or near thereabouts, assaying by all means to have the carnal knowledge of her body, and in the end seeing that this jurate at no hand would consent to his attempted devilish purpose, he left her and went his way.

[And further she deposes and says] that on the next Sunday then following in the afternoon, the said Thomas Hellyer again opening the back door came into the hall of the said house, and there finding this deponent took her by the arm, and requested her to go into a certain chamber of the same house within the hall, this deponent demanding him with what she should do there, he (after many foul and unseemly speeches, uttering and bewraying his lecherous intent) told her saying I'll occupy thee. But this deponent utterly refused the same and requested him to depart and suffer her to go about her master's business. And thereupon he took her by main force in his arms, and violently and altogether against her will, carried her into the said chamber, and threw her down upon the bed, notwithstanding that as he was bearing of her in that sort, this examinant caught hold of a certain cupboard standing in the said hall. And there kept her upon the said bed for the more part of an hour, and notwithstanding that she continually resisted him with all the might she possibly could, yet he pulled all her clothes very near as high as her middle leaving her body bare so far. And when this examinate strived to hide her shame, and to put down her clothes again, the said Hellyer took both her arms and wrested them back over her head. And all this whiles he continued sometimes entreating by all lecherous, and lustful means and sometimes violently, and forcibly striving, and wrestling with her to have the carnal knowledge of her body: but in the end departed without his purpose as aforesaid.

And she further deposeth and saith that on the Sunday then next following at evening prayer time the said Thomas Hellyer came to this deponent the third time as she was dressing of her masters grist[1] in the kitchen of the said house, and again very earnestly did solicit this deponent's chastity, and again by force carried her in his arms into the said chamber threw her upon the bed, pulled up her clothes, and in all respects both in words and deeds, used himself, and her, for the space of half an hour or thereabouts as he had done the second time: But at that time this deponent being willing to be discharged from his company told him saying I pray thee be gone, my master will come anon and find us, whereunto the said Henry carelessly made this answer following, or the like in effect Whiewe, is that such a matter, I know I have

1. Corn.

been playing here with Mary at one door whiles thy master hath been coming in at the other and could be welcome still, and she hath let me out at one door when her master hath been coming in at the other, meaning one Marie Loxton as this jurate doth verily believe, for that the said Marie Loxton dwelt with the said Thomas Quarman not above half a year, or thereabouts next before this deponent came to dwell with him. . . .

6

MARRIAGE

In the early modern period marriage was an economic as well as a personal decision. It determined female identity in both legal and social contexts; for women of all social classes, the ramifications of marital choice extended into every area of their lives. For the vast majority of women and men, marriage was 'until death us do part'. Separations, which did not allow remarriage, were possible but rare; divorce with remarriage was virtually impossible, at least in law. Death, however, ended marriage as frequently as divorce does today.

Entering into marriage generally involved a process of careful, slow negotiation and a series of recognised stages of commitment. Until the mid-seventeenth century at least, couples continued to make formal betrothals, which could constitute binding contracts of marriage, and which were treated by at least some people as effective marriages which made sex permissible. Our fullest records of ordinary courtships are of those which never became marriages, but ended instead with one partner trying to force the marriage through litigation at the church courts. These were atypical outcomes, but the stories of such cases record the social worlds of unmarried people and the processes of their courtships, the public and private promises they made, and the extent of physical relationships before marriage. While gentry and noble couples were expected to follow their parents' wishes in the matter of marriage, those at the lower end of the social scale had a good deal more freedom, partly because they tended to marry later, in their mid to late twenties. Many young women and men were living and working away from home, and it was their employers, older friends, or distant kin who supervised their courtships; others made their own marriages. On the whole, most young women expected to take the advice and help of parents and friends, but not necessarily to be ruled against their will.

Marriage was understood to be a central plank in the social order of early modern England: orderly households (ruled by men) made for an orderly kingdom. Conduct books prescribed a hierarchical relationship of duties and responsibilities between husbands and wives, as between parents and children or servants and masters. One influential historical model described the sixteenth and seventeenth centuries as a time of emotional distance, patriarchal authority, and lack of family privacy, with a corresponding lack of intimacy in marital relationships.[1]

Companionate, more egalitarian marriages, it was argued, only came into being with the new ideals of domesticity and romantic marriage of the eighteenth century. More recently, this chronology and the distinctions on which it depends have been disputed.[2] The romantic ideal of the eighteenth century did not replace patriarchal marriages with more equal relationships; nor was the sixteenth- and seventeenth-century model of patriarchal order incompatible with ideals of companionship and intimate, loving marriages. For most early modern people, marriage necessarily involved both partnership and hierarchy, love and mastery. Gentry women and men have left letters in which they speak of the expectations, disagreements, negotiations, and compromises of marriage; but we still have only piecemeal evidence for the ways in which the majority of women and men negotiated their emotional, economic, and physical relationships. As with courtship, we can often only guess how things worked from the evidence of what happened when they went wrong.

When marriages broke down, there were few possibilities. It was against church law to live apart without a decree of separation. Separations might be granted on the grounds of extreme cruelty or adultery, as those requested in the suits here, but they were rare, and did not allow remarriage. Adultery, a complaint almost always made by men against women, might involve only one incident; but cruelty had to involve a risk to life, and was necessarily difficult to prove. Early modern households tended to be more public than modern ones, and violence was often witnessed by neighbours, friends, and servants; testimonies in suits for separation suggest the degree to which marriage was seen as a matter of public concern, and the expectations of wives and husbands, parents and friends for marital relations. All the same, many more violent marriages must have gone unremarked or unchecked. The limits on male mastery were not clearly defined.

For other marriages, informal separation, abandonment, or illegal bigamy provided a solution. But it was death that was most likely to end a marriage early, and to lead, sooner or later, to a new partnership: one out of every two marriages was a remarriage for at least one partner. Widows experienced more freedom in their marriage choices, especially if they had inherited enough money to be independent. Nonetheless, they might find themselves – as some did here – under pressure from children and from their first husband's kin, and some, like Katherine Austen, felt that to remarry would be a betrayal. Such ideas might be related to the decreasing marriage and remarriage rates in the seventeenth century. As well as the high proportion of women never marrying, the proportion of widows who remarried was decreasing. The early eighteenth century saw marriage rates rising again and women marrying younger. Restricted work opportunities for women meant that it was no longer feasible or sensible to spend so long working and saving, and for some, marriage was the only way to survive. Some choices were narrowing, others were opening up.

COURTSHIP

6.1   Love magic: Margaret Bridge, 1609

Margaret Bridge, Mary Tomson, Mary's mother Christian, and Mary's brother William were questioned at the Somerset quarter sessions for trying to procure for Margaret the 'unlawful love of William Decon of Kingston' with 'sorcery, witchcraft, charm, or enchantment'. Love charms were used by many cunning men and women; the penalty was a year's imprisonment for a first offence, death for a second, but in practice courts tended to be more lenient.

Somerset Quarter Sessions Rolls, Somerset Archives, Q/SR 7/49–51 (1609).

The examination of Margaret Bridge of Haygrove, in the parish of Bridgwater, in the said county spinster, taken the first of June, as aforesaid,

Who saith, that about three weeks sithence,[1] she laid out for Mary Tomson, three shillings, and four pence to give her stockings, and shoes. And that the said Mary hath relieved this examinant, of a gold ring, worth 12s. 6d., and then persuaded this examinant, to go with her, unto the gallows, near Bridgewater, which this examinant did, and when they came near thereunto, the said Mary willed this examinant to go aside into a close, adjoining; And that after, the said Mary came unto her, in the said close, and shewed three pieces of earth, spit with a knife, and carried the same in the company of this examinant, unto the house of William Bridge of Haygrove aforesaid, and there kept the same, until the next day (as this examinant now remembered) when it was burned, And that on Saturday after the cutting of the said earth, the said Mary likewise persuaded this examinant, to get her a bone, of some dead man or woman. And that then this examinant, (to content, and for fear of the said Mary) did deliver unto the said Mary a bone, which she found in the highway between Bridgewater and Haygrove, and that on Sunday then following, this examinant delivered the said Mary a gold ring, which then the said Mary told her, she would use with the ashes of the said earth, and bone, as she thought good, and would throw the same, at the door of William Decon, to the intent, to procure the said Decon, to marry with this examinant, which she then affirmed, to effect, or else, to lose her head. And saith that this examinant went in the company of the said Mary unto the barn, near the dwelling house of the said Decon, where she did see the said Mary throw some of the ashes in the orchard near the door of the said Decon. And further saith, that William Bridge, her brother, did lately bring home a bird, and delivered it unto this examinant, to pull,[2] And saith, the bird was strange unto her, and knoweth not what bird it was.

1. Since.
2. I.e., to pluck.

The examination of Christian, the wife of Thomas Apler, of Thurlington, in the said county, taken the first of June as aforesaid,

Who saith that Mary Tomson within a month, now last past, in the house of William Bridge, her son, did burn three little spits of turfie earth, and one bone, which she received of Margaret Bridge the daughter of this examinant. And that the said Margaret told her she could not be quiet until she had brought the said bone unto the said Mary. And further saith that the said Mary did tell this examinant, that the ashes of the said earth and bone, and a ring, which the said Margaret had delivered unto the said Mary, would make Decon so in love with Margaret her daughter, that he should marry her, and fetch her away shortly. And that the said ring should be her wedding ring. And that, on a Sunday, after the burning of the said earth, and bone, the said Mary and Margaret, went unto Kingston aforesaid, to strew the ashes, and delivered the ring, (as they said unto Decon), And that at their return, the said Mary told this examinant they had had a joyful day.

6.2   Be well advised: Elizabeth Jackson, 1609

Elizabeth Jackson became betrothed to Thomas Thorpe without her parents' knowledge in 1609. Her teacher, Mary Sprigge, who deposes here, and another neighbour, John Mullins, took typical roles as 'friends' to ensure she was properly and suitably contracted, and did not 'default' on her suitor; nevertheless, Mary Sprigge also admitted that Elizabeth's parents were unhappy that 'she did not break this matter to them before they had so many meetings', and that her mother made her send back the ring discussed here. Other gifts included a bowed sixpence and a silk lace worth ten pence. The couple had planned to run away and be married at Bartholomew Fair, but did not do so, and Thomas sued Elizabeth for a broken marriage contract. In cases like this, proof of love tokens, words of marriage, and signs of affection were crucial to proving the bond of betrothal; the evidence also indicates the ways in which women might hesitate over making the decision to marry, the influence of friends and parents, and the publicity and social ritual that accompanied the process of marrying.

London Consistory Court Deposition Book, LMA, DL/C 219, fos 15v–17v.

[Mary Sprigge of Waltham Cross in Hertfordshire, wife of Gilbert Sprigge, where she has lived for about a year and a half and previously in the parish of St James Clerkenwell and in the parish of St Andrew Holborn and in Hunsdon in Hertfordshire for about the same time and previously in Cork in Ireland for 10 years, born in Throcking near Buntingford, Hertfordshire, aged 40 or thereabouts, she has known the litigants viz Thomas Thorpe for about half a year and Elizabeth Jackson for a year and more.]

[To the first article of the libel she deposes and says] that the articulate Elizabeth Jackson in the month of August last past and before Bartholomewtide was this jurate's scholar about 3 weeks whom this jurate learned to work with her needle and in that time the articulate Thomas

Figure 12 **Marrying couple**

From the Pepys Ballads, vol I, no. 489. By permission of the Pepys Library, Magdalene College, Cambridge

The late sixteenth and seventeenth centuries saw efforts on the part of the church to define marriage in church, rather than the prolonged courtship and marriage rituals of the earlier period. However, as in those rituals, the marital union involved not just the marrying couple, but also their friends, relatives, and neighbours.

Thorpe resorted to her the same Elizabeth, to this jurate's house diverse times, and sat talking with the same Elizabeth insomuch as this jurate thought that there was goodwill between them and that the said Thomas was a suitor to the said Elizabeth in the way of marriage but what their communication was she cannot tell [for she] could not well hear what they said. She overheard some words and heard the said Thorpe say to her give me thy hand or the same and thereupon this jurate looked toward them and saw the said Elizabeth offer him her hand and thereupon this jurate bad her be well advised what she did and then Thorpe said I would have her be well advised what she doth and then they joined hands together, and the said Thomas Thorpe kissed the said Elizabeth Jackson and said he would never forsake her while he lived. And presently after this the foresaid John Mullins looked into the same room and then the said Thomas Thorpe called the said John Mullins to him and they performed as much in the presence of the said John Mullins and this jurate . . . she verily thinketh by their gestures and behaviours they did then and there contract matrimony together . . . but being thick of hearing she could not well understand what they said. . . .

[To the third article she deposes and says] that immediately after the premises before by her deposed of they all went to dinner together, one of the company drank to this jurate in a cup of sack and this jurate then drank to the articulate Elizabeth Jackson and bad her drink to her self and thereupon the said Elizabeth Jackson took the cup and drank to the said Thomas Thorpe, whereupon this jurate laughed and said Now I see that he and you are all one, I willed you to drink to yourself and you drink to Thomas Thorpe it should seem that he is yourself . . . and he likewise drank to the said Elizabeth very kindly twice at the least that dinner time. . . .

[To the fourth article she deposes and says] that about a week after this their meeting and contracting together (as this deponent was then persuaded) her precontest John Mullins wished this jurate to send for the articulate Thomas Thorpe speedily and hasten his marriage for otherwise he said he feared the said Elizabeth Jackson would fault. Whereupon this jurate did write a letter to the said Thomas Thorpe to come over speedily and dispatch his marriage, but she did not write it in the said Elizabeth's name but in this jurate's name and after she had written to him she told the said Elizabeth that she had written for him and that he would be with her by a day then named which was not above 4 days off, and she then seemed to be well contented therewith and at that time appointed the said Thomas Thorpe came and brought with him a ring which he said he had bought for the said Elizabeth for her wedding ring, and prayed this jurate to carry it unto her as a token from him which this jurate offered to her, who so soon as she saw it said Hath he sent me this ring, what shall I do therewith? You told me he would come to me himself this day, and asked if it were for her wedding ring. And this jurate said she could not tell and then she required this jurate to keep it, and this was upon a Sunday morning and before service and this jurate left the said Elizabeth at home at her father's house and walked hastily toward church, and in the meantime the said Elizabeth looking out at her father's window saw the said Thomas Thorpe pass by and soon after the said Elizabeth came away to go to church and overtook this jurate and as they went by the way this jurate offered her the ring again and told her if she would not receive it she would redeliver it where she had it (meaning to the said Thomas Thorpe who went on not far off before them), and this jurate making an offer to go on with the rest, the said Elizabeth Jackson called this jurate back again and received the ring very lovingly and thankfully.

[To the seventh article she deposes and says] that since the contract aforesaid the said Elizabeth came to this jurate and said Now Mistress how like you my sweet heart? meaning the said Thomas Thorpe and said diverse times if ever she were married to any she would be married to the said Thomas Thorpe. . . .

[To the interrogatory:]

[To the sixth she answers] that she never heard any mention of any condition until about a week after their joining hands and other the premises before deposed of . . . and a week after she seemed to repent and said she would not marry unless she might have her father's good will, but yet she saith if ever she married she would be married to Thomas Thorpe.

6.3   Love and duty: Dorothy Denne, 1640s

Dorothy Denne, an heiress of Denne-Hill in Kent, wrote a series of letters in the 1640s to her suitor William Taylor, her father's serving-man. They did not marry, and after William's death (his mother later claimed Dorothy had poisoned him), her letters came into the possession of Henry Oxinden of Barham. When Dorothy married Roger Lukin, a London draper, Oxinden threatened to expose the story and despite Dorothy's pleas, he kept the letters. Dorothy's dilemma of balancing love, duty, and financial interest are echoed in the words of many other women of the period; her biblical references provide a particular spiritual context of sacrifice and obedience.

Oxinden Correspondence, BL, Add. MS 28,003, fos 143, 173.

Friend,

I have stolen so much time as to write a few letters unto you. I may say with David the sorrows of my heart is enlarged, for I think there lives not a sadder heart than mine in the world neither have I enjoyed scarce one hour of contentment since we happened to be discovered at our last meeting for I know that William told his sweetheart of it and she is as lying and prating wench as any that is in the town. If you had borne any true and real affection to me or valued my reputation you would never have run that hazard, knowing that that woman which has lost her good name is dead while she lives, (Timothy the first the fifth and sixth verse) but it seems you care not what becomes of me so you may compass your end though it be with the utter ruin of my soul and body hath not the Lord commanded children to obey their parents do you not think it is a sin of a high nature for me to be disobedient and rebellious to my father and run away with you, or can I expect to have the blessing of God if I should do so especially seeing my father have so often warned me to avoid your company and to have a care of you and he saith that if I have made any promises or vows to you he doth utterly dislike them and hath dissolved them, you wrote me word of a gentlewoman that you might have worth a thousand pounds for the Lord's sake take her or any other, and make not yourself or me forever miserable, you speak of having me without my clothes or one penny in my purse, people would think me either stark mad or a fool now I have the possibility of a fortune and may live happily to bring myself to beggary and contempt of all that know me, I beseech you for the Lord's sake make me not a shame, a dishonour to my sisters and kindred, that I shall not dare to look them in the face, my sister Jackman which is condemned and slighted and accounted as a castaway yet her husband is a gentleman, and shall have near £200 a year after his mother's death, do you think that the rent of £200 a year if it were clear gains would maintain me like as I have been bred and brought up, and as I live, it must needs be an extreme grief to me to have my sisters marry knights of great estates. . . .

If I had time I should have written a great deal more but shall reserve it till a nobler time I desire to speak with you before I go to London some-time next week at Mrs Kenard's house which is my friend and will say nothing of it in haste I leave now God bless you.

6.4 'The saddest day': Sarah Savage, 1687

Sarah Savage (1664–1745) was the daughter of an ejected Cheshire Nonconformist minister, Philip Henry. In 1687 she married a widower and distant cousin. The marriage seems to have been broached around November the previous year, and Sarah records some weeks of worry and perplexity 'with thoughts about the changing of my condition, not knowing what to do'.

Diary of Sarah Savage, Chester City RO, DBasten/8 fos 10–13v (extracts).

[12 March] 1687 Brother [Matthew Henry] in his letter to me comforts me as to a change of circumstances. . . .

Friday [18 March] Cos. Savage was here, and I had more than two hours discourse with him yet, to my shame and sorrow I speak it, scarce a word that I remember of any spiritual things. I fear this will be bitter in the reflection, but if God should dispense blessings and comforts as narrowly as I perform duties then were no hope. The Lord will perfect. My heart's desire is that I may have grace to fill the new relations he shall put me in.

Memoranda. Wednesday March 23 Cos. Savage came here and we had two or three friends present and were solemnly contracted, a step toward marriage.

Many hearty petitions offered up for us both first by our brother and then my father. God hear in heaven my dwelling place – we desire solemnly to knock at thy door, heartily have I begged Christ to be present at the wedding. Dear Jesus accept thy invitation. We were solemnly exhorted to prepare for the comforts, crosses and duties of that new condition. That night my Friend prayed with me in private to my satisfaction.

Thursday, he went home.

Friday was then appointed to be the day of marriage, a surprise to me to have it so soon, but having left the matter with God, and trusted him, I acquiesce in his disposition of me. That night begged heartily for the two great graces of wisdom and humility. I find I shall have special need of these – Lord keep me humble that I may now often look on my wants and imperfections. Surely if those among whom I shall be had but had the means of improvement that I have had, that difference would have been much more the other way. Very sensible I am that my improvements have not been according to my receivings. . . .

Monday, March 28 1687. We were solemnly married to Whitewell Chapel with the consent and approbation of most of our friends by Mr Green. At night I used this argument with God (to this purpose) Lord I have had the presence, blessing and approbation of my earthly parents in what I have been doing today and I beg thine. At night Father gave us a short sermon on Genesis 2.22 'and brought her to the man'; I hope God hath manifested himself in a special manner in bringing us together. Therefore I hope he will make it comfortable – whatever God bring to us – 1. he will bless to us. 2. he will fit for us. I am very sensible what I need I have of thy special help (oh my dear God) to fill up my new relations with duty, especially the great need of wisdom and humility. The night I was married a little surprised with my Dear not being well. I heartily resigned my interest in him to God, 'twas quickly over God be praised. I was about that time like one come into a new world. God give me a new heart[1] for my new condition, and help me to discharge the duties of it, as a wife, a mother and a daughter-in-law. I still find comfort by referring myself to God and trusting the whole matter with him.

Tuesday April 19 I left Broad Oak, the saddest day that ever came over my head, heart ready to burst but God I found to be the strength of my heart and trust he will be my portion for ever.

When I took leave with Sis. Anne she had two scriptures ready which were seasonable and I did greedily catch at one, I will never leave thee nor forsake thee. The other – All things shall work together for God. On these two I desire to act faith[fully] and to take them along with me into my new condition.

1. A heart is drawn for this word.

WIVES AND HUSBANDS

6.5 Marital breakdown: Margaret Littleton, 1606

The most detailed information we have about ordinary marriages comes from the histories of marriages that went seriously wrong and ended up in court. From these, historians can deduce not just what went wrong in extraordinary cases, but also what was expected of marriages in ordinary circumstances. Margaret Littleton's petition to the Staffordshire quarter sessions in 1606 was supported by a minister and six of her neighbours. She requested maintenance from her husband, who had allegedly evicted her from the marital home; his own petition complained that she had taken their household goods unlawfully. The justice ordered 'that Mr Littleton take his wife home and use her as befits a husband'.

Staffordshire Quarter Sessions Rolls, Staffordshire RO, Q/SR 98/31, 32 (Trinity Sessions 1606).

Lamentably complaining sheweth unto the honourable and right worshipful of this his majesty's court of justice and equity wherein many a poor distressed person is relieved and misdemeanours reformed I do most humbly crave justice forth of this court because the state of my life and maintenance lieth in the hands of authority which doth consist in justice.

That it may please the honourable and worshipful to consider of my poverty and want being distressed and wanting maintenance of my husband whom by the law of God is to maintain me being his lawful wife and he hath diverse and sundry times cast me off into the world and ever I did with patience endure the wrong by him unto me done so long being not able to use any means wherein I should maintain my self and withall void of friends in regard of my years and poverty and my husband putting me from him of no offence and contrary to law. Wherein for maintenance I am constrained to beg and be relieved abroad so long as I might have my neighbours' charitable devotion both in diet and lodging and now doth my said husband by threatening words cause all my neighbours to refuse me for that he sayeth law is against any man that taketh in his neighbour's wife and yieldeth her any maintenance without his consent by which means all my neighbours have refused me and doth maintain and keep in his house a lewd and bad woman whom causeth my husband to put me from him which person is by the churchwardens presented both to the king's advocate and ordinary of the jurisdiction of Penkridge and they both stand excommunicate and say they will live together in denial of law. Thus humbly craving that justice that shall belong to such offenders that will live so openly to the undoing of me and three motherless children and that I may have some order by our worships set down for my maintenance I shall be daily bounden to pray for you with long and happy days: whom I pray God bless and keep for ever.

6.6   Male violence: Anne Younge, 1608

Anne Younge, alias Lyngham (probably her maiden name), went to the London consistory court to sue for separation from her husband, a tailor in Ludgate Hill, in 1608, on the grounds of his violence. Canon law in this area demanded proof of lethal danger; 'moderate correction' was legal. The first witness, Margaret Bonefant, had lodged the couple in her house in 1607, and continued to be a close friend of Anne's. To some extent, what went on in such marriages was a public affair. However, it was also open to a variety of interpretations. While wives pleaded for separation on the grounds of both physical and mental cruelty, supported by the detailed stories of their witnesses, husbands defended their actions on the grounds of justifiable anger, reasonable correction, or occasionally, desperation. The results of these cases varied. The most a wife could hope for was to be granted the right to live apart from her husband, with a sum of alimony decided by the court; it was the settlement of alimony that provoked disagreements such as that here over the husband's pecuniary worth. Many judges, following the Protestant stress on keeping married couples together, aimed to reconcile rather than separate couples and frequently ordered them to go home and live quietly.

Consistory Court of London Deposition Book, LMA, DL/C 218, pp. 50–2, 88 (June 1608).

[Margaret Bonefant, wife of James Bonefant, woolman, of London, for the last twelve years, aged about 32; she has known Anne Younge for 9 or 10 years and James Younge for 3 months.]

[To the 2nd and 3rd articles she deposes and says] that in the month of February last past upon a Sunday in the afternoon . . . this deponent went to the articulate Anne Younge alias Lyngham to her own house in St Bride's parish in London to visit her and to see how she did and coming to her she found the said Anne Younge alias Lyngham so beaten and bruised and swollen about her head face and body that she was not able to speak nor go nor stir any of her limbs to help her self and her jaws were displaced or otherwise so hurt with beating that she was not able to stir them and the gristle of her nose was so bruised that until by the help of a surgeon it was raised and the flesh suppled she could not well fetch or take any breath at the nose, but seemed as though she were more like to die of that beating than to recover and live. And soon after that this jurate came and saw the said Anne in this miserable case, the said James Younge her husband came in, to whom this jurate said she was sorry to see his wife in this miserable case. Whereunto he answered that he did think her estate had been better when he married her than he did then find it, as he said, and then she this deponent asking him if he had so used her, he said that that which was done to her he had done, and so she this deponent then said unto him that was not the way to know or understand of her estate but if he would know that it must be his kind usage of her and not that severity for that was a way to make an end of them both. Aye, quoth he the same Younge, I am told I shall be hanged if she die within a year and a day[1] but if I be there

---

1. Death within a year and a day after an assault would be accounted manslaughter.

is but one out of the way. And this speech of his acknowledging his so beating of his said wife he the same Younge did avouch once or twice after within a week after walking with this deponent in the street homeward towards her this deponent's house in St Olaves parish from his the same Younge's house. And she saith there was present and saw her the same Anne Younge alias Lyngham in that pitiful sort as aforesaid Mrs Anne Cotes one Mr Grace and divers others. . . .

[To the 5th article she says and deposes] that both at the time afore by her deposed of upon the Sunday and twice after the same week when she this deponent came to see her the same Anne Younge alias Lyngham she hath been in sad want as that she this deponent did see Mrs Cotes and others that came to her give her money and send for drink wood and coals and for meat and likewise for ointments for her and for divers things that was fit for her comfort she having no money herself but being in great want and need. . . .

[To the 11th article she says and deposes] that for the reasons by her deposed of she saith that she verily believeth and that not without cause the said Anne dareth not nor may not live safely with her said husband in one house for fear of death or at least such cruel usage as she is not able to endure. . . .

[To the 13th article . . .] she saith she never heard any body ever say better of him than that he was and is such a severe cruel man to his wife.

[To the 14th she says and deposes] that at such time as the articulate James Younge and his said wife lay in her this deponent's house . . . he hath acknowledged and confessed both to her this deponent and in her hearing that he was worth four hundred pounds. . . .

[Personal Answers of James Younge . . .]

[To the 2nd and 3rd articles he answers] that Anne Younge this respondent's wife articulate having given him this respondent many vile and bad speeches, he this respondent hath sundry times in the time articulate chidden her and given her many angry words again. And he sayeth that the week before Shrovetide last she . . . having taken up a thing of wood like unto a bowl to strike him this respondent, he this respondent sayeth that he did strike her the same Anne with his fist in so much as her face was black and blue. Whereupon she the same Anne forsook his this respondent's bed, and that night and the next following lay by herself and the next morning he this respondent going up into her chamber and seeing her purse lying there took out two rings or three that was in it, and when she arose and found that he this respondent had taken away her rings, she became so sullen that she counterfeited herself sick and went to bed and kept her bed a week after whereby she caused him this respondent to spend 40s. in keeping of her in that her counterfeit sickness.

[To the 4th . . . he answers] that the same day that he this respondent did so strike his said wife, presently after one Mrs Cotes one of his said wife's acquaintance being there told him this respondent that if his wife did otherwise than well he this respondent should be hanged, whereupon he this respondent said unto her that if she would not be quiet it were well she were gone out at doors, but she went away none the sooner.

[To the 8th and 9th . . . he answers] that such hath been and was the wickedness of the articulate Anne his this respondent's said wife towards him this respondent as that . . . diverse times when he this respondent hath gone out of doors she hath fallen down of her knees and prayed to God that he this respondent might never come in at the doors again whereby this respondent was in a desperate mind about the time articulate for which he is now heartily sorry and desireth almighty God to forgive him as that in the morning when he arose out of his bed (he lying alone as he had done long before and after his said wife refusing his company) he did stab himself with a knife which he carrieth to bed with him in the breast in two places.

[To the 14th . . . he answers] that he this respondent is a tailor and getteth thereby 2s. 6d. a week and not above 3s. and is not worth forty shillings his debts paid, but he saith that [if] his said wife would be quiet and live quietly with him in the face of God as he this respondent desireth to do, he doubteth not but he should get much more and be better able to keep and maintain both himself and her than now he is to keep himself, his mind is so unquiet by reason of this trouble.

6.7   Pressing after the knowledge of the Lord: Mary Penington, *c.* 1640

In a time when religious commitment was central to many women's sense of their identities, religious belief could be the basis for marriage, religious dissent the foundation for an independent marital choice. Mary Proude (1624–82), born into a Puritan gentry family in Kent, was orphaned before she was 3 years old. She was educated by her guardian, Sir Edward Partridge, and his widowed sister Mrs Springett, who practised medicine and oculistry. Here, Mary writes of Mrs Springett's son William, who became a colonel in the Parliamentary army, and whom she married when she was about 18, he 20. Their first child died but their second, Gulielma, was born shortly after William's death at 23. Mary went on to become a prominent member of the Society of Friends and the wife of Isaac Penington; Gulielma married Sir William Penn. Two editions of the text she left survive, both clearly edited from the original; see also her dream in Chapter 10.

Mary Penington, *A Brief Account of my Exercises from my Childhood: Left with my Dear Daughter, Gulielma Maria Penn*, Philadelphia, 1848, pp. 4–5.

I minded not those marriages that was propounded to me by vain persons, but having desired of the Lord that I might have one that feared, I had a belief that though then I knew none of my outward rank that was such a one, yet that the Lord would provide one for me; and in this belief I continued, not regarding their reproaches that would say to me, that no gentleman, none but mean persons was of this way, and that I would have some mean one or other; but they were disappointed, for the Lord touched the heart of him that was afterwards my husband, and my heart cleaved to him for the Lord's sake. He was a man of a good understanding, and had cast off those dead superstitions that were manifest to him in that day beyond any I then knew of his rank and years, which were but small for that stature he was of in the things of God; being but of about twenty years of age. We pressed much after the knowledge of the Lord, and walked in his fear: being both very young, were joined together in the Lord, and refused the ring and such like things then used, and not denied by any that we knew of. We lived together about two years and a month; we were zealously affected, daily exercised in that we judged to be the service and worship of God. We scrupled many things then in use amongst those that were counted honest people: as for instance singing David's Psalms in metre, and when we tore out of our Bibles the common prayer and form of prayers at the end of the book: we also tore out the singing psalms, as being the inventions of vain poets as in metre, not being written for that use; and we found that songs of praise must spring from the same source as prayers did; so we could not use anyone's songs, no more than their prayer. We were also brought off from bread and wine and baptism with water, we having looked into the independent way,[1] saw death there, and that it was not what our souls sought; and looking into the baptism with water, found it not to answer the cry of our hearts. In this state my husband died, hoping in the promises afar off, but not seeing or knowing him that is invisible to be so near him; and that it was he that showed unto him his thoughts and made manifest the good and the evil. When he was taken from me I was with child of my dear daughter Gulielma Maria Springett.

6.8 Affectionate wife and faithful friend: Mary Clarke, 1675

Mary Clarke, born Mary Jepp, was a cousin and life-long friend of the philosopher John Locke. In 1675 she married Locke's friend Edward Clarke, and lived very happily with him until her death in 1705. Since Mary oversaw the household and estate at Chipley in Somerset during Edward's frequent absences in London as a Member of Parliament, there was an extensive exchange of letters between the two throughout their married life. The following is the first letter from Mary to her husband which has survived. At the end of her life, Mary was still writing to Edward in loving terms, signing herself 'your truly affectionate and faithful wife M Clarke'.

Clarke Papers, Somerset Archives, DD'SF 4515/1.

This document and its note supplied by Sara Mendelson.

1. I.e., the autonomous congregations that were appearing in the 1640s.

Sutton the 20th of August 1675

My Dear Husband

I return you my hearty thanks for sending Hugh to me that I might hear how you have done ever since you left Sutton and I am extremely sorry to understand by him and your letter that you have been so much troubled with the pain of the head but I hope you will be perfectly recovered at your return which [I hope] may be sooner than the time you have appointed for I cannot possibly live any longer without the sight of him that is most dear to me and therefore pray make all the haste you can to dispatch your business in those parts. My dear I have taken great care to send you a letter the last Tuesday which is in Taunton now and I hope will come safe to your hands and therein I gave you a little account of your affairs here and therefore will trouble you the less now but give me leave to tell you that there is no horses to be got that is fit for your use but I hear that there is a very great horse fair at Glastonbury about a fortnight hence where you can hardly miss of one to serve your occasions. This day Tom Lukins is come to Falston and I wish I could know your mind concerning the horse there but that is impossible and therefore I must content myself till I see you and in the mean time I subscribe my self my dear Neddy your affectionate wife and faithful friend

Mary Clarke

My duty to my father and service to my sister not forgetting little Grisse and Mr Treble. My Aunt Strachey and Mrs Swaine presents their service to you. My service to all at Holcombe. I have received a letter from my brother and all your friends there are well.

6.9   'More like a lover than a husband': Lady Peregrina Chaytor, 1697

In 1697 Peregrina Chaytor, wife of a Yorkshire baronet, was preparing to lie in in London, with a child who died shortly after birth. Nancy, her eldest child, aged 20, was staying with her and her three younger boys (mentioned in the letter) were at home in Croft, North Yorkshire. Peregrina's letters are long and unpunctuated, and range across a wide variety of local and personal affairs. This extract is part of a three-page letter.

Chaytor Papers, North Yorkshire County RO, ZQH 9/12/52 (published in *Sir William Chaytor (1639–1721)*, Northallerton, North Yorkshire County Council 1984).

London August 14th [1697]

My Dear

I give you thanks for your long and kind letters and must assure you they are more pleasing to me than any diversion here and though you write more like a lover than a husband yet I must believe you real having had your affection for above these twenty years and not in the least lessened by the charms of those who endeavour to captivate your sex though I have been in contrary

circumstances these many years you may be confident of the like return from
me which nothing but death can dissolve. I hope our dear children will be
a comfort to us and that they resemble you in your good inclinations which
will be more to my satisfaction than to be like me for I am sensible of my
faults. . . . Nancy I think looks better than when you left her Mr Nickola
comes now punctually he was here this day and gives encouragement enough
saying he will make her sing as well as any and that she has a melancholy
voice fit to sing Te Deums and anthems. He is learning her the second song
and will have a pair of harpsichords brought for her to sing to which he
said would advantage her voice. . . . You must order the goods as well as you
can to make them keep well and if you leave any in the house they should
be careful people but I do not like Ned Robeson. Mrs Croft might let 3 or
four of the best beds lie under hers. I think the proposal Mr Croft makes
about horses and cattle is very good but Nancy desires to have the best of
hers kept that she may still have a breed to bring her in a little monies and
if we come down betwixt Martinmas and Christmas then we must have cows
and some sheep and if nobody lives in the house for that time I hope things
will not take much harm and if we do not come perhaps some gentleman
may take the house and that may do as well. I must have one of the calico
sheets which we laid upon strangers' beds brought up and Nanny may consider
what I have had about me when I laid in and send it though I do not name
it for I cannot remember all. You may give her fleeces one of wool if you
think fit and if there be any yarn spun for the boys stockings they should
get them knit for Tom and Clarvax and must get shirts made for them all
and you must make Nanny Peacock see what cravats and handkerchiefs they
have. . . . I reckon but now about five weeks so I hope you will not be long
in letting me see you for if I should fall sick and you not hear what would
become of me Nancy gives her duty and love to her brothers I pray God
bless you all I am

yours ever
Pe. Chaytor

6.10 The oppressions of marriage: Anne Dormer, 1688

Anne Dormer wrote regular letters to her sister, Lady Elizabeth Trumbull, whose
husband was ambassador in Constantinople. She had married Sir Robert Dormer
in 1668. Many of her letters look back on her married life with deep unhappiness,
portraying her marriage as a 'cage'. This one lays bare a relationship fraught with
jealousy and distrust. After twenty years of marriage, her husband is still suspicious
about an incident before their marriage which seems to him to suggest Anne's guilt
of some 'roughness' or 'immodesty'. Anne's protests at his interpretation reveal, too,
the degree of modesty of mind that young women of her social status cultivated.
Anne's husband died the following year, but her letters continue unhappy. Two later
letters are reproduced in Chapter 8.

Trumbull Papers, BL, Add. MS 72516, fos 194–7.

Nov. the 29th [1688]

My dearest soul,

The desire I have had to keep all things from thy knowledge that would grieve thee has made me write to thee both seldomer and shorter since we parted than I wished to have done, but finding these oppressions I have lain under this last four months do daily increase and considering that friendship requires a communication of all concerns without reserve I will no longer conceal these sorrows from thee I am so grievously afflicted with, for since I hope they will prove as profitable to my soul as they are tormenting to my body I have reason to be thankful for them and patient under them; I have this comfort that I find compassion and kindness from every body and I cannot accuse my self of having brought upon my self any of these cruelties that person shews me from whom I deserve better than I do from all the world, besides, his usage of my father this last summer and the occasions he gave him to write a very sharp letter to him instead of a thanks for his kind entertainment, I suppose my dear father has given you an account of, and therefore I will not by repeating renew the smart of these wounds but I find my miseries then only at the height when I see the best of fathers and one of the worthiest of men barbarously used by him who owes him so much. . . .

By believing ill of all the world he makes a shift to keep up a high opinion of his own worth though he spends his days in idleness or quarrelling, is every way uncharitable and no way useful to no creature, nor ever like to be better, but every day worse these nineteen years. . . . I bless God for it the pity I have for him [hath] taken away all my anger against him, and though the injuries I have received and do every day receive are of the most cruel sort, yet I can with sincerity and a good conscience say forgive me as I forgive them that trespass against me. I beseech God shew him his errors, and give him grace to amend, for nothing but a ray from heaven can soften that heart which is made of such a piece of stone as is not in this world again to be found. His inveterate habits, his little sense of religion, his great pride and obstinacy and resolution to believe well of himself in spite of all, makes him appear to me an object of great compassion and to see a man that seems to have his senses, act in everything so like a mad man would almost turn one's brains. . . .

It is impossible to oblige when I am with him, no discourse can please him but all is thwart and cross. If he says such a woman's a whore because I don't second it and always be just of his opinion then he rails and reviles me and when any company is here he doth say so many rude contemptible things to me that it is almost insupportable though I know by it he doth himself more harm than he doth me, for while he is catching at every thing to turn it to my disgrace he doth me more justice than all the world could do, for they that know what a constant spy he is over me and see what poor shifts he makes to lessen that kindness all my neighbours ever shew me, they is sure themselves he would not let more material things pass could he find them. It concerns me to be always on my guard which though it is safe it is most tormenting not to able to set a step or speak a word but I am engaged in a laborious task to vindicate myself from some strange suspicion which if I do not immediately clear he takes for granted and then I must have been upbraided with it for ever, as one day after having cleared many of his extravagant fancies, after I had expressed my wonder that he would still give way to such unjust thoughts after I had so many years lived with him as I did and had always taken such care to satisfy him in every thing and that he had always seen me clear every suspicion he had ever fancied of me, to which he answered no for when he came up to London to marry me he remembered very well I had a foul scratch upon my arm and he asked me how it come and he was not satisfied with my answer and had thought of it many times since, and did believe there was something in it he did not expect I should own, it was great pity I had lost my mother she would never have let a crew of such young fellows as Mr Colt have come to the house, I told him as for the scratch if he had not so often refreshed my memory that I had one then ... I should scarce have now remembered how it come but running hastily out of the room hung with gilt leather into the next, the hasp of the door did that he has been so often concerned about, and tho I have now forgot whether upon being called or to fetch somthing made me run but this I well remember I was alone when I did it and that was the truth if he pleased I would not only take an oath it was so, but another that not only then, no man was rude to me, as he fancied, but that in my whole life, I never had any rudeness offered me, nor no kind of affront put upon me throughout the whole time I have lived, to which he answered to shew the great tenderness he had for me, that though my lord Chesterfield put his wife to her oath to damn her he would not do so to me, but he was satisfied a man was not fit to breed daughters so well as a woman. I had then a large theme to speak in justification at my dear father's breeding. . . .

I knew my innocence was so entire that at the same time he accused me his conscience as hardened as it was must fly in his face, for when I married him if I were never to speak a word more I would say I guessed no more what a man was than Fanny[1] now doth nor knew no more of anything that was immodest, and still from his extravagant jealousies he used to tell me what odious intentions wicked men had could they find opportunities, I could never have had such an imagining for if I had believed men such brutes I would as soon have gone into a den of lions as ever have come where a man was to be seen, and though since he had represented them such creatures I had often rejoiced in my mind that my innocence which feared so ill had never occasioned me to have a rudeness offered me, now I had

1. Her daughter, aged 7.

reason to wish I might have suffered some one affront, that I might have been secured by the hatred I should have taken against all men never to have married any as I am sure I never should could I have guessed what a man in his nature without virtue is. I could not but tell him such an innocence as mine, and such a worthy friend as my father, was ill bestowed upon him ... heretofore I have been such a fool as almost to wish that I had been guilty of some little indiscretion since I was his wife than to find him so harsh in his sense of a creature that have always in everything satisfied even him, as to any conversation with mankind, but since he resolved for ever to be unjust to me I would not always be a fool but for the time to come be as I had been, careful of even the appearance of evil, I would satisfy myself, and if he pleased to believe I got that scratch at a tavern ramping with my Lord Rochester and Sir Charles Sedley[2] it should be indifferent to me.

Much such kind of discourse we had that day and the next, and after of himself, for I did not creep nor ever will more, he fell to kissing my hand and so a little calm I had for a while which can never last with a man that lives by his fancy and doth everything by chance. . . . I hope my condition is safe though indeed it is often very tormenting to be as the other day surprised with seeing him like a lion in his house and frantic amongst his servants as well as often so with me, the particulars I would give thee of many things but the fear the carrier will be gone and the ship that is to bring this to thee if I keep it till the next return, therefore I cannot say all those kind things my heart is full of to thy self and my dear brother which I hope you will guess at for never sister loved more passionately than thy

A.D.

REMARRIAGE

6.11 A widow and her servant: Agnes Holloway, 1615

Agnes Holloway, a widow from Cheshunt, Hertfordshire, was sued in 1615 by her ex-servant Henry Rich, who claimed she had contracted to marry him. In her defence she claimed that, instead, she had allowed a number of affectionate exchanges (which she specifies), but that, pressured by her father, she had never accepted him as suitor. Especially interesting here is the balance between Agnes's autonomy and her apparent submission to the wishes of her father, even in her second marriage with some financial independence. Reproduced here are Agnes's answers to Henry's charges, and the testimony of one of Henry's witnesses, Ann Cordwell.

Consistory Court of London Deposition Book, LMA, DL/C 223, fos 201v–202v, 216v–217v (10, 19 June 1615).

---

2. Two notorious 'rakes'.

[Personal Answers of Agnes Holloway widow made to the charges and articles alleged on behalf of and by Henry Rich]

[. . . To the second article she answers and believes] that her husband George Holloway died on New Year's day last past in the morning and that the articulate Henry Rich continued with this respondent as her servant until about mid-Lent then next following all that while living in this respondent's house. . . .

[To the third article she answers and believes] that in the time that the said Henry Rich dwelt in house with this respondent they the said Henry and this respondent were free from all contracts of matrimony, and being so free the said Henry Rich made love to this respondent and became a suitor to this respondent to have her to become his wife. . . .

[To the fifth article she answers] that the said Henry Rich moved the question to have this respondent to his wife as she responded previously to the third article and this was at such time as he the said Henry attempted by force to ravish her. . . .

[To the sixth article she answers and believes] that the articulate Henry Rich in the time this respondent was a widow, he dwelling with her, was sick about two days, in which time this respondent was very careful of his recovery and did herself go often to him to look to him in his sickness he lying then in bed, and was with him there sometimes an hour or more and sometimes at nine or ten or the clock at night. . . .

[To the seventh article she answers and believes] that she never bore any affection to the said Henry Rich more than was fit for her to perform to a servant. . . .

[To the eighth article of the aforesaid allegation she answers and believes] that after the said Henry Rich was recovered of the sickness before specified in the sixth article she this respondent did sit up with the said Henry in her this respondent's hall of her dwelling house in Cheshunt articulate until ten of the clock at night as she believes at which time the said Henry Rich being alone with this respondent the rest of her family being in bed he the said Henry attempted to ravish this respondent as she says. . . .

[To the tenth article she answers] that in one of the months articulate this respondent going into her barn to her tasker[1] that was at work where the said Henry Rich was also to fetch some straw her upper coat being turned up the said Henry Rich put into this respondent's coat a pair of gloves which this respondent refused to receive yet afterwards they lying on the ground likely to be spoiled this respondent took them up and put them in her pocket and she this respondent did afterwards give to the said Henry Rich a shirt but not as any token of contract of marriage or love as she says and otherwise she does not believe. . . .

---

1. Labourer (paid by the task).

[To the eleventh article she answers] that when this respondent's father heard that the said Henry Rich did claim a contract of this respondent and said he had lain with her, he was much moved against the said Henry and said that he would have him before a justice, hereupon this respondent fell down on her knees and said good father be content I will pay him his wages and send him away and she said further that which the said Rich did in seeking to get a contract of her was for lucre to get that which she hath. . . .

[Ann Cordwell, the wife of George Cordwell of Cheshunt, Hertfordshire, tanner, where she has lived for the last 12 years, born at Felstead in Essex, aged 40 or thereabouts, she has known the plaintiff for 6 years and the defendant well for 6 years]

[. . . To the eleventh article she says and deposes] that in the month of March last past this deponent being a near neighbour to Agnes Holloway in this article mentioned went to her the said Agnes' house within the parish of Cheshunt in the county of Hertford, and at her coming thither and being in the entry of the said house, heard the said Agnes Holloway and one Ward the father of the said Agnes conferring together in the hall of the said house about a marriage which as it seemed to this deponent was intended between Henry Rich the party producent and the said Agnes Holloway and this deponent then plainly understood and heard the said Ward father of the said Agnes find fault with the said Agnes for sitting up late in the night and keeping him the said Rich company at such disorderly times and that he the said Ward would call him the said Rich in question for the same, whereupon this deponent could plainly hear the said Agnes weep, and did much commend the said Henry Rich for an honest man, and she the said Agnes then told her said father, that the love and goodwill which the said Henry Rich shewed to her the said Agnes was first sought for by her the said Agnes, and he the said Henry had done nothing but what she had solicited him thereunto and prayed her said father to be content, and said that she the said Agnes had rather spend ten pounds than he the said Henry should spend forty shillings, and then the said Ward the father of the said Agnes persuading the said Agnes to forsake the said Henry Rich telling her that if she should be married unto him the said Henry she would rue the time that she was ever born, and whereunto the said Agnes replied that she had known one in the like case grow mad and then also wept, all which premises she this deponent did well hear standing in the said entry. . . .

[To the fourteenth article she says and deposes] that she this deponent ever since she heard the conference between the said Agnes Holloway and her said father as previously disposed she this deponent for her part hath taken the said Agnes Holloway and Henry Rich to be lawfully contracted together and to be lawful man and wife.

6.12 Considering remarriage: Katherine Austen, 1665

Katherine Austen's personal writings record her reflections, material concerns, and prayers as a widow with means in late seventeenth-century London. In the eighth year of her widowhood, aged 38, she was considering remarriage to Alexander Callender, a physician.

Katherine Austen Collectanea, BL, Add. MS 4454, pp. 132–5 (1665).

For my part I do no injury to none by not loving. But if I do I may do real injuries where I am already engaged. To my deceased friend's posterity.

As for my body it can be enjoyed but by one. And I hope it's the worst part of me and that which every servant maid and country wench may excel mine, and can give the same satisfaction as mine. But that which my desire is should far excel my body is my soul, and the virtues and quality of that. And this I think may be useful to more than one and not confined to a single person, and if anything in me is to be loved I hope 'tis my mind. And if that I deny not a friendly correspondence to you, nor to any beside, thus all my friends may partake of me and enjoy me, and be married in the dearnesses and usefulness and benefits of friendship. And more than one can be satisfied with those lawful intimacies of friendship, and correspondencies of lawful public safe conferences, which is the better part of me, and which true virtue should most affect. And thus I may be partaker of the nobleness of your parts by an open and free amity.

And thus that person which pretends so great affection to me may be satisfied with an honest conversation and such lawful allowed conferences.

I was in discourse with a gentleman.[1] He had many arguments to prove. The papists had not idolatry by their pictures. This he said Monsieur Amaruth[2] did prove in a book he set out, wherein he shews, the idolatry of several nations, as the ancient Egyptians, to be perfect idolatry, but of the papists not to be such. I answered diverse things to it. And though at last I did not disapprove according as it might be the having a picture of Christ or of Saints, yet let Mr Amaruth say what he pleased, I must condemn the Romanists of superstitious and idolatrous adoring theirs. He then said to me and protested if I was a very beggar women if I would have him he would have me, and he would discourse with me all day, for he never talked with me but learned something of me. I told him he was mistaken and if I was so indeed he would not.

For my part I declined all things might give him a vain encouragement, and told him I was like Penelope, always employed. Aye says he her lovers could not abide her for it.

When I was returning home from Mrs Al. he said, You would not take pity if one should grow distracted for you. There is no fear of that said I.

1. Her suitor.
2. A French theologian.

Then as he took me by the hand, he said, What a hand there was to be adored. I answered him looking upon a tuft of grass which had growing in it a yellow flower: that that spear of grass was fitter to be adored than my hand. Aye alas says he we are all but grass, but shadows. And whenever we see the grass we are to adore the creator in it. I think at this time he was not very well; for afterwards he said that on that evening he first began to feel his head ache, which grew for four days very painful. So that eleven days after he ended his life on the eighth of October 1665 at Tillingham in Essex.

6.13   A change of condition: Elizabeth Burnet, 1700

Elizabeth Blake (1661–1709) married first Robert Berkeley, who died in 1698. She remarried in 1700. Her second husband was Gilbert Burnet, Bishop of Salisbury. This extract is from her personal writings.

Bodl., MS. Rawl. D1092, fo. 136–136v.

A reflection on the change of my condition of widowhood for a second marriage.

O Lord forgive me if I erred if I left a more solitary for a more secular state. Thou O my God knowest my intention was upright, I desired to choose the best, the life most useful most for thy glory, nor was or am conscious that ease, pleasure or honour had any influence in my choice, my temper and genius never affected a married state, which was first an act of obedience to my parents, and now an act rather of my will and understanding than of passion or inclination; I considered the circumstances of the person I chose made it, as far as I could judge, best for him to marry, with respect to the age of his children, the place he held in the court, where for one of his free and generous conversation a good nature, free from cunning or deceit, and so easily imposed on by those who had made a sincere and faithful friend of great advantage, and though I wanted all other qualifications, I thought myself capable of sincerity, and of sometimes preventing the too hasty impressions of others, or errors of inconsideration which ill designing men might unwarily engage him in; also I hoped I might have more power to do good in a more public part; so if I have descended to a lower place, as a second marriage in its own nature ever appeared to me to be, and as it has been generally esteemed by the wisest and most pious, except some particular circumstances supply that defect, if I have taken a lower place, it was out of a too great desire to serve my brethren; if I erred, pardon, O Lord, my error and bless my endeavours and punish not my presumption by withdrawing thy assistance and direction, without which I can do nothing successfully. I am indeed unworthy to be an instrument of doing good, who so often neglected past opportunities and calls to it, but in mercy pardon my past sins and omissions, and bless me, the least and lowest of all thine, and let thy power be shown in my weakness, for the glory of thy servants and my brethren.

7

MATERNITY

Maternity was the almost inevitable consequence of heterosexual activity in adult women: desired in some cases, not wanted or feared in others. Maternity was also a social relationship involving care of children. Here we have enlarged the subject of maternity to include childcare by women – aunts, grandmothers, and wet-nurses – who were responsible for overseeing the health and welfare of children.

Documents have been selected to illustrate a range of mothering experiences – licit, illicit, and surrogate – and to raise questions about maternity at various social levels in early modern England. Starting with Anne Glyd's record of the births and deaths of her children, a reminder of the mortality rates of seventeenth-century England, the documents have been arranged roughly according to the life stages of the child.

Mortality rates in seventeenth-century England were high: approximately one in five children died before they reached 10 years of age, with the highest mortality rate in the first year of life, especially in the first hours after birth.[1] Some historians have claimed that parents did not love their children; Lawrence Stone has suggested that parents could not 'invest' much love in their children, and that the mortality rates help explain a lack of affection in the family.[2] Most recent historians have challenged his conclusions, but in the debates about the early modern family, few distinctions have been made between mothers and fathers. Here we have focused on women's attitudes to the children in their care. In the early years at least, children were very much in the daily care of women; although we do not mean to imply that men were unloving, as fathers they were absent from the nurseries. There was a division of labour in all families. In the elite circles many fathers were away from home on various kinds of legal and political business; the sexual division of labour required the majority of fathers to earn a living for their families while their wives cared for the household and children in addition to any paid work they might undertake themselves.

Maternity has been more intensively studied in relation to childbirth and infancy, and to some extent our selection of documents illustrates this. The birth of her first child marks an important life stage for a woman. In the case of illicit maternity, a single mother might abandon her child and deny the relationship, or the parish authorities might insist that she wet-nurse the child and then place it into the care of others. A single mother sometimes kept her child with the father's financial support compelled by the courts. In most cases, mothers were married, and their relationships with their children were influenced by social and material circumstances, by the number of children they had already, and by the sex of the baby. If parents sent the baby out to be wet-nursed, the child might be away from home for over a year. Whatever relationship a mother developed with her children changed over time and varied with each child; the pleasures or griefs usually concluded only with the death of either mother or child.

Although motherhood may have been a bond between women, as they shared many feelings, and sympathised with each other's pains and sorrows, women could be divided by profound differences over maternity or its absence. Those who were not married were excluded from childbirths, and those who had not borne a child themselves were deemed to lack authority. Midwives who delivered babies could be the focus of blame when things went wrong. Tensions over maternity could be significant in witchcraft accusations, as Lyndal Roper's work has shown.[3]

Maternity was viewed seriously in early modern times. Children were expected and taught to respect and obey both their parents, and to seek their blessing. Adults expressed their duty to their parents in correspondence, and conventional notions of respect shaped the language in which maternal relationships were expressed. Furthermore, in many families where ideals of discipline may seem harsh, the context was again one of duty. Mothers such as the Nonconformist Sarah Meadows struggled against her own affections in determining to breed her children 'as hardy as I can'.[4]

Religious faith provided a context and a meaning for the work of motherhood. Biblical texts promised salvation through maternity: 'It comforts me as to nursing inconveniences, that bringing up of children, lodging strangers, and washing the saints' feet, are put together as good works 1 Tim. v. 10.'[5] Religion supported mothers through the illnesses, accidents, and deaths of their children. Prayer provided comfort and hope. Indeed, in many circumstances there was little else mothers could do but pray, as medical assistance, while it might be sought, availed little, for medical practitioners had little to offer beyond blood-letting. A child's death was a terrible test of Christian faith. Ultimately, the godly resigned themselves to the will of God, but not without a bitter struggle. As Sarah Savage wrote of her sister-in-law whose child had just died, 'Poor sister Henry . . . is sitting alone and keeping silence. The consideration of her giving it up to God in baptism, when she was asked by my father [the minister, Philip Henry] whether she could freely do it, hath had an influence upon her submission.'[6]

Evidence for ordinary women's attitudes to their children and their practices of childcare is rare. Incidental references in legal records suggest communal supervision of children, and that from the age of 2, children might stray quite far from home.[7] Nevertheless, mothers could be very jealous about who disciplined their children, as fragments of evidence show. In 1607 a children's quarrel ended up in the London church courts: when Marie Barwick's small boy injured Alice Ansley's little daughter, Alice was so angry she gave the boy 'a little pat upon the hand', Marie Barwick abused Alice as a whore, and Alice sued for slander. One witness was deemed to be a supporter of Alice because she had nursed Alice's child.[8] In poorer families, children left home earlier than among the elite, often around the early teens. Yet although mothers lacked the means to travel or to correspond, if they lived into their fifties they remained an important influence on their adult children, especially their daughters. Mothers supervised marriage negotiations even into their daughters' twenties and thirties, supported daughters against violent husbands, and attended their daughters' lyings-in.[9]

Maternity was an extraordinarily diverse experience, which could be a source of joy and pleasure to women, as well as of grief and even boredom: 'I heartily sympathise with you in the tediousness of your nursery', observed Sarah Savage to her sister, 'but take heed of complaining as Rebekah: if it be so why am I thus?'[10]

Delight and pleasure in children shines through much of the correspondence of literate women, and we have no reason to think that such feelings were class specific. We owe much of our evidence about maternal joy to the letters women wrote to their absent husbands, in which they described how 'the pretty harmless mirth' of their children refreshed their spirits.[11] As children grew older, mothers enjoyed their company: 'Ned is grown a very good companion,' wrote Lady Brilliana Harley to her husband, Sir Robert, in 1626.[12] However, during adolescent years there were frequently conflicts of will between mothers and children. Elite mothers had more opportunities than poorer women to enjoy a relationship with their adult children and even their grandchildren; married younger than their plebeian counterparts, they might be in their forties rather than their fifties when their children reached their twenties. While sons of the gentry were away at school and university, daughters remained at home longer, sometimes until marriage, although they too might move to another household. Sometimes a female relative or servant's mistress might fulfil part of the maternal role, offering advice to the young people in her employment.

7.1 Anne Glyd: a family record, 1650–97

Many literate women kept a personal record of the births and deaths of children and other immediate family. Anne Glyd (see document 1.7) bore seven children before her husband died in 1658; when the record ceases, only one of her daughters, Anne Brockman, was living. Children were often named for relatives, and should they die, another child would be given the same name. Entries relating to the births and deaths of her grandchildren by her daughter Martha Drake have been included.

Recipe book of Anne Glyd, Brockman Papers, 'Anne Glyd Her Book 1656', BL, Add. MS 45196, fos 82–83v.

A memorial of our children's births: Sep. 22 1650.
John Glyd born Sept 22 being Saturday 1650

Elizabeth Glyd born the 24th day of August being the Lord's day [1651] who lived no longer than till she was just 7 weeks old.

Anne Glyd born the 8th of October 1652 who lived no longer till she was just 6 weeks old.

Richard Glyd born the 26th day of October 1653 being Thursday.

Martha Glyd born the 10th day of February 1655 being Saturday.

Laurence Glyd born the 2d day of March 1656, being the Lord's day.

Elizabeth Glyd born the 6th day of September 1657 being the Lord's day.

Anne Glyd born the 7 of October 1658 being Thursday.

My dearly beloved husband Mr Richard Glyd and eminent Christian and a dear loving loyal exceeding eminent in the relation of a husband both to the soul and body of me his wife whose good counsels and instructions if my God will be pleased to give me the grace to follow I shall have cause to bless my good God to all eternity for him. He left this life for an eternal happy life the 24 of November 1658 about 5 a clock in the m[orning].

Laurence Glyd departed this life May the 3 about 9 at night being 3 years 2 months and one day old.

Richard Glyd departed this life June the 13 1662 about 12 a clocke at night being 8 years 7 months and 3 weeks old.

Elizabeth Glyd departed this life the 7 of November 1681 about 10 a clock in the morning. She was twenty-four years and nine weeks lack a day old. A good and gracious child, praised be thy name O my gracious God for making her such a one.

12 June 1684 my granddaughter Ann Drake June the 12th being Thursday. Lord my God be pleased to work in her the new birth, amen, amen, and for Christ's sake make her eminently thy servant from her infancy, amen, amen. Gracious God hear and grant.

My grand-daughter Martha Drake was born the thirtieth day of September 1686 . . .

November 10 1688 My grandson Ralph Drake was born the tenth of November 1688 being Saturday between seven and eight a clock in the morning.

[Margin] The 4 of November the Prince of Orange began to land his army.

Although he [Ralph] was born at a time that looked sad and dark and we were under great confusion: yet of thy mercy be pleased to spare him that he may live to see good and gracious times, thy Church to flourish in peace and holiness.

23 November 1689

My dearly beloved and extraordinary dutiful son John Glyd departed this life November 23 1689 about two a clock in the morning, being nine and thirty year old the 21 of September before. He was useful in his generation to man. And truly served God in his generation. O my God help me his sorrowful mother to rest satisfied with thy will. Dr Hampton preached his funeral sermon his text was Philippians 1: verse 21, For me to live is Christ and to die is gain.

August 4 1690 my daughter Drake was brought abed of a second son . . . and named John in remembrance of his uncle John Glyd.

June 8 1692 my daughter Drake was brought abed of a daughter who was named Elizabeth in remembrance of her aunt Elizabeth Glyd.

April 23 1694 my daughter Drake was brought abed of a daughter who was named Sarah in respect to her cousin Sarah Stoughton.

July 31 1694 my daughter Drake died of the small pox being the fortieth year of her age. She was a virtuous, pious, good woman. She left six small children behind her. The Lord in mercy take care of them and bestow on them all what is truly good for their souls and bodies.

13 July 1695. My son Drake died and left the six children behind him which his wife left and now that father and mother hath left them, good God for Christ's sake take them up into care and provide for them whatever thou knowest to be good for their souls and body.

July 20 1695. My son [in-law] Drake being dead I came to his house to try what I could be assisting in for good their poor 6 orphans my grandchildren. I was frustrated much in my thoughts by the unkind and I may say evil carriage of their trustees to me. But trusting to the Almighty having no evil ends: but a hearty desire to do them good, souls and bodies and do my duty. My God hath wonderfully helped me this year and almost a half, it being now November 24, 1697. O Lord my God ever assist in my duty to thee my God and man, keep me in my right reason and true understanding and spare my life so long as I am able truly [to] serve and please thee and be useful for the true good of the souls and bodies of these orphans. Receive me to thy mercy through the merits of thy son when I breathe out my soul.

LYING-IN

7.2   Need for linen: Lettice Gawdy, 1620s

A mother required linen for swaddling her baby. Lettice Gawdy, daughter of Sir Robert Knowles, wife of Framlingham Gawdy of West Harling, Norfolk, bore eight children before her death in 1630. Through her father, she asked assistance with clothes for her expected infant.

Lettice Gawdy to her father, Sir Robert Knowles, in Weston. (n.d. later 1620s), BL, Add. MS 27,395 fo. 125.

Dear father, I do hear you are going into Oxfordshire. I humbly beseech you to remember my humble service to my lord and my lady[1] and that you will

1. Unclear to whom this refers.

speak to my lady to send me some clouts and I shall think myself much bound to her for she promised me some when I was with child of my first but I was so well provided that I thought to reserve them till I had need of them, which is now, for I have had so many children that they have worn through all my things and therefore I must try my friends again for I trust that you have some old shirts in a corner for me or some old things and I do here give you many humble thanks for the two wrought stools you sent me by my husband and I beseech you to send me the yellow taffeta quilt that is to the black velvet bed if you do not use it, which I do think you have no cause to use it, being the bed is gone, with my humble services to yourself craving your blessing remain your dutiful daughter to command Lettice Gaudy.

7.3   The birth of a son: Lady Brilliana Harley, 1626

Brilliana Conway became the third wife of Sir Robert Harley. Her first son, Edward, was born in 1624. Here she announces the birth of their second son, Robert, to her husband who was in London attending Parliament.

Brilliana Harley to her husband Sir Robert, Brampton, 15 April 1626, BL, Add. MS 70110, fo. 23.

Dear Sir, I make haste to tell you under my own hand that it has pleased the Lord to bless us with another son, and tomorrow being Sabbath he shall be given to the Lord: and in his ordinance. I pray God make us both thankful for all the blessings, and do you love and long to be with me as do [I?] you, and I pray God preserve you, and do you pray for me
your most faithful wife
Brill: Harley
I desire to have the name Robert
Let me hear from you
my humble duty to my Lord[1] and tell my sister I am reasonable well
Ned is well

7.4   'We have failed in part of our hope':
Lady Anne D'Ewes, 1641

Anne Clopton (1612–41) married Sir Simonds D'Ewes in 1626 when she was 14 years of age. The young couple spent time apart, as Simonds' studies of records and his duties as an MP for Suffolk caused absences. D'Ewes kept many of his wife's letters. Their only son Clopton had died in 1636. Anne D'Ewes wrote the letter below when Simonds was attending the Long Parliament which had met in November 1640. She died in 1641.

Anne D'Ewes to Sir Simonds D'Ewes, [n.d.: 1641], BL, Harleian MS 379, fo. 112v.

1. My Lord probably refers to her father, Viscount Conway (d. 1631).

My dear love,

It hath pleased God now again the ninth time to restore me from the peril of childbirth, and though we have failed in part of our hope by the birth of a daughter, yet we are likewise freed from much care and fear a son would have brought. Let us wait patiently on God; he will in his good time vouchsafe us issue male if he see it good for us. I am through his gracious providence grown pretty strong though I was somewhat feverish at the beginning. Your three daughters with me and your fourth at nurse are, I bless God, pretty well. Thus with my dearest affection of you, hoping shortly to come to you, I rest

your faithful affectionate wife

Anne D'Ewes

7.5 Midwife's care for mother and child: Agnes Fisher, 1631

Agnes Fisher's baby died within a quarter of an hour of delivery. Agnes complained about her midwife, Elizabeth Bessy, and an office suit was undertaken which could have led to Bessy losing her licence. In her defence, Bessy argued that she had attended when required, that the labour had been long, and that Fisher seemed unwilling to help herself to delivery. Fisher, suffering from the loss of her baby, may have been in no mood to appreciate Bessy's ill-advised attempt to cheer her, suggesting that she too might have died.

Diocese of London Consistory Court, Personal Answer Book, LMA, DL/C 194, fo. 83.

[10 May 1631. Elizabeth Bessy responds to the charges contained in the articles presented against her by Agnes Fisher as follows:]

[To the third charge of the articles aforesaid she answers and believes] that in the months articulate this respondent (being sent for to come unto the articulate Agnes Fisher, who was then great with child and near the time of her delivery) came to her the said Agnes so soon as she had notice thereof or could well leave such other women as she had then in labour or were under her hands to be delivered and remained and continued with her at times needful duly helping and assisting her in her labours until such time as she was well and safely delivered of her child which was as this respondent believeth the next morning after this respondent came to her as aforesaid she coming unto her (as she believes) about six of the clock in the morning. . . .

[To the fourth charge of the articles she answers and believes] that she this respondent during the time that the said Agnes was in her pains of travail did not any ways neglect her but used all the best means she possibly could to assist and help the said Agnes in her delivery. [And otherwise she does not believe any of the rest to be true] saving that she believeth that whilst the said Agnes was without pain she this respondent might and did sometimes (being wearied with labour and her former watching with other women) take a short nap which could not be hurtful to the said Agnes in regard she this respondent upon the least motion or calling (being very wakeful) was ready to assist her and did help her the said Agnes.

[To the fifth charge she answers and believes] that although this respondent and the other women who were present with the said Agnes in the time of her labour and at her delivery used all the possible means that could be to assist the said Agnes in her deliverance, she the said Agnes was not withstanding so dull and slow in her pains and so unapt or unwilling to help herself and to set forward the production of her child that her child was born very weak and feeble and albeit she this respondent used the best means she could to save the life of the said child, it died within less than a quarter of an hour after the birth thereof but the life of the said Agnes was no ways endangered thereby for as this respondent hath been confidently informed she the said Agnes did within three days after her said deliverance forsake her bed and do some painful and toilsome work about her house which a weak and sick woman could not have done. . . .

[To the sixth charge of the articles presented as aforesaid she answers and says] that on the day of the burial of the child articulate, this respondent being in the house of the said [Agnes] with her she the said Agnes grudgingly and repiningly said to this respondent that if she, this respondent, had been careful the said child might have lived whereupon this respondent without malice or any discontent and thinking rather to cheer her up than to dishearten her did jestingly reply that she might give God thanks for sparing, for if she had not as many lives as a cat she might have died too. . . .

[To the seventh charge of the articles presented as aforesaid she answers and believes] that within six days after the delivery of the said Agnes of her said child this respondent sent her daughter to see the said Agnes and at her coming she found the said Agnes in good health and strength of body and up about her household employment whereat (as she believeth) her said daughter rejoiced in regard she had heard that the said Agnes was then very ill and likely to die. . . .

BEING A MOTHER

7.6   Abandoning a child: Mary Coyne, 1692

Mary Coyne was probably a single woman. She would be unlikely to find work to support herself and her child, and being a mother placed her at risk of punishment as a bastard bearer, so with the advice of two other women, she abandoned her child, leaving the baby girl in a basket at the porch of the minister's house. Such a public action might have led to Mr Beaton being suspected as the father. In areas closer to London, women were able to abandon their babies more anonymously. Hospitals such as Christ's placed the foundlings out to nurse, and supervised their education. (Note that the Christian name 'Denis' was used for a woman.)

Somerset Quarter Session Rolls, Somerset Archives, Q/SR 190/12.

The examination of Denis Fleming late of Weyly in the County of Wiltshire taken the 9th day of July 1692.

Who saith upon oath about three weeks since she left Weyly aforesaid and intended to go to Wishford in the county of Wiltshire aforesaid, but meeting with one Mary Coyne on the way and after some discourse she told this deponent that she was travelling to Exeter; and this deponent told her she would go with her, and accordingly they travelled on the way to Exeter until they came to Chard in this county where this deponent told her that she would go no further but return back to her own county and they parted there but after this deponent had left Chard and gone about a mile the said Mary Coyne overtook her and told this deponent she would go with her

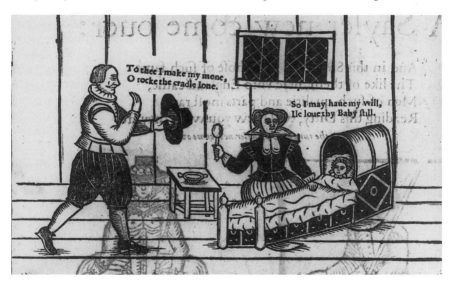

Figure 13 **Parents and baby**

From the Pepys Ballads, vol I, no. 397. By permission of the Pepys Library, Magdalene College, Cambridge

The ballad which this image illustrates ('Rocke the Cradle, Joane') tells of a husband who has persuaded his wife to take on his lover's child as her own. Such tales of husbands' concerns for their illegitimate offspring belong more to literature than to life; much more common was the single woman and her child abandoned by the father and his wife. The clothes, cradle, and their furnishings suggest a middling-status household. The print's poor quality is typical.

back again and they came both together to the parish of Linington where the said Mary Coyne was delivered of a female child where she stayed about a week after childbirth; and was going away with this deponent out of the said parish with an intent to return to their legal home but they meeting with one Joan Hocky of the said parish [she] advised them to leave the said female child there telling of them if the Devil were not in them they would not carry it with them; and told them if they would consent to leave the child behind then she would lend them a basket to put the child in and go with them to one Mr Beaton's of the said parish and leave it in the porch of the door of his house; and the said Joan Hocky told the said Mary Coyne that if she would stay there, (they being in a ground near the parish) she would come to her in the evening with a basket; and the said Joan Hocky went away from them and the said deponent left the said Mary Coyne and child there and went to Ashington; and came back to Linington that night and informed the said Mr Beaton with the whole design.

Mary Coyne late of London saith upon oath that what the abovesaid Denis Fleming hath sworn concerning her the said deponent is true and the abovesaid Joan Hocky returned to her that evening with a basket and they put the child into it and carried it to the minister's house of the said parish of Linington and left it in the porch of the door of the said house; and the said deponent with the said Joan Hocky went about a mile from the said parish and lay in an old house until a man came there that was sent in search of them and brought this deponent back to the said parish.

7.7 A mother's duty to breastfeed: Jane Sharp, 1671

The use of a wet-nurse was class specific: the majority of women could not afford to employ someone to feed their babies. Wealthier women and others with profitable employment might have used a wet-nurse. The practice was censured by ministers and others such as Jane Sharp, who believed that part of a mother's duty was to feed her child herself. Sharp here reflects the view that a mother's qualities of character were transmitted to the child by her milk, which was widely believed to be blood made white in her breasts.

Jane Sharp, *The Midwives Book*, London, 1671, p. 353.

The usual way for rich people is to put forth their children to nurse, but that is a remedy that needs a remedy, if it might be had; because it changeth the natural disposition of the child, and oftentimes exposeth the infant to many hazards, if great care be not taken in the choice of the nurse.

There are not many women that want milk to suckle their own children; so there are some that may well be excused, because of their weakness; that they cannot give suck to their own children: but multitudes pretend weakness when they have no cause for it, because they have not so much love for their own, as dumb creatures have.

7.8 Remedies for the health of babies and children: Katherine Packer, 1639

The commonplace books of elite women contain remedies for a range of the miseries and problems of children's health. Teething, fits, and rickets were common problems. Remedies for teething might include lancing the gums to allow the teeth to come through, or a hard object for the child to chew on. The wolf's tooth recommended here, being the tooth of a wild animal, was believed to have special piercing qualities. The fits which worried early modern parents were probably febrile convulsions caused by a high temperature, and are still common in children between 2 and 4 years of age. In some early modern cases (see document 1.5), we know that the baby was given blood from the navel string as a preventive.

Katherine Packer, 1639 [a leather book with 2 metal clasps], Folger, MS V. a. 387, pp. 9, 46, 94–5.

To make children's teeth grow with little pain
Hang about the neck a wolf's tooth that the child may rub the gums therewith.
For the rickets in a child
Take a pint of white wine and boil therein a handful of liverwort, as much water-wort [purslane?], and maidenhair, half as much brown sage, half a handful of brown fennel and yarrow. Boil them till half be consumed then strain it and sweeten it with 2 ounces of fine sugar, and let the child drink of it morning and evening 4 or 6 spoonfuls at a time.
For convulsive fits
[symbol] the innards of a hare viz heart liver lights and blood with the gall and the inward skins of the gizzards of pigeons and put them in a new glazed pipkin and dry them in an oven so that they may beat to fine powder and searse[1] them. Take of this powder morning and evening as much as will lie on a groat and mix it with a little black cherry water in a spoon, temper it so together that you may fit it upon a knife's point, and after it drink a good glass of poppy and black cherry water mixed together. Fast an hour or 2 after it; let it be the 1st thing you take in the morning and last at night. [symbol] repeat it for 2 months together.
For a young child, take as much of the powder as will lie on 2d. and give it mixed in a spoonful of the 2 waters and when it hath taken it down give a spoonful of the waters after it.

7.9 Death of a child: Mary Roberts, 1661

Infant life was beset with crisis and consequently maternal fears; teething, fits, and weaning all had a large lore about them. Mary Roberts (d. 1666) here seeks to negotiate the meaning, 'the uses', of her son's death. While she discussed the symptoms of his teething, the Lord's punishment for her own sins she believed to be the cause of his death.

Devotional diary of Mary Roberts, East Sussex RO, Dun 52/10/3, 1662, pp. 7–11.

1. Sift through a cloth made of bristles.

This is May 17 1661: but my dear first child John Roberts perished the 15th day being about teething as we thought: he had 3 great teeth broke flesh in the time of his illnesses 2 after the shaking took him which was plainly to be perceived on the Lord's day in the morning about the fifth day of the same month: in one of his arms, his right arm and it continued shaking from the time I dressed him by fits, without it were[1] when he was asleep almost all the day: in the night he kept reasonable well I think: but it came into both arms on the morning and left him not but when he was asleep in a sound sleep very little but he was very merry by fits and quiet a whole week till Easter day then it begin to be in his body more than formerly ... but he knew us very well till Tuesday night: I went to bed about 10 a clock or more though he had been very sick for the 3 nights before: with a kind of a stirring to vomit but brought away very little: till about a hour after he departed this life I hope for a better: this is the [illegible] to my remembrance I should live to forget it. . . .

Now I desire to make the uses of this late affliction: that he began to shake on a sabbath day morning for I desired to walk earlier on that morning: and to be humbled for all my sins which is the cause of miscarriage; and for ought I know the cause of this affliction though I know it may be for chastisement and I have great cheer to think God loves me as [much?] as he hath made me look towards him: for forgiveness of all my sins. . . .

I desire the spiritual presence of my good God to forgive me: and prepare me for danger: O it is not a small mercy to enjoy the life of children: I have the life of one at present and of a loving husband and a loving father and I believe the life and love of as many sisters and brothers according to their apprehension ... and other friends as most women have. Blessed is my good God, my husband and sisters sick, mother, all must in time perish.

7.10   'In danger of being weaned': Lady Brilliana Harley, 1626

The son Ned to whom Brilliana refers was the couple's eldest son and heir, born in 1624. He was aged about 17 months at the time of this discussion about his weaning.

Lady Brilliana Harley to Sir Robert Harley, BL, Add. MS 70110, fos 17, 21v.

Brampton, 14 March 1626

... Ned is well, I thank God, but was in danger of being weaned, for this last night his nurse was very much out of temper being inclined to an ague: and he lay in my chamber from her: but this day she is well: and if it prove to be an ague, he shall be weaned and I hope God will bless to him the food which man lives by: as he has done in mercy hitherto that of a child:

---

1. Except.

I must beg your blessing for him: and I pray God preserve you to the great comfort of your most faithful affectionate wife, Brilliana Harley
my humble duty to my father.

8 April 1626
. . . Ned by signs begs your blessing. I thank God he is very well and so is his nurse and I purpose, an it please God, to wean him the week after Easter.

7.11   'So full of pretty play and tricks': Katherine, Marchioness of Buckingham, 1623

Many literate women expressed their delight in their children, referring to 'their pretty harmless mirth' as refreshing to the spirit (BL, MS Harleian 379 fo. 137). Katherine, Marchioness of Buckingham, was married to James I's favourite, George Villiers, later Duke of Buckingham. In 1623 Buckingham and Prince Charles embarked on a journey to Spain to woo the Infanta. Katherine's letter dates to this absence.

Katherine, Marchioness of Buckingham, to her husband, 16 July [1623], BL, Harleian MS 6987, fos 119–22.

. . . my lord indeed I must crave your pardon that I did write you no more particulars of our pretty Mal, I did tell our dry nurse what you write to me and she says you had one letter from her and she has sent you word by every one that has gone that she was well and what she could do, but if you will pardon this fault I will commit the like no more, she is very well I thank God and when she is set to her feet and held by her sleeves she will not go softly but stamp and set one foot afore another very fast that I think she will run before she can go, she loves dancing extremely and when the Saraband is played she will set her thumb and her finger together offering to snap and then when tomduse is sung then she will shake her apron and when she hears the tune of the clapping dance my lady Frances Huberd taught the prince she will clap both her hands together and on her breast, and she can tell the tunes as well as any of us can and as they change the tunes she will change her dancing, I would you were here but to see her for you would take much delight in her now she is so full of pretty play and tricks and she has gotten a trick that when they dance her she will cry hah hah and Nicolae will dance with his legs and she will imitate him as well as she can she will be excellent at that for if one lay her down she will kick her legs over her head but when she is elder I hope she will be more modest, everybody says she grows every day more like you than other, you shall have her picture very shortly I am very glad you have the pearl and that you like them so well and am sure they do not help you to win the ladies' hearts. . . .
I rest your most dutiful wife till death K. Buckingham

CHILDCARE, HEALTH AND ADVICE

7.12 Maternal admonitions: Sarah Meadows (d. 1688)

Sarah Meadows (1654–88) was the granddaughter of Benjamin Fairfax of Halesworth, Suffolk, and the second wife (1675) of John Meadows. Both her father and her husband were ministers who were ejected from the Anglican church in 1662. Sarah wrote this advice for her seven children – four sons and three daughters – just before her death. Like her male relatives who had experienced persecution for their refusal to worship in the Anglican church, she emphasised the importance of family piety and godliness. Such ideas were significant in framing a Nonconformist conscience and morality among the emerging middle classes. Her daughter, Mrs Judith Meadows, who died in 1719 aged 41, commended this work to her own children: 'As to the well ordering of your selves . . . I refer you to the serious perusal of your dear grandmother Meadow's book.' There were two contemporary transcriptions of the manuscript, one of which is now in the Beinecke Library, Yale.

Edgar Taylor, *The Suffolk Bartholomeans: a Memoir . . . of John Meadows*, London, Pickering, 1840, pp. 137–8, 139–44.

This is the last gift and hearty well-wishes of Sarah Meadows to her beloved children, John, Daniel, Philip, Sarah, Rebecca, Thomas, and Mary Meadows.

The great miscarriage of youth in these days hath made me very solicitous how I might bring up these children the Lord hath graciously given me and continued to me, for the honour of that God from whom I received and to whom I have given them; and also what might render them most serviceable in their generation; and also what in all probability might be the best preservative against the evils of the days wherein they are cast. I therefore set myself to consider what were the evils they were most likely to miscarry by, and also what might be the most efficacious means to prevent them.

1st. Ignorance, . . .

2d. Irreligiousness;

3d. Another sin this age is apt to is too great a delicateness and tenderness, and an overvaluing the body, and giving too great indulgence to that manifest enemy of the soul, whose motions are always opposite, contrary, and in enmity to the motions of the spirit. The continual cries of indulged flesh will be 'a little more sleep, a little more slumber; a little more ease, a little more indulgence'; till at last we justly merit the doom of slothful and unprofitable servants.

4th. Pride; . . .

5th. Ungovernableness, . . .

6th. Idleness, . . .

7th. wicked, ensnaring, and tempting company; . . .

Now, since these are such dangerous evils, I do charge myself in the name and fear of God, to set myself, as much as in me lie, to be instrumental to prevent these great evils which my children are in so much danger of: and, in order to the right discharging of my duty towards them as a parent, I charge myself,

1. To teach, instruct, and principle my children in the fundamentals of religion, according to that knowledge, capacity, and ability that God hath given me: and further, that I bring them up in all school-learning, that their understandings and capacities may receive the greatest improvement they are capable of; that they may not at last be found to stumble and fall for want of light, or to go astray for want of being directed in the way of truth. Having endeavoured thus to furnish their heads, though this and much more will not better their hearts, yet,

2. I charge myself to bring them up so piously that they may conscionably perform the several parts of God's worship, . . .

3. I charge myself to bring them up as hardy as I can; with as little indulgence to the body as may be; . . .

5. I charge myself to exercise that due authority over my children which God have put into my hands; to endeavour the breaking of their wills betimes; and not easily pardon a fault that is directly in opposition to the wills of their parents, though otherwise it be small. . . .

As to the bringing up my children as hardy as I can, the arguments I will urge myself withal are these:

1. Because I think such persons have the greatest enjoyment of themselves. What renders us more uneasy to ourselves than too great delicacy and tenderness of the body? . . .

2. They have also great advantage above others, with respect both to their soul and body. A person that can rise early, go to bed late, endure heat and cold without any considerable discomposure or disorder, what advantage have such an one for his soul! how many hours may he gain, which another cannot possibly attain to; because use and custom render it exceeding difficult, if not utterly impossible to them. Besides, who, that knoweth anything of themselves, know not how great an influence the body hath on the soul, in all its motions? If the body be discomposed (and what render it more liable to discomposure than too great tenderness, delicacy, and an over love of ease?), how quickly are its malignant influences discovered in the soul. . . .

3. Such persons as have been used to least delicacy, and most hardiness, are likely to be most useful in church and state: . . .

As to the maintaining that authority over my children which God hath given me, I urge the necessity of this upon myself by these arguments:

1. It is a duty commanded and commended in Scripture. . . . And though it be chiefly the *father's* work, yet I know not but it may be first the *mother's*; and I suppose both jointly are to carry on this work.

7.13 Substitute mother: Abigail Harley, 1660

When his wife died, Sir Edward Harley, who was serving as governor of Dunkirk, entrusted their baby to the care of his sister-in-law, Abigail, the wife of his brother Thomas.

Abigail Harley, wife of Thomas Harley, to her brother-in-law Sir Edward Harley, 9 October 1660, BL, Add. MS 70115 (formerly Portland loan 29/76).

Honoured Sir, I am troubled that I am not able to tell you your sweet babe is better than when you went. She was brought up immediately after you were gone and has not since been out of her chamber, yet the distemper seemed to grow much upon her so that on Saturday, that choke or rattling in the throat was always to be heard. I gave her the syrups you sent and made a drink of maidenhair, and violet leaves and hyssop and sweetened it with syrup of violets and sugar candy. I sat up with her that night and finding that she slept very unquiet and had no stool I made a glister and gave her next morning it wrought very kindly once, I used to anoint her stomach with orange flower butter: yesterday morning we sent for the Dr finding she still grew worse, the distemper of stoppage in her water also troubled her, for that she has saxifrage water and star-wort which did good: that and altogether put her into such violent fits that we feared she would not live till now, I sent in the mean time for Mrs Davies of Wigmore and Mr Davies of Ludlow. Here is Mr Smith of Hereford who oft and earnestly prayed for her, all of us gave her up for dead having for some hours in the night symptoms of nothing else, but it pleased the Lord after the taking oil of sweet almonds 2 or 3 times that she much revived and grievous sick fits were not so long as before, between whiles she looks a little lightsome in the midst of great extremity, she is now very weak, we are waiting to see what the Lord will do with her, and in hopes of the doctor's coming this day, I pray God fit you and us to submit to his will if another sad providence must now pass upon us, it would be a very great trial to me yet I have comfort in that I hope nothing has been neglected that I knew to be good for her, and as soon as we apprehended danger we sent away Ned Perks, indeed before lest something might be more than we knew of. She did not change till about noon yesterday. If it please God I shall be glad to write next post of her recovery. I trouble you no further now, but assure you my care shall be to the utmost of my skill who am, Sir, your most affectionate humble servant,
AH

7.14 Convulsive fits: Jane Elyott's advice, 1635

Clopton D'Ewes was the only son and heir of his father Sir Simonds D'Ewes. His fits caused his parents terrible anguish. In this instance, his aunt Jane Elyott offers advice to her brother about treatment of the fits, and incidentally reveals a differential attitude to the weaning of boys and girls. Jane's recommendation of making 'an issue' meant making a cut in the child to let blood. Dr Mayerne, to whom she refers, was a prominent London physician who was consulted by King Charles I among others. Clopton D'Ewes subsequently died in 1636. As a good aunt, Jane also sends news of a possible 'match' for her niece.

Jane Elyott to Sir Simonds D'Ewes, London 9 [Ju]ne [1635], BL, MS Harleian 382, fos 45, 55.

Worthy Brother, . . . for the forwardness of my little nephew I hope tis never the worse, for mine was so after the fits, and although she were older than your son, yet she would cry extremely at the dressing of the issue, when it was first made she had seven fits in one day, when she was a year and [a] half old and presently fell into an ague and had no more fits, till that time twelve month then she had one and a show of 2 or 3 more, then we made an issue and doctor Maherne said it might be stopped, any time before the child were seven years old without any danger. I never had any other of my children had such fits but at the point of death, and I think few children die, without them. I know the grief and care, for the loss of my children, was a great cause of the loss of more. I think it was very ill for your child to suck again, after so long being kept from it. I desire to hear whether it had fits, before you tried to wean him, I know not what cause you had but methinks it was somewhat soon to wean a boy. The best way I found was to change the complexion of the nurse. When you have another, a brown ruddy complexioned woman I found best for my children. The starting in the sleep as it threatened more fits, so it is a sign of teeth. I have had my children when they have been about teeth start in their sleep exceedingly and yet never had touch of convulsion. I have been so fearful ever since my daughter had them, that I have never been without something good for those fits, I had waters and powders my cousin Charles Latham helped me to (his children being subject to them), for Paul he being a great fat pale boy, but I thank God I had no cause to use it, and that being naught, I got a glass of spirits which doctor Flud prescribed but never yet used it. My youngest boy Richard once fainted away in the maid's arms at the cutting of his eye teeth, having a strong fever and extremely forward, but now I praise God, well and lusty again. I took not anything when I was with child, the only good and great physician of us all cured me and my poor innocent children. The Lord hath sent me many afflictions with my children and now hath given me comfort of his great mercy as long as he pleases, I verily hope my sweet cousin shall no more feel the terror of that cruel disease, neither is it always sure, that if one have the rest will be subject to it, our gracious God is not tied to any thing his mercy being over all his works: to him my best prayers, and wishes shall be sent up for the perfect recovery of your dear boy, I hope this long letter will be accepted having herein strived to show the truth of my affection, to yourself, my worthy sister; and all yours. Mr Elyott remembers his kind love to you and my sister. Now tis time to subscribe my self your ever faithful hearted sister: J: Elyott

[ps] If my lady Denton and yourself have not a better match for my sister Betty I desire to make known some particulars of one by us, tis a knight's son a young man free from vice about 3 and 20 his father will settle 13 hundred pound a year and offers four hundred a year maintenance he has a great store and is a very near husband, he has another son who has three hundred pound a year given him [the remainder cut off in binding?]

2 June [1635]

Good brother

I do sincerely partake with you of your care and grief and my devoutest although poor prayers shall ever attend you and your sweet innocent for freedom from those cruel fits which my heart trembles to think on. I doubt not but your child will outgrow them I having seen great experience of these fits in children of late but not in my own I thank God but so common are convulsions grown with children that very many physicians about us cure it. An issue is in my judgment the surest way to prevent it, my daughter never had any after the issue was made … if it were mine I would by no means wean him till he had some teeth not knowing how he may breed them. … I have known children have as bad fits only with breeding teeth yet the teeth not appear a long time after. It may be if the nurse be a pale complexioned woman her milk is too weak. Pray as little as you can tamper with the tender body of so young a child.

7.15   Another remedy for convulsive fits:
Johanna St John, 1680

Women's commonplace books include many remedies for a range of children's ailments. In the example below, we might wonder how commonly used such a remedy might have been. The comments in Jane Elyott's letters seem more directly based in experience, yet the remedy here, even if unlikely to do much good, would have been less harmful.

Johanna St John 1680, Wellcome MS 4338 (for a description of the MS see document 1.14).

C. For convulsion fits: A stone growing in gall of an old ox, and the same quantity of a dead man's skull that comes to an untimely end, mix an equal quantity as much as will lie on 2 pence a little before the fit comes and give the child the hair that grows between the hinder legs of a her-bear boiled in brandy till the brandy be consumed, lay it warm to the soles of the feet.

7.16   Teaching literacy: Abigail Harley with her nieces
and nephew, 1695

Abigail Harley (1664–1726), who wrote this letter, was the unmarried daughter of Sir Edward Harley (1624–1700), the eldest son of Sir Robert and Brilliana. (Abigail's father is the 'Ned' whose weaning was discussed above in document 7.10. The Harley family's habit, common among the gentry, of naming their children after other family members, makes for some confusion). Abigail looked after her father's household and supervised her nephews and nieces at Brampton Bryan, Herefordshire. The children she cared for were those of her brother Robert, later 1st Lord Oxford, yet interestingly she reports the children's progress to her father, the children's grandfather.

Abigail Harley to her father Sir Edward Harley, BL, Add. MS 70117.

[2 February 1695] Before you went to London you were pleased to speak of having one to teach Betty and Taby to write. There is one at Leominster his name is Tyler, nephew to Mr Henry Tyler, he has sent some copies hither of his writing that I think are very well writ, I suppose will come over thither, if you please we shall agree with him to teach them to write and cast accounts. . . .

[2 March 1695] Through mercy we are all very well here. Taby has been so ever since her vomit and purge, I hope will have no return of pain in her stomach. They are very busy now at their writing have made a very good progress in it for one week. Neddy would needs have a copy book but cannot be expected to make much out, follows his reading very well now and desires with his humble duty you may know it. . . .

[9 March 1695] The children follow their writing very close. Neddy will not be contented without a copy book, yet is not like to do any great matters at it, but follows his book very well and is very orderly. They all present their humble duties to you, their father and mother. . . .

[6 April 1695] Betty and Tabby could not be satisfied till they had presented their duties to you and their father that you might see what progress they have made in their writing I hope they will mend every day. . . .

[30 April 1695] Through mercy the children are pretty well of their colds. Tis great mercy God gives us any cause to hope we may yet be delivered from our fears and dangers, though I know not which is more astonishing, that people have been so long blind, or how they now come to see, but God reigns even in the midst of his enemies, and in this we may rejoice.

THE MATERNAL RELATIONSHIP

7.17   Lady Elizabeth Petty: letters to her children, 1684

Elizabeth Petty, the daughter of Sir Hardress Waller, widow of Sir Maurice Fenton, married Sir William Petty in 1667. She bore a number of children, but when she died in 1708 only three survived her. Petty's work took him to Ireland. Assuming his business to be brief, she accompanied him there, leaving two of their children, Anne, aged about 11, and Henry, about 9, in their London house, under the care of a nurse. The following is one of a series of letters to her children showing her concern for their daily activities.

Petty papers, vol. 8, Lady Petty's correspondence with her children, 1684, BL, Add. MS 72857, fos 3–4, 21–21v, 47.

For Mistress Anne and Mr Harry Petty at Sir William Petty's house in Piccadilly London

Dublin, 24 January 1684

My Dear Children, We all praise God to hear you continue in good health. Your Pa-Pa as well as myself, and your Bro: Charles think it very long till we see you, and desire you to believe that tis for your own sakes that we do it, for to leave our affairs unsettled would but make us uneasy when we were with you. You forget to say anything of Derrick Pain and Owen, you must always read your letters just before you answer them, and then you will be able to answer to every particular. Let Mr Banworth take care to buy you good ink, paper, pens, and wax, and then you will take pleasure in writing, I would have you tell me everything you hear, and where you go, and who comes to see you, and what clothes you have, and what your Bro: Harry does. Tell my Sister Ingold: that I am very glad to hear she is well of her lameness. My niece Blundell's boys are very well, the youngest has been a little ill with his teeth and had two cut 3 days since and is now very well, though a little fallen of his flesh which is never the worse. I do not approve of Sir Francis forbidding them to take the air in mild fair weather, if they were my own and that I had no more in the world, I would not shut them up so, and this is also Sir William's opinion, and therefore when tis fair weather they shall have my coach about noon, and stay out about an hour at a time and so by degrees use them to the air, which is the most refreshing thing in the world. You never say a word of Mistress Brooke nor my Bro: Tommy, don't forget it for the future. I intend to bring you Sarah Knight. God send me a happy meeting with my dear children, Adieu, make my compliments to all those you think I owe them, and go visit Madam Justell.

Dublin 21 June 1684

. . . Your Pa-Pa sends you both his blessing, we expect to hear that you are both very good, and observant of those things that are taught you. . . .

I hope your nurse will take care to keep you from running in the streets, and fighting with one another. . . . You tell me nothing of Mr Isacke[1] nor Seigneur Bartholeme, methinks Harry should be always present when you sing and dance.

[PS] Be sure nurse does not let you go abroad in the heat of the day, nor never alone.

Dublin 8 Nov 1684

I am very glad, My Dear Children, to find by yours of the 28 past that you are in good health, though I hear my girl has had a little cold, God be praised that tis past I hope, I need not tell your nurse that you should take no physic, a rosemary or raisin posset is enough, if your beds be warmed be sure you do not go into them whilst they are hot. I do not doubt your nurse's care, I only put her in mind of what I would have done.

7.18 'So much a woman': Lady Ann North, 1676–77

Ann North was the wife of Dudley, 4th Baron North. Her weekly letters to her daughter Anne, the wife of Robert Foley of Stourbridge, discussing a range of subjects, illustrate her relationship with one of her own adult children.

Ann North to Anne Foley, BL, Add. MS 32500, fos 15, 18, 24.

31 December [16]76
Dearest Daughter,
I am very glad to hear that my son and you and pretty Missy are so well upon your removes which must needs have been great trouble. . . . I am sorry to hear there is not a boy towards but I hope there will be in good time. I am your most affectionate Mother, A. North.

25 March 1677
. . . I am sorry that your cousin Foley's lady hath a girl, a boy would have been a good pattern for you. But I suppose the next generation women will be very considerable, for there will be so many of that sex that if they have not their will, sure it will be their own faults, for either by love or luck they may hope for great things. . . .

29 August [?1677]
. . . I am glad pretty Missy is so much a woman as to be able to speak her mind.

---

1. The dancing master.

7.19 'My blessing to all your sweet children': Ann Temple, 1641

Two months after the meeting of the Long Parliament, Ann Temple expresses her concern for both the souls and bodies of her children and sees in the reforming work of the Puritan party a sign of the longed-for reformation of the church.

Ann Temple to her daughter, 16 Jan. 1641, East Sussex RO, DUN 51/54.

Dear daughter

I thank you for your kind letter I received long since, but could not then write to you if I would, and now have not your letter here and almost forgotten the substance of it only 2 things I partly remember you mentioned; the one was about the gold was sent, which I have been as sorry for, as you could be in regard I perceive it was a grief and trouble to you and offence to your husband and I did much blame Humfrey that he did not bring it back again, But being it cannot be helped I hope you will rest satisfied and make a charitable construction of that which love was the point [?] of, and hereafter I hope we shall be more wary of transgressing in the like kind. I was very glad to hear of all your good healths and shall be again thinking it long now since we heard of you which I hope for this week. I am at Broughton and have been this 3 weeks and more, my cousin Carte is not yet delivered but now I hope she draws nearer that good time; my Lady hath desired me to be with her she being absent herself and cannot be here, in regard my Lord is apt to be ill, and she dares not leave him.

I am in reasonable health I praise God, and so I hope are all the rest at Hanwell and little Sara, only I am troubled with a cold and so are some of them, for it is a general disease I think, yet Sara is free for aught I know, God is exceeding good to us every way, both for bodies and souls; and hath done wonderful things among us already; and gives us hope of more, and that we shall see idolatry and superstition rooted out; and God's ordinances set up in the purity and power of them; altars begin to go down apace and rails in many places, and yours must follow if it be not down already. Let us labour to be shameful[1] and continue our prayers; hold up our hands that Israel may prevail and not let them fail lest [evil] prevail. It concerns us much to be earnest with God, sweet daughter if we live till spring I hope we shall see my son and you here, and that he will give you leave once more to come and see me, and bring pretty Nan and Moll with you, I should be very glad to have them both here that they might go to Church, which they cannot do with you especially in winter, they shall be most welcome to us, but if I may not have both, yet I pray you not to let Nan come, Sara goes daily and will remember her doctrines, one is that God is the giver of all grace, and she will set me of it, and her other also, she is a pretty child and I hope

---

1. Conscious of our sins, and so full of shame.

you will have much comfort of her, she is so loving to me and enquires after me and sends to me to come home, Sin was grown to great height, but let it be our case to keep our hands close to God in the use of his ordinances, and to avoid every sin, and seek to him to keep us from the temptations of Satan and the power of our own corruptions, and to preserve us by faith unto salvation. And so being in heart I can only commend my dear love and affection to my good son, and your self, with my blessing to all your sweet children, I take leave and rest
your most loving mother
An Temple

Broughton this 16th of January 1640[1]
My service to my Lady and my cousins, as occasion serves you, and my kind love to Hanna

7.20 'Only you can decide': Mary Evelyn to her daughter Mary, 1684

In gentry circles, parents played a major role in finding suitable marriage partners for their children. Gentlewomen would marry younger than the bulk of their contemporaries. Mary Evelyn, born on 30 September 1665, was of marriageable age, so her parents had been seeking a suitable match. Here the mother is advising her daughter to choose for herself about the potential husband proposed to her. Mingled with so weighty a business was a range of common domestic concerns between mother and daughter. Mary decided in the negative, and died unmarried in March 1685. Her mother's draft memoir of her daughter survives in a very fragmented form.

Mary Evelyn to her daughter Mary, [1684], BL, Evelyn MS ME12.

My dear,
I have so real a concern for your present and future good that you are part of my daily care. I rejoice in all your improving, I wish you all that is happy, and will to the utmost of my power contribute towards it. The affair in discourse last night is of such a nature that you only can decide the point, since you are chiefly to receive the advantage or bear with the inconveniencies of the married state when once engaged, your parents will comply with reasonable desires for or against this choice, be discreet weigh every circumstance and if upon due consideration you cannot comply, refuse an honest gentleman with as much civility that he may not charge you with want of good nature. I left you in good hands last night and I hope you will do for the best. Your lace I have measured, it wants near a half a yard which if not exactly matched will be seen especially when the coat is at any time turned the hind part before, therefore I believe you had best take all of a piece or you may try if such as Mrs Leader's would not look well upon the silk. John will go to Mr Martins for if you desire him or do any thing else for you.

Remember me kindly to all your sisters and particularly to my daughter.[1]
M. E.

Pray do not omit to visit your godmother tell her I designed to see her very
suddenly
[ps] I send you a bottle of femetory[2] water, drink a little draught every
morning and with it a spoonful or two of syrup of violets, so not eat presently
after it, not that it is in any way physic-al, but upon a general account never
eat within half an hour after any remedy.

7.21 A daughter in service: Joane and Anne Graves, 1603

From further down the social scale, this poignant fragment hints at a disturbance
in the relationship between a London mother and her daughter when the daughter
was in service. The mistress here has replaced the mother as the daughter's confi-
dante.

Bridewell Hospital Records, Guildhall, BCB 4 (microfilm), fo. 373v (25 May 1603).

Anne Graves servant with one Mrs Rixman near the Exchange being with
child and examined in court who is the father of her child, saith that Robert
Woolstoncraft a tailor is the father thereof and that she was servant with Mr
Feild half a year ... and above, and the first time he had the use of her
body two months before [Christmastide] last.

Joane Graves mother to the said Anne Graves being examined saith that her
daughter never made this examinant acquainted with her being with child,
but her mistress she dwelt with, made it known to this examinant and thereupon sent for the officers and caused Feild to be sent to the Counter.

7.22 Multiple roles: Elizabeth Turner as daughter, mother, step-mother, and aunt, 1668–76

Elizabeth Brodnax married Thomas Turner on 14 February 1660, and became a
stepmother and mother. In addition, she and her husband undertook the care of
her orphaned nephews and nieces. Each year, on her wedding anniversary, she
reviewed the state of her children's souls, struggling to view all her charges as 'her
own'. Betty was her stepdaughter. In June 1668 she recorded her grief at the death
of her own mother. Among her relatives were gentry in Cheshire and the London
merchant and MP Thomas Papillon.

Elizabeth Turner's Journal, CKS, U1015 F27, fos 83, 135, 149–52.

1. The sisters and daughter referred to may have been Lady Mary Tuke and her daughters;
   the two mothers were close friends, and their daughters, as in many other gentry families,
   might stay at each other's houses for long periods.
2. Fumitory, a plant, usually *Fumaria officinalis*.

June 1668 toward the end of this month the Lord was pleased to try me by the death of my dear and endearing mother. She died at my house whereby I had the satisfaction of being serviceable to her in her sickness for which opportunity I desire to be thankful, and cannot yet charge mine heart with any neglect towards her therein, but desire to walk humbly before the Lord all the remainder of my days in the sense of my non improvement of my mercies in her while I enjoyed her. Oh what rich advantages might I have reaped from her soul experiences, had I delighted more in spiritual converse with her, and how much victory might I have observed over my corrupt heart and increase of grace in my barren withering soul had I more freely improved her interest at the throne of grace. . . .

14 February 1674 Being the day in which my God set me in the estate of marriage, and gave me therein opportunity to serve him and approve myself useful in my generation, opportunity to which I had coveted it is now 14 years since my settlement in this station, and upon the review of time I find my self to have been a very unprofitable instrument and to have done little service to my God with reference to the souls committed to my charge with not as yet being able satisfyingly to discern the work of grace brought forth in any of their souls; and that at any time I have been more solicitous for their temporal than spiritual welfare, I desire to look upon as sin to be humbled for (Lord humble me therefore). I hope I may conclude it has all along (from the very beginning that I undertook this charge) been in my aim and design to promote their souls' welfare, and see Christ brought forth in them, but though the prevalence of corrup[tion] and sometimes multiplicity of worldly affairs, I have too too much failed in pursuing that design by constant vigorous endeavours. This sin hath affected me of late and I have endeavoured to stir up my self anew to all endeavours that may be conducible thereunto. . . . In those 14 years God had blessed me with many children also, whom to have made heirs of his grace and covenant love is my great ambition, and to be made an instrument to promote the same is such a privilege as my soul longs after in its settled bent and course. But am oft at a loss in endeavours through the inconstancy and treachery of my heart for this. I desired this day to be sincerely humbled also to bless God who of late hath in some measure quickened my heart to duty upon that account, and particularly with reference to my eldest son, who is now 13 years of age, and blessed be God, a capable child who from his infancy hath in a measure inclined unto goodness, but as he grows up seems to be full of pride and self conceit, and carried forth with expectation of applause and vain glory in all things, wherein meeting with disappointment, knows not how to bear it, corruption being strong proportionable to parts, and this disproportion renders my work difficult towards him, the Lord makes me to see a continual need of his wisdom to be imparted: my present endeavour towards him is to convince him of the necessity of making particular appli-

cation of the truths made known to him by the ministry of the word, as well as to retain them in memory, hoping in this way my God would by his powerful and secret working gradually subdue him to himself, and the sovereignty of his own grace; for though the pride and frowardness of his spirit nonplus me many a time, yet my God hath said nothing is too hard for him, and when he will work none can let. I desire therefore to wait on him in his own way, and hope in his mercy and according to that measure of wisdom he shall give me to persevere and deal with him from time to time this whole year ensuing. . . .

14 February 1676. According to custom I did attempt to spend in my closet in a solemn review of the dealings of my God with me and mine in the year past. . . . And here I judged it meet to remark the particular state and condition of each of their souls according to my best judgment and observation upon them, that I may the better discern what steps grace shall gain upon them in this following year, and where my work lies toward each of them.

As for Betty, I am still in hope God hath begun his good work upon her, but still her iniquities prevail, a lying tongue, and passionate spirit are too strong for her, also an unsatisfied spirit in her station leads her into many temptations: yet saying my God is able to subdue the strongest corruptions, and fully establish his own throne in spite of nature's bent, I esteemed it my duty with faith and hope to wait on him for the perfecting his own work in her through his mighty grace. My heart was also much in desire that by his good providence he would dispose her to an happy alteration of her station, the which I should esteem a great happiness, and in the mean season I coveted wisdom.

For poor Ned I have great cause to fear atheism. Oh my God possess him with the fear and dread of thy great name, and teach thy servants how to act duty towards him with all prudence and faithfulness.

In Nell I can yet observe little or nothing of the workings of grace, nor can I yet find out the proper way to deal with her, Lord teach and quicken me in that duty and help me to look up and wait on thee for the operation of thy free spirit who blows where and when it listeth.

My poor Will Providence having removed a distance from me I cannot so well judge whether he go backward or forward in the things of God, but my fears are that the power of godliness doth not prevail in him according to desire, and here my soul designed to commit him to the keeping of my God who is able to deliver him from his own corrupt[ion] and the hazard of temptations and by his mighty power preserve him to his heavenly kingdom. Sure I would be much in this duty in the ensuing year. Lord be my strength and assistance therein.

As for James I have not been able to fasten any thing upon him for good, my fears for him are high, endeavours taking no impression upon him, his own purposes and promises in the day of visitation proving abortive, and he remaining (as I fear) under the power of a lying tongue and proud stubborn spirit, hardening himself against correction. . . .

My poor Harry (blessed be the Lord) hath been more tractable and ready to receive and embrace instruction since his visitation with the small pox than formerly, and I hope my good God will in his due time make him partaker of real saving grace. . . .

For my poor Ralph, my fears increase and I am very jealous least a lying spirit get ground upon him and his delight in learning decline. Oh I find great need of much wisdom to order myself aright in the discharge of my duty towards them. . . .

The other 3 are not yet towardly and give hope through the grace of my precious God and my soul ardently covets that my tender father would begin his own great work upon them betimes and carry it on to the day of his power. . . .

And as for those children of my dear brother's committed to my charge, I have found little opportunity as yet to influence good upon them, the eldest being at a distance from me and I apprehend what I should do in that kind would accidentally be abused to their prejudice, which holds me under much difficulty in that respect. . . .

As for the little ones, I hope I may say my endeavours in their education are as for my own.

8

RELATIONSHIPS

Few sources remain to tell us explicitly about women's relationships with friends, lovers, marriage partners, neighbours, and enemies. For literate women, the seventeenth century saw a rapid increase in letter and diary writing. Partly inspired by the encouragement Puritanism gave to self-reflection, the 1600s saw women beginning to write detailed spiritual and worldly diaries, commonplace books, and reflections. Some of the earliest women's writings we have are letters; by the seventeenth century many elite women were prolific correspondents, spreading news and passing messages up and down Britain, and sometimes across the world. Their letters are full of references to their roles as correspondents, complaints about the post, and messages or errands for distant acquaintances: letter writing positioned gentry women at the heart of a whole series of county and national networks.

Elite women had also a written language in which to express a wide range of emotions for their friends and families. Mothers and grandmothers wrote articulately and tenderly about their children and grandchildren. Friends and sisters-in-law expressed their depth of connection in an idiom of passionate love that could serve for both heterosexual love and female friendship. For early modern people, the words 'friend' and 'lover' might overlap in meaning: neither was exclusively sexual or non-sexual. This flexibility opened up a spectrum of intimacy that is further explored by Mary Beale's treatise on friendship, with a feminist slant and a plea for companionate marriage.

For non-literate women, we have much less evidence. We might speculate that, for them, friendship was based on proximity and need: it was neighbours who loaned food and money, watched children, and advised on love, pregnancy, and illness. Bequests in wills confirm the significance of those who were close by.[1] The practice of chain migration ensured that young women moving into a town were often welcomed and watched by old acquaintances from their birthplace. At the same time, kin from several counties away might remain significant figures, sending and receiving oral messages or gifts by friends. The everyday friendships of women were, like men's, based on proximity, functionality, and reciprocity. Rather than money, goods or services would be exchanged: cleaning, sewing, or knitting, nursing or helping at a lying-in were all services that one woman could offer or expect from another. Women's friendships may also have revolved around their own houses more than men's did: where men consolidated bonds by eating and drinking, women spent less time in alehouses and would have recognised different signs of friendship, such as visiting each other's houses, or talking 'as neighbours do' at the doorstep. Some spaces and rituals – the water conduit, the birthing-room – were specifically female.[2]

Particularly for non-elite women, the immediate family was likely to be small and depleted by the time of adolescence. Wills and other documents confirm the importance of siblings and step-siblings; high mortality and remarriage rates meant that many households and families included orphaned nieces and nephews, stepchildren and remarried parents. Outside the household, historians have also identified a wide range of 'kin': in many communities, it has been argued, geographical closeness was as significant as blood ties in determining a person's immediate support network. This was particularly so in the case of marriage, where 'friends' had a special meaning. It was friends whom women named as those responsible for overseeing their final marital decisions, helping them with their portions, seeing off unwelcome suitors, or welcoming suitable ones. To stress the term 'kin' rather than 'friendship', though, runs the risk of emphasising the functionality of such relationships at the expense of warmth of feeling, intimacy, and attachment.[3] In the absence of detailed records of the emotional lives of non-elite women, we need to allow for complex, deep feelings in our readings of the limited documents we have.

In the close-knit communities of early modern society, enmity and anger were as powerful as friendship and attachment. Neighbourhood relations involved frequent disputes, some handled between individuals and families, others mediated by local magistrates, clergymen, or, eventually, the courts. The church courts were particularly important as a forum for cases of damaged reputation, and as such, they were used more by women than any other court.[4]

The parish church, where we start, was the stage for neighbourhood relations: women and men had their own seats and the gender and social organisation of the parish was made visible in seating arrangements.[5]

NEIGHBOURS

8.1 Brawling pewmates: Elizabeth Fontstone and Joan Butcher, 1604

Like many disputes between women, this one took place in church, as two women sat in their pew. Joan, who is testifying, had known Elizabeth since her childhood; the two may have been much of an age as they ended up fighting over their daughters, and since they were pewmates they had probably been friends. Jostling for place in church, and fighting for seats in pews, where the order of seating was often firmly established by family, social position, and gender, were the sources of many neighbourhood disputes, particularly, apparently, amongst women.

Consistory Court of Bath and Wells Deposition Book, Somerset Archives, D/D/cd/34 (1604)

Figure 14 **Two women talking**

From the Pepys Ballads, vol III, no. 290. By permission of the Pepys Library, Magdalene College, Cambridge

An extremely rare woodcut image of two women. They may be wearing mantuas, are holding fans, and have elaborate head clothes. It is used here to illustrate 'Sweet-faced Jenny', a 'country lass' telling her mother of her plans to leave her spinning wheel for 'a more pleasant employment', prostitution.

[Joan Butcher, wife of John Butcher, smith, of Yeovil in Somerset, where she has lived for 7 years and where she was born, aged 28 or thereabouts . . .]

   . . . She deposes that on a certain Sunday happening near about the beginning of Lent last past before . . . the above named Elizabeth Fontstone and this examinant being seat or pewmates in the parish church . . . and present in their seat hearing divine service the said Elizabeth Fontstone fell out with this examinant and brawled with her in the said seat saying, dost thou pull thy daughter over my daughter's back thou proud beggarly jade, pride will have a fall, and thy pride is falling already, and I hope to live to see thee pulled lower yet, go home jade, and pluck down thy pride, for it is for no devotion that thou comest to the church mistress turdpie. . . .

8.2 Ancient seating customs: Frances Brown and Elizabeth Clark, 1607

Testimonies in this pew dispute between two women in Allestree, Staffordshire, in 1607 reveal something of the construction of women's places in the community through seating arrangements in church. As in many parish churches, the parishioners of Allestree were accustomed to sit in ancestral seats, men on one side of the church and women on the other. But women, as the churchwarden testifying here reveals, do not sit in the seats of their ancestors, but those of their husbands, and this can produce a quite different sense of tradition and custom. So, here, the two wives of Robert Brown succeed one another in a seat on the women's side. The seating of women in church is thus both ostensibly rigid, and by its very nature subject to change; perhaps this different tradition can be traced in pew disputes between women. The relationships *between* women in various seats are also complex and not easy for everyone to remember: Elizabeth Clark, the grandmother of the husband of the Elizabeth fighting this suit, may have been yielded her place by the courtesy of her daughter, or she may have had it by right; Elizabeth also attempted to defend her use of the seat on the grounds that her husband paid twice as much towards church rates as Robert Brown. Frances won the suit in January 1608: Elizabeth may then have been assigned a penance.

Consistory Court of Coventry and Lichfield, Lichfield RO, B/C/5 1607.

[John Tailor of Allestree aged 60. . . .]

. . . he says there is an ancient and long continued custom observed and kept within the parish of Allestree articulate for every householder in the said parish to sit kneel and hear divine service in the parish church of Allestree aforesaid in the seat or pew there wherein his predecessor inhabitant in the said parish did usually sit and kneel, and saith this custom hath continued throughout the parish aforesaid for the space of forty years and upwards in this deponent's time of remembrance . . . all other inhabitants of Allestree articulate have rooms or pews in the church belonging to their houses and there do usually sit and kneel and have successively so done time beyond the memory of man if so they please. . . .

He says there is within the church of Allestree articulate a seat being the nethermost saving one on the south part of the middle aisle, in which seat the articulate Frances Brown hath possessed and enjoyed for a certain space until she was interrupted by Elizabeth Clark the defendant in this cause the next room or place saving one on the left hand towards the south And saith the same room or place did belong and appertain to Johane Browne and

Alice Browne the first and later wife of Robert Browne articulate in their times and there they did sit and kneel viz. the said Johane in the time of Queen Mary and the aforesaid Alice in all the late Queen Elizabeth's time without the disturbance or interruption of any other.

... He says the articulate Elizabeth Clarke hath divers times sithence Our Lady Day last past hindered the aforesaid Frances Browne so that she could not come to sit or kneel in her room or place aforesaid but hath been forced to kneel without her seat in the common aisle he knoweth it for he saith that he this deponent being one of the churchwardens of Allestree articulate hath observed so much and been present in the time aforesaid when as the aforesaid Elizabeth Clark hath in time of divine service sat in the place where the aforesaid Frances Browne and her predecessors have used to sit and caused the said Frances to look some other place to sit and kneel in. . . .

[Roger Mould, vicar of Allestree, aged 57 . . . testifying on the supplementary evidence of Elizabeth Clark against Frances Brown]

... He says that sithence the death of Margaret Smart which was about Candlemas last past to this deponent's now remembrance the articulate Elizabeth Clark hath used to kneel and sit most commonly in the uppermost room on the left hand in the seat in question whereby Frances Brown articulate hath not been hindered to go into her room in the said seat where she useth to sit being the second room on the left hand towards the middle aisle but hath had free liberty to come and go into her room without disturbance for aught that this deponent knoweth to the contrary. And further saith that he hath seen one Elizabeth Clark the grandmother of William Clark husband to the plaintiff in this cause in her time to sit and kneel in the uppermost room on the left hand next to the font in the aforesaid seat, but whether it were on the sufferance of Margaret Smart her daughter who might in courtesy yield her the highest room on the left hand or whether it were of right she there sat he knoweth not.

... He says the articulate Johane and Alice Browne were wives of Richard Brown and not of Robert Brown for the said Robert Brown had nor hath no other or more wives but Frances Brown his now wife.

8.3   Insults at the door: Mary Daintrey, Elizabeth Hulme, and Margaret Keeling, 1697

Insults between women and men were a stock part of the currency of neighbourhood dispute, and only occasionally ended up in lawsuits: they could be sued at the church courts on the grounds that they imputed sexual sins and hence damaged reputation. In such cases, both the words used and the circumstances in which they were spoken can be revealing. Here, as so often, the insulting words are exchanged at the entry of the house, on the doorstep, and in this case they led to two separate lawsuits, one betweeen Mary Daintrey and Elizabeth Hulme, a neighbour, and one between Mary and Sophronia Daintrey, her husband's sister.

Consistory Court of Coventry and Lichfield, Lichfield RO, B/C/5 1697.

Mary Daintrey *v.* Elizabeth Hulme

Margaret Keeling [of Mayfield in the county of Stafford, spinster, aged 25, who has known the parties in the case for three years]

[To the second and third articles of the aforesaid libel she says and deposes] That this deponent having ever since Christmas last been as now she is domestic servant to Mary Daintrey, party agent in this cause and the said Elizabeth Hulme alias Homes having all the time aforesaid been domestic servant to Sophronia Daintrey wife of Thomas Daintrey (brother of the said Brian Daintrey the said Mary's husband) who with his wife and family have all the time dwelt in one end of the same house where the said Brian with his wife and family have all the time aforesaid lived in the other end of the said house being divided into two dwellings, this deponent knows that about March last to the best of her remembrance as to the time, a little girl that was with the said Sophronia at her house happening to be playing with this deponent's mistress's children at her mistress's house being hurt by some of the children fell a crying and thereupon the said Elizabeth Hulme coming for the child in a passion took the child away from among them and said, What canst expect amongst these whores and bastards? And after she had put the child into their own house the said Elizabeth came to the said Mary her door again and asked her the said Mary, When will you have another kissing bout in Stone Meadow? and the said Mary asking her with whom, away the said Elizabeth went saying no more to the said Mary at that time. And that within this fortnight or three weeks as she thinks, but is sure within a month at furthest . . . this deponent and Joseph Sale her precontest sitting in their own home one evening after their master and mistress were gone to bed and hearing some talk in the said Sophronia's house suspected she and the said Elizabeth were talking of the said Mary this deponent's mistress and so went into the entry which is betwixt the two dwellings aforesaid to harken what they said and peeping in at the door into the said Sophronia's house plain this deponent saw and heard Elizabeth Hulme alias Homes the said Sophronia's maid say, Mary Daintrey (meaning the party agent in this cause) is a whore, and the said Sophronia reply, Aye; so she is a whore, and I can prove her one when she has all done. By which speaking of which words spoken by the said Elizabeth as this deponent has predeposed, she the said Elizabeth must mean that the said Mary was an adulterous person . . .

[To the interrogatory]

. . . [she answers] at the speaking of the words which happened upon the crying of the child the plaintiff was sitting in the house, and when the defendant and her mistress were talking of the plaintiff in the said Sophronia's house the defendant was walking about the house and her mistress sitting in her chair near the fireside. . . .

. . . [she answers] . . . Joseph Sale this deponent's precontest dwells in the same house with this deponent and she never saw any carriage betwixt him and his mistress but such as is used and ought to be betwixt mistress and servant, nor believes nor ever heard of any familiarity betwixt them more than ordinary. . . .

Mary Daintrey *v.* Sophronia Daintrey
Margaret Keeling . . .

[To the second and third articles of the libel she says and deposes] That this deponent having ever since Christmas last been as now she is domestic servant to Mary Daintrey party agent in this cause who with her husband and his family have all that time dwelt in one end of the same house where the defendant Sophronia Daintrey and her husband Thomas Daintrey (brother of the said Brian) with his family have all the time aforesaid lived in the other end thereof . . . this deponent knows there has been frequent differences betwixt those two families and in the beginning of May last the said Sophronia coming to the said Mary's door saw a poor man begging there and the said Mary telling him she would not relieve him the said Sophronia asked her why she would not and the said Mary said she would not to please her, and the said Sophronia thereupon replying, Not to please any you whore, the said Mary and Sophronia fell into hot words amongst which the said Sophronia called the said Mary Whore several times, and whilst she was so calling her Mr William Jarvis the younger came in and heard her. And this deponent was in the house with her mistress all the while and saw and heard all that passed at that time and about a fortnight after . . . this deponent being in the garden the said Sophronia being there also and finding that the said Mary's children had fouled her water which she had set there for whitening her cloth, called one of the said children Bastard and said to him Thy mother is a whore, over and over. And a third time . . . since this suit was began, this deponent and Joseph Sale her precontest sitting, one evening after their master and mistress were gone to bed, in their own house and hearing some talk in the said Sophronia's house suspected she and her maid were talking of the said Mary this deponent's mistress and so went into the entry, which is betwixt the two dwellings aforesaid, to harken what they said and peeping in at the door into the said Sophronia's house plain this deponent saw and heard Elizabeth Hulme alias Homes, the said Sophronia's maid, say Mary Daintrey (meaning the party in this cause) is a whore and the said Sophronia reply Aye, so she is a whore, and I can prove her one when she has all done; and just after they had so said the said Elizabeth coming to shut the door this deponent and her precontest Joseph Sale went back again into their own house.

8.4   Revenge and witchcraft: Margaret Eccleston, 1645

Witchcraft accusations typically grew out of long histories of tensions and grudges. This case, from England's largest witch-hunt, in East Anglia between 1645 and 1647, emerged from atypical circumstances, with the involvement of the witch-hunter Matthew Hopkins in the locality; but it also reflects familiar local conflicts. Here, these focus particularly on threats, guilt, and the dangers of failing to forgive enemies.

'Examinations of Wizards and Witches (com: Suffolk) in August 1645', BL, Add. MS 27402, fo. 121 ff. (A transcription of the manuscript is published in C. L'Estrange Ewen, *Witch Hunting and Witch Trials*, London, Kegan Paul & Co.,1929).

Margaret Eccleston of Linstead . . . upon the testimony of Smith, that upon a difference with his daughter Jane Smith she threatened a revenge and forth-with immediately this Jane Smith fell lame, and after upon a second threat the pain increased and after Ecclestone came to her and laid her hand upon Jane's head and told her if she pleased she would ask her forgiveness, but she, putting her by, refusing to let her touch her, she grew worse and worse for two or three days and then died. Upon the testimony of Thomas Legate she confessed that she had an imp that did suck on her and would often urge her to employ it in doing hurt and that she sent [it to] Jane Smith and it killed her, and that she would have called her imp from Jane Smith again and saved her life but she could not for she came too late.

***Figure 15* Women with familiar**

A Rehearsal 'both Strang and true, of hainous and horrible actes . . .', frontispiece. By permission of the British Library

This image from a witchcraft pamphlet of 1579 shows two women, with shopping baskets, with a familiar, which looks like a dragon, in the hands of one. It may have been cut from an earlier publication, but it seems to illustrate perfectly the themes of early modem witchcraft: women's relationships, consumption, and housewifery, an older and a younger woman.

8.5 Stealing with a friend: Mary Pond and Elizabeth Ruskin, 1635

Mary Pond was examined at the Essex Quarter Sessions in 1635 for theft. She was indicted for the theft of a ewe worth 10d., but Elizabeth Ruskin was not found guilty.

Essex Quarter Sessions Bundles, Essex RO, QSba2/22.

The examination of Mary Pond the wife of John Pond ... 25 Sept. 1635

This examinate confesseth that upon Friday about two of the clock in the morning being the eight and twentieth day of August last Elizabeth Ruskin the wife of William Ruskin came to this examinant's door and called upon her to rise she being abed (they having agreed overnight to go into the grounds of Thomas Say of Roxwell to steal a sheep which the said Ruskin's wife had moved this examinant often to do) saying that her husband would not take his wages until his month was come out being in harvest work, and she could not tell how to do whereupon she this examinant arose and went into the said grounds together with the said Ruskin's wife and stole one ewe belonging to Thomas Shettlewood a servant of the said Thomas Say and divided the mutton between them, and together put the skin into a bag and carried it into the grounds of Robert Haggsley and there hid the same under a stub in a ditch and farther she confesseth that they two have often conferred of such things, but never did any act of this nature before.

8.6 Violence between women: Cesily Pope and Alice Rawlins, 1652

Women fought not only with words but also with violence. In this case, Cesily Pope, probably a young woman, complained to the quarter sessions of Alice Rawlins, an older widow. As well as undermining the simple correlation of men's disputes with violence, women's with words, this case suggests that women, like men, had issues of pride and honour relating to violence and self-defence. Cesily's father also testified that Alice threw her into a ditch of water where she bit the top of one of her little fingers to pieces and cut her nose with a knife.

Somerset Quarter Sessions Rolls, Somerset Archives, Q/SR 84/21 (12 April 1652)

Alice Rawlins of Keynsham ... widow being examined saith That on Thursday last in the afternoon, as she was gathering of mint in a ditch near to the said close called Breaches, the said Cesily came to this examinant and said unto her, Thou base whore get thee out of my father's ground, to whom this examinant said, if I am in your father's ground I will go forth of it; Thereupon the said Cesily took up a stake and swore that she would flat out this examinant's brains and said moreover, Thou didst beat my sister and though she could not have her opportunity, I will, and forthwith she did strike this examinant on the head, whereupon both of them fell into the

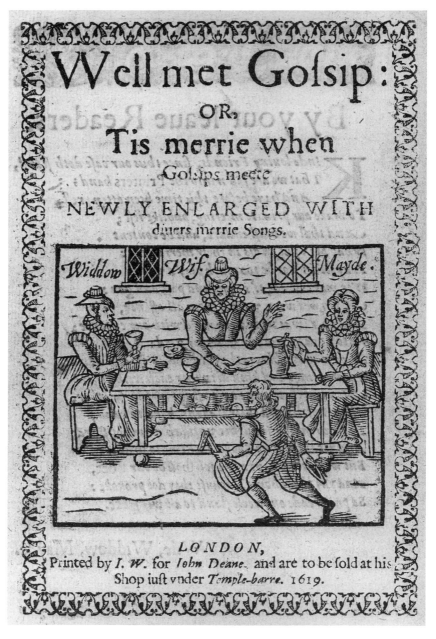

Figure 16 Women drinking together

Samuel Rowlands, *Well met Gossip: Or, 'Tis merrie when Gossips Meete*, frontispiece. By permission of the British Library

Female sociability often focused around events such as a childbirth or christenings; but women, even those of similar social position, were also divided by marital status. This image marks out women through the three life stages of maid, wife, widow.

ditch. But this examinant denieth that she did strike the said Cesily or tread upon her or cut her with a knife or other such thing, she having none then about her; And this examinant further saith that when the said Cesily called her whore she asked her whose whore she was to whome the said Cesily answered you are my father's whore for aught I know; And that the said Cesily perceiving herself to be bloody, said to this examinant, Thou dost think that thou hast fetched this blood of me but I did hurt myself with the stake, And lastly this examinant saith that the said Cesily went away well enough from her and was at home before her.

8.7   Leisure life: Tymothye Wright, 1604

A suit at the Court of Requests led to a series of testimonies about the reputation of the litigants. The original case alleged theft and bawdry by a servant, Elizabeth Deane, and also accused two other men and women of being in league with her to defraud her employer. Tymothye Wright, one of the women, was accused specifically of episodes of lewd living. Jane Collines came to testify in support of the allegations. Her deposition records an episode which was clearly disorderly, but perhaps also related to familiar, acceptable rituals of transgression, as well as to the customs of charitable support for other women.

John Springe *v.* Elizabeth Deane *et al.*, Court of Requests, PRO, REQ2 308/17, m. 10. (15 October 1604).

Jane Collines the wife of Peter Collines of the parish of Great Allhallows, London, merchant tailor, of the age of thirty-six years or thereabouts sworn and examined the day and year abovesaid.

. . . To the 12th interrogatory this deponent saith she knoweth that Tymothye Wright the wife of Humphrey Wright did go into the country in the company of diverse women neighbours thereabouts with a young man of the age of two-and-twenty years or thereabouts disguised in women's apparell, she and the rest knowing that he was so disguised. And it was upon this occasion viz there was a poor woman lying in childbed in the country, and Tymothye Wright and she this deponent with some twenty or thirty women more went to spend their money to do her good. And the maids [at]tired the said young man in women's apparel to make them merry and he went a little way with them but they were not well pleased to have his company wherefore they made him undress himself and go home in his hose and doublet. And more she cannot depose.

FAMILIES

8.8   Step-sisters: Marian and Margerie Barbour, 1606

In middle or old age, Marian Barbour of Tutbury in Staffordshire was reduced to dependence, and chose to live with her sister-in-law (step-sister). The petition of Marian Barbour is a plea for help against the circumstances that have forced a blind woman into indigence and poverty. But it also reveals the ties between step-siblings, who, here, leave each other money and make choices to live with and help each other. The petition was presented by Margerie Barbour on Marian's behalf, and £12 10s. 5d. was awarded for Marian to live on during her life, supplemented where necessary by the parish.

Staffordshire Quarter Sessions Rolls, Staffordshire RO, Q/SR 98/48 (1606).

To the right honourable and worshipful his majesty's justices of peace for the county of Stafford

Humbly complaining showeth unto your honour and worships your poor oratrix Marian Barbour of Tutbury, being a poor blind woman, and having in her youth and before such time as she became blind gotten some substance

Figure 17   A woman with men in a tavern

From the Pepys Ballads, vol. IV, no. 130. By permission of the Pepys Library, Magdalene College, Cambridge

This image of a woman drinking with men in a tavern is used in several ballads (this one is 'The Catalogue of Contented Cuckolds'); it might represent a prostitute, but it could also be an everyday social scene, as there are many records of women drinking with men for business or pleasure.

presently of her self, and presently left unto her by her sister, as hereof the greatest part being £20, and more in ready money was left your said oratrix by her said sister towards her maintenance. But so it is that your said oratrix finding great kindness and love to be in one Margerie Barbour her sister-in-law, did make choice to live with her and that little substance and money which she had did commend to the keeping of the said Margerie, yet nevertheless one Humfrey Mathew of Tutbury aforesaid without any manner of colour or right in Lent last entered the house of the said Margerie, being accompanied with one Christopher Granger William Greaves Humfrey Barnes and John Allcocke, and there did break open a chest of your said oratrix's and out of the same took £20 in ready money of your said oratrix's which the said Humfrey detaineth in his custody. Humbly therefore she beseecheth that she may be herein relieved and have her goods restored unto her, as also that the parties may be bound over to appear before his majesties justice of peace before whom she will open further matter against the said Humfrey Mathew and the rest, and in the meantime that the peace may be taken of them, in regard, they have not only taken from her the money aforesaid out of her chest, but also did most violently handle and entreat your said oratrix by force breaking her purse from her, with divers other wrongs whereof she prayeth redress, as to your wisdom shall be thought fitting, So shall she be very bound to pray to the Almighty for the increase of your healths and happiness.

8.9 A widow and her sons: Katherine Venables, 1633

Katherine Venables of Staffordshire was one of many widows who had problems with their inheritance. Hers were compounded by conflicts between herself and her eldest son. Her complaint reveals something of what was expected of sons, as well as how this relationship went so badly wrong. Her words suggest the revolution a spouse's death could cause in emotional, familial, and economic relationships and status: from, presumably, a mother in a stable marriage exerting quite effective parental authority, she has become a 'poor widow', open to being 'molested' and 'troubled' by her child, whose resort is the law and a request for her son to be bound over to keep the peace. The second document gives a more detailed picture of her story, her other options for negotiating or confronting her son, and her economic relationship with him as a neighbour with all the possible problems of bad neighbours.

Staffordshire Quarter Sessions Rolls, Staffordshire RO, Q/SR 211/21, 22 (1633).

To the right honourable and worshipful his majesty's justices of peace and quorum within the county of Staffordshire
The humble petition of Katherine Venables widow.

Humbly shewing that whereas Thomas Venables your petitioner's oldest son hath for the most part ever sithence the death of her late husband Richard Venables being the space of one year and a half now last not only carried and behaved himself in such undutiful manner towards her as well in his actions and behaviour in threatening troubling and molesting her from time to time but also therein hath shewed and stirred up so many crosses and troubles in hindering her many ways that she cannot quietly enjoy that small living and means which her said late husband left her to maintain herself upon that she is weary of her life if some present course be not taken for her relief all which appeareth by several articles hereunto annexed which your petitioner is now ready to prove by oath before your honour and worships.

She therefore humbly desireth your honour and worships for God's cause to take some such speedy course for her safety from him either by awarding the good behaviour against him or otherwise as to your honour and worships shall seem expedient And your petitioner shall daily pray to God for your honour and worships etc.

Articles preferred by Katherine Venables widow against Thomas Venables her eldest son as followeth:

[Especially] the said Katherine Venables upon or about the last day of October last past having hired a workman to cleave wood and to do such work as she then had to do the said workman having made a ladder and wanting staves to put therein William Venables youngest son of the said Katherine went with the said workman to cut staves forth of a tree that lay in the ground of the said Katherine whereupon the said Thomas Venables came in most violent and outrageous manner (having a broom hook in his hand) into the said close and then and there threatened the said workman that if he offered to work any longer there or to strike over another stroke he would cut off his hands and head and vowed so to do with many heavy vows and oaths whereupon the said workman being in great fear durst not work any longer there but was enforced to leave of and give over his work to the great prejudice of the said Katherine.

Item the said Katherine having set diverse rails and posts to preserve her corn from the cattle of the said Thomas for eating the same forth of her barn the said Thomas the day in the precedent articles did cut down the said rails and did likewise cut the said ladder into diverse pieces so that the said Katherine by that means had a great part of her corn destroyed by the cattle of the said Thomas.

Item the said Thomas upon or about the said last day of October coming to the house of the said Katherine and finding the door shut and having an axe in his hand did in most violent manner break down the door of the said house into diverse pieces (the said Katherine with her family being in peace and quietness in her said house) the said Thomas having broken down the said door and having a great pitching pikel[1] in his hand held and shook the same towards the said Katherine insomuch that she and her family being

1. A pitchfork.

in great fear and peril of their lives were enforced to cry for help of their neighbour.

Item the said Thomas upon or about the six and twentieth day of May last past came to the house of the said Katherine and threatened the said Katherine and her whole family that whosoever came forth of the door of the said house he would make them forever going in again and swore most heavily for that purpose and likewise would have killed the son of the said Katherine, with a great bill[2] and endeavoured himself to that purpose also.

Item the next day having been at the alehouse and being almost drunk came into the fold belonging to the said house and there cut a stone trough into pieces having laid a great pitching pikel by him whereat the said Katherine was very sore affrighted and in great fear.

Item the said Thomas doth so threaten and terrify the said Katherine and her son William and other workmen insomuch that no workmen dare work with her to her great discomfort and hindrance.

8.10   The love of sisters: Lady Elizabeth Poley and Lady Anne D'Ewes, *c.* 1639

This is one of a series of letters between two sisters, playing on precisely those difficulties of communication and distance that could both interrupt and enhance friendships. Lady Elizabeth Poley was the second wife of Sir William Poley, and died in 1698, having had three daughters and three sons; her sister Lady Anne D'Ewes was the wife of Sir Simonds D'Ewes, MP, and died in 1641, aged 29.

Elizabeth Poley to Anne D'Ewes, BL, Harleian MS. 382, fo. 173 (1639/40).

For my Lady D'Ewes at her lodging in Aldersgate Street at Mr Johnson's a tailor at the Hand in Hand
Worthy sister
I could wish we might always enjoy each other which is one of the greatest comforts I take in this life especially where I find so much nobleness with so many realities as distance of place or length of time doth rather unite our hearts than accuse them of any neglects which is the truest love and though I have not those ways and means of expressions that others have yet God knows the truth of it to you and my dear brother for in my saddest thoughts which are not few it is such comfort to but wish myself with you. . . .
Your affectionate sister and servant Elizabeth Poley

8.11   My dearest soul: Anne Dormer, her sister and son, 1691

These letters from Anne Dormer to her sister Lady Elizabeth Trumbull and her son Jack were written three years after her husband's death, while she was at

2. A long-bladed tool.

Tunbridge for her health. She discusses her relationships with both of them, but also those with the servants whose lives are dependent on their relations with the family. The first letter was written by one of the servants, perhaps Robin, who is elsewhere recorded as running to fetch glasses of the Tonbridge water for her to save her appearing in the public rooms. Other letters (e.g. document 6.10) describe her unhappy marriage in much detail.

Trumbull Papers, BL, Add. MS 72516, fos 235–6, 233–4.

Anne Dormer to her sister Lady Elizabeth Trumbull

Tonbridge October 2 [1691]

My dearest soul

Just now I received thine of September the tenth from Lazareto and since love and joy are passions as well as grief which often hinders us from expressing our thoughts as we wish, so the transporting pleasure I received in the kindness of thine, and in hearing you were all well, and got so much nearer me, makes me neither able to write as I would, nor to forbear saying something to satisfy thee that thine came safe, and found me I bless God in much better health than I have been a great while, though I make use of another hand to tell thee so because I have my belly full of water, and dare not stay till I am rid of it least the post should be gone; you tell me unless I write immediately it will not come to you time enough before you leave the place where you are; I have been here a tedious time, ever since the 26 of May last, and truly till very lately I can scarce say the water did me any good, it passed so ill, and it plagued me so much, that I look like a gridiron, and were it not for the scar in my forehead it were impossible for you to know me. I resolve now to try if I can learn, to laugh a little; now I hope once more to enjoy thy beloved company, for you know I never could be so truly merry as when thou wert one of the company and I think to use my poor cousin Ward's expression, my eyes ever since we parted have been buttonholes of grief, or as she said at other time fountains fraught with tears. . . .

Before this I imagine thou hast heard that my dear brother has been married above these three months, and is not only a most extraordinary woman whom you will love and delight in, but she is really in her ingenuity, will, good nature, readiness to oblige in that way and manner infinitely like her predecessor, whom she dearly loved and highly values, and is so infinitely kind to my niece Fany that I hope this Betty and she will live as the other did with good Mrs Burwell who is Frances you know. I had begun to answer dear Jack's most affectionate letter which the post will not allow me to finish therefore here dear heart let him read my true love and assure him that as never son can better deserve a mother's kindness than he has done, so no son shall find a greater share of mine than he shall ever have. To my most worthy brother I owe so much that I can say nothing which equals my sense of his kindness to my and all mine, Jack I hope will do his endeavour to help me return some part of his share and I am sure I will never fail of

doing all I am able to shew myself grateful. His most affectionate letter I have answered several times and am sorry to hear he now enquires whether I had his and that you have received so few from thy
passionately loving sister and faithful friend
Anne Dormer

Fany[1] who is here with me a tall small sprat desires her duty to you and her dear uncle whom she says she is sure she loves tho she doth not remember but for her dear brother Jack she makes love to him daily and well remembers his fair face and his white locks and next to seeing him there is nothing she longs for like having her brother Jack married because then mamey, says she, I shall be an aunt within a year or it will be very strange. Pray give my respects to good Mr Halley.

Anne Dormer to her son Jack

Tunbridge August 10 1691

Dear Jack

Tho' the advantage you had in being my first love was so great it needed no addition, yet I have received so very many expressions of your affection to me that I should be unjust if I did not own the share you have in mine grows daily greater, not my dear child that I set so high a value upon the increase you have added to my fortune which was full as large before as I ever desired to have it, or intended to have made it, but that I am truly pleased with the proofs you have given of a most generous temper, love to a mother that tends you above her own flesh, and kindness to brothers and a sister who all will I hope deserve so well of you as never to give you cause to repent what you have done for them. I am still at Tunbridge where I should not have stayed so long, but that the hopes of gaining better health and as well to avoid many inconveniences that would have entailed some upon you has made me bear with such as I found here, for it is a place I should never have chosen for my delight, the company which most come hither for being a burden which I have always avoided in the public meetings neither did I bring a coach hither because I would have that just excuse not to visit any but such very particular friends as would find me out and which lay very near me and truly I met with so many of them that I could not get the time to myself I wished for and which I hope to enjoy when they are gone.

Do not dear heart believe that I want care of your father's reputation or yours in that I come hither now without a coach for I saw last year so many of the best quality and fortune that sent back their own and kept none here that I had very good examples doing so this. . . . I bless God I am better

1. This Fanny is her daughter rather than the niece mentioned earlier.

now tho' not well for I lived so many years with very little sleep that I had such a languishing indisposition of body as I find will not soon be removed, I cannot say to have any particular disease but my spirits are very low and my body weak and like Samson when I think to rise up and go out as heretofore I see I cannot. Oh my dear child mayst thou never afflict a wife that loves thee nor make her suffer what I have undergone . . . in short the little care your father took (which you could not but see) to oblige any of my friends and the thousands of obligations you all had to them and in particular to my excellent father, together with the very great intimacy he kept up with all my Papist neighbours from whom I daily received most friendly offices or all you had been very miserable, I have been put upon very many difficulties; I owed so much to my good father, to whom yours had kept me almost twenty years like a stranger, that I had all the reason in the world to go up into London when he desired it, tho' I knew my sickly health would be impaired in that close place in winter, where to increase my sorrows that dear saint in heaven mine and your excellent friend my sister Cottrell lay upon her deathbed seven weeks; how her dying groans pierced my heart and what an addition her death gave to the trouble I had upon me for your fathers (whose worst humours would have been more supportable to me forever, than I found his death at that time, and in so sudden a manner), I cannot in this compass describe; but besides this I had an arrear of obligations to all my neighbours whose religion and interest so different from ours, made it very hard for me to be so just to them as I desired. . . . I scorned me to fall off from then when I had no longer need of their help . . . but to be just to two such obligations as my friends and neighbours which the Revolution here in England has made of very different interest required more time and strength than I could well spare . . . but I have so disposed of all those servants which would have been of no use to you that Doll and Robin only which I am sure now are most necessary to you, are all that you can think has any expectations from you, and Robin who values his good qualities at a very high rate has done very well for himself . . . he is a nimble pated fellow and you will find him very craving if you do not keep him at a distance as your father did and the more you give him the more he will still ask, for pride and covetousness can never be satisfied. . . . Little Fanny is here with me she says she doth remember [you] longs to see you as I do and says many kind things to you as your brother Robin doth who is here to drink the waters but my paper will not allow me now to tell thee more dear that art thy A. D.

FRIENDS AND LOVERS

8.12 'This sweet good woman': Katherine Austen, 1665

Katherine Austen, widowed young, commemorated her relatives and friends, young and old, in her personal writings. Here, in the spring of 1665, when she was 36, her friend's death and her survival are part of a year of deaths.

Katherine Austen Collectanea, BL, Add. MS 4454, p. 86 (1665).

The last week I attended a friend of mine (cousin Birkenhead's wife Mr Prier's daughter), to her grave. And when I recollect my distemper which began in Feb. last about the beginning, and continued till the middle of March. By a violent cold in my head, took away my hearing, my speech, my eye sight, and vapours flew up almost continually, as dossed[1] me in that manner, I had feared the benefit of my understanding.

This cold and illness meeting with troublesome business the more discomposed me, that I could not tell whether my occasions had augmented my illness, or my illness made my business so tedious to be endured. And coming upon that time I sometimes had the persuasions I should die at. And yet the Lord was pleased to let my glass run longer, and give a final stop to this sweet good woman, adorned with the graces and true humble virtues of a christian and a wife. The original of her illness only a cold in her head, caused the same effects as fell to me in my head: yet death became in earnest to her, and after 3 or 4 days the sickness was contracting at her outward senses, in 2 or 3 days more grew violent by convulsions, which deprived her of her life the 3d of April 1665. God hath saved me, and my two sons. All three having felt severe effects of the sharp winter: and how many gone, and withered as grass. And the places know them no more.

The 5th March 1665, my brother in law Mr Edward Cropley died: the same month little infant Rowland Walteres. And Sir Thomas Bides' eldest son of 13 yeares; the 21 April Aunt Wilson, aged 79, died, mother to Cousin Samuel Wilson.

8.13 'That immortal beauty friendship': Mary Beale, 1667

Mary Beale, painter (1632–97), sent this 'very imperfect draft after that immortal beauty friendship' to her 'dear friend' Mrs Elizabeth Tillotson in 1667. Her notion of friendship imagines a kind of 'companionate marriage'; but it also encompasses a much wider range of relationships, including Plutarch's love between warriors and the friendship of David and Jonathan.

'Thoughts on Friendship', BL, Harleian MS 6828, fos 510–13v.

1. Overwhelmed.

Figure 18 **Mary Beale: self-portrait (1673–80)**

By permission of Manor House Museum, Bury St Edmunds

Mary Beale painted a number of self-portraits of herself as a working artist. Her husband and sons worked with her in her studio, and she had a number of women friends. The slightly odd posture of her arms may have derived from the alabaster casts that she and her husband made of them, as he recorded in his diary.

Friendship is the nearest union which distinct souls are capable of; (and is as rare to be found in sincerity, as it is excellent in its qualities) though next to the glorifying our Creator, man seems to be made for nothing more. For when God had at first created him, It is not fit, said he, that Man should be alone, and then he gave him Eve to be a meet help, and what can that imply but that God gave her for a friend, as well as for a wife? A wife and friend but not a slave; for we find her not in the beginning made subject to Adam, but always of equal dignity and honour with him, till by her own credulity, sinning herself and the seducing her husband, she lost her shame . . . and as a just reward of her transgression had both her desires and person subject to him. . . .

Between friends' words and actions must always be allowed the best and most candid construction. For if we give ourselves once the liberty of harsh and unkind thoughts, twice doing so will beget an habit, and evil habits usher in bad affections, which oft times end in disunion. Or if the breach be made up again, it seldom becomes so firm, or looks so beautiful as before. A mutual bearing thereof with one another's infirmities and conforming to those dispositions which bear sway in such we love, as it is a great part of wisdom, so it is one of the surest ties and clearest evidences of friendship. . . .

As touching the ends of friendship, self love must not be wholly excluded from being one, though but sparingly to be used; for that seems to be the centre from which all the lines of friendship are drawn. For did I not love my self first, I could scarce be capable of loving my friend. . . . This is requisite for the beginning of Friendship, but as that grows more perfect, the love of my self is swallowed up in the love of my friend.

8.14 Loving too much: Anne Flower, 1666

Ellen Eliot was one of the witnesses in a church court disciplinary prosecution of Thomas Pinder, accused of fornication and fathering Anne Flower's illegitimate child.

Consistory Court of York Cause Papers, Borthwick Institute of Historical Research, CPH 2690 (1666).

[Ellen Eliot of Tadcaster, wife . . . aged 50 . . .]

[To the first article she says] That about two years ago this examinate being in company of the articulate Anne Flower she the said Anne took occasion to speak of the kind love and affection which then was betwixt herself and the articulate Thomas Pinder, and there said, that she loved him exceeding well, To whom this examinate replied and said Well, Nanny, but take heed you do not lie it over hard on, least you cannot take it off again, whereto the said Anne replied, and said, Nay I care not who knows it I do love him well and will do so although it cost me my life for it, And this examinant further saith that about eight or nine weeks ago this examinant with other women was called to the labour of her the said Anne being then with child begotten in fornication, and being there, did heare this examinant's precontest Ellen Watson being her midwife, demand of her the said Anne in her greatest extremity, who was the father of her child, and she the said Anne replied and took it on her death that Thomas Pinder articulate was the only father of it and she never knew other man but him, there and then being present six or seven other women besides this examinate and the said midwife.

8.15 'Never more passionate affectionate lovers': Constance Fowler and Katherine Thimelby, 1636

This letter is one of a series from Constance Fowler, youngest daughter of Walter, first Lord Aston, and wife of Walter Fowler of St Thomas Priory near Stafford, to her second brother the Hon. Herbert Aston, then at Madrid with his father who was ambassador to Spain. From encouraging her brother's courtship of Katherine Thimelby, whom he eventually married, she has moved into a relationship with Katherine that, apparently predicated entirely on their potential relationship as sisters-in-law, nevertheless has its own weight of secrecy, tension, and passion. Later letters from Katherine to Henry refer to Constance: 'I do not wish you here when you are with her. I hope she will not when you are here.' It is an extraordinary testimony of how much passion was allowable between two women – particularly when it is stimulated, supposedly, by love for a man. The original is over three times this length.

Arthur Clifford, *Tixall Letters; Or the Correspondence of the Aston family, and their friends*, London, Longman, Hurst, Rees, Orme and Brown, 1816, vol I, pp. 107–28.

My dearest Brother,

The story that I must now make you acquainted with does nearly concern us both. For my part, I am sure the happiness of my life depends on it; therefore I beseech you read it, and mark it with your best attention. . . . Therefore to begin, I must first put you in mind that all the letters I received from you when you were at London afore your going into Spain were full of nothing more than praises of Mrs Thimelby, and so infinitely did you extoll her in them, that I had no desire more than that I might be happy in her esteem; and the more because my love was so infinite to you, and I saw that you so much wished I were so. For you did desire me many times in most sweet words, that I would write often to her to make my self happy in her acquaintance, assuring me I could not more oblige you than to honour her; and you told me you knew I would not repent my pains in striving to get in to her esteem. I would find her so rare a creature, full of unmatched worth, that I would bless the time that first brought the thought in to your mind of writing to me of her, and so I have indeed a thousand times, for never creature was more fortunate then I in gaining affection from her. For I believe I am blest with the most perfectest and constant lover as ever woman was blest with. Oh, if you would know the story of our affection, you must come hither and read volumes of it, afore you can be able to understand half the dearness of our love. I keep them apurpose for your sight, and no creature breathing but my self ever saw them or knows of them else. You will say, I am certain, when you peruse them that there was never any more passionate affectionate lovers than she and I, and that you never knew two creatures more truly and deadly in love with one another than we are. . . . For after I had made known to her by letters how infinitely I honoured her, and how I had done so since I first saw her here, she writ me the sweetest answers, that from that very hour I confess I have been most deadly in love with her as ever lover was. . . . Therefore to go on with my story, you must know that many letters having passed between us of only complimental friendship, it was my happy fortune to meet her by chance with Sir John and my Lady Thimelby at Tixall, they staying there only dinner and some two hours after, I having no more time than this to possess the company of her whom I honoured more than all the world; and such was our misery that we could not have that time to converse more than by silent expressions . . . and therefore she durst not take notice of me, but as one she honoured being her choice's sister; and so she sat betwixt us all the time, and she was fain to answer to the entertainment my sister gave her of compliments, which she seemed to take little delight in but that by obligation she was compelled to answer them, which she did indeed expressing most sweet gratitude. But as she thus discoursed to her as she sat between us, she would sometimes give a look to me as if by chance her eye had so wandered, and then she would steal the prettiest words to me, that you would have been taken extremely if you had seen and heard her. . . . Truly, I have a great deal of reason to labour hard in persuading you to esteem her, as she is the only wonder of this age. For in the success of your affections depends the happiness of my life; for I have nothing in this world that I can receive contentment in, if this prosper not as I wish. For you two are dear partners in my heart, and it is so wholly divided betwixt you, that I have so much ado to get leave of it to place any other friend of mine there. Oh then, in pity of this heart which has been so faithful to you, and which has suffered so extremely for you, do what you can to compass that happiness for yourself which I so thirst after, that my dearest friend and you being united in one, your hearts may likewise be come one, and so I may keep them with more ease in my breast than now I can, they being divided. . . . I know my lord does most dearly love you, and if he be anything able, he will not sure deny to make you happy in any way you desire. . . . But if he should be not able, then all the world could not have invented a more killing news than this will be to me; therefore for godsake let me not know it if you have any hope to find it otherways. For I speak it to you with my eyes drowned in tears; I think, nay, I am certain the grief of it would kill me, yet pray do not forget to let me know something from you as sure as may be, for I live in infinite affliction with fear of the success of this business, which I have every way taken such pains in for your sake, and for her sake who so highly prizes you, and

who you have reason to value and more esteem than all in this world; and I command you to do so, and to make her happy in your affection, if it be possible, as you tender the life and happiness of her who has ever been most constant in being
Your dear affectionate lover
Constance F.

8.16 'My dear dear husband': Mary Stuart and Frances Apsley, 1678

Mary Stuart, daughter of James II, and later Mary II, and Frances Apsley, later Lady Bathurst, were close friends from childhood. Letters between the two survive from the early 1670s, when Mary was around 9 and Frances eight years older. Throughout the correspondence, which continued throughout their marriages, Mary wrote as 'Clorine', Frances as 'Aurelia'; and from the first letters until shortly before Frances' marriage, Mary writes of Frances as her 'husband'. The roles were playful, but also expressed the depth of intimacy between the two. Mary's sister Anne, later Queen, was also a friend of Frances, and Mary's letters express some conflicts and jealousies among the three. Later, Anne was to have a long, loving friendship with Sarah Churchill, Duchess of Marlborough, and then Abigail Masham; when Abigail replaced Sarah, Sarah warned Anne that her display of 'no inclination for any but of one's own sex' endangered her reputation. In very many ways, and provided they were not politically threatening, the intimate relations, roles, and communications between these two queens and their favourites were an acceptable aspect of women's close friendships in this period: to compare the love of women favourably to that of men, even to call another woman husband, did not necessarily constitute lesbianism. Nevertheless, modern categories of sexuality, such as 'lesbianism' or 'romantic friendship', do not do justice to the range of erotic and emotional intimacy and conflict that might be encompassed in such relationships. This letter, from Mary Stuart to Frances Apsley, was written in 1678, when Mary, at 16, had just married William of Orange, and when Frances was 25. In a previous letter Mary had written, 'you see though I have another husband I keep the name of my first'; in this, she intimates the secret of her pregnancy. Trust and secrets were the currency of their relationship, as they were that of Anne and Sarah. The original uses very little punctuation, so commas and full stops have been inserted.

Mary Stuart to Frances Apsley, Benjamin Bathurst (ed.), *Letters of Two Queens*, London, Robert Holden [1924], pp. 91–2.

Honslerdyck August the 9th [1678]

I have a hundred thousand pardons to beg of my dear dear husband, who if I did not know to be very good and hope she loves me a little still, I could not so much as hope to be forgiven, but those considerations make me, though very criminal for not having writ since I was well again, begin to believe that so charitable a body as yourself can't believe how sorry I am for the fault and continue long angry, but if anything in the world can make amend for such a fault, I hope trusting you with a secret will, which though in itself 'tis not enough, yet I tell you 'tis one that I would hardly give myself leave to think on it nor nobody leave to speak of it not so much as to myself, and that I have not yet writ the Duchess word, who has always charged me to do it in all her letters. It is what I am ashamed to say but seeing it is to my husband I may, though I have reason to fear because the sea parts us you may believe it is a bastard but yet I think upon a time of need I may make you own it, since 'tis not out of the four seas. In the meantime, if you have any care of your own reputation consequently you must have of your wife's too, you ought to keep this a secret since if it should be known you might get a pair of horns and nothing else by the bargain, but dearest Aurelia you may be very well assured tho' I have played the whore a little I love you of all things in the world. Tho' I have spoke as you may think in jest all this while yet for God sake if you love me don't tell it because I would not have it known yet for all the world, since it cannot be above 6 or 7 weeks at most, and whenever you do hear of it by other people never say that I said anything of it to you. In the meantime I beg of you to say nothing as you hope ever to be trusted another time.

ANIMALS AND SPIRITS

8.17 'A pretty sensible creature': Lady Isabella Wentworth, 1706–8

Isabella Wentworth was a lady of the Bedchamber to Mary of Modena, James II's wife. These extracts are from letters to her son Thomas, Lord Raby (later Earl of Strafford), who was ambassador to Berlin. Her 'little family of creatures' included in 1711 a monkey, a parrot, and five dogs.

The Wentworth Papers 1705–39, ed. J. Cartwright, London, Wyman & Sons, 1883, pp. 42, 45, 55, 64.

Twickenham, April 2, 1705

Fubs is a mighty favourite; at first my niece was afraid of her jumping upon her, but Fubs is so subtle as to fawn upon her, and kiss her, and comes gently to her, that she cannot stir without her; and last Sunday would have her go with her to church, and I will assure you, Fubs sat very orderly; and Pug is very kindly treated but at great distance, for my niece is very much afraid of her. . . .

June 5, 1705

. . . Fubs is fonder of my niece Hanbury than ever she was of you. She cannot move out of one room to another, without her following; and is very still till the water is put upon the table, then she jumps up and drinks out of a glass. She will bite her friend Betty if she offers to meddle with my niece, and I could fill a whole sheet of paper, should I tell you all her subtle tricks.

February 27, 1706

. . . I shall be glad [to return to Twickenham] also for poor Fubs, for here I am in a great fright whenever she is out of sight, and especially if a dog happens to be shot, then I am out of my wits till I see her. She is a pretty sensible creature, but I fear has forgot all her tricks, for I cannot practice her. Pug never was so diverting and beautiful as now. In my last I told you that Lord Huntingdon was dead, I wish you had his sister, she is young and handsome; she had left by her father ten thousand pound, and six hundred a year by some relation I think her grandmother, and now by the death of her brother six hundred a year more. . . . One of Fubs's puppies the Duke of Beaufort has got, and designs to put him out to learn all tricks.

November 16, 1708

My dearest and best of children . . .

I have a most dismal story to tell you, God forgive me for it. I cannot help being more than I ought concerned. I had rather lost a hundred pound, nay all the rest of my dumbs[1] I would have given to have saved poor charming Fubs, never poor wretch had a harder death. As it lived so it died, full of love leaning its head in my bosom, never offered to snap at any body in its horrid torture but nuzzle its head to us and look earnestly upon me and Sue, who cried for three days as if it had been for a child or husband. . . . Sure of all its kind there never was such a one nor never can be, so many good qualities, so much sense and good nature and cleanly and not one fault; but few human creatures had more sense than that had. . . . I could write a quire of paper in her commendations. I have buried her in this garden, and there is a stone laid at her head.

8.18 Familiars: Ellen Greene, 1619

Ellen Greene was one of the women accused in the trial of Margaret and Phillipa Flower for witchcraft against the Earl and Countess of Rutland and their family in 1619. Like many other witches, her relationships with her familiars fulfil special needs, and seem to rely as much on the folklore of fairies and spirits as on the demonological ideas of familiars. The success of these familiars is unusual: frequently, they promise money or food which never materialises. The trial documents were published in 1619 in a pamphlet; as in most witchcraft cases, the original legal records do not survive, and the published version may be rather different.

The Wonderful Discovery of the Witchcrafts of Margaret and Phillipa Flower, daughters of Joan Flower near Beaver Castle: Executed at Lincoln, March 11, 1618, London, 1619.

---

1. I.e., dumb beasts.

The examination of one Ellen Green of Stathern in the county of Leicester
... [17 March 1619].

She saith, that one Joan Willimot of Goadby came about six years since
to her in the Wolds, and persuaded this examinate to forsake God, and
betake her to the Devil, and she would give her two spirits, to which she
gave her consent; and thereupon the said Joan Willimot called two spirits,
one in the likeness of a kitlin[1] and the other of a moldiwarp[2]: the first the
said Willimot called *puss*, the other *hiss, hiss*, and they presently came to her,
and she departing left them with this examinate, and they leapt on her
shoulder, and the kitlin sucked under her right ear on her neck, and the
moldiwarp on the left side in the like place. After they had sucked her, she
sent the kitlin to a baker of that town, whose name she remembers not, who
had called her Witch and stricken her; and bade her said spirit go and bewitch
him to death: the moldiwarp she then bade go to Anne Dawse of the same
town and bewitch her to death, because she had called this examinate witch,
whore, jade, etc and within one fortnight after they both died. . . .

And for her self, this examinate further saith, that she gave her soul to
the Devil to have these spirits at her command; for a confirmation whereof,
she suffered them to suck her always as aforesaid about the change and full
of the moon.

1. Kitten.
2. Mole.

9

POLITICS
AND PROTESTS

Politics should be understood broadly in seventeenth-century England. Recent studies of the political activities of ordinary people have both extended our notion of the political and shown how the actions of rulers were influenced by public perceptions of their behaviour.[1]

Women considered themselves to be citizens, members of their society, with rights and duties, and demonstrated a degree of sophistication in their political actions and protests.[2] Documents have been selected and ordered chronologically to demonstrate the range and variety of female political activities. Gender and social level shaped the repertoire of action available to women. Gentlewomen had access to the households in which much of the elite's political activity took place, and followed the affairs of the court, parliaments, and foreign policy as best they could. The mass of women, of middling and labouring status, were more engaged in local action, and frequently took direct action. Depending on whether they lived in the cities or countryside, they protested about religious and political issues, about food prices and common rights.

At the middling and lower social levels, some women's political protests were imaginative and varied. Some individual and collective actions involved patterns of learned behaviour: groups of women organised, petitioned, and gathered together to make their demands. They resisted with what James Scott has described as the 'weapons of the weak', staying silent, refusing to co-operate, and making their opponents act.[3] Quaker women infuriated their contemporaries by their defiance of gender stereotypes and their lack of deference for their social superiors. Their wordless defiance could drive some magistrates crazy.

The bases for women's political interventions were several. According to the law and to political theorists, women, like men, were born free in the sense that they were not slaves or villeins. Since only marriage, and its consequences, coverture, deprived women of their legal freedom, single women and widows continued to claim whatever privileges were appropriate for their social level. Thus in some instances single women, *femes soles*, with property voted for Parliament in the first half of the century on the basis of their property rights.[4] However, women also claimed rights as Christians and as mothers. During the Civil Wars, which began in 1642 between King and Parliament, women of all

243

Figure 19 **'The Parliament of Women'**

From the Thomason Tracts, 14 Aug. 1646. By permission of the British Library

In 1646, female activism so alarmed contemporaries that they joked about the idea that women might sit in Parliament. Here an anonymous satirist envisaged women passing laws so that they might live in greater ease 'but especially that they might have superiority and domineer over their husbands'. Women's petitions demonstrate, however, that women were concerned about their rights as Christians and as citizens.

ranks were visible participants. Like men, they manifested their political and religious views, choosing sides, and tried to influence the actions of their male relatives. One mother tried to dissuade her son Samuel from enlisting, going 'along with him a quarter of a mile ... she besought him with tears not to go'.[5] In a civil war, there was less distinction between homes and battle sites, so women participated by supporting their favoured cause with provisions and shelter. In many areas adult women, irrespective of marital status, considered themselves to be citizens and swore oaths of allegiance and loyalty to the authorities.[6] In 1649, women as well as men expressed horror at the execution of the

King. Like their male contemporaries, again in the Interregnum of the 1650s, women were found on both sides. At the Restoration of monarchy in 1660, and during the political disputes of later seventeenth century they espoused different religious and political causes. Their contemporaries believed females were strong supporters of the exiled Stuarts against William, Mary, and Anne, and later the Hanoverian monarchs.

Collective action by women had antecedents in earlier periods. Women and men were accustomed to take direct action over certain rural grievances, such as shortage of grain and high prices, enclosures of common land, or embankments for fen drainage. There was a widespread popular belief that if women acted alone, without men's involvement, they would not be indicted for riot. However, on many occasions women were indicted for the felony, and the women leaders hanged.[7]

Religious belief was fundamental to women's sense of themselves as human beings with rights, and their religious convictions frequently determined their allegiance during the Wars. Furthermore, religion authorised women in public political action. As the 1649 petition of women on behalf of the imprisoned Levellers shows, women claimed rights as Christians to petition and to demonstrate. Women were more numerous than men in the range of religious movements which developed during the 1640s and 1650s, and were especially prominent among the Quakers. Those with more radical religious beliefs were involved in more extreme public action. Partly for this reason, radical women have attracted notice from both their contemporaries and later historians out of proportion to their numbers.

Women of higher social status were able to express their views publicly in print. Included are a few brief extracts from writers who expressed views we might label feminist. Feminism, a protest at the social disadvantage of women compared with men, did not involve a movement at this date, but nevertheless, individual writers expressed their views in a variety of angry and ingenious ways. Some female poets wittily mocked the deficiencies of female education: ''Tis hard we should be by the men despis'd, Yet kept from knowing what would make us priz'd'.[8] Hannah Wolley, a woman of middling status, expressed herself more bluntly on the sexual politics of daily life: 'Vain man is apt to think we were merely intended for the world's propagation, and to keep its human inhabitants sweet and clean.' She refused to accept the notion of female inferiority: 'I have already endeavoured to prove, that though Nature hath differed mankind into sexes, yet she never intended any great difference in the intellect.'[9] Compared with the attention accorded to endless treatises by men about the nature of the female sex, women's words about the female condition have had little public space.

Divisions of class and race between women were marked. Only the Quakers in the North American colonies believed that all human beings, irrespective of their social status, had the right to Christianity, and they attacked the colonists' refusal to baptise their slaves. However, the Quakers did not challenge the acts of the colonial assemblies which decreed that Christianity did not free slaves from bondage.

Early modern men found the whole subject of women in politics inherently ridiculous. They satirised women's political actions, imagining such world-turned-upside-down scenarios as *The Parliament of Women*, and acted as though any remarkable deeds must have been done by 'men in petticoats'. How women's political activities and protests relate to the political history of the seventeenth century is an important question which awaits some answers.

The documents in this chapter have been organised chronologically, unlike other chapters. This complements the political history of the seventeenth century, and allows the reader to observe women's involvement in shifting political issues. A chronological account also allows us to see the persistence and adaptation of women's traditional forms of protest.

9.1 'This is not good government': Catherine Mylls, 1605

Catherine Mylls of Beckenham, widow, was indicted for seditious words when she questioned the legitimacy of the Stuart monarchy. Furthermore, she considered that as neither James, his wife, or his heir Henry were born in England, they lacked rights, which was legally correct for all Scots until Calvin's Case of 1609. Criticisms of King James for favouring the Scots who had accompanied him to England were common. The original document was damaged.

J. S. Cockburn (ed.), *Calendar of Assize Records. Kent Indictments James I*, London, HMSO, 1980, p. 26.

[On 17 August 1605 at Beckenham she publicly said] That King Henry the eight, King Edward, Queen Mary and Queen Elizabeth were born in the land and came rightly to the crown. But King James, Queen Anne and Prince Henry were not born in the land . . . [not] so rightly to the Crown by inheritance but by gift. . . . that she had delivered unto King James petitions, and could not be accepted of him and he would not relieve her, for English men and English women cannot be accepted but Scottish men and Scottish women are accepted and believed, and that this is not good government but whether it will . . . the said Catherine knoweth not.

9.2 Refusal of church rituals: Joan Whitcop, c. 1610

A number of women in late sixteenth- and early seventeenth-century England resisted the custom of being 'churched' after childbirth, feeling it was an unscriptural cere-mony. The ritual could represent thanksgiving, cleansing, and re-entry into the wider community after the secluded time of childbirth, and most women seem to have accepted it; Joan Whitcop's form of protest perhaps negotiates her own, subversive way between acceptance and rejection.

Archdeaconry of Essex Act Book 1612–14, Essex RO, D/AEA 27, fo. 38.

Curingham: Joan the wife of Nathaniel Whitcop presented for that she being admonished that when she came to church to give God thanks for her safe deliverance in childbirth that she should come with such ornaments as other honest women usually have done, she did not, but coming in her hat and a quarter[1] about her neck sat down in her seat where she could non [not] be descried nor seen unto what the thanksgiving was read, which being done she did as disorderly walk out of the church as she came in. And also for that she said that none but whores did wear veils and that a harlot or a whore was the inventor of it, or that first wore a veil.

9.3 'The cry of the country and her own want': Anne Carter and others, 1629

The case of Anne Carter and her associates represents both typical and exceptional women's roles in politics. Essex in 1629 had suffered a period of depression. Clothworkers were particularly badly damaged by the European trade slump, and grain prices were high. Grain intended for export and those planning to ship it out were particular targets of local resentment. The women of Maldon, who boarded Flemish ships exporting grain and seized some for their families' use, were in part following the established tradition of female participation in food riots, which traded partly on the belief in women's responsibility for food and partly on the belief that married women's ambiguous legal status allowed them a certain licence (in fact this custom was countered by a number of harsh legal responses to such disorders). The 1629 grain riots, though, were also atypical. The disturbances recorded here, in March 1629, were followed by another riot in May 1629, which was taken much more seriously. Large numbers of clothworkers were involved, and Anne Carter, involved again, was reported to have toured the clothing townships to gather support, styling herself 'Captain'. After this second riot, Carter and seven others were hanged.

Maldon Court Leet Records, Essex RO, D/B 3/3 208, m. 14, 16. (The incident is examined in detail in John Walter, 'Grain riots and popular attitudes to the law: Maldon and the crisis of 1629', in John Brewer and John Styles (eds), *An Ungovernable People: The English and their Law in the Seventeenth and Eighteenth Centuries*, London, Hutchinson, 1980.)

The examination of Anne wife of John Carter of Maldon butcher taken the 28th day of April anno 1629 before &c. The said examinate confesseth touching the late assembling of many women and their taking away of corn out of the ships at Burrow Hills in Totham that before the said assembly, her self heard one Phillip Ewdes a hoyman[2] of Lee complain that the owners of the said vessel were Dunkirks[3] and that it was pity they were suffered to lie there, by occasion of which speech and of other men sailors, herself and divers other women to the number of above a hundred of Maldon, Heybridge and Witham and from the heath called Totham Heath assembled together

1. A piece of cloth.
2. Man in charge of a small sloop.
3. Dunkirk privateers.

to the said Burrow Hills in the parish of Totham Magna where the said vessels did lie in the channel and she and the rest of the women entered into one of the said ships, and the Flemings who were therein filled the rye which was therein into the aprons and coats of many of the women and some children who were in the company which they carried away but that herself took not any whit thereof. And she denieth that she did draw any company of women from Witham to the said Burrow Hills.

Anne the wife of Thomas Speareman of Maldon fisherman examined the fourth day of May before his majesty's bailiffs and justice of the said borough: The said examinate confesseth that she with others (because she could not have corn in the market and certain Flemish ships lying at Borrow Hills in the parish of Little Totham there to receive in corn to carry beyond sea) did go down about the 23th day of March last past and there being assembled divers women to the number of about seven score they did enter into one of the said ships and did take away a quantity of corn which was therein but how much she knoweth not, and denieth that any did set her on the said action, and being demanded why she stayed not when she was required and charged by one of the bailiffs of the said town to depart home she saith she saw the rest go and she followed them.

Elizabeth the wife of Samuel Sturgion of Maldon labourer examined the said fourth day of May saith that she being in poverty and wanting victual for her children and being called out of her house by Anne the wife of Thomas Spearman of Maldon and Dorothy the wife of John Berry of the same town about the said 23th of March she went with them and other women to the beforesaid place called Burrow Hills in Little Totham where the said Flemish ships did lie where there were a great many of women met and they entered into one of the same ships and took out a quantity of corn whereof herself had about half a bushel and she denieth that any did set her on but only the two women aforesaid.

Margaret the wife of George Williams of Maldon cordwainer examined the day abovesaid and saith that corn being dear and being carried away and she being a poor woman amongst others of her own accord, went the day aforesaid to the said Burrow Hills in Little Totham and there she with other women did enter into one of the Flemish ships there lying and took out certain rye therein being whereof she saith she took away about a peck and she saith she was not procured thither by any.

Dorothy wife of John Berry of Maldon shepherd examined the day and year abovesaid saith that there being want of corn in the market and she being a poor woman and hearing that there were Flemish vessels at Burrow Hills at Little Totham which lay to carry away corn she with other women went to the said place where they entered into one of the said Flemish vessels where they had filled into their aprons a quantity of rye and being demanded who procured her thither she answereth the cry of the country and her own want.

9.4 The political interests of a gentry wife: Lady Anne D'Ewes, 1640

Sir Simonds D'Ewes was elected to the Parliament, known as the Long Parliament, which assembled in November 1640. Like many other wives, Lady Anne was aware of the importance of the religious and political issues before the House of Commons. (For details of Anne, see document 7.4.)

Anne D'Ewes at Ixworth to her husband, Sir Simonds D'Ewes, 5 Dec. 1640, BL, MS Harleian 379, fo. 111.

My dearest, I have with great joy received your letters full of good news and fair hopes of a happy success of the parliament. I wish that you may find as good success every day after as you did the first morning you went in. Myself and our three daughters are at this time in health, I bless God, but our two youngest have not been well since our removal to Ixworth. All is well at Stow: I chiefly want your company for the best things but I hope and pray that after a few months we may meet again with comfort and that in the meantime God may enable you to discharge your place in Parliament to his glory and the public good. Thus with my dearest affections to you I rest your faithful wife
Anne D'Ewes
[p.s.] All here desire to be remembered to you.

9.5 Mother and son: Susan Fielding, Countess of Denbigh, 1642

Susan, Countess of Denbigh, was the close friend of Queen Henrietta Maria. Sister of George Villiers, Duke of Buckingham, the favourite of two kings, the countess had been at court since the 1620s. Her husband, William Fielding, first Earl of Denbigh, fought for King Charles I during the Civil War, and was killed in 1643. Their son Basil chose the Parliamentary side. Internal evidence suggest that this anguished letter dates from mid-1642, when many peers were joining the King at York, prior to the outbreak of formal hostilities on 22 August 1642.

From Cecilia Mary Fielding, Countess of Denbigh, *Royalist Father and Roundhead Son*, London, Methuen & Co, 1915, pp. 164–5.

My dear son, I was very glad to receive a letter from you, but when I found how little my persuasions had wrought upon you I was much afflicted. Methinks you spoke Mr Pym's[1] language, and I do long to hear my dear son Feilding speak once again to me in the duty he owes to his Master and dread sovereign, the master of your poor afflicted mother, banished from the sight of you I do so dearly love. Let me entreat you look back upon me and on yourself whose ruin surely I see before my eyes. All that is here does more wonder at you than at all the rest, your fortune being but weak, and the many obligations you and your best friends have to the King and Queen. I hear my Lord Paget and many other lords are going to York. Oh that I might be so happy as to hear you were gone too. Let my pen beg that which, if I were with you, I would do upon my knees with tears. If you will come hither I know the Queen will make your peace with the King, but that I leave to you, though I do not think it would be a very good way. You will, I do believe, be left [illegible] all, and were it not better to do it in some reasonable time to my comfort and your own good. The King is now in a very good condition, and doth daily grow better, his people being every day more and more his. Do not deceive yourself, he shall not want men nor money to do him service. All good men begin to see how he hath been abused, and none are undeceived, and I hope you will be amongst them. I want language to persuade with you, though I do not love and reason. Therefore for the Great God of Heaven's sake let me prevail with you. Do not let me be made unhappy by you, my dear son. I have suffered grief and sorrow enough already, let me reap comfort from you in this action. Remember it is a loving mother that begs for the preservation of her eldest son. I hear my Lord of Holland is gone to the King. I hope the next news it will be you, and so with my blessings to you, and my daughter, I take my leave.

9.6   Disturbance of war: Lady Elizabeth Poley, *c.* 1643

Elizabeth Poley directed her letter to the Parliamentarian Sir Simonds D'Ewes in Aldersgate, but the contents are for her sister-in-law, D'Ewes's second wife Elizabeth. The letter probably dates to around 1643.

Lady Elizabeth Poley to Sir Simonds D'Ewes, n.d., BL, MS Harleian 382, fo. 174.

Sweet Sister, I have received as from yourself so from my lady Poley and my brother Poley letters to comfort me with an earnest desire of my company, but it is not many places that 'twill at this time please me but if I may be so happy to hear you are safe at Stow,[2] I shall without doubt visit you there, and I shall with great fear and joy expect to hear from that battle which is my daily conflict. Here are many that partake with me, some for their husbands, others for sons and servants, some crying, others much troubled for servants. One hath drowned herself for fear they are resolved never to return again. Being sorry I have such harsh complements as these so daily to attend you both, if I had come up my company had been three but before

1. John Pym, a leader of the Parliamentary party in the House of Commons.
2. D'Ewes's house in Suffolk.

250

I should have set a time to come up I much hope you will be come down. With my love and service to my brother and your self I end ... [torn] [p.s.] I have sent a box. I pray let it be called though it be not worth your remembrance.

9.7   *The King's Cabinet Opened*: Henrietta Maria to Charles I, 1644

In 1645 the Parliamentary New Model Army won a significant victory over the King's forces at Naseby. In addition, they captured the King's correspondence, from which they learnt that their suspicions of the Queen's influence upon her husband were justified. Parliament published the letters. The one printed here shows Henrietta Maria's intimate knowledge of the current political situation, and her own views about the peace negotiations. Henrietta (1609–69) was the youngest daughter of the French King, Henry IV, and his wife Marie de Medici. She married Charles in 1625, and bore several children. The 'perpetual' Parliament to which she refers was the Long Parliament assembled in November 1640 which was not finally dissolved until 1660. She offers her detailed political advice to Charles about the peace negotiations, particularly about what he should demand by way of security of his correspondence, as a sign of her love.

Henrietta Maria to Charles I, from York, 30 March 1644, *The King's Cabinet Opened*, 1645, reprinted in *The Harleian Miscellany*, 12 vols, London, 1808–11, vol 5, 536–7.

My Dear Heart,

I need not tell you, from whence this bearer comes; only I will tell you, that the propositions, which he brings you, are good, but 260[1] and I believe that it is not yet time to put them into execution; therefore, find some means, to send them back, which may not discontent them, and do not tell, who gave you this advice. Sir Hugh Cholmley is come, with a troop of horse, to kiss my hands; the rest of his people he left at Scarborough, with a ship laden with arms, which the ships of the parliament had taken and brought thither, so she is ours; the rebels have quitted Tadcaster, upon our sending forces to Wetherby, but they are returned, with twelve hundred men. ... Between this and tomorrow night, we shall know the issue of this business, and I will send you an express. I am more careful to advertise you of what we do, that you and we may find means to have passports to send; and I wonder, that upon the cessation, you have not demanded, that you might send in safety. This shows my love. I understand to-day, from London, that they will have no cessation, and that they treat, at the beginning of the first two articles, which is of the forts, ships, and ammunition, and afterwards of the disbanding of the army. Certainly, I wish a peace more than any, and that with greater reason: But I would have the disbanding of the perpetual parliament, first; and, certainly, the rest will be easily afterwards. I do not

1. A cipher of numbers was used to conceal the identities of individuals.

say this of my own head alone, for generally, both those who are for you, and against you, in this country, wish an end of it; and I am certain, that if you do demand it at the first, in case it be not granted, Hull is ours, and all Yorkshire, which is a thing to consider of; and for my particular, if you make a peace and disband your army, before there is an end to this perpetual parliament, I am absolutely resolved to go into France, not being willing to fall again into the hands of those people, being well assured, that if the power remain with them, it will not be well for me in England; remember what I have written to you in three precedent letters, and be more careful of men, than you have been, or at the least dissemble it, to the end, that no notice be taken of it. Adieu, the man hastens me, so that I can say no more.

9.8 'The King's children are bastards': Anne Smith, 1648

Although Parliament had fought against the King and defeated him in two Civil Wars, the justices remained protective of his honour. It was seditious to question the legitimacy of the monarch's heir. Anne Smith was found guilty, fined 100 marks, and reimprisoned till she should find sureties for good behaviour.

J. C. Jeaffreson (ed.), *Middlesex County Records*, London, Middlesex County Records Soc., 1888, vol. iii, p. 103.

2 August, 24 Charles I – True Bill that, at St Giles's-in-the-Fields co. Midd. on the said day, Anne Smith, late of the said parish spinster, being diabolically affected towards the said Lord the King Charles and towards our most serene Lady Mary[1] now Queen of England and towards Prince Charles the Prince of Wales and the other children of the said King and Queen, publicly spoke and uttered these false and seditious words, to wit, 'The King's children are bastards, And that the Queen was delivered of a child at Oxford when the King had not been with her a twelvemonth before.'

9.9 'To judge of such high things': Katharine Whitstone, 1649

Katharine Cromwell, the third sister of Oliver (Lord Protector of England in the 1650s), was baptised in 1597. Her first husband was Roger Whitstone, by whom she bore three sons and two daughters. Her second was John Jones, a regicide who was executed in 1660. Her letter is fascinating on two counts: one is her extreme distress at the execution of the King, and her intention of discussing the matter with her brother, who had been so actively involved in the proceedings; and the second, her allusions to gossip about her having engaged in an illicit affair with Captain Pye. Bergen is in the Netherlands.

Katharine Whitstone to Mrs Wind at Bergen, Ely, 16 Feb. 1649, Folger, MS X. c. 53.

1. Henrietta Maria.

Sweet cousin, I acknowledge myself extremely obliged to you for your kind letter, and had satisfied your noble father and husband with your own desires with the news of these parts, but there needs not my pen to declare what is so in the mouths and ears of all men. Alas dear cousin, I am very dark and know not what to judge of such high things. They are far above my capacity I confess. I was very much troubled at that stroke which took the head of this poor kingdom from us, and truly had I been able to have purchased his life, I am confident I could with all willingness have laid down mine. But God's word hath silenced me, for till I was set down by that I did nothing but murmur, neither indeed could I contain myself, so that I have now gotten a name here which I never had in Bergen. They say I am a Royalist. The Lord make me what he will have me to be, for I shall submit to his will in all things, and let us strive to possess ourselves with patience, as well in the public as our more private affairs, because will we, or nil we, the counsel of the Lord shall stand. Oh how happy are they that can say from a ~~true~~ single heart, the Lord's will and ways are best. I wish and pray I may attain to it. Truly cousin you have not a friend or servant that should or would more faithfully serve you than myself but so long as I am in the country I cannot perform your commands. I hope ere long to go to London to see and speak with my brother who I have not seen as yet since my coming over, and then I shall be your humble servant to my power. As for the news about Captain Pye, I much rejoice I confess at any good that shall befall him, but I believe he follows the good, or bad counsel of some, who intended to work me discontent. I beseech God forgive them but I am afraid God will in the end let them feel what now peradventure they little dream of, I leave to the Lord and their own consciences, and it may be in time he will find the wrong he hath had and done in listening after so unworthy people, for my part they shall find I will not run after him, as they peradventure imagine, yet if I had been with child as some of them spake, I might have been inforced to it. I suffered more in Bergen, than ever I did in any place in my life, but I am now gotten by providence under the wings of a dear and tender mother, where I neither feel nor see the greatness of the world, for I live not in any want, save what pleaseth the Lord to deny me, tis not just a husband, for if it were, happily I might have my desires, but were I worthy of the best man of this kingdom, and might have him if I would, I deal truly with you, all the friends I have in the world should never alter my determination, and yet I have a brother tenders me as dearly as a brother can do, and I know will not deny me anything, upon good and just grounds. I could and would say more but I am afraid you will let me letter be seen by some that I desire should not see it, for my noble cousin your husband if he should peruse I am content and desire it. He can but laugh at this foolish, at best weak expressions of a poor woman, yet his true friend and servant. Dear cousin I much rejoice to hear of the health of your whole family, the Lord in mercy continue it, I see you are careful to increase the world still, the Lord make you a joyful mother, to the comfort of you and yours, I could wish I were near to serve you in your need, to my power, be pleased to present my respects to Sir Robert Wind and my worthy cousin your husband with your self, kiss little Bette from me, my love to all yours, assuring you I am, dear cousin, your faithful friend and humble servant, Ka Whistones

I pray cousin be pleased to present my respects to all that wish well to me, Lavena[1] presents her due respects to you and all yours, she is ere long to go from me, my children have and do find a loving and careful uncle I praise God.

9.10 'A proportionable share of the freedoms of this Commonwealth': women petitioners, 1649

In 1649 London women organised a petition on behalf of the imprisoned Leveller leaders. When they came to Parliament to present it, they were told to 'go home and wash your dishes'. A week later they returned with an even more strongly worded petition which was printed in several editions and newsbooks.

To the supreme authority [5 May 1649], BL, Thomason Tracts 669 f. 27.

That since we are assured of our creation in the image of God, and of an interest in Christ, equal unto men, as also of a proportionable share in the freedoms of this Commonwealth, we cannot but wonder and grieve that we should appear so despicable in your eyes, as to be thought unworthy to petition or represent our grievances to this honourable House. Have we not an equal interest with the men of this nation in those liberties and securities contained in the Petition of Right,[2] and other the good laws of the land? Are any of our lives, limbs, liberties, or goods to be take from us more than from men, but by due process of law . . . ? And can you imagine us to be sottish or stupid as not to perceive, or not to be sensible when daily those strong defences of our peace and welfare are broken down and trod under-foot by force and arbitrary power?

Would you have us keep at home in our houses, when men of such faith-fulness and integrity as the four prisoners, our friends, are fetched out of their beds and forced from their houses by soldiers . . .? . . . And are we Christians, and yet must we sit still and keep at home . . . and shall we show no sense of their sufferings? . . . Let it be accounted folly, presumption, madness, or whatsoever in us, whilst we have life and breath, we will never leave them.

1. Lavena, Katharine's daughter, married Richard Beke in 1656 (Mark Noble, *Memoirs of the Protectorate – House of Cromwell*, Birmingham, 1784, vol ii., pp. 264–5).
2. The Petition of Right, claiming among other things that no freeman should be impris-oned but by due process of law, was passed by Parliament and agreed to by Charles I in 1628.

9.11 Refusing obedience: Margaret Killen, 1655

Margaret Killen, a Quaker (for which see Chapter 2), travelled to Devonshire to speak to people of the inner light. The magistrates attempted to evoke the vagrancy laws against her. In her defence here, she argues that she had been treated without regard for modesty. The Society of Friends solicited records of what they termed 'Sufferings for the Truth' which were entered in large folio volumes, by county. Subsequently, some were published. Quakers had reformed the dating system. Thus the 11th month mentioned below would usually have been given as January.

The Great Book of Sufferings (MS), Friends House Library, London, i, 366.

Devonshire, For Speaking the Truth in several places, 1655
On the third day of the eleventh month, between the 9th and 10th hour at night came a sergeant and would have her open her chamber door, but it being so late in the night, and she alone, she told him she was not free to open her chamber door, so he bid her prepare to be going to Exeter prison at six of the clock the next morning, and about four a clock the next morning came the constable and some others with him, and bid her open the door, which she was not free to do, being alone as had been said, and it being two hours to day, but such was the immodesty and unreasonableness of the officer that he called for a smith and broke open her chamber door at such an unseasonable and unlawful hour and haled her out of the room through the street to a stable where was a carrier's horse, and kept the stable door fast refusing to let friends come in to her.

9.12 Rogues and knaves: Alice Bent, 1660

Ordinary women had views about their rulers. Alice Bent came to court for an attack on the regime of Richard Cromwell, Lord Protector, on 14 April 1659. Richard abdicated at the end of May 1659.

J. C. Jeaffreson (ed.), *Middlesex County Records*, London, Middlesex County Records Soc., vol iii, 1888, p. 277.

[7 March 1659 – Recognizances, taken . . . in the sum of £40 each; For the appearance of Alice Bent, wife of William Bent of Shadwell aforesaid seaman, at the next Sessions of the Peace for Middlesex, to] answer for assaulting and striking in the face Capt. Valentine Jowles, Commander of the Waxford frigate in the service of the state, making his face to bleed; Charged also by the said Valentine Jowles upon his oath of [calling him] rogue and horse-turd, and further saying that the Lord Protector and [they] that employed him (meaning the said Valentine) were rogues and knaves.

9.13   Going naked for a sign: Sarah Goldsmith, 1655, and Katherine Hearne, 1666

In the 1650s, Quakers were spreading their message all over England. Quaker women engaged in a number of dramatic public actions which were highly effective in publishing the truths they sought to witness, including 'going naked for a sign'. To go naked was not the modern equivalent of 'streaking'. Goldsmith undid her hair and wore it uncovered, and was dressed in a coat of sackcloth and shoes. Even so, her action so outraged contemporary views of female modesty that she attracted a crowd. Later Quakers regarded 'going naked for a sign' as immodest and denied that it ever occurred. These two examples of political activity for a religious cause are a decade apart. To the Quakers, the form of government – Protectorate in 1655 or monarchy in 1666 – made little difference; their task was to bear witness to the Lord.

Abstract of the Sufferings, Friends House copy, vol. 1, p. 15; The Great Book of Sufferings (MS), Friends House Library, London, i. 548.

On the 3d of the 3d month [May], 1655, Sarah Goldsmith, being moved to put on a coat of sackcloth of hair next her, to uncover her head, and put earth thereon, with her hair hanging down about her, and without any other clothes upon her, excepting shoes on her feet, and in that manner to go to every gate, and through every street within the walls of the city, and afterward to stand at the High-Cross in the view of the town and market, as a sign against the pride of Bristol, and to abide so in that habit seven days, in obedience thereto, though in great self-denial, and in a cross to her natural inclinations, she cheerfully prepar'd her garment, being long and reaching to the ground; and on the 5th of the 3rd month early in the morning, two friends accompanying her, passed through the streets to the several gates, some people following them, but doing no harm: then she return'd home: and about the ninth hour came to the High-Cross, and one friend with her, a great multitude of people following; there she stood about half an hour, till the tumult grew so violent, that some bystanders, in compassion, forced them into a shop, out of which the multitude call'd to have them thrown, that they might abuse them; but by the intervention of the chamberlain kept out of their hands, and carried to the Tolzey. The Mayor came thither, and ask'd her, why she appear'd in the city in that habit? She answered, in obedience to the light in my conscience. What if you, said the Mayor, in your obedience had been kill'd by the rude multitude? She replied, I am in the hands of Him that ruleth all things. I have harm'd none, yet have I been harm'd; neither have I broken any law by which I can be brought under just censure; if I had appeared in gay clothing you would [not?] have been troubled. In conclusion, the Mayor, at the instigation of Joseph Jackson one of the aldermen sent her to Bridewell, and with her Anne Gunnicliffe and Margaret Wood, for owning and accompanying her.

In the 3rd month [May] in the year 1666 It was laid upon Katherine Hearne by the Lord to go through the streets and market of Dover on a Market Day upon her bare feet, with sackcloth on her body, and ashes upon her head, and to say, Repent for the Kingdom of Heaven is at hand, Fear and dread the living God.

9.14 'Moved by the Lord': Dorothy Waugh, 1656

In 1656 the Quaker Dorothy Waugh published an account of how the Mayor of Carlisle had treated her when she spoke in the market place. It is a rare first-person account of being 'bridled' with a scold's bridle, but it is also transformed by Waugh's perception of the whole event through her faith: she is spiritually guided both to protest and endure.

Dorothy Waugh, *The Lambes Defence Against Lyes*, London, 1656, pp. 29–30.

. . . I was moved by the Lord to go into the market . . . to speak against all deceit and ungodly practices, and the Mayor's officer came and violently haled me off the cross, and put me in prison, not having anything to lay to my charge, and presently the Mayor came up where I was, and asked me from whence I came; and I said out of Egypt where thou lodgest;[1] But after these words, he was so violent and full of passion he scarce asked me any more questions, but called to one of his followers to bring the bridle, as he called it to put upon me, and was to be on three hours, and that which they called so was like a steel cap and my hat being violently plucked off, which was pinned to my head, whereby they tear my clothes to put on their bridle as they called it, which was a stone weight of iron, by the relation of their own generation, and three bars of iron to come over my face, and a piece of it was put in my mouth, which was so unreasonable big a thing for that place as cannot well be related, which was locked to my head, and so I stood their time with my hands bound behind me with the stone weight of iron upon my head, and the bit in my mouth to keep me from speaking. And the man that kept the prison-door demanded two-pence of every one that came to see me while their bridle remained upon me; Afterwards it was taken off and they kept me in prison for a little season, and after a while the Mayor came up again and caused it to be put on again, and sent me out of the city with it on, and gave me very vile and unsavoury words, which were not fit to proceed out of any man's mouth, and charged the officer to whip me out of the town, from constable to constable to send me, till I came to my own home, when as they had not anything to lay to my charge.

1. A reference to Moses leading the Israelites, the chosen people, out of Egypt which represented bondage; Exodus 13.

9.15   Seven thousand Quaker women petition against tithes, 1659

Tithes, the taxes which supported the ministry, were bitterly resented by those who denied the established church and worshipped apart. Although the Anglican church had been replaced by Presbyterian and Independent congregations in the 1650s, the ministers continued to collect tithes. Believing that the word of the Lord was present in everyone, the Quakers considered that ministers who took money for spreading 'the Truth' were cheats. Protest against tithes could take the individual form of direct action, refusal to pay, or be a more organised collective action – namely, a petition to Parliament. The women's petition here, supported by 7,000 signatures, county by county, respresented a major feat of organisation, and was probably the largest organised petition of the period 1640–60. The petition was highly insulting to the Protestant congregations who had been accustomed to refer to their Catholic opponents as 'the Beast' and 'the great Whore' spoken of in the Book of Revelation. Quakers were prosecuted by the governments of the 1650s as well as those after the Restoration.

These several papers was sent to the Parliament . . . Being above seven thousand of the names of the Hand-Maids and Daughters of the Lord, London, Printed for Mary Westwood, 1659, pp. 1, 38–9.

It may seem strange to some that women should appear in so public a manner, in a matter of so great concernment as this of tithes, and we also should bring in our testimony even as our brethren against that Anti-Christian law and oppression of tithes, by which many of the servants of the Lord have suffered in filthy holes and dungeons until death; But let such know, that this is the work of the Lord at this day, even by weak means to bring to pass his mighty work in the earth, that all flesh may be silent, and the Lord alone may be exalted in them who can truly say, Now I live, yet not I, but Christ liveth in me . . . ; Behold our God is appearing for us, and they that be in the light may see him, choosing the foolish things of the world to confound the wise, weak things to confound the mighty, vile things, and things that are despised hath God chosen, yea and things which are not, to bring to nought things which are. . . .

And Christ did provide another maintenance for his ministers and disciples than tithes. . . . The true church is coming out of the wilderness again, and the Beast as the false prophet cast alive into the lake of fire, and the Judgment of the great Whore is come, the false church; The Lamb, the Saints shall have the victory, the Lamb, the Bride is known again, preparing for her husband's coming out of the wilderness, and the daughters of Abraham are meeting of her, who gives in their testimony against this oppressive church, ministry and maintenance.

9.16   Refusal of tithes: Dorothy Neele, 1659

An individual woman who refused to pay tithes had goods confiscated, and then would be further punished for her contumacy. For a poor woman, a cow might make the difference between survival and destitution.

The Great Book of Sufferings (MS), Friends House Library, London, i, 3.

. . . the same bailiff took from Dorothy Neele widow one cow worth £5 rendering no overplus.

Dorothy Neele was summoned to appear in the upper bench at the suit of the same priest Faireclogh, and he caused Thomas Sam bailiff to arrest her, And have her to the common gaol the 13th of the 9th month [November] 1659 where she remained this 11th month [January] 1661 for not paying tithes.

9.17   Signs and witnesses: Elizabeth Adams, 1660–68

Street demonstrations such as those of Elizabeth Adams allowed the dramatic perfor-mance of the Lord's message. Her own account attributes the public nature of her demonstrations to the Lord. Addressing the magistrate as a fellow creature rather than one whose authority was to be respected was a further offence. Her posses-sion of a horse indicated that she was not poor and could not be dealt with as a vagrant. After the Restoration of Charles II in 1660, the Quakers were persecuted until the Toleration Act of 1689. Activities for which women were punished included holding meetings, refusing to pay tithes, and not taking oaths.

The Great Book of Sufferings (MS), Friends House Library, London, i, 547, 549.

In the year 1660, in the same year which the King came in, it was required by the Lord for the said Elizabeth Adams to go to London, and to buy a great painted earthen vessel, and to carry it to the Parliament-House, which thing in obedience she did and stood there two days with the vessell at the first on her head, and afterwards she sat down on it. The second time coming in obedience to the Lord, she stood below, and laid her vessell the bottom upward. And that day there came many people both priests and others, and asked her many questions, unto which the Lord opened her mouth to answer. Amongst the rest one asked her, What was in the pot? She answered that he saw it was the bottom upward as many things were turned, and a-turning. So at night when the House broke up, she was moved to break the vessell, which she did at the bottom of the stairs, before many people that came down out of the Parliament House, and all that she had to say, was, Here is a Figure, and they that live well know what it meaneth. It was the very day that they gave way for the secluded members[1] to sit amongst them again. . . .

1. The secluded members were those MPs who had been excluded from Parliament by Colonel Pride in December 1648. They were readmitted on 21 February 1660.

ELIZABETH ADAMS aforesaid, having been at London in the year 1661. Returning homewards, it was required of her to buy two torches at Gravesend, and to light them both at once; and to carry them in Gravesend streets, which in obedience she did, and carrying them almost through all the chiefest streets in silence, until a man with a halberd laid violent hands on her, and took her torches away, and haled her before the Magistrates. Who demanded of her the reason for her so doing. Her answer was, Friend, I seek or look for an honest man that truly fears the living God and will stand up to vindicate the truth, who presently said, You would be hanged. Her answer was, He was not the man that she looked for. So he threatened to send her away by officers to the place of her abode. She said, she should not be so dealt withall, for she had a horse in town. So he sent an officer to see if she spoke true, and to warn the host not to give her entertainment upon his peril.

In the year 1668 it was upon Elizabeth Adams aforesaid to go to the great Mass-house called Christ Church in Canterbury, and to warn them to leave off their idolatry, and that the Lord was angry with idolators, and that his wrath was and is ready to break forth, and that God would not always be mocked. So the priest stood still till she had near freed herself. Then a priest's wife stood up, and said she was an old Quaker. She answered her, That if the power of the Lord God seized on her, that she must quake and tremble also. Whereupon the Keeper came to her, and threatened to knock her down, saying, Do you come here to seduce people? so a bad man haled her out, and pushed her, and said she was a Jesuit; and that he warranted she had a good sum of money to do that service. So coming out, the priests were in that they called the body of their church, there was 4 of them there, and one of them said, Bedlam is most fittest for you, and the man that before called her a Jesuit, said, He would he had an order he would soon carry her to Bedlam, with many other railing speeches.

9.18 'The Lord God Almighty will set them free': Alice Curwen and the rights of slaves, 1680

Alice Curwen married Thomas Curwen around 1641. She became a Quaker, and in 1660 experienced the Lord's command to travel to Boston. Initially, Thomas refused to accompany her, but the Lord convinced him, and he travelled with her. Alice died in 1679. Here, in her autobiography, she recounts her contest with Martha Taverner's ruling over slaves' consciences.

A Relation of the Labour, Travail and Suffering of that faithful Servant of the Lord Alice Curwen. Who departed this Life the 7th Day of the 6th Month, 1679. and resteth in Peace with the Lord, London, 1680, p. 18.

There was a widow-woman in Barbados that had negroes to her servants, who were convinced of God's Eternal Truth, and I hearing of them was moved to go to speak to the woman for their coming to our Meetings; and when I did speak to her she did deny me, and then I did write to her as followeth.

Martha Taverner:

I cannot pass by, but in love write to thee, for in love we came to visit thee, and to invite thee and thy family to the Meeting; but thou for thy part art like him that was invited to work in the vineyard, and went not: And as for thy servants, whom thou callst thy slaves, I tell thee plainly, thou hast no right to reign over their conscience in matters of worship of the Living God; for thou thyself confessed, that they had souls to save as well as we: Therefore, for time to come let them have liberty, lest thou be called to give an account to God for them, as well as for thyself: So in thy old age choose rather, as a good man did, that both thou and thy whole family may serve the Lord; for I am persuaded, that if they whom thou call'st thy slaves, be upright-hearted to God, the Lord God Almighty will set them free in a way that thou knowest not; for there is none set free but in Christ Jesus, for all other freedom will prove but a bondage.

From thy Friend,

Alice Curwen

9.19 'Oh, that I were but a man!': Mary Alder, 1688

Throughout the seventeenth century, women were among those prosecuted for seditious words. As wives, women were sometimes but not always named as accessories. The husband and wife here accused pleaded not guilty and were acquitted by a jury. The description of the wife as 'spinster' might refer to her occupation, but probably represents a legal fiction to enable a married woman to be sued in her own right at the common law (as, technically, she could not be).

J. C. Jeaffreson (ed.), *Middlesex County Records,* London, Middlesex County Records Soc., 1892, iv, pp. 319–20.

29 October, 3 James II [1688] True Bill that, at St. Martin's-in-the-Fields co. Midd[lesex] on the same day, Cornelius Alder yeoman and his wife Mary Alder alias Mary Alder spinster, both late of the parish, being pernicious and seditious persons, in order to bring the Lord King James II and his beloved consort the Lady Mary the Queen into odium and contempt with the lieges and subjects of the said Lord the King spoke certain malicious and seditious words: that on the 29th Oct. the said Cornelius Alder in the presence and hearing of divers of the said King's lieges and subjects said in the said parish these seditious words, to wit, 'Oh, what a fit opportunity the city hath to shoot them, as they go by any corner!' and that afterwards on the same day the said Mary Alder of her most wicked mind spoke these malicious and seditious words, to wit, 'Oh, that I were but a man!'

9.20 Political differences among kin: Margaret Standish, 1689

The flight of the Catholic King James II was followed by the accession of his Protestant daughter Mary and her husband William. Margaret Standish here expresses her hope for the security of the Protestant religion and peace. The dangers she feared were from the Catholic supporters of James in Ireland and France. The commandeering of horses troubled her, as it seemed like the arbitrary proceedings which she associated with the French.

Margaret Standish to Thomas Worsley, JP, 1689, Worsley Papers, North Yorkshire County RO, ZON 13/1/31.

I am extremely glad my dearest cousin always to hear from Hovingham but especially to have so full an account of all your healths [there]. . . . It would have pleased me much better to have had it from your own mouth. It is really a troublesome time to travel and leave one's house which together with my husband's London journey must be my excuse for not waiting on you in Yorkshire this summer and not any dislike I took either to the place or persons: I'll hope if we live till another summer we shall be in a more settled condition: free from sudden alarms and afrightments which would interrupt our pleasure if we were together if they be as frequent with you as they are here: if I durst set my heart upon it I could almost long to see your little flock: but must not hope for it yet: I am very glad my cousin has recovered her health. I hope you will both live to see your children's children and peace and true religion flourish in England: for I really believe Popery will be extinguished in a short time unless it please God to deliver us into the hands of our French and Irish enemies which would certainly be the greatest judgment that could befall us and what every good man ought to do his utmost to prevent in this land: Hayes yet in the country in hopes to see our new Lord Lieutenant who is expected every day: and tho I believe there is but few of this country gentlemen that have any kindness for his person yet they will rather submit and take commissions under him than stand for ciphers in their county and let the militia be put in worse hands: we have dragoons here which seize all Papists' horses I had a sad complaint from Lodge by 4 a clock this morning they had been there yesterday and taken all they have of horse kind. I must needs own I am very sorry for them though I cannot help them. I think this way of dragoons is too like the French fashion and which troubles me most my sister is so hardened and exasperated by this kind of usage that I am afraid it will increase her aversion to the Protestant religion: for she says it has lost one of its best principles viz (loyalty) all I or any of her friends can do for her is to pray that God will open her eyes and let her see her beliefs her self for she is abundantly more vehement in her way than ever she was and looks upon herself as suffering for righteousness sake . . . my daughter Frances says 'her dodfada is very dud baby', which is the best way she has to keep her kindness. She is mighty fond of her token for which I give you hearty thanks. I believe you will begin to think me impertinent in this long letter therefore dare say no more, but that I am with greatest sincerity Your most affectionate cousin and servant whilst Margret Standish

Durbury May the 6th
My husband is all your servant and if you send your letters by Robart Wright the Manchester carrier redirects them for me to be left at Mr Heyes house in back Salford they will come safe.

9.21   The value of history: Mary Astell, 1705

Here Mary Astell shows her awareness of the writing of history as a political act, as feminists are still pointing out. And just as Astell knew that any women who distinguished themselves were said to be 'above their sex', so some historians still characterise any woman in the past whose eyes rise above her sampler as 'formidable' or 'redoubtable'. For biographical information about Mary Astell, see document 1.12.

[Mary Astell], *The Christian Religion*, London, 1705, pp. 292–3.

But to what study shall we apply ourselves? Some men say that heraldry is a pretty study for a woman, for this reason, I suppose, that she may blazon[1] her Lord and Master's great achievements! They allow us poetry, plays, and romances, to divert us and themselves; and when they would express a particular esteem for a woman's sense, they recommend history; though with submission, history can only serve us for amusement and a subject of discourse. For though it may be of use to the men who govern affairs, to know how their forefathers acted, yet what is this to us, who have nothing to do with such business? Some good examples indeed are to be found in history, though generally the bad are ten for one; but how will this help our conduct, or else excite in us a generous emulation? Since the men being the historians, they seldom condescend to record the great and good actions of women; and when they take notice of them, 'tis with this wise remark, that such women *acted above their sex*. By which one must suppose they would have their readers understand, that they were not women who did those great actions, but that they were men in petticoats! The business, to learn the weakness and strength of our minds; to form our judgments, and to render them always just; to know how to discover false reasonings, and to disentangle truth from those mazes of error into which men have hunted her; whatever tends to this end ought to be pursued.

---

1. To describe in proper heraldic language.

9.22   Challenge to political theorists: Mary Astell, 1706

In this extract Mary Astell shows the inconsistency of Whig doctrines of a social contract between free individuals and the patriarchal family structure. She herself was a Tory, and supported the Stuart monarchy and the Anglican church.

Mary Astell, *Some Reflections upon Marriage*, 3rd edn, London, 1706, preface, p. 5.

That the custom of the world has put women, generally speaking, into a state of subjection, is not deny'd; but the right can no more be prov'd from the fact, than the predominancy of vice can justify it. . . .

Again, men are possess'd of all place of power, trust and profit, they make laws and exercise the magistracy . . . women think as humbly of themselves as their masters can wish, with respect to the other sex. . . .

If absolute authority be not necessary in a state, how comes it so in a family? Or, if in a family, why not in a state. . . . Is it not then partial in men to the last degree to contend for and practise that arbitrary dominion in their families which they abhor and exclaim against in the state?

If all men are born free, how is it that all women are born slaves?

10

MENTAL WORLDS

In early modern thought, minds and bodies were intimately related. Women's physical experiences, their illnesses and disturbances, were connected with their psychological states, and the humours that constituted the body had a profound effect on both physical and mental health. The women who consulted physicians and astrologers told stories of griefs and upsets or disturbing dreams, followed by disrupted menstrual periods, aches in the back, stomach, or heart, and sleeplessness. Alice Chapman, a 30-year-old woman, went to consult Richard Napier in 1607, complaining of what he noted as 'A grief taken some three years ago about her friends, short-winded, pain in the breast and back, ill by fits, no child this ten years, her sickness [menstruation] not above a day, but only a show, urine white and thin'.[1] In humoral explanations of the female constitution, melancholy was associated with an imbalance in humours, and the remedies were physical.

For women, the periods of adolescence and that of childbearing were understood to be times of especial vulnerability. Greensickness, believed to be largely caused by sexual abstinence, was seen as a mental as well as a physical malady, a sign of the frustrations of adolescence; widows were believed to be subject to similar diseases. It was in late adolescence that many women experienced religious conversions, some of them occasions of great trauma and mental anguish, as well as of social and familial upset. Young women also tended to be the most likely subjects for possession. A series of celebrated cases involved girls from gentry families demonstrating all the signs of possession – starvation, fits, spitting up bent pins. Some contemporaries recognised in such behaviour cries for attention. In contrast, premenstrual syndrome does not seem to have been widely expected or recognised.

The time of courtship and marriage could be stressful. For many women, balancing their choice with their family's, economics with affection, could be hard, and once they had decided, pre-marriage anxieties and fears were by no means uncommon. In London in 1591, Katherine Hawfield found her friend Joan Mortimer sitting in the kitchen 'very dumpish and grievously weeping' because, in promising to marry against her parents' wishes, 'she had cast herself away, contrary to all her friends' goodwill'.[2] Another of Richard Napier's patients suffered a 'griping and pulling' in the chest and stomach and 'sigheth much' after her match had been broken off when her father would not meet her prospective husband's demands for a jointure.[3] Both women and men were recognised to suffer, occasionally, extreme love-sickness.

Pregnancy and childbirth might give rise to deep anxieties and fears. Most women would have known someone who had died in childbirth: their fears for delivery were in many ways rational ones, and resulted for some women in panic, dread, or depression. The widely accepted idea that a mother's moral and mental state in pregnancy had direct, visible effects on her child must have been another cause of pre-natal tension. Contemporaries were less interested in the mental state of women after giving birth, but women's own testimonies convey some evidence of post-natal depression. Spiritual diaries and confessions dwell anxiously and sometimes guiltily on feelings of unhappiness after giving birth. More obliquely, some witchcraft trials suggest that accusations of bewitching and maleficium were particularly likely to grow out of tensions and anxieties between mothers, midwives, and wet-nurses after birth.

The deaths of children, husbands, family members, or friends were expected to cause depression and sadness, but some women expressed guilt for taking such deaths so deeply to heart. In the minister Vavasor Powell's collection of exemplary 'spiritual experiences', women are provoked to a greater closeness with God by a realisation that they had cared too much for an infant, or grieved too hard for a husband. The obligation to accept God's will gave some women comfort in grief; but others found themselves tormented with anxiety about the guilt and sin that had led them to be so punished. Spiritual understanding gave women both structures through which to understand mental states and much of the vocabulary in which they expressed their psychological experiences.

Mental disturbances might be related to the stages and stresses of life-cycles; but throughout life, the mind was understood to be open to many influences and invasions, most of them not easily explicable through simple causes. Possession, by which the soul was taken over by the devil, was only one of the most dramatic. Women's constitution was supposed to leave them more open to such influences: 'empty vessels', they could be both more open to the word of God and positive spiritual influences, and more subject to the dangers of demonic possession. Women were also recognised to be particular authorities on the interpretation of dreams, and it may well be that they felt themselves more likely to see ghosts and visions. The distinction between dreams and visions, or between daydreams and nightdreams, was less clear than it is today. Often, early modern writers are unclear about whether they themselves conjured up a vision, or experienced it involuntarily.

DEPRESSION AND DESPAIR

10.1 Many crosses increasing upon me: D.M., 1652

Vavasor Powell's *Spiritual Experiences* collected the testimonies of believers in his London Independent Congregation, describing moments of religious conviction or revelation. Many of them came from women. The despair of 'D.M.' at her widow-hood 'discovered' to her her own sins: a fleshly love for her husband. Like many other women reflecting on their lives, she found her salvation through understanding 'the mind of God' in her life, and through tracing his dealings with her. Alice Thornton wrote her autobiography with the same aim in mind (Alice Thornton, *The Auto-biography of Mrs Alice Thornton of East Newton, Co. York*, Yorks, Surtees Society, vol. 62, 1873). D.M. was also helped through a godly woman friend.

Vavasor Powell, *Spiritual Experiences, of Sundry Believers, Held Forth by them at Several Solemn Meetings, and Conferences to that End*, London, 2nd edn, 1652, pp. 33–8.

About forty years since, through many crosses increasing upon me, like an armed man, I flew unto God to seek his mind by prayer, and he discovered to me that it was my sins, which were then set before me; which caused me to feel the hand of God by afflictions upon me, that sin was the cause of my sufferings, which lay very heavy upon me, and terrified me, so that I thought I had been in the way to damnation: and that if I had been in the way to salvation, every affliction would not come so upon me, greater than I thought I could be able to bear. In particular, the Lord discovered to me, that I had too much loved my husband in a fleshly love, making an idol of him, and therefore he justly became a great terror to my spirit, first he became an enemy to goodness, and so an hindrance in me in coming to Christ. And also, that while I thus doted on him, he went away from me: I feared, through the sense of that and other sins, together with the aggravation of my afflictions, that God did not love me. Yet it struck into my heart, that God did not strike willingly, and therefore I endeavoured to see what was the mind of God in it, who had taken away my husband, goods, and all, from me; namely that he had done it, that I should not hang upon husks, but that I should love him.

And I found that I had loved the world too much, and set my heart too much upon these creature-comforts, and therefore the Lord took them away from me. This wrought upon me great troubles, and despair; that I cried until I was almost blind. And I had great fear and trembling upon me, that I could not pray, nor hear with profit, but thought it was in vain for me to pray, whom God loved not, and whom I had so offended.

And about a quarter of a year after, I had a temptation by Satan to drown myself in a pond near Leeds in Yorkshire, whither the devil led me, telling me that I might do it there; it being a private place where no body could see me; and I was by him drawn out thither, and came to the pond side, but by the providence of God, having a great love to a young infant I had then, I took that child in my arms; and when I came to the place, I looked upon the child, and considered with my self, what, shall I destroy my self and my poor child? and cried unto God, Lord, what wilt thou have me to do? and I had a sore conflict at that time with the Devil; But me thought at last, I heard the Lord saying to my soul, as he did to Paul, *Trust in me, my grace is sufficient for thee.* And then I found some comfort, which enlarged my heart, through the assistance of God's Spirit, to call upon the name of the Lord, for further assistance and comfort, and so I went away back with much joy, believing that I should have the favour of God.

And the Lord put it into my mind to go to one E.B. that dwelt by a moor side near Leeds, whom I knew was a godly woman, and she opened to me the troubles of David, and Job and gave me sweet comfort, saying, God is by me, and I did not see him, as Job wished, so she wrought upon my heart to wish, *O that I could see him, O that I could behold him*; and my heart was full of joy, and I cried, and was much grieved, with very great repentance that I had been so seduced, and did so despair of God's mercies, and had been so blinded. And the Lord set it upon my spirit, that though I had laid all aside, yet now I would come out of the *wilderness leaning on my beloved*; and had a greater affection to the ways of God than ever; and delighted in them more than ever. Before they were a burthen to me, now they were easy and sweet.

10.2 The temptation of despair: E.C., 1652

From the same work as the previous testimony came the story of 'E.C.', recording her depression and despair at the birth of her child and later at one of her children's deaths.

Vavasor Powell, *Spiritual Experiences, of Sundry Believers*, 2nd edn, 1652, pp. 25–7.

About some nine years ago at the birth of a child I had very great temptations, of destroying myself, and have had oftentimes a knife put into my hand to do it, so that I durst not be left by myself alone; and when I had considered what the causes of it might be, my conscience did hint most my neglecting of duties, the which I had many opportunities to have performed they being the ordinances of God.

Thus I continued till two years ago I buried a child, which was a very great trouble to me to part with, and then was I more fully convinced of sin, which caused my burthen to be the greater, so that I could seldom have any other thoughts but of desperation; but the Lord kept me by his great mercy, so that sometimes I could pray with devotion, and discern the Lord to remove this great trouble from me, I did plainly find that those great temptations were very much lessened, which was a great comfort unto my spirit; but yet this still was upon me, that I could read the promises, but I found none of them to me; I could not say, God was mine, or had discovered himself unto me, in pardoning my sins; yet this I had often thoughts of, that I would throw my self upon Christ, if I perished I perished; and not long since, I had a very great desire to join myself to that society which was truly godly, and Providence ordered it so, that I had my desire in it; which was of great use and encouragement unto me, in believing the promise of the Gospel; and since, I bless God, I have found some satisfaction in several places of scripture.

10.3   Inner conflict: Hannah Allen, 1683

Hannah Allen's autobiographical narrative records her melancholy and illness before God allowed her to triumph over the Devil's temptations. Born a merchant's daughter in Derbyshire, she was sent to school in London in 1650, aged 12, after which she returned to live with her mother, a widow, where her depression started, and continued over several years, during which time she married and was widowed when her first husband died abroad. She eventually joined a Presbyterian congregation in London and married a Mr Hatt. These sections concern particularly her experiences of inner conflict. This extract starts at the death of her first husband, Hannibal Allen.

Satan his Methods and Malice Baffled. A Narrative of God's Gracious Dealings With that Choice Christian Mrs. Hannah Allen, London, 1683, pp. 12, 15–17, 60.

. . . in few months after I heard of the death of my husband (for he died beyond sea) I began to fall into deep melancholy, and no sooner did this black humour begin to darken my soul, but the Devil set on with his former temptations, which at first were with less violence and frequent intermissions, but yet with great strugglings and fightings within me. . . .

[The next sections contain, Allen says, some of her shorthand writings 'written in my deep distress'.] The sixth of April 1664. The truth is I know not well what to say, for as yet I am under sad melancholy, and sometimes dreadful temptations, to have hard thought of my dearest Lord (The least assenting to which by his grace I dread more than hell itself). Temptations to impatience and despair, and to give up all for lost; and to close with the Devil and forsake my God, which the Almighty for Christ's sake forbid: these temptations were with dreadful violence. Besides, my melancholy hath bad effects upon my body, greatly impairing my health: truly there is sometimes such a woeful confusion and combating in my soul, that I know not what to do; And now my earnest prayer to my Lord is this (which I trust for Christ's sake he will not deny me, though I cannot beg it with such earnest affections as I should, yet I hope my heart is sincere), that for my sweet Redeemer's sake he would preserve me from sin and give me strength of faith; and self-denial and patience to wait upon him, and submit to him; and let him do with me what he pleaseth. . . .

[Later passages record her dialogues with her aunt on her spiritual state.]

My aunt sometimes would tell me; that my expressions were so dreadful she knew not how to bear them; I would answer roundly, but what must I do then, that must feel them; I would often say to my aunt, Oh, you little know what a dismal dark condition I am in; methinks I am as dark as hell itself. My aunt would say, Cousin, would you but believe you were melancholy it might be a great means to bring you out of this condition. Melancholy, would I say, I have cause to be melancholy, that am as assuredly damned as that there is a God. . . . One fit my humour was such, that when friends would have argued with me about my condition, I would not speak, but only give them some short scornful answer and no more; but I would be sometimes in one temper and sometimes in another; my aunt would take the advantage of my best humour, to talk with me then, and the main thing she designed in most of her arguments with me was, to convince me of the fallacy and delusion that was in my opinion; that it was so infallibly revealed to me that I was damned; but alas all took no place with me; but when she began to speak with me of such things, I would generally fling away in a great fume, and say; Will you not let me alone yet, methinks you might let me have a little quiet while I am out of hell; this was almost my daily practice while I was with my aunt; I was usually very nimble in my answers, and peevishly pettinacious to please my own cross humour.

10.4 Soul and body: Mary Carey, 1650

Like many other early modern women, Mary Carey feared death in childbirth. Before the birth of her fourth child, and after the deaths of three earlier children, she wrote a book of meditations, in the form of a dialogue between the body and the soul, in which she recounts her own spiritual development. Carey was the daughter of Sir John Jackson of Berwick; the dialogue is addressed to her second husband, George Payler. The pattern of a sinful early life followed by a religious conversion in adolescence gave a typical structure to early modern spiritual experience. Here, as in other texts and conversion narratives, a consciousness of oppressive sin is followed by joy at the hope of mercy.

Meditations of my Lady Carey, Bodl., MS Rawl. D 1308 (transcript by Charles Hutton, 1681) pp. 17–21, 23.

Soul. Mark then what was the Lord's dealing towards me, which I shall briefly and truly relate. It was the Lord's pleasure to smite me with a sore sickness (in my apprehension it was unto death) when I was about 18 years old, in the midst of jollity, when I was taking my fill of worldly contentments, and restrained my heart from nothing it fancied to follow, delighting myself, and spending my time in carding, dice, dancing, masquing, dressing, vain company, going to plays, following fashions, and the like. In this sickness I began to think that God had given me a time in the world, which I was now quitting. God did please to call back my life from the grave, and restored me to health and strength, but I knew not God, nor what would be become of me for Eternity. . . . God did please to call back my life from the grave, and restored me to my health and strength, which free mercy did so win upon my heart; that I found my resolutions in the time of my sickness much strengthened, but I knew not how to set one step forward in this great work, only I sequestered my self from all my former company, and sinful delights, and my spirit was very restless, and full of enquiry.

Body. But what couldst thou do in this condition? thou wert a stranger unto God, to his Word, to his people, to all means, and helps.

Soul. 'Tis very true, I neither did nor could do anything, but God did all, and thus he removed my dwelling, and set me under a powerful ministry, powerful I may call it, even the power of God, sharper than a two-edged sword, piercing, dividing soul, and body, joints, marrow, a discerner of my heart, and thoughts; Heb. 4.12 & Rom. 1.16. This Word, I say, even every sermon I heard, did so find me out, and discover me unto my self, that I thought there was no reprobate in Hell more sinful than I;

I found myself equal with them in original sin, beyond most in actual sin, my sins were laid before me, Satan let loose upon me, so far as to tempt me, terrify, upbraid, and challenge me for his own, and worst of all, I believed God mine enemy, his wrath, and Hell my portion for eternity; O what confusion was in my thoughts day and night; I durst not eat, nor drink, but to keep life, nor take any comfort from any creature; that I could want; I thought I had no interest in Christ, & therefore no right to any creature, but was confident to suffer for the least refreshment I had [either from meat, drink, sleep, clothes, fire, company, etc.] in Hell. . . .

. . . Truly, long it was, as I thought, many months, almost a year, before I got any abiding, or firm comfort; and all the means I used made me still worse; for I could use none aright. . . .

I could not believe a promise, or pray, but in this sad condition of desertion, I lay under the arrest of divine justice, the Lord being so gracious to me, as not to let me fall back again. He also kept me from those violences, that the malice of my spiritual enemy desired. Now the first glimpse of mercy was, a secret thought, or wish, or poor hope; yet, what if the Lord will be gracious, and freely merciful, even to me the chiefest of sinners. And, methinks those that verily believe the people of God, and know they dare not lie, have been something after my manner; this a little stayed me.

FITS AND DISORDERS

10.5   Fits: Isabel Armestead, 1692

Occasionally, mental disturbance served as an explanation, partial or full, for law-breaking.

North Riding Quarter Sessions Working Papers, North Yorkshire County RO, QSB 1692/231.

The examination of Isabel Armestead . . . upon the twenty-first day of May 1692 touching some linen clothes, which were stolen from Mr Whitehouse of Ackendale.

First the said examinant saith, that she hath no kind of thing to say for herself, but begs mercy for Christ Jesus sake; for she confesses that she stole those clothes which she pulled out of her knapsack about day-break on Friday morning (which was the twentieth of May 1692) and says that she will not deny the matter though she were to go up the stile to the gallows for it. And further she saith that she doth often have fits, and that she was madled in her mind when she stole them, or else she would not have taken them.

10.6   Light-headedness: Sibill Fisher, 1603

Sibill Fisher visited the astrological physician Richard Napier in August 1603. His notebook records her horoscope and his diagnosis. Like many women, her mental disturbances seemed connected partly to disturbances in childbirth: in this instance, jealousy is suspected to have led to witchcraft. The majority of Napier's patients were female, and many of them complained of a combination of physical and mental sufferings. Diagnosis was made using horoscopes and examinations of urine, and they were prescribed specific remedies.

Notebooks of Richard Napier, Bodl., MS Ashmole 207, fo. 113v.

Sibill Fisher of Cokenho., 24 years, August 1, 12.15 p.m., 1603.

Light headed, laughs, but at first took it with a weeping look ghastly a fleering look, set her teeth. One night did nothing but swear and curse. She knows not of her husband's coming for her, knows no body. They bind her hands and feet – when she is loose she is so strong that they cannot deal with her. Sings idle songs, desires to dance. She had two midwives, the first unskilful, the second froward and would not meddle with her because she was not first sent for, suspected to be a witch, the woman well laid but a week after fell into these fits and at first speaking of her second midwife said what dost thou there with thy black hen? and such like speeches.

10.7 Eating feathers: E.R., 1652

Vavasor Powell's collection (see above) also presented the story of a young woman's delusions. E.R.'s 'desperation' developed after she told a lie, aged 11; it led her to threaten suicide and to display a form of *pica* (eating inedible objects, an established disorder in this period). Her parents asked first a doctor, then two ministers to help; the last stage in her recovery, though, involved a dream of Christ.

Vavasor Powell, *Spiritual Experiences, of Sundry Believers*, 2nd edn, 1652, pp. 357–66.

I was born and bred up of godly parents, yet Satan so far tempted me to commit that detestable sin of telling a lie, about eleven years of my age, against a sister of mine, and my sister was shrewdly and severely corrected by my parents for that fault, and that none of hers, but mine, and I had not grace at that time to lay it to heart; but within some three months after I had a fit of sickness, and a grievous touch in my conscience for that sin committed against God, and my sister, as that I saw nothing but desperation, and feared that the horrors of hell-fire would seize on my soul and body for this sin, and Satan told me, that there was no salvation for me, for God knew me not, neither would he own me; but if I would either hang myself, or cut my throat, or take the bedstaff to thrust down my throat, then I should never be tormented more, but look how an ox died, so should I.

Then I cried out to my parents, and said, that I was damned, and that there was no salvation for me, but that I must go to hell; then my parents watched me, and did search narrowly to see what instruments I had prepared. Then the devil did tempt me to rend the pillow, and pick out some of the feathers to swallow them down, which I did, which had like to have cost me my life, for I was very nigh dead by this means.

10.8 Melancholy and spiritual trials: Dionys Fitzherbert, 1608

Dionys Fitzherbert (*c.* 1580–1640) was the daughter of a gentry family who in her late twenties experienced a mental crisis lasting for around six months, involving a range of delusions and eccentric behaviour. On her recovery she wrote a long account of the experience, designed in part to refute those (her friends and family) who interpreted her breakdown as madness or melancholy, and to identify it instead as a spiritual trial of a special kind. The narrative was not printed, but the existence of a second (slightly amended) copy in a different hand, and her detailed instructions for circulation, make it clear that it was to some extent a public document. This extract from her original manuscript describes the beginning of the episode: she had apparently been living in the household of the Countess of Huntingdon, and had feigned illness to escape embarrassment at not having bought her a New Year gift.

Bodl., Ms. e.mus 169, fos 8–10v.

This document and its note supplied by Katharine Hodgkin.

Lo now indeed I began to play the hypocrite, which God did so punish in me that my soul trembles to think of it, and did indeed most justly lay open my sin and shame to all the world in this manner. At night when I was set by the fire one of my lady's women came to see me and gave me a baked apple, which I did eat, never thinking how ill it was for the disease I pretended to be troubled withall; so utterly was my senses and reason now bereft me, with all feeling of godliness and virtue, as if I had never felt the motions of it in my soul. A most fearful case, and a warning to every one to take heed that though they stand they fall not! When I had eaten it the core stuck in my throat and trembled me very much; and I, who now thought everything was a judgement of God upon me for my sin, persuaded myself it was gone up into the end of my mouth, and that undoubtedly it could never be gotten from there, but it would kill me. The miserable state of them may be seen in me that God leaves to themselves never so little. For I, who was not wont to fear in most apparent danger, but was able to comfort and encourage others (as many can tell which knows me), behold now the very conceit of death makes me to despair. The advantages were now very great the Enemy had to work upon, to cause me to speak those fearful speeches – if not blasphemous – I after did.

For going to bed in this mind, full of despair and terror of conscience, whether the apprehension of death did in this case make me sick or that it was the physic they gave me caused me to vomit as I did, I can no means remember. But the deadly adversary, taking the advantage of my miserable state, made me think assuredly no sin could be like mine, and that therefore I was ~~Antichrist~~ an adversary to God; which I did affirm and speak in the hearing of many, and complain that I was forsaken of God, that I was a firebrand of hell, and that I should be laid in the Charterhouse yard for all people to wonder at, and all the yard should flow with the matter that came out of my mouth; and did assuredly think all the bed and clothes were as wet with it as might be, and therefore did most instantly[1] desire them that were about me to carry me into the yard; for thither I knew I must go, and there I should die with such torments that I should pluck out my own eyes.

. . .

Lying in this lamentable case, how long I cannot tell, for I had not understanding to distinguish the day from the night; also they kept me somewhat dark, plying me with physic, which to give Doctor Lester (then my physician) his deserved due was in all likelihood undoubtedly under God the only means of the safety of my life, in purging by his skilful potions those pestiferous humours which came of so many deadly conceits, the least of which had been able to kill a far stronger constitution; and the immediate danger I was in, he himself did then testify. Now very many of my friends and

1. Insistently.

acquaintance came to see me which sometimes I knew and other times no more than if I had never seen them.

. . .

And so I continued I think two or three days, and then thought assuredly I should die; for to my thinking, imagination and feeling also, the palate of my mouth was quite broken away, and the gall within my body. Therefore I did assure myself it was impossible for me to live, and so did affirm, and thinking verily to die gave away my clothes.

But what I did or said while I was in that place afterwards I can by no means call to memory, nor how long I stayed before I was removed to Doctor Carter's, or why they did bind my hands. But most certain it struck an intolerable horror into my heart, thinking sure I had committed some crime they would put me to death for; and when I heard them say that I should be removed to Doctor C. I imagined I had been a loose liver and a thief and that therefore they would punish me, and had bound me so. But when they did remove me, which was in the night, they put a fair cloak and safeguard[2] about me that my Lady L. gave me; therefore I thought I had stolen it, and that they went to carry me to her; and when I should alight I cried out that I would not see my Lady L. by no means. My brother who was in the coach with me told me I was not near her, neither had I stolen those things from her, but she had given them me; but I thought he mocked me, beginning now to think that he was not my brother but I had been deceived in thinking so, which afterwards I did always affirm, and verily thought so (albeit I loved him dearly above all other), believing that he and another of my brothers that came to me were of the greatest enemies that I had.

They kept me a while at Doctor C.'s very dark, and I had some to watch me day and night, having in every respect as careful attendance as might be; but that did astonish me the more, especially when Doctor C. ministered physic to me, much to my dislike, thinking it was all done in scorn of me. After a while they removed me into a more lightsome room, where by reason of certain gestures of the company that were there at my coming, [I] conjectured that they would burn me; which opinion was every day increased by one accident or another.

Doctor C.'s wife, a very good gentlewoman and exceedingly carefully attending me many times with her own hands, with very great compassion ofttimes showed towards me, would stand and dress herself by me, imitating (at the least as I thought) my fashion and carriage when I was accustomed to dress myself, and that so perfectly as methought she expressed the pride I was then possessed withall. And her maid would do many things that to my thinking did so lively set out many of my follies and faults past that I know not how to express the astonishment they put me into.

2. A protective overgarment.

Also the children would stand and stagger by me after their childish manner as if they were ~~drunk~~ giddy, and one of them would say God made this gentlewoman's clothes, with many like words; which I thought their parents bid them do to show the vices I had been subject to, and that they said God made my clothes because I had stolen them, which I believed confidently I had done, and therefore would ask everyone that I knew if I had stolen aught from them. And all that my brother gave me I verily thought I had gotten from him by that means, calling him my master, imagining a great cause of my burning was because such an abject as I was durst challenge him for my brother, and other of worth for my kindred; which was the cause I would desire them to kill me always, and offer my neck to their swords when they came to see me, thinking I had deserved no less of them or any of my former acquaintance; as also to avoid the torment of the fire, that above all things I feared.

For I never rose out of my bed that I thought I should have gone into it again, but that they would set me in the chimney and make a small fire under my feet, and there should burn for ever and never die; believing most assuredly none did die otherwise, but by death was meant to be burnt, so as I should be. And therefore would I look upon my body, and then say to Mistress C., Is it possible this body should die? No, it can never die, but here you will burn me for ever.

All that I had ever heard or seen of God, the distinction of states, magistrates ordained for the defence of the oppressed, ministers for the comfort of the afflicted, did sometimes come into my mind; but then after much debatement would conclude that sure there was no such thing, but these things were feigned to deceive such as I am, and to bring them to that miserable state wherein I was; which I thought was meant by hell and to be a devil, and so would tell them they meant to make of me.

For the conceit of burning without order, judgement and in that form I imagined it should be, did so confound my understanding that I did not believe the most sensible things that be. No, not that I was child to my own parents, but sister to one Mistress H., whom I had loved dearly and been much beholding to, but now accounted her as one of my greatest enemies; as well because I was somewhat indebted to her, and that also by her procurement I came to Doctor C.; and now did verily think I was her own sister, and that my name was Mary, which was the name of a sister of hers that I had heard her often say was dead and she did much resemble me. Which words I did remember, and thought I was the same, and she said she was dead because the meaning was I should be burnt, which was all the deaths I could conceive of. And the chief cause was because of the words of atheism I had spoken, of which my conscience did extremely accuse and condemn me, tormenting me with unspeakable terror, well remembering how severely I had always judged them worthy of death that did not acknowledge their life's giver; and also for treason, which opinion came by this occasion.

As I was saying, which commonly I did, that they would burn me, Doctor C. said (or I thought he said), No, you may speak treason or anything and have no punishment; by which I gathered that I had spoken treason and therefore should die for it and that it should be by fire. The least occasion might easily persuade me to: as one of the servants giving me beer in a jug set it by the fire and heat it very hot, then putting it to my mouth willed me to taste it; and also the maid by Doctor C.'s commandment laid piggons[3] so hot to my feet that they almost scalded me; all which I conjectured was done to show me what end I must come to. Mistress C. and her children would many times read and sing psalms to me, but that I take as the greatest mockery to me that might be, because I had taken so singular delight in it in former time, and also now thought they hated me for nothing more; neither could they procure me by any means once to look upon a book.

DREAMS AND VISIONS

10.9   A dream after childbirth: Elizabeth Banebery, 1618

Elizabeth Banebery visited the Buckinghamshire physician Richard Napier three times in 1618. Like Sibill Fisher, Elizabeth Banebery suffered mental disturbances after childbirth. Hers were linked to a dream which reminded her of the social tensions of the birth; but they also suggest some familiar manifestations of postnatal depression. None of her symptoms (including the eventual loss of her milk) was regarded as a physical, but as a mental disturbance.

Notebooks of Richard Napier, Bodl., MS Ashmole 198, fos 53, 76, 83.

Eliz. Banebery of Fenny Stratford, 22 years, Jan. 17, 11 a.m. 1618
Brought abed well tomorrow night willbe fortnight. 3 days remained well and afterward dreamed and upon her dream grew mopish and feareth a woman that was ill thought of that she did not bid to her travail. Not sick in her body but troubled in mind. Cannot sleep well. Grudgeth her husband his victuals which she never did before. Is taken with a fit in the afternoon and will snarl [?] and lament that she should be driven to quit her house.

[March 1 1618] . . . mightily afflicted in mind, not sick body. Married a year hath a child and after childbearing 4 days troubled with a frightful dream and since much troubled in mind. . . . Her milk was suddenly dried up. She hath put out her child to nurse. Troubled with worldly businesses. Tempted to kill herself and had a knife in her hand.

---

3. Warming irons.

[March 13 1618] hath a child of 9 weeks old which another suckleth. After her child birth fell with a dream and was frighted as if something lay upon her and since hath been troubled with worldly matters. Over careful of the world. Well in health. but much troubled in mind.

10.10   A dream of Christ: Mary Penington, 1640s

Many women and men in the seventeenth century recorded intimate, personal dreams of Christ. Mary Penington, a Puritan and later a Quaker, recorded here a vision she had as a young woman in the 1640s, troubled about the form her religious practice should take. (See also her account of her marriage in Chapter 6.)

Mary Penington, *A Brief Account of my Exercises from my Childhood*, Philadelphia, 1848, pp. 9–10.

[I]n this state my mind being almost constantly exercised about religion, I dreamed that I was sitting in a room, alone, retired and sad; and as I was sitting, I heard a very loud, confused noise; some screeching and yelling, some roaring in a piteous doleful manner; others casting up their caps and hollowing in a way of triumph and joy. I listening what should be the matter, it was manifested to me, that Christ was come, and that this was the state people were in at his coming; some in joy, and some in extreme sorrow and amazement. I waited in much dread: at last I found, that neither the joy nor the sorrow of this confused multitude was that which truly knew of his coming; but it was the effects of some false rumour. So I abode in the room solitary, and found I was not to join with either, but be still and not affected with the thing at all, and not to go forth to enquire concerning it. Sitting thus a time, all was whist, and it was manifested to me it was so. I remaining cool and low in my mind abode in the place, and when all this distracted noise was over, one came and spoke with a low voice to me, Christ is come indeed, and is in the next room, and the Bride the Lamb's wife: at which my heart secretly leaping in me, I was ready to get up to express my love to him and joy at his coming; and was going into the next room, which I did, and stood trembling at the end of the room, which I found to be a spacious hall. I was joyed at the appearance, but durst not go near him, for it was said in me, stay and see whether he own thee and take thee to be such an one as thou lookest upon thyself to be so. I stood at a great distance, at the lower end of that great hall, and Christ at the upper end; whom I saw in the appearance of a fresh lovely youth, clad in grey cloth (at which time I had not heard of a Quaker or their habit) very plain and neat, he was of a sweet, affable, courteous carriage, and embraced several poor old simple people, whose appearance was very contemptible and mean, without wisdom or beauty. I beholding this judged in myself, that tho' his appearance be young, yet his wisdom and discretion is great; that he can behold the hidden worth in those people, who to me seem so mean, so unlovely, old and simple: at last he beckoned to me to come to him, of which I was very glad; but came lowly and trembling, and solid in great weightiness and dread. After a little time it was said, 'The Lamb's wife is come'. At which time I beheld a beautiful young virgin, slender made and grave, in plain garments becoming and graceful, and her image was fully answering his, as a brother and sister.

10.11   Interpreting dreams: Katherine Austen, 1665

The London widow Katherine Austen (1628–83) was a frequent and reflective inter-preter of her own and others' dreams. She used them to prophesy future events, and often looked back on previous dreams to make sense of her life. At this time Katherine's husband had been dead seven years and she was engaged in a battle through Parliament for his father's estate at Highbury (acquired by possibly illegal manoeuvres). The dream is full of symbols: the back stairs by which Katherine's husband leaves her, the card game, the wedding. Many of these would have had established meanings in popular dream interpretation; here, Katherine produces her own interpretations.

Katherine Austen Collectanea, BL Add. MS 4454, pp. 63–4, 70–1.

My Dream on 2nd of Jan. 1664:

I dreamt I was going to a wedding and took my leave of my mother. Then I went up a high pair of stairs and came into a room where was a long table in the middle at the upper end sat my husband a discoursing with a gentleman in a gown, sitting at the side of the table. I looked upon them and went down, as I went down a few steps I saw my husband again. I kissed him, and asked him how he could come down before me since I left him sitting. He told me by a back stairs. So down I went. And then I forget-ting my muff, I went up the back stairs for it. But I had not gone up above eight or nine steps but I waked.

This came in my mind diverse days afterwards, and I concluded, the first pair of stairs signified to me the end of Jan.: and the second was so many days in Feb.: and then something would fall out to me. And indeed I was troubled that some unhappy adventure would come, as I indreaded[1] every day, wishing Feb. out. It came to pass that on the 9th of Feb. I was appointed to be that day at the Committee of Parliament: and when I came into the room it was the same as I saw in my dream. The situation of the room the same with the table. And as soon as I cast my eye on Sir John Birkenhead, I was confided he was the very same man I saw my husband with.

This business was a wedding: for it was a contract, a confederacy to take away our estate. And I shall no more be of that opinion generally observed on dreams, that a wedding foretells a burning, and a burning a wedding.

1. Dreaded

Figure 20 **A woman's winter clothes, by Wenceslaus Hollar**
By permission of the Corporation of London, Guildhall Library

These might be the kind of winter outer clothes – a muff, gloves, and hand-kerchief – that Katherine Austen wore to the Parliamentary committee, as she had dreamed.

But that it is danger of conspiracy against one as this was to me. By my muff going for that I was to be lapped warm as it fell out – went in muff and velvet hat and mantle.

And certainly something might concern Sir J. by my husband's seeming to divert him that if he acted in so just a matter it would not be well to him. And by my husband sitting at the upper end of the table, as if he would be his judge. It proved a very troublesome time to me, for I was sick of an exceeding cold in my head. . . .

I dreamt I think it was about the 20th Aug. 1664, the last night before I came from Twickenham, that my father Austen and my brother Austen was partners at a game of cribbage and my husband and I: and as soon as the cards was dealt, my husband said he would deal again. I was unwilling and said I had a good game: for I had three aces and I said that was six; and this I thought intimated to me six months, and something would happen. Which now the six months is past. I think that and my four moons dream related to our estate of Highbury which then was called into a most dangerous question, by persons who is ready to do what they pleased if the special providence of God do not prevent them.

That troublesome business might well be compared to a game at cards, wherein my father Austen and all of us have been concerned in the taking case of and defending. Our adversaries do see our cause is so apparently

right, and yet they will essay to vex us more. I beseech God if it be his pleasure to divert their unjust pretentions.

I dreamt a while before, I had thieves came to my bedside. And there
was my husband came and gave me two rings. One his father's gold sealed
ring, the other a diamond ring of his brother's. And his father was in the
entry, but did not come in, and thus I was delivered from the thieves.

And when I waked I hoped I should have the better of my father's estate
of Highbury and of my brother's estate of the Red Lion, now at this time
which I am in law with by my sister Austen.

10.12   Ghosts: Susan Lay, 1650

Susan Lay was a servant in an alehouse in Battlebridge, Essex, from 1648 to 1650.
A widow, she had had two illegitimate children, one fathered, she said, by her
master Francis Beauty, the other by his son William. (The use of 'Gammer' to address
her here may indicate that she was nearer the age of her master and his wife than
their son.) By the beginning of 1650 both children, put out to nurse, had died, and
shortly after Francis's wife Priscilla, who had helped Susan, died also. In July 1650
Susan was examined by a JP and indicted for the theft of two geese with another
woman, Ann Hove, for which both were sentenced to be whipped in the market
place. Her testimony, reproduced here, also told the story of the birth of her bastard
children, for which she was later committed to the house of correction for a year;
but its essence is a long narrative of the visions she saw after her mistress's death,
corroborated by Ann Hove. Such a story was far from what those justices expected
to hear, but a clerk recorded it nonetheless. Susan reappeared in the sessions
records in July 1652 for stealing a woman's petticoat, for which she was whipped:
we do not know what happened to her next.

Essex Quarter Sessions Bundles, Essex Record Office Q/SBa 2/74 (3 July 1650).

The examination of Susan Lay of Sawcott, Essex . . .

Saith that she hath dwelt with Francis Beauty of Battlebridge near
Rettenden as a hired servant for the space of two years last past and that
she came out of his service about Christmas last past, and that about a year,
and a half since she had a male bastard begotten by the said Beauty which
died about Christmas last. And saith that she had another bastard since by
William Beauty, his son, which she was in travail of at Rettenden and was
presently sent away by his father in the company of the said William Beauty
to St Lawrence, but was delivered by the way and herself carried the child
to a house that the said Francis Beauty held there, where she remained for
about a week, at which time the said Francis Beauty sent for her back to
Battlebridge, and left that child with her first child at St Lawrence aforesaid in the keeping of the wife of Richard Ballard. And at this examinant's
coming back to Battlebridge her dame Prissilla Beauty went with her to
Hockley in Rochford hundred and left her at the house of one William
Corbet for about a fortnight after which she went away from Hockley to

St Lawrence to see her children, and from thence the next day to her master Beauty's at Battlebridge from whence her master carried her up by boat to London from Gray's intending to put her to service there, but she returned back with him to Battlebridge, and after that her master told her that her children were provided for, and that she might go shift for herself since which she never saw her children but going to St Lawrence about a month after found them both dead and the woman that kept them asked her whether she would have the clothes, but she would not but went back to her master Beauty's, who would not receive her into his house but her mistress took her in and kept her in her chamber a week together. And saith her said mistress died on Easter Day last having been ill about a week of a swelling about her face and saith that she went to St Lawrence to bid folks to her burial by her master's direction, but he wished this examinant not to come again till after the burial because if the people saw this examinant the people would laugh at him.

And she this examinant coming again to her master after Tuesday he having formerly promised this examinant some clothes but then refused to give her any, and that she hath lain in his barn ever since, and saith that the said Francis Beauty promised to marry this examinant, and made her say that she was his wife both at Gray's, and in London when he was with her, and his son William did likewise promise to marry her before he had the use of her body and her master and mistress bad her not say who she was with child by and she should never want as long as they had a halfpenny. And saith that the third night after her dame Beauty was buried her dame's ghost appeared to her all in white in her master's barn where she lay, and having appeared to her three nights, the third it called to her Sue, Sue, Sue and pinched her at her departure on the right arm, and saith that it appeared to her again on the last Lord's day in the night as she lay in the same barn in the sight of another woman, a boy and a girl that lay in the same barn. Whereupon this examinant got up and run to her master's door, and knocked and told them that her dame was a-coming, and the door being opened they went in, and she prayed William Beauty to go to reading and the other woman looking out of the window of the house said she saw the same ghost walking in the yard.

And saith that on Monday morning last she went with Ann Hove towards Basildon, and in the way as they crossed a field near Basildon Hall, she this examinant took up a couple of geese and killed them the said Ann standing the whilst to watch that no person might come to see them, and then she this examinant carried one of the said geese and the said Ann thother to Billericay where they offered to sell them, and afterwards carried them to one Batt's at Hutton, and there did eat them.

Saith further that the said Ann Hove told this examinant that she would carry her [to] a man in Maidenhead Court in Whitechapel in the house of the widow Reynolds that should tell her wherefore the ghost of her dame did walk and saith that the said William Beauty had carnal knowledge of the body of the said Ann Hove in the presence of this examinant, about two years since and saith that she lay in the said Francis Beauty's chamber, where the said Beauty lay himself for three nights the last week.

The examination of Ann Hove, servant to Henry Bennet of Canvey Island . . .

[she confesses stealing the geese.]

. . . and saith that on the last Lord's day at night she this examinant lying at the said Beautys' house at Battlebridge, and the said Susan lying in the barn near the said house, and another woman with a child, and another boy and a girl lying in the said barn, the said other woman boy and girl in the beginning of the night saw the likeness of a spirit in white come into the barn, and stand looking upon the said Susan where she lay, at which they cried out to the said Susan: Gammer Gammer[1] there she comes, whereupon the said Susan and the rest came out of the barn to the door of the house, and this examinant heard Susan cry aloud For God's sake open the door, here's my dame here's my dame, and the said Beautys soon opening the door and locking her in the said Susan cried bitterly Oh this is my master that brought me to this and sitting still crying in the house, the other woman came out of the barn with her looking out at the hall window into an inner yard saw as she told this examinant and the said Beauty that she saw the said Beauty's wife in the shape of a girl about a dozen years old walking up and down the yard whereupon telling it to the said Susan, and the rest they all came up into the said Beauty's chamber where this examinant lay in a bed by herself, and the said Susan wrung her hands and said to the said Beauty Oh Master this is you that hath brought me to this sorrow you will make me cut my throat, or run out of my wits with these frights and scares that you put me to, whereupon the said Beauty's son went to reading, and presently they heard a great noise below, and then the said Susan came again, into the chamber, and said, Ann Hove are you arising?, and saith that the said Susan and this examinant lying at Basildon on Monday at night, the said Susan was again troubled in her sleep and told this examinant, Oh this woman will be the destruction of me. You shall not need to fear her, if she comes she comes to me and not to you, and that she must conjure her into the red sea[2] or else she would be her destruction, and at her departure on Monday morning from Beauty's she told his son that she must cut her throat, drown herself or make herself away for she was never able to live in the condition that she was in. Whereupon the said Beauty's son said to her, Sue this is a just judgement of God upon you for if she walks she walks to you and to nobody else.

1. Gammer, a corruption of grandmother and a rural title for an old woman.
2. A metaphor for death (the sea of blood).

283

And saith that the said Susan told this examinant that she had had two bastards the one by the said Francis Beauty the father, and the one by William Beauty his son, and that the first bastard [s]he had about two years and a half since, and the last by the same she had about a month before Christmas last which died within six weeks after, and saith that the said Beauty's wife died about Easter last. The said Susan told this examinant that she said that she had broke the said Beauty's wife's heart in bringing home the said bastard to her, and saith that the said Susan saith that she cannot be out of her master's company and that she must have the blood of him, or hang him at one time or other, and saith that the last night lying in the barn with the said Susan at Hutton she heard a noise and the said Susan told her that her dame was there again and that she heard her below, and Mr Ammatt's man that watched them came out of the barn being frighted into a molehole and said that he would never come into the barn again. And saith that the said Susan lay did formerly steal a turkey cock in this examinant's company and saith that the said Susan confessed to this examinant that she the said Susan with another woman stole two geese and made them into pies the week before.

PROPHESYING THE FUTURE

10.13   Astrology: Sarah Jinner, 1658

Sarah Jinner, 'a student of astrology', published three 'women's almanacks' in the period 1658–61. Her preface acknowledged the oddity of a woman studying 'celestial science', but justified herself with examples of feminine achievement from the Amazons to the poet Katherine Phillips. As well as listing the lunar positions through each month, the almanacks gave recipes for women's diseases, monthly advice for 'good housewives', and prognostications for the year to come. After some general observations, these continue with enquiries 'more particular of our sex'.

Sarah Jinner, *An Almanac or Prognostication for the year of our Lord 1658*, London, 1658, sigs B2–B3v.

A Prognostication for the year of our Lord, 1658

. . . Now let us enquire of this position of the heavens more particularly of our Sex. And first we find Mercury in a feminine sign, in a feminine house, drawing towards a corporal conjunction with Venus, and therefore we shall allow Mercury a female in this case: The lawyer is no small servant of ours. Mercury to a quartile of Mars and Pisces and Gemini, giveth some of our sex (that are not poised with virtue) a rare faculty of scolding, in other some muteness and sullenness, Venus in the twelfth house, in exultation, but applying to combustion with the Sun, signifieth that end[1] women will be

---

1. Possibly a misprint for 'evil'.

more apt than ordinary in bestowing the pox upon their clients. Luna in going into Saturn in the sixth house in Libra, signifieth, that many an old coveteous grub will dote after young women, signified by Luna full of light. Let me advise you to beware marrying in the spring, for Scorpio being in the seventh house intercepted, denoteth unseemly wantonness, and lightness in women.

Of the Sun's entrance into Cancer

Mercury Lord of the Ascendant in Cancer, and the Moon, have significa-tion, that the Commonalty suffer much by their strife, dissension, and heart-burning one against another. Great ones suffer by having the Dragon's tail in the tenth house, it's fatal for some of the biggest of the City of London. Luna being in the seventh house in Pisces, a double bodied sign, is noteth frequent marrying, and it is a pretty lucky position, for oyster wives, fish wenches, and others, whose callings are signified by the sign of Pisces. The Moon and Jupiter being in reception, the Moon in Pisces and Jupiter in Cancer doth tell me that it is a fortunate time of marrying, that many of our sex shall obtain good rich matches: some of them better than they deserve: Mercury and Venus in Cancer, being in conjunction in the eleventh house, the house of friends: the which considered, to marry a seaman is fortunate, I advise thee to marry the trumpeter rather than the gunner: but have a care of Saturn, he casts a quartile into the fifth house, the house of children, but that may be over by the next quarter, if you chance not to lie down before the quarter ends.

Of the Sun's entrance into Libra

In the Sun's entrance of Libra, which will be Sept. the 12th. 25 min. past 12 at night, the general judgement of this figure I shall pass over briefly for as much as Jupiter is with the Moon in the first house nigh the cusp, it signifieth, that religion shall pass amongst the people with much credit, that the ministry shall have great power of persuading the people; yet for the most part this religion is but formal.

Jupiter and the Moon being in Leo upon the ascendant, giveth our sex rampant and fiery spirits, proud and ignorant dames that understand no better will strive for the mastery; but the Sun being near Mars in Libra, his fall and going towards Saturn, a crooked fellow, he will hamper you, and put the distaff in your hands and make you spin.

Venus being in Scorpio, I fear me that the naughty wantons of our sex as well as the other sex, will be peppered with the pox, and if so, woe be to your noses; it is malignant to catch it at this time.

In this figure, the Dragon's head being in Sagittary denoteth fruitfulness to honest women.

Of the Sun's entrance into Capricorn
In this figure I find Mars Lord of the ascendant in the eight house with the Dragon's head: it denoteth some loss of blood by battle, sore robberies, and inhumane murders, diseases, as coughs, sore eyes, and violent fevers, having Venus in the twelfth house in opposition to Jupiter in the first house, and the Moon in the seventh in Scorpio, doth foretell many diseases in women. You would now fain know, if it be good to marry this quarter: I tell you no, for Saturn is a tragical enemy to all comfort that way. You have the Moon lady of the fifth in Scorpio, your children will die, neither can I promise you any riches; for Mars is in the second house next the seventh, and consumes it all; but Mercury in the 9th house puts you a jogging to see your friends, and delight in discourse, as gossipings.

10.14   A vision for the Millennium: Mary Cary, 1651

'I am a very weak, and unworthy instrument,' wrote Mary Cary (Rande), a Fifth Monarchist prophet. But like other women prophetic writers, she uses the language of emptiness to create a space for her words and visions. Here, she glosses the biblical texts dealing with what she and her fellow millenarians saw as the 'New Jerusalem', into a very material vision of a new world for God's chosen saints. 'To a holy heart', Cary notes, such things are 'but secondary comforts': but in the context of the high mortality of seventeenth-century England, and the Interregnum turmoil, they must have had a special resonance.

Mary Cary, *A New and More Exact Map or Description of New Jerusalem's Glory*, published with *The Little Horns Doom and Downfall*, London, printed for the author, 1651, pp. 287–90.

But now more fully to declare what this external glory of this new world shall be; thus:

There shall be no outward thing wanting to the Saints, that may make their life outwardly comfortable: for what is it that can be desired or that heart can think of, that ever at any time maketh the lives of people comfortable, but the Lord hath promised that his people shall enjoy it, in these times.

And first, Doth the enjoyment of near relations, without losing of them, make the life comfortable? Are children outward blessings, in which men take much outward content and delight? And is it a very desirable thing to have our children the Lord's children, to be the blessed of the Lord? And is it a bitter thing to lose an only son, a sad thing to lose children and near relations, and is the contrary a desirable mercy? And is long life a blessing, and an outward favour lawful to be desired? According to that, Psalms 91.16 *With long life will I satisfy him, and shew him my salvation.*

Why, all these things hath the Lord promised to his people in these days, when these new heavens and new earth shall be, as we find in these Scriptures. Isaiah 65.17,18, etc. *Behold, I create new heavens & a new earth: and then what follows? I will rejoice in Jerusalem, and joy in my people: and the voice of weeping shall be no more heard in her, nor the voice of crying.* But if they should lose their children, and lose their relations before they come to a full age, there would be mourning and weeping: for these things usually prove sad afflictions to the best Saints; even to Jacobs and Davids. But they shall not lose these then: for, verse 20, it is said, *There shall be no more thence an infant of days nor an old man that hath not filled his days: for the child shall die an hundred years old.* So that this is clear, No infant of days shall die; none shall die while they are young; all shall come to a good old age. They shall not be afflicted for the loss of their children; for they shall live till they be an hundred years old; and not an old man shall die that hath not filled his days. Again Zechariah 8.3,4 etc. *Thus saith the Lord, I am returned to Sion, and will dwell in the midst of Jerusalem: and Jerusalem shall be called, A city of truth, and the mountain of the Lord of hosts, the holy mountain,* wherein the Lord will dwell. And what follows? *Thus saith the Lord of hosts, There shall yet old men and old women dwell in the streets of Jerusalem, and every man with his staff in his hand for multitude of days, and the streets of the city shall be full of boys and girls playing in the streets thereof.* Thus shall the Saints in those days enjoy those desirable blessings of children, and of long life; they shall have a numerous issue; *The streets shall be full of boys and girls*; and old men and old women shall live to they come to good old age till they walk with a staff in their hand for age.

NOTES

INTRODUCTION

1 See document 2.9.
2 For collections of these representations, see N. H. Keeble (ed.), *The Cultural Identity of Seventeenth-century Woman: A Reader*, London, Routledge, 1994, and Kate Aughterson (ed.), *Renaissance Woman: A Sourcebook. Constructions of Femininity in England*, London, Routledge, 1995.
3 Roger Coke, *A Survey of the Politicks*, London, 1662, pp. 76–8.
4 James Howell, *Proverbs, or Unsayed Sawes and Adages*, London, 1659, p. 11.
5 For more woodcuts, see *The Pepys Ballads*, ed. W. G. Day, Cambridge, Boydell and Brewer, 1986; on ballads and cheap print, Joy Wiltenburg, *Disorderly Women and Female Power in the Street Literature of Early Modern England and Germany*, Charlottesville, University Press of Virginia, 1992.
6 E. A. Wrigley and Roger Schofield, *The Population History of England 1541–1871*, Cambridge, Cambridge University Press, 1989, p. 249.
7 Roger Schofield, 'Did the mothers really die? Three centuries of maternal mortality in "The World We Have Lost", in Lloyd Bonfield, Richard M. Smith and Keith Wrightson (eds), *The World We Have Gained: Histories of Population and Social Structure*, Oxford, Oxford University Press, 1986.
8 Wrigley and Schofield, *Population History*, p. 217.
9 E. A. Wrigley *et al.*, *English Population History from Family Reconstitution 1580–1837*, Cambridge, Cambridge University Press, 1997, pp. 438–9.
10 For the complexity of family relationships in a household, see Miranda Chaytor, 'Household and kinship: Ryton in the late 16th and early 17th centuries', *History Workshop Journal*, 10, 1980, pp. 25–60.
11 Wrigley and Schofield, *Population History*, pp. 260–3. Rates of non-marriage were lower in the late sixteenth century and rose again after the 1650s.
12 Richard Wall, 'Women alone in English society', *Annales de Demographie Historique*, 1981, pp. 303–17. For a case study of one single businesswoman, see Pamela Sharpe, 'Dealing with love: the ambiguous independence of spinsters in early modern England', *Gender and History*, 11, 1999 [forthcoming].
13 On the brewing trade, see Judith M. Bennett, *Ale, Beer and Brewsters in England: Women's Work in a Changing World, 1300–1600*, Oxford, Oxford University Press, 1996; a fuller bibliography on women's work follows Chapter 3.
14 Amy Louise Erickson, *Women and Property in Early Modern England*, London, Routledge, 1993, p. 86.
15 Patricia Crawford, 'The challenges to patriarchalism: how did the revolution affect women?' in John Morrill (ed.), *Revolution and Restoration: England in the 1650s*, London, Collins and Brown, 1992.

16 Patricia Crawford, *Women and Religion in England 1500–1750* , London, Routledge, 1993.

17 Phyllis Mack, *Visionary Women: Ecstatic Prophecy in Seventeenth-century England*, Berkeley, University of California Press, 1992; Patricia Crawford, 'Public duty, conscience, and women in early modern England', in John Morrill, Paul Slack and Douglas Woolf (eds), *Public Duty and Private Conscience in Seventeenth-century England*, Oxford, Oxford University Press, 1993.

18 David Cressy, *Literacy and the Social Order: Reading and Writing in Tudor and Stuart England*, Cambridge, Cambridge University Press, 1980, chap. 3.

19 Margaret Spufford, 'First steps in literacy: the reading and writing experiences of the humblest seventeenth-century spiritual autobiographers', *Social History*, 4, 1979, pp. 407–35.

20 Sara Heller Mendelson, 'Stuart women's diaries and occasional memoirs', in Mary Prior (ed.), *Women in English Society, 1500–1800*, London, Methuen, 1985, p. 184.

21 *The Diary of Samuel Pepys*, ed. Robert Latham and William Matthews, London, Bell and Hyman, 11 vols, 1970–83, iv. 9–10.

22 *The Household Account Book of Sarah Fell*, ed. Norman Penny, Cambridge, Cambridge University Press, 1920, pp. xxvi–xxvii.

23 Benjamin Bathurst (ed.), *Letters of Two Queens* [1924], pp. 11–13 .

24 Quoted in Frances Harris, 'Living in the neighbourhood of science: Mary Evelyn, Margaret Cavendish and the Greshamites', in Lynette Hunter and Sarah Hutton (eds), *Women, Science and Medicine: Mothers and Sisters of the Royal Society*, Stroud, Sutton, 1997, p. 213.

25 Bodl., MS. Rawl. Q e 27, Book 4, fo. 27 (18 Oct. 1680).

26 Bodl., MS. Rawl. Q e 28, fo. 48v.

27 Natalie Zemon Davis writes of the family as 'an arrow in time': 'Ghosts, kin, and progeny: some features of family life in early modern France', *Daedalus*, 106, 1977, pp. 87–114: p. 97.

28 Patricia Crawford, 'Katharine and Philip Henry and their children: a case study in family ideology', *Transactions of the Historic Society of Lancashire and Cheshire*, 134, 1984, pp. 39–73.

29 Folger, MS Additional 590, fo. 2.

30 Folger, MS X d 477/28, Lydia Du Gard to Samuel Du Gard, 13 Feb. 1673. Thanks to Nancy Taylor for her kind reference to this collection of letters.

31 Harold Love, *Scribal Publication in Seventeenth-century England*, Oxford, Oxford University Press, 1993.

32 Edward Poeton, 'The Midwives Deputie', n.d., BL, Sloane MS 1954.

33 Jane Sharp, *The Midwives Book,* London, 1671, sig. A 6.

34 On the process and enforcement of the criminal law, see Cynthia B. Herrup, *The Common Law: Participation and the Criminal Law in Seventeenth-century England*, Cambridge, Cambridge University Press, 1987.

35 For discussion of ways of reading legal records, see J. S. Cockburn, 'Early modern assize records as historical evidence', *Journal of the Society of Archivists*, 5, 1975; Laura Gowing, *Domestic Dangers: Women, Words, and Sex in Early Modern London*, Oxford, Oxford University Press, 1996, chap. 7; Miranda Chaytor, 'Husband[ry]: narratives of rape in the seventeenth century', *Gender and History*, 7/3, 1995, pp. 378–407; Garthine Walker, 'Rereading rape and sexual violence in early modern England', *Gender and History* 10/1, 1998, pp. 1–25; Natalie Zemon Davis, *Fiction in the Archives: Pardon Tales and their Tellers in Sixteenth-century France*, Stanford, CA, Stanford University Press, 1987.

36 On church courts and their procedure, see Martin Ingram, *Church Courts, Sex and Marriage in England, 1570–1640*, Cambridge, Cambridge University Press, 1987; on women in the church courts, Gowing, *Domestic Dangers*, chap. 2.

37 On the Court of Requests, see Tim Stretton, *Women Waging Law in Elizabethan England*, Cambridge, Cambridge University Press, 1998. Central legal records are held at the PRO, Kew; local courts' records are held in county record offices. Selections of many local records have been published by local record societies.

1 BODIES

1 For an important discussion of this theme, see Lyndal Roper, *Oedipus and the Devil: Witchcraft, Sexuality and Religion in Early Modern Europe*, London, Routledge, 1994, pp. 1–34.

2 Ian Maclean, *The Renaissance Notion of Woman: A Study in the Fortunes of Scholasticism and Medical Science in European Intellectual Life*, Cambridge, Cambridge University Press, 1980, pp. 28–46; for a useful collection of medical texts on female physiology, see Kate Aughterson (ed.), *Renaissance Woman: A Sourcebook: Constructions of Femininity in England*, London, Routledge, 1995, pp. 41–66.

3 Thomas Laqueur, *Making Sex: Body and Gender from the Greeks to Freud*, Cambridge, MA, Harvard University Press, 1990.

4 Laura Gowing, 'Gender and the language of insult in early modern London', *History Workshop Journal*, 35, 1993, pp. 1–21.

5 Guildhall, MS. 9189/1, fo. 130v. It was believed that if a woman did not menstruate, letting blood in the foot would draw the menses down.

6 Jane Sharp, *The Midwives Book*, London, 1671, p. 103.

7 Dame Sarah Cowper noted that she had conceived without any particular pleasure (document 5.8); Patricia Crawford, 'Sexual knowledge in early modern England', in Roy Porter and Mikulas Teich (eds), *Sexual Knowledge, Sexual Science; The History of Attitudes to Sexuality*, Cambridge, Cambridge University Press, 1994, pp. 97, 87–8.

8 Roger Schofield, 'Did the mothers really die? Three centuries of maternal mortality in "The World We Have Lost"', in Lloyd Bonfield, Richard M. Smith and Keith Wrightson (eds), *The World We Have Gained: Histories of Population and Social Structure*, Oxford, Blackwell, 1986, pp. 231–60.

9 Sara Heller Mendelson, 'Stuart women's diaries and occasional memoirs', in Mary Prior (ed.), *Women in English Society 1500–1800*, London, Methuen, 1985, pp. 196–7.

10 [Thomas Gibson], *The Anatomy of Humane Bodies Epitomized*, London, 1682, p. 150.

11 Lynette Hunter and Sarah Hutton (eds), *Women, Science and Medicine 1500–1700: Mothers and Sisters of the Royal Society*, Stroud, Sutton, 1997.

2 RELIGION, BELIEFS, SPIRITUALITY

1 Christopher Haigh, *English Reformations. Religion, Politics, and Society under the Tudors*, Oxford, Oxford University Press, 1993.

2 Patricia Crawford, *Women and Religion in England, 1500–1720*, London, Routledge, 1993; Anne Laurence, *Women in England, 1500–1760*, London, Weidenfeld and Nicolson, 1994, chaps 12 and 13.

3 Claire Walker, *Gender and Politics in Seventeenth-century English Convents*, London, Macmillan [forthcoming].

4 Phyllis Mack, *Visionary Women: Ecstatic Prophecy in Seventeenth-century England*, Berkeley, University of California Press, 1992.

5 Patricia Crawford, 'Public duty, conscience, and women in early modern England', in J. Morrill, P. Slack and D. Woolf (eds), *Public Duty and Private Conscience in Seventeenth-century England*, Oxford, Oxford University Press, 1993.

6 Patricia Crawford, 'Women, religion, and social action in England, 1500–1800', *Australian Feminist Studies*, 13, 1998, pp. 269–80.

3 WORK

1 Alice Clark, *Working Life of Women in the Seventeenth Century* (1919), ed. Amy Louise Erickson, London, Routledge, 1992.
2 Ann Kussmaul, *Servants in Husbandry in Early Modern England*, Cambridge, Cambridge University Press, 1981; Ilana Krausman Ben-Amos, *Adolescence and Youth in Early Modern England*, New Haven, CT, Yale University Press, 1994; Paul Griffiths, *Youth and Authority: Formative Experiences in England 1560–1640*, Oxford, Clarendon Press, 1996.
3 E. A. Wrigley and R. S. Schofield, *The Population History of England, 1541–1871*, Cambridge, Cambridge University Press, 1989, pp. 255, 264.
4 Natalie Davis, 'Women in the crafts in sixteenth-century Lyon', *Feminist Studies*, 8, 1982, pp. 47–80.
5 Sara Mendelson and Patricia Crawford, *Women in Early Modern England, 1550–1720*, Oxford, Oxford University Press, 1998, chaps 5 and 6.
6 LMA, DL/C 225, fo. 326 (1618).
7 Judith M. Bennett, *Ale, Beer, and Brewsters in England: Women's Work in a Changing World, 1300–1600*, New York, Oxford University Press, 1996.
8 Dorothy McLaren, 'Marital fertility and lactation 1570–1720', in Mary Prior (ed.), *Women in English Society 1500–1800*, London, Methuen, 1985, p. 40.

4 POVERTY AND PROPERTY

1 Sara Mendelson and Patricia Crawford, *Women in Early Modern England, 1550–1720*, Oxford, Oxford University Press, 1998, p. 261.
2 Amy Louise Erickson, *Women and Property in Early Modern England*, London, Routledge, 1993, pp. 170, 178.

5 SEXUAL EXPERIENCES

1 Miranda Chaytor, 'Husband[ry]: narratives of rape in the seventeenth century', *Gender and History*, 7/3, 1995, pp. 378–407; but see Garthine Walker, ' "Strange kind of stealing": abduction in early modern Wales', in Michael Roberts and Simone Clark (eds), *Women and Gender in Early Modern Wales*, Cardiff, University of Wales Press, 1999.
2 Tim Hitchcock, 'Redefining sex in eighteenth-century England', *History Workshop Journal*, 41, 1996, pp. 73–90.

6 MARRIAGE

1 Lawrence Stone, *The Family, Sex and Marriage in England 1500–1800*, London, Weidenfeld & Nicolson, 1977; Randolph Trumbach, *The Rise of the Egalitarian Family*, London, Academic Press, 1978; Edward Shorter, *The Making of the Modern Family*, London, Penguin, 1975.
2 See, for example, Anthony Fletcher, *Gender, Sex and Subordination in England 1500–1800*, New Haven and London, Yale University Press, 1995, p. 395; Laura Gowing, *Domestic Dangers: Women, Words, and Sex in Early Modern London*, Oxford, Oxford University Press, 1996, pp. 172–7; Sara Mendelson and Patricia Crawford, *Women in Early Modern England, 1550–1720*, Oxford, Oxford University Press, 1998, pp. 131–2.

7 MATERNITY

1 Ralph A. Houlbrooke, *The English Family 1450–1700*, London, Longman, 1984, pp. 136–7.
2 Lawrence Stone, *The Family, Sex and Marriage in England, 1500–1800*, London, Weidenfeld & Nicolson, 1977, pp. 105–14.
3 Lyndal Roper, *Oedipus and the Devil: Witchcraft, Sexuality and Religion in Early Modern Europe*, London, Routledge, 1994, pp. 199–225.
4 Document 7.12.
5 Anne Radford, quoted in J. B. Williams (ed.), *Memoirs of the Life and Character of Mrs Sarah Savage*, London, 1821, p. 314.
6 Ibid., p. 313.
7 Barbara Hanawalt, *Growing Up in Medieval London: The Experience of Childhood in History*, New York, Oxford University Press, 1993, p. 65.
8 LMA, DL/C 217, fo. 100 (19 February 1607).
9 Laura Gowing, *Domestic Dangers: Women, Words, and Sex in Early Modern London*, Oxford, Oxford University Press, 1996, pp. 154–7; Sara Mendelson and Patricia Crawford, *Women in Early Modern England, 1550—1720*, Oxford, Oxford University Press, 1998, pp. 115–16, 209.
10 Ibid.
11 Elizabeth D'Ewes to her husband Sir Simonds D'Ewes, n.d, BL, Harleian MS 379, fo. 137.
12 BL, Add. MS 70110, fo. 35.

8 RELATIONSHIPS

1 Vivian Brodsky, 'Widows in late Elizabethan London: remarriage, economic opportunity and family orientations', in Lloyd Bonfield, Richard M. Smith and Keith Wrightson (eds), *The World We Have Gained: Histories of Population and Social Structure*, Oxford, Blackwell, 1986, pp. 150–1.
2 Sara Mendelson and Patricia Crawford, *Women in Early Modern England, 1550–1720*, Oxford, Oxford University Press, 1998, chap. 4.
3 Patricia Crawford, 'Friendship and love between women in early modern England', in Andrew Lynch and Philippa Maddern (eds), *Venus and Mars: Engendering Love and War in Medieval and Early Modern Europe*, Perth, University of Western Australia Press, 1995, p. 49.
4 Laura Gowing, *Domestic Dangers: Women, Words, and Sex in Early Modern London*, Oxford, Oxford University Press, 1996, chaps 3, 4.
5 Margaret Aston, 'Seating in church', in W. Sheils and Diana Wood (eds), *Women in the Church*, Studies in Church History 27, Oxford, Blackwell, 1990.

9 POLITICS AND PROTESTS

1 Some of the important studies include Buchanan Sharp, *In Contempt of All Authority: Rural Artisans and the Riot in the West of England, 1586–1660*, Berkeley, University of California Press, 1980; John Walter, 'Grain riots and popular attitudes to the law: Maldon and the crisis of 1629', in John Brewer and John Styles (eds), *An Ungovernable People: The English and their Law in the Seventeenth and Eighteenth Centuries,* London, Hutchinson, 1980; Keith Lindley, *Fenland Riots and the English Revolution*, London, Heinemann, 1982; David Underdown, *Revel, Riot and Rebellion: Popular Politics and Culture in England 1603–1660*, Oxford, Clarendon Press, 1985; Ralph Houlbrooke, 'Women's social life and common action in England from the fifteenth century to the eve of the Civil War', *Continuity and Change*, 1,

1986, pp. 339–52; Roger B. Manning, *Village Revolts. Social Protest and Popular Disturbances in England, 1509–1640*, Oxford, Clarendon Press, 1988.

2 Patricia Crawford, 'Women and citizenship in Britain, 1500–1800', in Patricia Crawford and Philippa Maddern (eds), *Inclusions/Exclusions: Histories and Contexts of Women's Citizenship in Australia*, Melbourne, Melbourne University Press, forthcoming.

3 James C. Scott, *Weapons of the Weak: Everyday Forms of Peasant Resistance*, New Haven, CT, Yale University Press, 1985.

4 Patricia Crawford, '"The Poorest She": women and citizenship in early modern England', in Michael Mendle (ed.), *The Putney Debates of 1647: The Army, the Levellers, and the English State*, Cambridge, Cambridge University Press, forthcoming.

5 *Some Memoirs concerning the Family of the Priestleys, written . . . by Jonathan Priestley*, 1696, *Yorkshire Diaries and Autobiographies*, Surtees Soc., vol. 77, 1886, p. 26.

6 Sara Mendelson and Patricia Crawford, *Women in Early Modern England, 1550–1720*, Oxford, Oxford University Press, 1998, pp. 397–9.

7 Bernard Capp, 'Separate domains? Women and authority in early modern England', in Paul Griffiths, Adam Fox and Steve Hindle (eds), *The Experience of Authority in Early Modern England*, Macmillan, Basingstoke, 1996, pp. 137–9.

8 [Mary Chudleigh], *The Ladies Defence*, London, 1701, p. 14.

9 Hannah Wolley, *The Gentlewoman's Companion*, London, 1675, sig A 6, pp. 1, 29.

10 MENTAL WORLDS

1 Bodl., MS Ashmole 193, fo. 190. For more on Napier and his patients, see Michael McDonald, *Mystical Bedlam: Madness, Anxiety and Healing in Seventeenth-century England*, Cambridge, Cambridge University Press, 1981.

2 LMA, DL/C 214, p. 32.

3 Bodl., MS Ashmole 404, fo. 185.

FURTHER READING

INTRODUCTION

Introductions and general works on early modern women

Jacqueline Eales, *Women in Early Modern England, 1500–1700*, London, UCL Press, 1998.

Olwen Hufton, *The Prospect Before Her: A History of Women in Western Europe,* vol. One, *1500–1800*, London, Harper Collins, 1995.

Anne Laurence, *Women in England 1500–1760*, London, Weidenfeld and Nicolson, 1994.

Sara Mendelson and Patricia Crawford, *Women in Early Modern England, 1550–1720*, Oxford, Oxford University Press, 1998.

Mary Prior (ed.), *Women in English Society, 1500–1800*, London, Methuen, 1985.

Merry Wiesner, *Women and Gender in Early Modern Europe*, Cambridge, Cambridge University Press, 1993.

Guides to the records

Maureen Bell, George Parfitt and Simon Shepherd (eds), *A Biographical Dictionary of English Women Writers, 1580–1720*, London, Harvester Wheatsheaf, 1990.

Colin R. Chapman, *Ecclesiastical Courts, their Officials and their Records*, Dursley, Lochin,1992.

Patricia Crawford, 'Women's published writings 1600–1700', in Mary Prior (ed.) *Women in English Society, 1500–1800*, London, Methuen, 1985.

Sara Heller Mendelson, 'Stuart women's diaries and occasional memoirs', in Mary Prior (ed.) *Women in English Society, 1500–1800*, London, Methuen, 1985.

Ian Mortimer (ed.), *Record Repositories in Great Britain*, London, HMSO, 1997.

Probate Jurisdictions: Where to Look for Wills, compiled by Jeremy Gibson, Birmingham, Federation of Family History Societies, 1994.

Quarter Sessions Records for Family Historians: A Select List, compiled by Jeremy Gibson, Birmingham, Federation of Family History Societies, 1995.

Anne Tarver, *Church Court Records: An Introduction for Family and Local Historians*, Chichester, Phillimore, 1993.

Janet Todd (ed.), *A Dictionary of British and American Women Writers, 1660–1800*, London, Methuen, 1987.

Modern publications of women's non-fictional writings

D. J. H. Clifford (ed.) *The Diaries of Lady Anne Clifford*, Stroud, Sutton, 1990.

Ann Fanshawe and Anne Halkett, *The Memoirs of Anne, Lady Halkett and Ann, Lady Fanshawe*, ed. John Loftis, Oxford, Clarendon Press, 1979.

Moira Ferguson (ed.), *First Feminists: British Women Writers, 1578–1799*, Bloomington, Indiana University Press, 1985.

Celia Fiennes, *The Journeys of Celia Fiennes*, ed. Christopher Morris, London, Cresset Press, 1949.

Valerie Frith (ed.) *Women and History: Voices of Early Modern England*, Toronto, Coach House Press, 1995.

Elspeth Graham *et al.* (eds), *Her Own Life: Autobiographical Writings by Seventeenth-century Englishwomen*, London, Routledge, 1989.

Elizabeth Viscountess Mordaunt, *The Private Diaries of Elizabeth Viscountess Mordaunt*, Duncairn, 1856.

Dorothy Osborne, *Letters from Dorothy Osborne to Sir William Temple, 1652–54*, ed. G. Moore Smith, Oxford, Oxford University Press, 1928.

Charlotte Otten (ed.), *English Women's Voices 1540–1700*, Miami, Florida International University Press, 1992.

Mary Penington, *A Brief Account of my Exercises from my Childhood: left with my dear daughter, Gulielma Maria Penn,* Philadelphia, 1848.

Mary Rich, Countess of Warwick, *Diary*, London, Religious Tract Society, 1847.

Barbara Rosen, *Witchcraft in England 1558–1618*, Cambridge, MA, University of Massachusetts Press, 1991.

Alice Thornton, *The Autobiography of Mrs Alice Thornton of East Newton, Co. York*, Yorks, Surtees Society, vol. 62, 1873.

Betty S. Travitsky and Patrick Cullen (general eds), *The Early Modern Englishwoman: A Facsimile Library of Essential Works*, Aldershot, Scolar Press, 1996– .

[Isabella Twysden] Rev. F. W. Bennitt, 'The diary of Isabella, wife of Sir Roger Twysden, Baronet, of Royden Hall, East Peckham, 1645–1651', *Archaeologia Cantiana*, 51, 1939, pp. 113–36.

1   BODIES

Patricia Crawford, 'Sexual knowledge in early modern England', in Roy Porter and Mikulas Teich (eds), *Sexual Knowledge, Sexual Science: The History of Attitudes to Sexuality*, Cambridge, Cambridge University Press, 1994.

—— 'Attitudes to menstruation in seventeenth-century England', *Past and Present*, 91, 1981, pp. 47–73.

—— 'Printed advertisements for women medical practitioners in London, 1670–1710', *Society for the History of Medicine*, 35, 1984, pp. 66–70.

David Cressy, *Birth, Marriage, and Death: Ritual, Religion, and the Life Cycle*, Oxford, Oxford University Press, 1997.

Mary Fissell, 'Gender and generation: representing reproduction in early modern England', *Gender and History*, 7, 1995, pp. 433–56.

Laura Gowing, 'Secret births and infanticide in seventeenth-century England', *Past and Present*, 156, 1997, pp. 87–115.

Thomas Laqueur, *Making Sex: Body and Gender from the Greeks to Freud*, Cambridge, MA, Harvard University Press, 1990.

Linda Pollock, *With Faith and Physic: The Life of a Tudor Gentlewoman, Lady Grace Mildmay, 1552–1620*, London, Collins and Brown, 1993.

Hilda Smith, 'Gynaecology and ideology in seventeenth-century England', in B. A. Carroll (ed.), *Liberating Women's History*, Urbana, University of Illinois, 1976.

Rachel Weil, 'The politics of legitimacy: women and the warming-pan scandal', in Lois G. Schwoerer (ed.), *The Revolution of 1688–1689: Changing Perspectives*, Cambridge, Cambridge University Press, 1992.

Adrian Wilson, *The Making of Man-Midwifery: Childbirth in England, 1660–1770*, London, UCL Press, 1995.

Keith Wrightson, 'Infanticide in earlier seventeenth-century England', *Local Population Studies*, 15, 1975, pp. 10–22.

E. A. Wrigley, 'Explaining the rise in marital fertility in England in the "long" eighteenth century', *Economic History Review*, 2nd series, 51, 1998, pp. 435–64.

2 RELIGION, BELIEFS, SPIRITUALITY

Patricia Crawford, *Women and Religion in England, 1500–1720*, London, Routledge, 1993.

—— 'Charles Stuart, that man of blood', *Journal of British Studies*, 16, 1977, pp. 41–61.

—— 'Public duty, conscience, and women in early modern England', in John Morrill, Paul Slack and Daniel Woolf (eds), *Public Duty and Private Conscience in Seventeenth-century England*, Oxford, Oxford University Press, 1993.

Claire Cross, '"He-Goats before the Flocks": a note on the part played by some women in the founding of some Civil War Churches', *Studies in Church History*, 8, 1972, pp. 195–202.

Phyllis Mack, *Visionary Women: Ecstatic Prophecy in Seventeenth-century England*, Berkeley, University of California Press, 1992.

Sara Mendelson, 'Stuart women's diaries and occasional memoirs' in Mary Prior (ed.), *Women in English Society, 1500–1800*, Methuen, London, 1985.

Marie Rowlands, 'Recusant women 1560–1640', in Mary Prior (ed.), *Women in English Society*, 1500–1800, Methuen, London, 1985.

W. Sheils and Diana Wood (eds), *Women in the Church*, Studies in Church History, 27, Oxford, Blackwell, 1990.

3 WORK

Lindsey Charles and Lorna Duffin (eds), *Women and Work in Pre-industrial England*, Beckenham, Croom Helm, 1985.

Alice Clark, *Working Life of Women in the Seventeenth Century*, ed. Amy Louise Erickson, London, Routledge, 1992.

Patricia Crawford, 'Printed advertisements for women medical practitioners in London, 1670–1710', *The Society for the Social History of Medicine*, 35, 1984, pp. 66–70.

Peter Earle, 'The female labour market in London in the late seventeenth and early eighteenth centuries', *Economic History Review*, 2nd Ser., 42, 1989, pp. 328–53.

Paul Griffiths, 'The structure of prostitution in Elizabethan London', *Continuity and Change*, 8, 1993, pp. 39–63.

Bridget Hill, *Servants: English Domestics in the Eighteenth Century*, Oxford, Oxford University Press, 1996.

Hilary Marland (ed.), *The Art of Midwifery: Early Modern Midwives in Europe*, London, Routledge, 1993.

Tim Meldrum, 'London domestic servants from depositional evidence, 1660–1750: servant–employer sexuality in the patriarchal household', in Tim Hitchcock, Peter King and Pamela Sharpe (eds), *Chronicling Poverty: The Voices and Strategies of the English Poor, 1640–1840*, Basingstoke, Macmillan, 1997.

Sara Mendelson and Patricia Crawford, *Women in Early Modern England, 1550–1720*, Oxford, Oxford University Press, 1998, chaps 5 and 6.

Margaret Pelling, 'Appearance and reality: barber surgeons, the body and disease', in A. L. Beier (ed.), *London 1500–1700: The Making of the Metropolis*, London, Longman, 1986.

Michael Roberts, 'Sickles and scythes: women's work and men's work at harvest time', *History Workshop Journal*, 7, 1979, pp. 3–28.

Pamela Sharpe, *Adapting to Capitalism: Working Women in the English Economy, 1700–1850*, London, Macmillan, 1996.

—— 'Dealing with love: the ambiguous independence of spinsters in early modern England', *Gender and History*, 11, 1999 [forthcoming].

Elizabeth Tebeaux, 'Women and technical writing, 1475–1700: technology, literacy and the development of a genre', in Lynette Hunter and Sarah Hutton (eds), *Women, Science and Medicine, 1500–1700: Mothers and Sisters of the Royal Society*, Stroud, Sutton Publishing, 1997.

Adrian Wilson, *The Making of Man-Midwifery: Childbirth in England, 1660–1720*, London, UCL Press, 1995.

4 POVERTY AND PROPERTY

Amy Louise Erickson, *Women and Property in Early Modern England*, London, Routledge, 1993.

John Henderson and Richard Wall (eds), *Poor Women and Children in the European Past*, London, Routledge, 1994.

Tim Hitchcock, Peter King and Pamela Sharpe (eds), *Chronicling Poverty: The Voices and Strategies of the English Poor, 1640–1840*, Basingstoke, Macmillan, 1997.

B. A. Holderness, 'Widows in pre-industrial society: an essay upon their economic functions', in R. M. Smith (ed.), *Land, Kinship and Life-cycle*, Cambridge, Cambridge University Press, 1984.

Geoffrey L. Hudson, 'Negotiating for blood money: war widows and the courts in seventeenth-century England', in Jenny Kermode and Garthine Walker (eds), *Women, Crime and the Courts in Early Modern England*, London, UCL Press, 1994.

Beverley Lemire, 'Consumerism in pre-industrial and early industrial England: the trade in secondhand clothes', *Journal of British Studies*, 27, 1988, pp. 1–24.

Sara Mendelson and Patricia Crawford, *Women in Early Modern England, 1550–1720*, Oxford, Oxford University Press, 1998, chap. 5.

Mary Prior, 'Women and the urban economy: Oxford 1500–1800', in Mary Prior (ed.), *Women in English Society 1500–1800*, London, Methuen, 1985.

—— 'Wives and wills, 1558–1700', in John Chartres and David Hey (eds), *English Rural Society, 1500–1800: Essays in Honour of Joan Thirsk*, Cambridge, Cambridge University Press, 1990.

Susan Staves, *Married Women's Separate Property in England, 1660–1833*, Cambridge, MA, Harvard University Press, 1990.

Tim Wales, 'Poverty, poor relief and the life-cycle: some evidence from seventeenth-century Norfolk', in R. M. Smith (ed.), *Land, Kinship and Life-cycle*, Cambridge, Cambridge University Press, 1984.

Lorna Weatherill, 'A possession of one's own: women and consumer behaviour in England, 1660–1740', *Journal of British Studies*, 25, 1986, pp. 131–56.

—— *Consumer Behaviour and Material Culture in Britain 1600–1760*, London, Methuen, 1988.

5 SEXUAL EXPERIENCES

Richard Adair, *Courtship, Illegitimacy and Marriage in Early Modern England*, Manchester, Manchester University Press, 1996.

Nazife Bashar, 'Rape in England between 1550 and 1700', in London Feminist History Group (ed.), *The Sexual Dynamics of History*, London, Pluto Press, 1983.

Miranda Chaytor, 'Husband[ry]: narratives of rape in the seventeenth century', *Gender and History*, 7/3, 1995, pp. 378–407.

Patricia Crawford, 'Sexual knowledge in England, 1500–1750', in Roy Porter and Mikulas Teich (eds), *Sexual Knowledge, Sexual Science: The History of Attitudes to Sexuality*, Cambridge, Cambridge University Press, 1994.

Patricia Crawford and Sara Mendelson, 'Sexual identities in early modern England: the marriage of two women', *Gender and History*, 7/3, 1995, pp. 362–77.

Emma Donoghue, *Passions between Women: British Lesbian Culture 1668–1801*, London, Scarlet Press, 1993.

Mary Fissell, 'Gender and generation: representing reproduction in early modern England', *Gender and History*, 7/3, 1995, pp. 433–56.

Tim Hitchcock, *English Sexualities, 1700–1800*, Basingstoke, Macmillan, 1997.

Martin Ingram, *Church Courts, Sex and Marriage in England, 1570–1640*, Cambridge, Cambridge University Press, 1987, chaps 4, 7, 8.

Thomas Laqueur, *Making Sex: Body and Gender from the Greeks to Freud*, Cambridge, MA, Harvard University Press, 1990, chap. 3.

Valerie Traub, 'The (in)significance of "lesbian" desire in early modern England', in Susan Zimmerman (ed.), *Erotic Politics: Desire on the Renaissance Stage*, London, Routledge, 1992.

Garthine Walker, 'Rereading rape and sexual violence in early modern England', *Gender and History*, 10/1, 1998, pp. 1–25.

Alison Wall, 'Elizabethan precept and feminine practice: the Thynne family of Longleat', *History*, 75, 1990, pp. 22–38.

6 MARRIAGE

Susan Amussen, *An Ordered Society: Gender and Class in Early Modern England*, Oxford, Polity, 1988.

—— '"Being stir'd to much unquietnes": violence and domestic violence in early modern England', *Journal of Women's History*, 6/2, 1994, pp. 70–89.

Vivien Brodsky, 'Widows in late Elizabethan London: remarriage, economic opportunity, and family orientations', in Lloyd Bonfield, Richard M. Smith and Keith Wrightson (eds), *The World We Have Gained: Histories of Population and Social Structure*, Oxford, Blackwell, 1986.

Vivien Brodsky Elliott, 'Single women in the London marriage market: age, status and mobility, 1598–1619', in R. B. Outhwaite (ed.), *Marriage and Society: Studies in the Social History of Marriage*, London, Europa, 1981.

Charles Carlton, 'The widow's tale: male myths and female reality in sixteenth- and seventeenth-century England', *Albion* 10, 1978, pp. 118–29.

Patricia Crawford, 'Katherine and Philip Henry and their children: a case study in family ideology', *Transactions of the Historic Society of Lancashire and Cheshire*, 134, 1984, pp. 39–73.

David Cressy, *Birth, Marriage and Death: Ritual, Religion and the Life-cycle in Tudor and Stuart England*, Oxford, Oxford University Press, 1997.

Anthony Fletcher, *Gender, Sex and Subordination in England 1500–1800*, New Haven and London, Yale University Press, 1995, chaps 8, 9.

John R. Gillis, *For Better, For Worse: British Marriages, 1600 to the Present*, Oxford, Oxford University Press, 1985.

Laura Gowing, *Domestic Dangers: Women, Words, and Sex in Early Modern London*, Oxford, Oxford University Press, 1996, chaps 5, 6.

Margaret Hunt, 'Wife-beating, domesticity and women's independence in eighteenth-century London', *Gender and History*, 4, 1992, pp. 10–33.

Martin Ingram, *Church Courts, Sex and Marriage in England, 1570–1640*, Cambridge, Cambridge University Press, 1987, chaps 4–6.

Sara Mendelson and Patricia Crawford, *Women in Early Modern England, 1550–1720*, Oxford, Oxford University Press, 1998, pp. 126–48.

Lawrence Stone, *The Family, Sex and Marriage in England, 1500–1800*, London, Weidenfeld & Nicolson, 1977.

—— *Road to Divorce: England, 1530–1987*, Oxford, Oxford University Press, 1990.

—— *Uncertain Unions*, Oxford, Oxford University Press, 1993.

Barbara Todd, 'The remarrying widow: a stereotype reconsidered', in Mary Prior, (ed.), *Women in English Society 1500–1800*, London, Methuen, 1985.

Barbara Todd, 'I do no injury by not loving: Katherine Austen, a young widow of London', in Valerie Frith (ed.), *Women and History: Voices of Early Modern England*, Toronto, Coach House Press, 1995.

Alison Wall, 'Elizabethan precept and feminine practice: the Thynne family of Longleat', *History*, 75, 1990, pp. 22–38.

7 MATERNITY

Toni Bowers, *The Politics of Motherhood: British Writing and Culture 1680–1760*, Cambridge, Cambridge University Press, 1996.

Patricia Crawford, 'The construction and experience of maternity', in Valerie Fildes (ed.), *Women as Mothers in Pre-industrial England*, London, Routledge, 1990.

Jacqueline Eales, *Puritans and Roundheads: The Harleys of Brampton Bryan and the Outbreak of the English Civil War*, Cambridge, Cambridge University Press, 1990.

Laura Gowing, 'Secret births and infanticide in seventeenth-century England', *Past and Present*, 156, 1997, pp. 87–115.

Ralph A. Houlbrooke, *The English Family 1450–1700*, London, Longman, 1984.

Roger Schofield and E. A. Wrigley, 'Infant and child mortality in England in the late Tudor and early Stuart period', in Charles Webster (ed.), *Health, Medicine and Mortality in the Sixteenth Century*, Cambridge, Cambridge University Press, 1979.

8 RELATIONSHIPS

Bernard Capp, 'Separate domains? Women and authority in early modern England', in Paul Griffiths, Adam Fox and Steve Hindle (eds), *The Experience of Authority in Early Modern England*, Basingstoke, Macmillan, 1996.

Patricia Crawford, 'Friendship and love between women in early modern England', in Andrew Lynch and Philippa Maddern (eds), *Venus and Mars: Engendering Love and War in Medieval and Early Modern Europe*, Perth, University of Western Australia Press, 1995.

Leonore Davidoff, 'Where the stranger begins: the question of siblings in historical analysis', in *Worlds Between: Historical Perspectives on Gender and Class*, Cambridge, Polity, 1995.

Laura Gowing, 'Language, power, and the law: women's slander litigation in early modern London', in Jenny Kermode and Garthine Walker (eds), *Women, Crime and the Courts in Early Modern England*, London, UCL Press, 1994.

Sara Mendelson and Patricia Crawford, *Women in Early Modern England, 1550–1720*, Oxford, Oxford University Press, 1998, chap. 4.

Diane Purkiss, *The Witch in History: Early Modern and Twentieth-century Representations*, London, Routledge, 1996, chaps 4–6.

Barbara Rosen, *Witchcraft in England, 1558–1618*, Cambridge, MA, University of Massachusetts Press, 1991.

9 POLITICS AND PROTESTS

Bernard Capp, 'Separate domains? Women and authority in early modern England', in Paul Griffiths, Adam Fox and Steve Hindle (eds), *The Experience of Authority in Early Modern England*, Basingstoke, Macmillan,1996.

Kenneth L. Carroll, 'Early Quakers and "Going Naked as a Sign"', *Quaker History*, 67, 1978, pp. 69–87.

Patricia Crawford, 'The challenges to patriarchalism: how did the Revolution affect women', in John Morrill (ed.), *Revolution and Restoration: England in the 1650s*, London, Collins & Brown, 1992.

Dagmar Freist, *Governed by Opinion: Politics, Religion and the Dynamics of Communication in Stuart London*, London, I. B. Tauris, 1997.

Frances Harris, *A Passion for Government: The Life of Sarah Duchess of Marlborough*, Oxford, Oxford University Press, 1991.

Patricia Higgins, 'The reactions of women with special reference to women petitioners', in B. Manning (ed.), *Politics, Religion and the English Civil War*, London, Edward Arnold, 1973.

Ann Hughes, 'Gender and politics in Leveller literature', in Susan Amussen and Mark Kishlansky (eds), *Political Culture and Cultural Politics in Early Modern England: Essays presented to David Underdown*, Manchester, Manchester University Press, 1995.

Carole Levin and Patricia A. Sullivan (eds), *Political Rhetoric, Power, and Renaissance Women*, Albany, State University of New York Press, 1995.

Sara Mendelson and Patricia Crawford, *Women in Early Modern England, 1550–1720*, Oxford, Oxford University Press, 1998, chap. 7.

Ruth Perry, *The Celebrated Mary Astell: An Early English Feminist*, Chicago, University of Chicago Press, 1986.

Simon Shepherd (ed.), *The Women's Sharp Revenge: Five Women's Pamphlets from the Renaissance*, London, St Martin's Press, 1995.

Hilda Smith (ed.), *Women Writers and the Early Modern British Political Tradition*, New York, Cambridge University Press, 1998.

10 MENTAL WORLDS

Elspeth Graham, 'Women's writing and the self', in Helen Wilcox (ed.), *Women and Literature in Britain, 1500–1700*, Cambridge, Cambridge University Press, 1996.

Katharine Hodgkin, 'Dionys Fitzherbert and the anatomy of madness', in Kate Chedgzoy, Melanie Hansen and Suzanne Trill (eds), *Voicing Women: Gender and Sexuality in Early Modern Writing*, Keele, Keele University Press, 1996.

Anne Laurence, 'Women's psychological disorders in seventeenth-century Britain', in Arina Angerman *et al.* (eds), *Current Issues in Women's History*, London, Routledge, 1989.

Michael McDonald, *Mystical Bedlam: Madness, Anxiety and Healing in Seventeenth-century England*, Cambridge, Cambridge University Press, 1981.

GLOSSARY

articulate   'Said', a formula used in legal records ('the articulate Mrs Smith')

bridewell   Generic term for punitive institutions, the first in London, others in county towns, for the whipping and setting to work of (for example) mothers of illegitimate children

clandestine marriage   A marriage ceremony that contravened any of the conditions of canon law, often undertaken in secret, but nonetheless usually legally binding

corporal oath   Oath ratified by the touching of the Gospels

deponent   Witness in a court case

deposition   Testimony of a witness in a church court case

examinate, examinant   Party being examined in court

examination   Examination of an accused party in a court case

Fifth Monarchists   Believed that the four kingdoms of the earth would pass away and that the fifth, that of Christ, was imminent

gentlewoman   One born into a family entitled to a coat of arms

groat   Fourpence

gross   144

impotent   'Unable to work' is the more common meaning

information   Testimony of a witness in a court case

interrogatories   Statements produced by the defendant in a church court case in their own defence, to be answered by the plaintiff's witnesses

jurate   Sworn witness in a court case

mark   13s. 4d.

Mistress   See below; also, a servant's employer

Mrs   Pronounced 'mistress', the title of married women and of single women of some social standing

naked   A variety of meanings, dependent on context, and rarely meaning entirely unclothed; often, wearing a smock

oratrix   Female petitioner

ordinances   In a religious context, refers to those practices authoritatively enjoined or prescribed. While most agreed that the Lord's Supper was an ordinance of the church, the status of baptism, for example, was disputed among different religious groups

303

points   Tagged laces for lacing bodices, etc.
precontest   Previous witness in court case
Quadragesima   First Sunday in Lent
respondent   Party answering questions in a court case
terms   Menstrual periods; legal terms, of which there were three per year
to be at nought   Frequently used to refer to sexual intercourse

INDEX

Note: Entries in italic are references to illustrations.

305